Meeting the Enemy

CRITICAL AMERICA
General Editors: Richard Delgado and Jean Stefancic

For a complete list of titles in the series, please visit the
New York University Press website at www.nyupress.org.

Meeting the Enemy

American Exceptionalism and

International Law

Natsu Taylor Saito

Maud —
looking forward
to the poetic complement
to this history...
with love & admiration,
Natsu

NEW YORK UNIVERSITY PRESS

New York and London

NEW YORK UNIVERSITY PRESS
New York and London
www.nyupress.org

Library of Congress Cataloging-in-Publication Data

Saito, Natsu Taylor.
Meeting the enemy : American exceptionalism and
international law / Natsu Taylor Saito.
p. cm. — (Critical America)
Includes bibliographical references and index.
ISBN-13: 978–0–8147–9836–2 (cl : alk. paper)
ISBN-10: 0–8147–9836–5 (cl : alk. paper)
1. United States—Foreign relations. 2. Exceptionalism—United States—
History. 3. Manifest Destiny. 4. United States—Territorial expansion.
5. International law. I. Title.
E183.7.S24   2010
973—dc22   2009041512

New York University Press books are printed on acid-free paper,
and their binding materials are chosen for strength and durability.
We strive to use environmentally responsible suppliers and materials
to the greatest extent possible in publishing our books.

Manufactured in the United States of America
10 9 8 7 6 5 4 3 2 1

In memory of Ruth Taylor Saito

Contents

Acknowledgments

This book was initially proposed by Richard Delgado and Jean Stefancic, whose support and encouragement ensured that it would come to fruition. I am deeply indebted and grateful to my editor, Deborah Gershenowitz, who maintained faith in the project through many years, and to the editorial staff at New York University Press.

Although I am responsible for the finished product, such projects are always collective efforts. Thanks must go to my research assistants Tiffany Bartholomew, Lisa Liang, and Shane Peagler, who always came through; to our ever enthusiastic librarian, Ron Wheeler; and to my dean, Steven Kaminshine. This work would not have been possible without generous research support from Georgia State University's College of Law.

I am especially indebted to Andrea Curcio for constant and constructive feedback, and to the work of the many scholars, especially Antony Anghie, Ruth Gordon, Tayyab Mahmud, Henry A. Richardson III, and Robert A. Williams Jr., which laid the foundation for my analysis. Special thanks go to Kathleen Cleaver, Pearl and Russell Means, George "Tink" Tinker, Sharon H. Venne, and Michael Yellow Bird for protecting spaces in which a "pluriverse" of understandings can flourish.

Finally, I cannot express the extent of my gratitude to Ward Churchill, my husband and partner in struggle, for his consistent support and innumerable contributions to this project, and to our daughter, Akilah Jenga Kinnison, who put in countless hours of research and editorial assistance and is always an inspiration to me.

This book is dedicated to the memory of my mother, Ruth Taylor Saito, whose internationalist spirit permeated her life and inspired all who knew her.

"We have met the enemy and he is us."
                                        —Pogo

Introduction

"A Distinctly American Internationalism"

> We remain the most prosperous, powerful nation on Earth. . . .
> We will not apologize for our way of life, nor will we waver in its
> defense. . . . Let it be said by our children's children that when
> we were tested . . . with our eyes fixed on the horizon and God's
> grace upon us, we carried forth that great gift of freedom and
> delivered it safely to future generations.
> —Barack Obama, Inaugural Address, January 2009

In January 2009 President Barack Obama took office "amidst gathering clouds and raging storms," with, among other things, the United States "at war, against a far-reaching network of violence and hatred."[1] According to U.S. officials, this so-called war on terror is being fought not only to secure the physical and economic well-being of the American people but also to preserve and extend freedom and democracy throughout the world. In his acceptance speech, Obama emphasized the "enduring power of our ideals: democracy, liberty, opportunity, and unyielding hope," and his inaugural address assured his worldwide audience that America was again ready to lead the world in realizing these values.[2] Similarly the *National Security Strategy of the United States* (*NSS*), a 2002 policy report of the Bush administration, stated that the aim of the U.S. international strategy "is to help make the world not just safer but better. Our goals on the path to progress are clear: political and economic freedom, peaceful relations with other states, and respect for human dignity."[3]

The aims described by both Barack Obama and George W. Bush correspond to the foundational principles and goals of international law—international peace and security, fundamental human rights, and the global rule of law—clearly articulated in the UN Charter, the Universal Declaration of Human Rights, and numerous multilateral treaties.[4] Nonetheless, as the *NSS* made clear, the United States was not making a commitment to international law per se but to what it called, echoing a 1999 Bush campaign speech, "a distinctly American internationalism that reflects the union of our values and our national interests."[5] The "path to progress" envisioned by Presidents Obama and Bush, as well as many of their predecessors, is considered uniquely American yet universally applicable. Barack Obama has repeatedly emphasized that the United States is "the last, best hope of Earth."[6] This sentiment was put a bit more bluntly by George W. Bush in the NSS: "The great struggles of the twentieth century . . . ended with a decisive victory for the forces of freedom—and a single sustainable model for national success."[7] In both cases claims are being made that freedom, democracy, and human dignity are peculiarly "American" values, and that human progress is dependent upon the universal implementation of the "single sustainable model" which the U.S. exemplifies.

The "cooperation" of the international community is seen as vital to the success of this mission, and the U.S. emphasizes that these values have been generally accepted in international law. In fact, one of the key attributes of "rogue states," as defined in the NSS, is that they "display no regard for international law . . . and callously violate international treaties to which they are party."[8] Since World War II, the international community as a whole has recognized that the maintenance of international peace and cooperation requires structures for developing agreements and resolving disputes between states, and it is generally accepted that the global stability necessary for the protection of fundamental rights and freedoms requires adherence to the rule of law, both within and between states.

Nonetheless, the United States has consistently distanced itself from many established principles of international law, as well as the international institutions that have evolved to implement such law. For example, despite playing an influential role in the drafting of all major human treaties, the U.S. took forty years to ratify the Genocide Convention, and fifteen to ratify the International Covenant on Civil and Political Rights.[9] It still refuses to become a party to many basic treaties such as the Convention on the Rights of the Child,[10] and it has ratified others with reservations that undermine meaningful participation.[11]

In the mid-1980s the United States withdrew its agreement to submit to the compulsory jurisdiction of the International Court of Justice, and, more recently, it has announced its intent not to become a party to the Rome Statute establishing the International Criminal Court.[12] Throughout the 1990s the U.S. insisted on sanctions against Iraq that are estimated to have resulted in the deaths of more than a million Iraqis, many of them children under the age of five.[13] In deciding to invade Iraq and hold detainees indefinitely at Guantánamo Bay in the current "war on terror," U.S. officials have asserted the right, ability, and even responsibility to act unilaterally when international bodies do not function in ways the U.S. believes most effective.[14] Simultaneously the U.S. has attempted to unilaterally reshape certain doctrines of international law, such as the rules precluding preemptive warfare,[15] while apparently disregarding others, including provisions of the Geneva Conventions and the prohibition on torture.[16] With respect to environmental matters, the U.S. is now the only "advanced" country that has refused to ratify the Kyoto Protocols.[17]

Selective self-exemption undermines not only specific legal institutions and norms, but it also leads to the decreased effectiveness of the global rule of law. Such exemption is therefore problematic when engaged in by any state, but the United States' practice of shaping, invoking, and selectively rejecting international law is particularly significant because of the extraordinary influence it currently wields as the world's sole "superpower." A fundamental premise of this book is that we have now been placed at a critical juncture because of the combination of certain factors: the unilateral prerogatives that the United States, as well as some of its key allies, are asserting; the increasingly desperate responses of those without comparable economic, military, or political power; and the fragile state of the environment on which we all depend. We face the choice between a world increasingly dominated by raw power, accompanied by the heightened levels of repression necessary to maintain that power, or one in which global relations are transformed and democratized, allowing international institutions to build the base for a peaceful, just, and sustainable world order.

This book is the result of my attempt to understand why the United States' frequent—if selective—disregard of international law and institutions is met with such high levels of approval, or at least complacency, by the American public. Some of this, of course, can be attributed to fear-mongering but I believe that the answer lies much deeper in our history, for attempts by the United States to invoke underlying principles of law while exempting itself from specific applications are not a new phenomenon, nor unique to any particular administration. The thesis of this book is that the United States' current approach to international law is not simply a response to a new crisis in world order but is best understood as the most recent extension of a consistent history in which international law has been both invoked and disregarded.

Since its inception, the U.S. has grappled with contradictions between its stated values and its actions, its constitutional framework, and its legal practices. The new republic was born in a state of exception to international law, needing to justify its otherwise illegal break with British colonial rule by claiming that it was more faithfully representing the underlying principles of "natural law." The "Founding Fathers" were clear that in order to be recognized as a legitimate state the U.S. had to comport with international law, a position confirmed by the text of the Constitution as well as by early Supreme Court opinions. Yet they were also determined to expand and consolidate a territorial and economic base as broadly and expediently as possible, often resulting in violations of international law as wars of extermination were waged against Indigenous peoples, treaties consistently broken to appropriate land and natural resources, and chattel labor imported in disregard of an international ban on the slave trade.[18] The United States has, as a result, consistently based its claims to legitimacy on advocacy of the principles of freedom, democracy, and the rule of law, while simultaneously developing policies and engaging in practices, often shored up by convoluted legal "interpretations," to exempt itself from compliance, thereby subverting the realization of these principles both domestically and internationally.

Rather than concretely reconciling these contradictions, it seems that Americans find it easier to remain in denial, dismissing the country's history with the assertion that it all happened "a long time ago" and moving on to some version of "well, the injustices were unfortunate, but we've ended up with the most democratic—or freest or richest—country in the world, so it must have been for the best." In this construction America is special, or exceptional, because it claims certain incontestable values; the possibility that its hegemony was consolidated and continues to be exercised at the expense of those values can be ignored in the name of a greater good. This is the conception of American exceptionalism that is addressed in this book, for the contradictions embodied within this formulation set the stage for the United States' assertion of a "uniquely American" posture toward international law today.[19]

The phenomenon of American exceptionalism in international affairs has, of course, been widely criticized. Many critiques focus on the hypocrisy evidenced by U.S. officials, dismissing their selective invocation of international law as a cynical means of enhancing political or economic power. Although this may be accurate in any given instance, such *realpolitik* arguments disregard the extent to which the United States–indeed, all states–rely upon legal structures to further their political or economic ends. More significant, this critique ultimately privileges the rule of power over the rule of law by presuming that power cannot be channeled through international institutions to enforce, and reinforce, law on a global scale.

A second line of criticism emphasizes the value of legal institutions but tends to focus on specific instances in which the United States has failed to comply with international law. It is undoubtedly important to challenge each assertion of American exceptionalism (the failure to ratify particular conventions, for example) and to make good the promise articulated by Supreme Court Justice and chief Nuremberg prosecutor Robert Jackson that "if certain acts in violation of treaties are crimes they are crimes whether the United States does them or whether [another country] does them, and we are not prepared to lay down a rule of criminal conduct against others which we would not be willing to have invoked against us."[20] Nonetheless, countering exceptionalist arguments on a case-by-case basis will not alter the underlying dynamic at issue. The problem cannot be solved simply by challenging its most current manifestation or by attributing blame to the latest political administration.

As a result, I believe that neither of the more familiar approaches to American exceptionalism effectively addresses the dangers posed by the perhaps distinctive but not especially new "American internationalism," and that we must, instead, recognize and confront the historical patterns and structural dynamics that make such policies seem right, natural, even inevitable to the American public. The questions addressed in this book are not of recent origin, but they take on a heightened urgency in light of the current war on terror, the pervasive reach of global economic institutions, the rapid expansion and dissemination of military technology, and the realization that "civilization" as we know it poses an imminent threat to the environment of the entire planet. Under these circumstances, it is hardly a radical position to assert that our collective survival and well-being require effective systems of international justice and that these cannot be achieved as long as the most powerful state on the globe exempts itself from their application.

While advocating adherence to the global rule of law as well as the U.S. Constitution, I believe it is critical to remember that each of these legal systems emerged in large measure to rationalize and regulate imperial expansion and to consider the extent to which they continue to replicate colonial relations. Quite consistently the advance of "civilization" has been posited as the goal of these legal systems, and those deemed "uncivilized," or Other, constructed as the enemy. Only recently have legal frameworks posited by both the Constitution and international law evolved sufficiently through their guarantees of equality and self-determination to offer a truly liberatory potential. Nonetheless the ideology of colonialism, with its presumption that only one viable path of human "progress" and "development" exists, continues to constrain our thinking. It is important, therefore, to disentangle freedom, equality, and democratic governance, which I believe are fairly characterized as universal aspirations, from the "civilizing mission" that has characterized both European colonial expansion and the consolidation and extension of U.S. hegemony. Similarly the "enemies of freedom" must not be conflated with those who resist being "civilized."

The question is not whether we should struggle for freedom or democracy but, instead, what those values actually mean and how they can best be ensured and sustained in a diverse and rapidly changing world. In the following chapters I attempt to identify key points at which U.S. practice has diverged from its stated principles in the domestic and international arenas and how the gaps between principle and practice have been rationalized. This history is essential, I believe, to understand both the dangers inherent to the assertion of American exceptionalism and the ways in which it can most effectively be countered.

Chapter 1 begins with a brief overview of the justifications asserted for American exceptionalism in the context of the current "war on terror," with the purpose of identifying some of the asserted values, identity, and mission of the United States that have remained remarkably consistent throughout its history. It focuses, in particular, on the precepts undergirding the construct of civilization that U.S. officials are invoking, presumptions that, to many Americans, appear simply as "common sense" but rely on a particularly "Western" understanding of human progress, measured by development along a unilinear path and juxtaposed to conditions of savagery or barbarism. It is this construction of human purpose that provides the underlying ideology for the United States' establishment and expansion and the framework of Euroderivative international law addressed in this book.

George W. Bush sparked international controversy when he alluded to the war on terror as a "crusade." Yet in many ways this was an apt reference, for it was in the context of the Crusades that contemporary international law emerged. Chapter 2 considers the notion of civilizing the infidel Other that provided the ideological underpinnings not only of the Crusades but of Europe's "Age of Discovery," and summarizes how this mission became a foundational premise of international law. Chapter 3 begins with the earliest English settlers' belief in their divinely ordained mission to bring progress and civilization to the wilderness. Their vision of establishing a "city on a hill," a beacon of freedom for the world, was perpetuated in the faith of the American colonists that their new republic was taking European civilization to a higher level. By thus situating themselves in the "genealogy" of Western progress, the founders quite literally created a "state of exception," justifying their divergence from prevailing norms of international law by claiming to better represent the fundamental values, such as freedom and democracy, of a higher law.

The United States was then forced to confront the contradictions between its stated commitment to the "American" values of freedom, democracy, and the rule of law, and the reality that it was a settler colonial power whose legitimacy was necessarily grounded in the legal framework of European colonialism which it was purporting to supersede. Chapter 4 addresses how this new government "of the people" reconciled its decimation of Indigenous peoples, the appropriation of their lands, and the institution of chattel slavery with its foundational principles by invoking the premises of "civilization" to construct racialized identities that excluded American Indians and Africans from the American polity. In this process, the arguments made to justify American exceptionalism in the international sphere were being made within domestic law to justify internal colonial practices.

This convergence of the ideological framing of U.S. domestic practice and foreign policy is illustrated in chapter 5, which addresses the consolidation of U.S. claims to what are now the "lower forty-eight" states, from the "conquest" of the more than four hundred Indigenous nations on the continent to the "acquisition" of Florida and the northern half of Mexico. In realizing what was envisioned as America's "manifest destiny" of continental expansion, however, the tensions between appropriating additional territories and incorporating their inhabitants became increasingly problematic, given the racialized construction of American identity discussed in chapter 4. Within U.S. law these contradictions became more acute when, following the Civil War, the Constitution was amended to extend formal equality and civil rights to a much larger sector of the American populace. At the same time, however, the "internal frontier" would soon be declared closed, bringing early U.S. visions of extending beyond the continent much closer to realization. At this point the United States began its explicitly imperialist project of acquiring external colonies, such as Hawai'i, Puerto Rico, and the Philippines, inaugurating a new phase of its "civilizing mission." This development, and the legal justifications accompanying it, is the subject of chapter 6.

The international legal system, meanwhile, was struggling with similar tensions in the wake of the Great War, as European and American leaders attempted to create structures of international order that maintained the dominance of Western civilization and colonial ideology within a new paradigm of self-determination that envisioned the emergence and assimilation of additional "civilized" states. With the decolonization and national liberation movements that followed World War II, the international legal regime was even more significantly restructured. Chapter 7 looks at the dominant role the United States played in this process, from the League of Nations and its mandate system, through the establishment of the United Nations and the international financial institutions, such as the World Bank and International Monetary Fund, which have become increasingly influential forces in the global project of "development."

Since the end of the Cold War U.S. claims to and justifications for American exceptionalism, articulated since its inception, have been writ large. The attitude in the United States toward "foreign" relations and global law has often been characterized as isolationist, with intermittent bursts of internationalism, but the history considered in this book indicates that those advocating for unilateral or multilateral policies and practices virtually always have agreed about the underlying principle of "America First." If the United States is presumed to be the exemplar of Western civilization and therefore human progress, it becomes reasonable, indeed desirable, that it bring its uniquely American but nonetheless universal values of "freedom" and "democracy" to the rest of the planet. It becomes appropriate, moreover, to do so by whatever means, unilateral or multilateral, it deems most effective. Chapter 8 proposes that American exceptionalism can be seen as fraught with practical contradictions but nonetheless quite ideologically coherent when viewed from this perspective. Observing that "civilization," as it has emerged over the past several centuries, has given us a world in which human well-being is threatened by armed conflict, poverty, and disease, and the planet itself appears to be on the verge of imminent environmental collapse, it suggests that these problems will not be solved by remaking the world in the image of the United States.

The tensions between colonialism and self-determination reflected within the trajectory of American exceptionalism provide a lens through which contemporary relations of law and power can be understood and perhaps changed. The lesson I take from the history outlined in this book is that the principles and structures of international law, as they have emerged over the past century, provide as viable a starting point as any currently available for the creation of a sustainable and just world order. Still, realizing this potential will require a willingness to confront the continuing influence of colonial ideology honestly and to take seriously the many alternative visions of human purpose and social structure that have resisted assimilation into the paradigm of Western civilization. These ideas are discussed in chapter 9, which summarizes the dangers posed by American exceptionalism and the liberatory potential of a decolonized international legal framework.

Saving Civilization

The War on Terror

The transformation of "the other" has been the continuous goal
of the "civilizing mission," but this task has acquired an unprecedented urgency, an imperative character, precisely because it
is now so powerfully linked to the idea of self-defence and survival, not only of the United States but of civilization itself.

—Antony Anghie, *Imperialism, Sovereignty and
the Making of International Law*

Every nation, in every region, now has a decision to make.
Either you are with us, or you are with the terrorists. . . . This
is not, however, just America's fight. And what is at stake is not
just America's freedom. This is the world's fight. This is civilization's fight.

—George W. Bush, Presidential Address to Congress,
September 23, 2001

On September 11, 2001, nineteen hijackers flew three airplanes into
the Pentagon and World Trade Center towers, resulting in approximately
twenty-nine hundred deaths.[1] These attacks could have been treated as
criminal acts and prosecuted within the existing framework of law, domestic
or international. As legal scholar Anthony Cassese has explained, international terrorism has been recognized as a crime in times of peace; in times of
armed conflict it is a war crime; and it may also be a crime against humanity,
whether committed during times of peace or war.[2] However, the attacks of
September 11, 2001, have been used by the United States, wielding its superpower status, to formally usher in a new era of international law and political
relations defined in terms of a global "war on terror."

While many of the specific actions taken in this "war" have been cast
as emergency measures necessary to protect against imminent threats to

national or international security, it has become increasingly clear that the government's intent has been to ensure the consolidation of a framework of international law in which American exceptionalism is structurally embedded. As George W. Bush announced in February 2002, "Our Nation recognizes that this new paradigm–ushered in not by us but by terrorists—requires new thinking in the law of war."[3] In this process, not only international but U.S. norms are being reshaped, prompting one scholar to observe that the war on terror "is also a catalyst for a process through which the identity of the United States is being constituted or shaped, although not always self-reflectively."[4] This process will continue to have lasting effects, regardless of the particular polices of future administrations, unless the underlying dynamics and rationales for these changes are significantly altered.

The emerging paradigm, within both domestic and international law, has many unique features. Nonetheless, in critical ways, it is best understood as the latest extension of a number of historical trends. In some respects, this reconfiguration can be characterized as the military capstone of a process of political and economic consolidation, often shorthanded as "globalization," which has been occurring for several decades, a subject addressed in more detail in later chapters. But the "new paradigm" has much deeper roots and, therefore, to fully appreciate and appropriately respond to the implications of this emerging world order, we must consider not just its recent history but the more fundamental constructs of international law and the visions of "civilization" and human progress upon which it relies.

In light of the many criticisms of the crudity of the "us versus them" arguments put forth in this so-called war on terror, the interesting question becomes why these arguments have had so much traction, at least in American public opinion. The answer lies, I believe, in the reality that, despite the discomfort many Americans feel with such a stark articulation, the underlying concepts do, in fact, resonate with deeply held beliefs about "human nature," "progress," and "civilization" and, more specifically, about American identity within that paradigm. I begin, therefore, with these arguments—not because they provide a convenient "straw man," but because I believe they reflect core beliefs which undergird arguments for the maintenance of the status quo, even when articulated in a more sophisticated manner. This chapter begins by outlining some basic presuppositions of the current war on terror, focusing particularly on what is meant by the claim that it is a war to preserve and protect civilization. The following sections consider the presumptions underlying this notion of civilization and look briefly at how the assumption of a "civilizing mission" informed the early development of a universalizing yet distinctly Eurocentric international law from which contemporary legal norms and institutions have evolved.[5]

Six Precepts of the War on Terror

Within a few days of the attacks on the Pentagon and the World Trade Center, George W. Bush, forty-third president of the United States, announced that "our responsibility to history is . . . to answer these attacks and rid the world of evil."[6] What materialized was a shape-shifting "war on terror." As both a military and an ideological struggle, it has been a conflict with neither geographical boundaries nor a clear definition of what would constitute victory, and therefore a "global enterprise of uncertain duration."[7] Named enemies have taken various forms—Osama bin Laden and the al Qaida network, the Taliban government of Afghanistan, the state of Iraq and its president, Saddam Hussein, an "axis of evil" consisting of North Korea and Iran as well as Iraq, "radical Islam," the hundreds of men and boys of several dozen nationalities indefinitely detained at the U.S. Naval Base at Guantánamo Bay, Cuba, and select U.S. citizens declared without proffer of evidence to be "enemy combatants."[8] Perhaps because its scope is so broad and its campaigns so numerous, this war on terror has been analyzed in many different ways. In order to understand its relationship to American exceptionalism, however, it is useful to focus on six of its basic precepts.[9]

The War on Terror Is a Confrontation with Evil

The first precept is that there is an enemy, and that enemy is "evil," the term being used in this context as both a noun and an adjective. Invoking, at least obliquely, President Ronald Reagan's Cold War rhetoric describing the Soviet bloc as the "evil empire,"[10] George W. Bush announced in his June 2002 West Point commencement address, "We are in a conflict between good and evil, and America will call evil by its name."[11]

By establishing this as their most basic premise, the architects of this project have laid the groundwork for avoiding any discussion of motivations, legitimate or not, that might prompt attacks against the United States, as well as any debates concerning the morality or legality of actions taken in the course of the "war." As President Bush told a gathering of Federal Bureau of Investigation employees, "The people who did this act on America, and who may be planning further acts, are evil people. They don't represent an ideology, they don't represent a legitimate political group of people. They're flat evil. That's all they can think about, is evil."[12] Shortly thereafter, he emphasized the imperative of responding rather than analyzing: "We cannot fully understand the designs and power of evil. It is enough to know that evil, like goodness, exists."[13]

Terrorists and Those Who Harbor Them Are the Enemy

Well before the inauguration of the war on terror, President Bush informed the American people that we had enemies, even if we had difficulty identifying them: "When I was coming up, it was a dangerous world, and you knew exactly who they were. It was us versus them, and it was clear who them was. Today we are not so sure who they are, but we know they're there."[14] The unseen enemy is, of course, often the most frightening, a psychological phenomenon frequently taken advantage of by the makers of Hollywood "westerns" and horror movies.[15] After September 11, 2001, the enemy now has a name, if not a clear identity. The evil being fought is embodied in terrorism, which is defined in the *NSS* as "premeditated, politically motivated violence perpetrated against innocents."[16] The second precept is that terrorists are the enemy, and "we make no distinction between terrorists and those who knowingly harbor or provide aid to them."[17]

This enemy is nonetheless elusive, operating, in President Bush's terms, from "shadowy networks" which are "organized to penetrate open societies and to turn the power of modern technologies against us."[18] Individually identified terrorists, such as bin Laden, have proven remarkably difficult to locate and capture, and large-scale round-ups of "suspects," such as the thousands of immigrants detained in the U.S. shortly after September 11 or those since detained at Guantánamo Bay, have yielded few individuals against whom credible charges of terrorism can be made. According to David Cole,

> As of January 2004, the government had detained more than 5000 foreign nationals through its antiterrorism efforts. By any measure, the program has been spectacularly unsuccessful. None of these detainees has been determined to be involved with al Qaeda or the September 11 conspiracy.[19]

Perhaps as a result, the U.S. has also targeted states accused of harboring or supporting terrorists. In October 2001 Afghanistan was subjected to a bombing campaign, followed by an invasion that forced its Taliban rulers from power, and soon thereafter the groundwork for the invasion and occupation of Iraq began to be laid.[20] The message being forcefully delivered was not directed solely at the Taliban or Iraq's Saddam Hussein, but at all states whose rulers might consider acting in defiance of the United States or its allies.

A "rogue state" has generally been recognized as one "whose identity is to some extent defined by acting outside of the standard rules of international law."[21] U.S. officials, however, have expanded on this definition by describing rogue states as ones that "brutalize their own people and squander their national resources for the personal gain of the rulers[; d]isplay no regard for international law, threaten their neighbors, and callously violate international treaties to which they are party[; a]re determined to acquire weapons of mass destruction. . . [; s]ponsor terrorism around the globe[; r]eject basic human values and hate the United States and everything for which it stands."[22] Because such states and "their terrorist clients" must be stopped "before they are able to threaten or use weapons of mass destruction against the United States and our allies and friends,"[23] they have been viewed as legitimate targets in this Manichean conflict.

War Is the Appropriate Response to Terrorism

By September 12, 2001, barely twenty-four hours after the September 11 attacks, President George W. Bush had declared, "The deliberate and deadly attacks which were carried out yesterday against our country were more than acts of terror. They were acts of war."[24] Soon thereafter James Woolsey, a director of the Central Intelligence Agency under President Bill Clinton, concurred: "It is clear now, as it was on December 7, 1941, that the United States is at war. The question is: with whom?"[25] In his inaugural address, President Barack Obama agreed with the premise and answered the question by saying, "Our nation is at war, against a far-reaching network of violence and hatred."[26]

This third precept, that war is the most appropriate response to terrorism, is an ideological choice, not an inevitable conclusion. If the long-term goal is prevention of terrorist attacks, many scholars and political analysts have pointed out that the underlying causes of terrorism must be addressed.[27] Despite the fact that states can and have regularly engaged in "premeditated, politically motivated violence perpetrated against innocents," those deemed terrorists are usually individuals or groups frustrated by perceived injustices and effectively excluded from other forms of political power.[28] The general principle enunciated in the UN Charter that international peace and security cannot be achieved without safeguarding fundamental human rights and dignity, seems equally applicable to state and nonstate actors.

To some extent this is acknowledged by the United States' emphasis on the idea that its war on terror is being fought to defend liberty and justice and the recognition that a "world where some live in comfort and plenty, while half of the human race lives on less than $2 a day, is neither just nor stable."[29] Nonetheless, in his introduction to the *National Security Strategy (NSS)*, Bush was careful to note that poverty is not the cause of terrorism; the problem lies in its ability to create environments hospitable to terrorists. "Poverty does not make poor people into terrorists and murderers. Yet poverty, weak institutions, and corruption can make weak states vulnerable to terrorist networks."[30] Thus, although "legitimate grievances . . . must be addressed within a political process," the bottom line is that "no cause justifies terror."[31] The U.S. focus, therefore, has not been on identifying and addressing the root causes of terrorism, whatever they may be in any given case.

Even if the focus is to be on punishment rather than prevention, there are alternative methods that could be employed. Since well before September 11, 2001, the United States has had numerous laws under which terrorists, including those responsible for the attacks, could be criminally prosecuted.[32] As noted in a 2004 report of a UN High-Level Panel on Threats, Challenges, and Change, "virtually all forms of terrorism are prohibited by one of the 12 international counterterrorism conventions, international customary law, the Geneva Conventions or the Rome Statutes."[33] And, as the Panel added, if a military response was deemed necessary, the adequate procedures for the use of self-defense or collectively sanctioned force were available under Article 51 of the UN Charter.[34] Instead, however, the United States has claimed a unique, or exceptional, prerogative to respond with overwhelming military force designed to "shock and awe"[35] in a manner that exceeds legally permissible responses.[36]

The Usual Rules of Engagement Do Not Apply
Because the Enemy Is Uncivilized and Irrational

According to the United States, the laws of war, developed over several centuries by "civilized" states, cannot be adhered to in the current war on terror because "the enemy" consists of individuals, nonstate organizations, or "rogue" states that are motivated by "evil" rather than by discernable political or economic interests and because their leaders are irrational, or "madmen."[37] This fourth precept has been used to justify the United States' deviation from standard international norms because, presumably, an irrational enemy will not "play by the rules" either. From this perspective, there is no point in engaging in routine diplomacy or the politics of deterrence of the sort that characterized the Cold War. As the president stated in a 2002 West Point commencement address, "Deterrence—the promise of massive retaliation against nations—means nothing against shadowy terrorist networks with no nation or citizens to defend. Containment is not possible when unbalanced dictators with weapons of mass destruction can deliver those weapons on missiles or secretly provide them to terrorist allies."[38]

One of the most significant manifestations of American exceptionalism today is the assertion by the United States of a right to engage in "preemptive self-defense," at such times and in such manner as it deems appropriate. The UN Charter, acknowledged to be an international treaty that "trumps" all other agreements,[39] carefully delimits the circumstances under which armed force may be used by member states. Military actions undertaken in self-defense are permitted by Article 51 of the Charter, but this does not extend to preemptive use of force under the circumstances faced by the United States to date.[40] Rejecting the stance previously assumed by the United States,[41] the *NSS* declared: "While the United States will constantly strive to enlist the support of the international community, we will not hesitate to act alone, if necessary, to exercise our right of self-defense by acting preemptively against such terrorists."[42] In other words, "we recognize that our best defense is a good offense."[43]

Rejecting a "reactive posture," U.S. officials explained in 2002 that "the concept of imminent threat" must be adapted "to the capabilities and objectives of today's adversaries."[44] Because these adversaries—"the enemies of civilization"—use unconventional means and attack without warning, "anticipatory action" may be necessary "even if uncertainty remains as to the time and place of the enemy's attack."[45] Indeed, the goal is to "act against such emerging threats before they are fully formed," for "we cannot let our enemies strike first."[46] This, of course, was the rationale given for the subsequent U.S. invasion of Iraq in March 2003.[47]

Legal scholars Jeanne Woods and James Donovan point out that rationality is viewed in Western philosophy as the defining characteristic of civilized human beings, and therefore the characterization of the enemy as "uncivilized" justifies a preemptive attack because of the nature, rather than specific acts, of the enemy.[48] Thus they note that weapons of mass destruction "in the hands of 'civilized' governments is normal, even comforting," but their possession by "wild uncontrollable, irrational madmen" is inherently a crisis.[49] As Antony Anghie notes, the terrorist has now been constructed not only in terms of race or economics but of war: "It is principally through the language of war-as-self-defence that the 'other' is constructed, excluded from the realm of law, attacked, liberated, defeated and transformed."[50]

The other primary example of the exercise of American exceptionalism in the war on terror is found in the Bush administration's position, backed by lawyers in the Department of Justice, that the war on terror justified the administration's disregard for, or "reinterpretation" of, the Geneva Conventions and the prohibition on torture. Despite objections from the State Department and U.S. military officials, in January 2002 President Bush announced that members of al Qaida and the Taliban captured by U.S. forces would not be treated as prisoners of war protected by the Geneva Conventions.[51] Shortly thereafter White House Counsel Alberto Gonzales sent a memorandum to Bush that supported this position by arguing, among other things, that the "new paradigm" occasioned by the war on terrorism "renders obsolete Geneva's strict limitations on questioning of enemy prisoners and renders quaint some of its provisions."[52]

This position laid the groundwork for the subsequent torture of prisoners held at Guantánamo Bay, in Afghanistan and Iraq, and in secret prisons in undisclosed locations around the world,[53] most notoriously at the Abu Ghraib military prison in Iraq.[54] In perhaps its most flagrant assertion of a unique prerogative to disregard the norms of international law applicable to the rest of the world, the United States dismissed as inapplicable the laws of war embodied in the Geneva Conventions and significantly undermined the prohibitions against torture articulated in the Convention Against Torture, ratified by the United States[55] and accepted as a *jus cogens*, or preemptory, norm of customary international law.[56] Again, these decisions were rooted in the notion that the enemy is uncivilized and therefore less than truly human. As Woods and Donovan put it, "if the 'other' is nonhuman enough to kill with impunity in an unprovoked war, why would mere torture be objectionable upon capture? This is the background against which the degradations of Abu Ghraib should be viewed."[57]

Civilization Is at Stake and therefore Freedom and Democracy Are as Well

A fifth precept is that the war on terror is being fought to preserve civilization. "America will help nations that need our assistance in combating terror. And America will hold to account nations that are compromised by terror, including those who harbor terrorists—because the allies of terror are the enemies of civilization."⁵⁸ Civilization is the "good" being protected against "evil." Beyond that, "civilization" is not precisely defined, but it is clear that a Euroderivative conception, what we commonly call Western civilization, is being referenced and that it is intimately associated with certain values. As President Bush said in a speech to the German Bundestag, "America and the nations in Europe are more than military allies, we're more than trading partners; we are heirs to the same civilization. . . . Our histories have diverged, yet we seek to live by the same ideals. We believe in free markets, tempered by compassion. We believe in open societies that reflect unchanging truths. We believe in the value and dignity of every life."⁵⁹

Historian Richard Drinnon has noted in other contexts that the term "civilization" is not used "interchangeably with *culture*, so that other peoples might have 'civilizations.' Instead, [it is used] to distinguish Western superculture, or the one true 'civilization,' from so-called primitive cultures."⁶⁰ Or, as a former Bush administration legal adviser put it, the threat of terrorism can be likened to the "Goths' sacking of Rome," threatening "the possible emergence of another 1,000 years of religious obscurantism and the destruction of our liberal values."⁶¹ Despite their European origin, however, these values do, or should, apply to all. As George W. Bush added in his presentation to the Bundestag, "These convictions bind our civilizations together and set our enemies against us. These convictions are universally true and right."⁶²

The war on terror, therefore, is being fought for principles that are "right and true for all people everywhere," principles summarized in the *NSS* as "the nonnegotiable demands of human dignity: the rule of law; limits on the absolute power of the state; free speech; freedom of worship; equal justice; respect for women; religious and ethnic tolerance; and respect for private property."⁶³ Freedom is the touchstone to which justifications for the war have predictably returned, and democratic government has been posited as the key to its protection.⁶⁴ Antony Anghie observes, "Democracy plays a crucial dual role in this [war on terror]: it liberates the oppressed people of Islamic states and it creates law-abiding societies that would be allies rather than threats to the United States."⁶⁵ The concept of democracy also justifies the actions taken against the enemy:

Consider the ways in which U.S. officials . . . use the term "terrorist" as a way of defining a shifting and amorphous group of people characterized by their lack of civilization, their inhuman nature, and their bestiality. In the words of President Bush, Vice President Cheney, other executive branch officials, and members of Congress, terrorists are "fanatics," "brutal," "barbaric," "evildoers," "uncivilized," and "animals." The point of this rhetoric must be to classify terrorists and their supporters as "incapable" of participating properly in the social institutions or practices that are central to liberal democracy.[66]

Thus, within this paradigm, the purpose of the war on terror is to preserve civilization and, because freedom is a "right" that can be realized only through the structures of formal democracy adopted exclusively by "civilized" states, if civilization is lost then freedom and democracy will be lost as well.

There Is One Path of Human Progress and the United States Represents Its Highest Stage

As noted in the previous section, the war on terror has been characterized consistently as a struggle for a universalized, hegemonic construct of civilization, not just one particular culture, people, or way of life. It is simply presumed, not argued, that there is one path of human progress leading to ever higher forms of civilization. To again quote President Bush's introduction to the NSS, "The great struggles of the twentieth century between liberty and totalitarianism ended with a decisive victory for the forces of freedom—and *a single sustainable model* for national success: freedom, democracy, and free enterprise. . . . These values of freedom are right and true for every person, in every society—and the duty of protecting these values against their enemies is the common calling of freedom-loving people across the globe and across the ages."[67]

Thus a sixth basic precept of the U.S. war on terror has been the notion that the American model of social, political, and economic organization is the only truly viable option for any society and, as such, represents the highest stage of human development. Framed in that way, the United States has not only a right but a responsibility to remake the rest of the world in its image. President Bush said to the West Point graduating class in 2002, "The 20th century ended with a single surviving model of human progress." That model, clearly, was the American one, and he indicated a preference for extending it to the rest of the planet in relatively benign terms: "America cannot impose this vision—yet we can support and reward governments that make the right choices for their own people."[68] Nonetheless "support and reward" are powerful terms in light of the United States' immense political, economic, and military status, and the United States' clear intent to preserve its military options.

As frankly stated in the first sentence of the *NSS*, "The United States possesses unprecedented—and unequaled—strength and influence in the world,"[69] and it intends to preserve and expand this power. "The United States must and will maintain the capability to defeat any attempt by an enemy. . . . Our forces will be strong enough to dissuade potential adversaries from pursing a military build-up in hopes of surpassing, or equaling, the power of the United States."[70] Those who wish to be considered allies are warned to concentrate on economic development, conceding military primacy to the United States. In his West Point commencement address, President Bush emphasized, "Competition between great nations is inevitable, but armed conflict in our world is not. More and more, civilized nations find ourselves on the same side—united by common dangers of terrorist violence and chaos. America has, and intends to keep, military strengths beyond challenge . . . thereby making the destabilizing arms races of other eras pointless, and limiting rivalries to trade and other pursuits of peace."[71] While President Obama's Inaugural Address had a more conciliatory tone, he similarly emphasized that "we remain the most prosperous, powerful nation on Earth," adding by way of warning: "We will not apologize for our way of life, nor will we waver in its defense, and for those who seek to advance their aims by inducing terror and slaughtering innocents, we say to you now that our spirit is stronger and cannot be broken; you cannot outlast us, and we will defeat you."[72]

As is discussed in the following chapters, the belief that the United States represents the apex of civilization is not a recent development but a consistent theme throughout its history. What *is* new is that the United States apparently has the military, economic, and political capacity, for the first time in history, to impose its will on the entire planet. In Richard Falk's words, "The United States is by circumstance and design an emergent global empire, the first in the history of the world."[73] It is thus particularly important to understand the dynamics underlying the claim that the United States represents the forefront of civilization and therefore is justified in taking extraordinary measures to preserve it. The present inquiry begins by considering the notion of civilization that is invoked in this process.

The Construct of Civilization

"Civilization" undergirds each of the precepts of the war on terror outlined in the previous section and therefore U.S. justifications for deviating from international legal norms in responding to terrorism. However, the construct itself is rarely discussed; it is presumed that we know what "civilization" means, and that it is an inherently positive and desirable goal. Given its centrality to the discourse, this bears some scrutiny.

Civilization is often associated with the notion of living in cities. In describing the "founding legend of Western civilization," Richard Waswo notes that "[c]ities are literally what qualify us as civilized, and their prominence in the story suggests the precise nature of the civilization they embody."[74] According to the *Oxford English Dictionary* (*OED*), the word "city" derives from the Roman *civ'tade, civitas*, and *civis*. "Its primary sense was therefore 'citizenship'; thence concretely 'the body of citizens, the community'; only in later times was the word [associated with] the town or place occupied by the community."[75]

Because the terms "civic" and "civil" pertain to people living together in a community,[76] "civilization" could simply be a descriptive term applying to all human societies and cultures.[77] However, as the *OED* notes, it "more usually" means "a developed or advanced state of human society"; the first definition of "civilize" includes "to bring out of a state of barbarism; to instruct in the arts of life, and thus elevate in the scale of humanity."[78] Cities represent settlement, a benchmark by which "civilized" societies can be distinguished from "wandering savages," and "[s]ettlement in a new, unknown, uncultivated country is equivalent to an act of Creation" because it signifies "the transformation of chaos into cosmos."[79] Civilization has become, therefore, a term that connotes a measurable progression of human development with both substantive and normative implications.

As discussed in the previous section, the war on terror is portrayed by U.S. officials as a battle not just for civilization in a generic sense but for Western civilization. This brings into play the West's history of itself, one shaped in large measure by more than five centuries of European imperialism and colonialism.[80] Maori scholar Linda Tuhiwai Smith points out, "While colonies may have started as a means to secure ports, access to raw materials and efficient transfer of commodities from point of origin to the imperial centre, they also served other functions. . . . Colonial outposts were also cultural sites which preserved an image or represented an image of what the West or 'civilization' stood for."[81] Thus the "civilizing mission" invoked to justify the "new paradigm" of international law in the U.S. must be seen in the context of this history. First, however, to meaningfully assess and respond to claims of American exceptionalism, it is useful to clarify some of the presumptions upon which the construct of Western civilization rests. As noted below, each of these has been contested, factually as well as conceptually, but their ideological significance must be acknowledged.

Humanity Is Defined by Difference from and Domination over Nature

In the worldview common to Western civilization "human-ness" is defined by distinction from nature. People have linguistic and conceptual abilities that animals do not, allowing the development of art and literature; we cultivate the earth, which provides the material basis for our highly organized societies, distinguished particularly by cities; we have scientific understandings that allow us to produce goods, provide sophisticated services, and control our environment.[82] Each of these achievements is evidence of humanity's having "risen above" and subjugated nature.

This dichotomy is deeply rooted in the Judeo-Christian tradition, which tells us that, from "the Beginning," human purpose and well-being is correlated to the control of nature. Witness its Creator's initial instructions to humanity:

> So God created man in his *own* image, . . . male and female created he them. And God blessed them, and God said unto them, Be fruitful, and multiply, and replenish the earth, and subdue it: and have dominion over the fish of the sea, and over the fowl of the air, and over every living thing that moveth upon the earth.[83]

The message conveyed by this directive is, first, that people are separate from animals and have an essentially antagonistic relationship to nature. Further, all living beings have a clear place within a unitary and hierarchical ordering: God is the Creator and ultimate authority; he has charged humans, created in his likeness, with dominion over other living beings. Their mission is to "subdue" the earth.

This is clarified in a second passage from Genesis: "And out of the ground the Lord God formed every beast of the field, and every fowl of the air; and brought *them* unto Ad'am to see what he would call them: and whatsoever Ad'am called every living creature, that *was* the name thereof."[84] As most cultures apparently recognize, the act of naming defines what is named and, in that process, situates or places it within a particular understanding of the world. As such, it also carries with it the power to change that understanding, for languages are not simply collections of words or names capable of being individually correlated to the words of other languages; rather, they are holistic ways of organizing understandings, histories, and relationships.[85] According to educator Paolo Freire, by speaking their word, people transform their world.[86]

In the Judeo-Christian context, as Christian theologian Harvey Cox notes, the responsibility given to Adam for naming animals means that "man" is "their master and commander."[87] In this tradition the distinction between God, despite his anthropomorphic characterization, and his creation—people and the natural world—is signified by Adam's "fall from grace" by virtue of eating the forbidden fruit. Lakota theologian and attorney Vine Deloria Jr. points out that this sets the stage for the introduction of evil into the world, and also implies that humanity must overcome the corruption of nature in order to become closer to God.[88] Emphasizing the very different understanding of the relationship between people and nature in American Indian traditions, he says, "For many Indian tribal religions the whole of creation was good, and because the creation event did not include a 'fall,' the meaning of creation was that all parts of it functioned together to sustain it."[89]

By contrast, within the dominant Western paradigm, the civilized are juxtaposed to the savage who, by definition, live in a "state of nature." As summarized by English professor Richard Waswo, "Opposed to cultivation, which is civilized, is savagery, which isn't. And what is savage (*silvestris, silva*) is literally 'of the woods.' . . . Our languages thus encode the forms of fear and contempt felt by a settled agricultural community for other modes of material and social organization."[90] Perhaps even more fundamental, in this worldview civilization and human-ness are measured by distance from nature and thus defined by what they are *not*. Legal philosopher Peter Fitzpatrick explains that, when identity is thus created through negation, an "uncivilized" Other must always exist to confirm the existence of the civilized. This leads, he notes, to the creation of dichotomies, including savage/civilized, mad/normal, and child/adult, from which "there emerges a 'natural being,' a sub-social, sub-human sphere, the image of which underpins the affirmation of a society above nature."[91] As discussed throughout the following chapters, the construction and maintenance of such an Other is a recurring theme in both U.S. history and the development of international law.

Rationality, Particularly as Embodied in Science and Technology, Is the Benchmark of Civilization

Once we presume that people are defined by their distinction from nature, it follows that human progress or development is rightfully measured by the extent of their conquest of nature. This is implicit in the association of civilization with cities, but reaches much further with the bifurcation of mind and body and the status given to "reason," which is defined as a distinctly human attribute.[92] Rationality, facilitated by the presumptively unique human asset of language, is what allows human conquest and control of the earth through scientific and technological advances. Standard histories of civilization tend to draw the line between "prehistory" and history at the emergence of Neolithic culture, defined primarily by its substitution of chipped with polished stone tools. This is followed by the agricultural developments that allow for the accumulation of surplus, the establishment of more permanent settlements, and the development of metallurgy.[93]

Reason, manifest through science, gave us the steam engine, followed by an accelerating ability to convert natural substances such as coal and oil, and even atomic particles, into "fuels" whose energy was harnessed to industry. Industrialization propelled the growth of markets, ever more "efficient" modes of transportation, and urbanization.[94] As the Kenyan legal scholar Bosire Maragia emphasizes, in the Western paradigm,

> Science became the social context for producing the knowledge essential to the development of technology which in turn drove industrial production that came to be identified with social progress. The ideas of progress, civilization, and development required privileging science and technology as well as the systematic obliteration of all types of knowledge that were identified with primitive, uncivilized, and, today, underdeveloped societies.[95]

Conquering, settling, and productively transforming nature also, in this understanding, required the recognition of property and a system of law that would protect it. As Fitzpatrick puts it, property is, "to summarize various formulations of the Enlightenment, the foundation of civilization, the very motor-force of the origin and development of society, the provocation to self-consciousness and the modality of appropriating nature."[96]

Creation stories, whether classified today as "myth" or "science," define human understandings of origin, purpose, and identity. Cherokee author Thomas King's playful retelling of the "naming" passage from Genesis highlights some of the presumptions embedded within Western origin stories:

> First Woman's garden. That good woman makes a garden and she lives there with Ahdamn. I don't know where he comes from. Things like that happen, you know. . . .
> Ahdamn is busy. He is naming everything.
> You are a microwave oven, Ahdamn tells the Elk.
> Nope, says that Elk. Try again.

You are a garage sale, Ahdamn tells the Bear.
We got to get you some glasses, says the Bear.
You are a telephone book, Ahdamn tells the Cedar Tree.
You're getting closer, says the Cedar Tree. . . .
Wait a minute, says that GOD. That's my garden. That's my stuff.
"Don't talk to me," I says. "You better talk to First Woman."
You bet I will, says that GOD.[97]

King reminds us that we could take the notion of the absolute, all-controlling God less seriously; that other peoples did not need scientists to "discover" that chimpanzees or dolphins can communicate; that there is nothing inevitable or inherently superior about a world of microwaves, phonebooks, or "my stuff."

In other words, we could pay attention to the fact that there have been, and still are, a multitude of societies with very different understandings of human purpose—cultures that thrived for millennia in a sustainable manner, some of which have managed to avoid elimination or assimilation by more "advanced" civilizations. From their perspectives, science and technological developments may not be presumed inherently positive, but their potential judged and utilized in accordance with a wider range of values.[98]

This is not simply a hypothetical proposition. One recent example of the "triumph" of Western science over indigenous understandings is found in the conflict over the placing of an astronomical observatory on what is called Mt. Graham in Arizona. To the Apache, this site has long been known as *Dzil nchaa si an,* the center of their spiritual universe, "home of the Mountain spirit and other sacred beings which gave creation, guidance, strength, knowledge and direction to the Apache people."[99] Since the 1980s the Apache have resisted the placement of the observatory, including what was to be named the "Columbus Scope," on the summit of the mountain by a consortium that included the Vatican. The Vatican, however, unswayed by the protests, responded: "We are not convinced by any of the arguments thus far presented that Mt. Graham possesses a sacred character which precludes responsible and legitimate use of the land." Further, the statement continued by reading scientific advances back into its definition of what is sacred: "In fact, we believe that responsible and legitimate use of the land enhances its sacred character."[100]

We have been inundated recently with studies indicating that the scientific and technological advances of civilization, combined with the industrial development and population increases they have enabled, are killing the planet, and humanity with it.[101] To quote a few statistics,

Approximately half of the world's original forest is gone, and another 30% is degraded or fragmented. There are now 200 "dead zones" in the world's oceans, covering tens of thousands of square miles. Nearly one-third of the sea fisheries have collapsed, with the rate of decline accelerating towards complete loss of wild seafood just four decades from now. . . . [G]lobally, 20% of all mammals, 31% of all amphibians, and 12% of all bird species are threatened. . . . [T]he Earth's natural ecosystems have declined by 33% over the last thirty years. . . . Scientists warn that temperature increases world-wide may send more than a third of the planet's species into extinction within the next forty-four years.[102]

Nonetheless, science and technology continue to be considered the bench-marks of civilization.

A significant feature of Western science is that it "creates or 'discovers' order, even if that order is always held provisional, and it extends a unifying order presumptively to all that is yet to be discovered."[103] It is, in other words, all-encompassing, as illustrated by the fact that science and technology are most frequently proffered as the solution for impending ecological disas-ters.[104] Thus, for example, in President Obama's Inaugural Address, he prom-ised to "restore science to its rightful place, and wield technology's wonders to raise health care's quality and lower its cost. We will harness the sun and the winds and the soil to fuel our cars and run our factories."[105] Although this may have been a promise of "greener" technology, the president clearly intended to rely on scientific "advances" to maintain what may well be an unsustainable way of life. Even when it seems that the quest to dominate and subdue the earth will result in its destruction, the Western understanding of rationality, with its presumption that scientific and technological advances are inherently good, appears unshakeable.

Human History Is a Universal and
Linear Path of Progress toward Increased Civilization

Within the paradigm of Western civilization, history is the record of change insofar as it relates to people. Summarizing this view, J. M. Roberts introduces his one-volume *History of the World* by noting that despite our awareness of vast planetary and evolutionary changes, "commonsense" tells us that "history is the story of mankind. . . . We all know that dogs and cats do not have histories, while human beings do," and that "when historians write about a natural process beyond human control . . . they do so only because it helps us to understand why men and women have lived (and died) in some ways rather than others."[106] Once it has been established that controlling nature is humanity's primary purpose, it follows that human progress can and must be measured in terms of the achievement of that goal.

Incorporating the dichotomy between people and nature, the mandate to "subdue" the earth, and the central role of rationality, Roberts continues, "Humanity's unique achievement is its remarkably intense level of activity and creativity, its cumulative capacity to create change. . . . Human history began when the inheritance of genetics and behaviour which had until then provided the only way of dominating the environment was first broken through by conscious choice."[107] "Primitive" societies are regularly characterized as "static," stuck, as it were, in a state of nature. Having no marked changes to point to, no "development" from one stage to another, they are said to have no real histories, only myths and stories.[108]

Whether framed in terms of the religious traditions which posit a God who literally resides separately and above the natural world, or in the Enlightenment's "substitution of knowledge for fancy,"[109] there is a general consensus in the West that humanity shares a common objective called "civilization" and that its achievement is measured by the extent to which people have succeeded in controlling nature. Because it is a universal purpose, posited as true for all peoples, it can be judged "from above," by some rational and objective standard, rather than from a multiplicity of human perspectives. Thus framed, all of human history is assessed in terms of a linear progression toward higher forms of civilization, and the multiplicity of human histories are collapsed into one teleological narrative.[110] As noted by philosopher Ludwig Wittgenstein, this notion of progress is of the essence of Western conceptions of civilization: "Our civilization is characterized by the word 'progress.' Progress is its form rather than making progress being one of its features."[111]

Once one has accepted this unilinear path, at any given moment each society or culture can be ranked as more or less advanced, and it is the responsibility of those more "developed" to eliminate the less civilized or to "uplift" them through absorption or assimilation. Those who have not advanced toward this goal have no history worth telling; their histories begin, within this worldview, at the time of their "discovery" by "civilized" powers.[112] Native Hawaiian historian Haunani-Kay Trask captures this concept when she notes that, "burdened by a linear, progressive conception of history and by an assumption that Euroamerican culture flourishes at the upper end of that progression, Westerners have told the history of Hawai'i as an inevitable if occasionally bitter-sweet triumph of Western ways over 'primitive' Hawaiian ways."[113] In the context of the emergence of an international law that only recognized European sovereignty, Antony Anghie says, "The only possible history of the non-European world is the history of its absorption into the European world in order to move toward acquiring sovereignty."[114] Or, as Kwame Toure (Stokely Carmichael) put it a bit more bluntly: "History books tell you that nothing happens until a white man comes along."[115]

Once human history has been collapsed into a universalized narrative of progress, our options collapse into the either/or choice between more progress or less. Of course, one need not eschew all belief in progress to break out of the unidimensional and highly constricted linearity defined by the purveyors of Western civilization. As literary theorist Terry Eagleton warns in his critique of postmodernism,

> It is a mistake to believe that all grand narratives are progressive. . . . But to argue against History as progressive is not, of course, to claim that there is never any progress at all. . . . You do not need to believe in a golden age to hold that the past was in some respects better than the present, just as you do not need to be an odiously self-satisfied Whig to argue that the present is in some respects better than the past. . . . Nobody in this sense disbelieves in historical progress, and anyone who did would be making quite as meta-narrational a claim as someone who thought that history has been steadily on the up since the sack of Rome. But this is different from believing that, say, there is a universal pattern to history characterized by an inexorable growth of productive forces.[116]

It is possible to develop analyses that reject the vision of a grand Eurocentric "march through history" while still believing that one state of affairs can be characterized as more desirable than another, but this would require a rethinking of the premise that all human history falls into a singular and linear trajectory.

Western Civilization Represents the Highest Stage in the History of Human Development

If one accepts a universally applicable definition of human progress as leading to higher forms of civilization measured, in large part, by material or scientific development, one then has "objective" and "rational" means by which to judge a society or culture's relative degree of civilization. A fourth premise underlying not only the current war on terror but much of contemporary international law is that Western civilization represents the highest stage yet attained on that scale of human history. In making this case, arguments are generally presented of the relative material well-being of people in "civilized" states, as well as the extent to which freedom or human rights are espoused by their governments. In addition, Darwinian notions of evolution are often invoked to portray the Western powers' conquest of huge portions of the planet as evidence of their superiority.

J. M. Roberts gives a typical example of this in *History of the World*:

> By 1900 European civilization had shown itself to be the most successful which had ever existed. Men might not always agree on what was most important about it but no one could deny that it had produced wealth on an unprecedented scale and that it dominated the rest of the globe by power and influence as no previous civilization had ever done. Europeans (or their descendants) ran the world.[117]

As framed somewhat less glowingly by anthropologist Eric Wolf, the triumphalist "genealogy" of the West that we are generally taught converts history "into a tale about the furtherance of virtue, about how the virtuous win out over the bad guys. Frequently, this turns into a story of how the winners prove that they are virtuous and good by winning. If history is the working out of a moral purpose in time, then those who lay claim to that purpose are by that fact the predilect agents of history."[118]

As noted above, numerous peoples and cultures have been dismissed as "lesser" in the course of the past several centuries of European expansion on the ground that they were "savage," that is, "living in a state of nature," and therefore possessing no history. To some degree, this was accomplished by defining history as the record of advances along a given axis of material, social, or political change. Peoples whose ways of life had not significantly changed for hundreds or thousands of years had no history worthy of note, regardless of what they might believe. Thus, for example, the Hopi's placing of their history in the context of ecological changes brought about by fire, ice, and floods, and their ancestors' subsequent migrations, has routinely been relegated to the status of myth or legend, despite periodic "scientific" confirmation of various aspects of this history.[119]

In the process of collapsing all human history into the narrative of the ascendancy of the West, the histories of non-European peoples have "disappeared" in various ways. Often they have been overwritten by narratives which so consistently paint their subjects as backward, illiterate, or savage that they are presumed to have been incapable of producing anything "civilized." Methodologically this process has been greatly facilitated by Western scholars' insistence that only written history is "scientifically" verifiable and therefore reliable.[120] At the other extreme, the extraordinary libraries of those deemed Other—such as those maintained by the Egyptians in Alexandria,[121] the Moors in Cordova,[122] or the Aztecs at Tenochtitlán[123]—were intentionally destroyed in attempts to eliminate the histories documented therein.

It has proven difficult, however, for even the most Eurocentric historian to completely disregard the reality that other civilizations have not only existed but had extended geographic reach, built large cities with impressive infrastructures, and made significant scientific, medical, and artistic advances. As Fitzpatrick notes, evidence challenging the unique supremacy of Western civilization has not only been disregarded but has also been "re-cast."[124] Sometimes, the achievements of non-Europeans are dismissed as inconsequential because they did not, after all, result in the conquest of the planet. Roberts, for example, dismisses the Olmecs and the Chavin culture of Peru as "early lunges in the direction of civilization" which mysteriously disappeared and therefore are of little significance to history.[125] In other cases the achievements are acknowledged, but the people are not credited, a process that is simplified by constraining historical "evidence" to that which is verifiable by European scholars or scientists.[126] Thus Peter Tompkins could say in introducing his extraordinarily detailed account of the science embodied in the Great Pyramid of Cheops: "Till recently there was no proof that the inhabitants of Egypt of five thousand years ago were capable of the precise astronomical calculations and mathematical solutions required to locate, orient and build the pyramid where it stands."[127] From this perspective, the existence, age, and location of the Great Pyramid, to say nothing of Egyptian understandings of history, simply added up to "no proof."

Attempts have regularly been made to appropriate others' accomplishments into the master narrative of Western supremacy by giving them a European origin. Thus, despite their extensive contact with and reliance upon North African civilizations, the Greeks are credited with inventing mathematics, philosophy, and political democracy.[128] Even today a mainstream historian can glibly assert that "no doubt a primitive mathematics is part of the explanation of the sterility of the Egyptians' astronomical endeavors," dismissing this as yet "another field in which posterity, paradoxically, was to credit them with great things."[129] The incredible contributions of the Indigenous peoples of the Americas to agricultural production are routinely overlooked,[130] as are the extensive civilizations of the Olmec, Toltec, Aztec, Mayan, and Incan peoples.[131] In the Mississippi and Ohio river valleys of what is now the United States, tens of thousands of mounds existed prior to European contact. Seneca historian Barbara Mann reports that these were "myriad complexes of earthen mounds comprising graded highways leading out from geometrical circle-and-square earthworks, all platted across miles," enormous mounds in the shapes of birds, or badgers or serpents, and containing pipes, pottery, and artistic goods.[132] Mann explains not only how these mounds were systematically destroyed by American settlers, but documents in extensive detail a long history of attempts to prove that they were constructed by anyone except the Indigenous inhabitants of that area: "Indeed," she says, "had I set out to parody western scholarship, I could not have devised a better satire than that provided by the Euroamerican imagination, as it led the country on a wild-goose chase through ancient Greece, Rome, Egypt, Malaysia, Japan, and Atlantis in quest of the 'lost race' of American Mound Builders."[133]

Some older civilizations have been incorporated into the genealogy of the West and subsequently excluded to ensure that the narrative maintains a European hegemony. Linda Tuhiwai Smith observes that, "for this purpose, the Mediterranean world, the basin of Arabic culture and the lands east of Constantinople are conveniently appropriated as part of the story of Western civilization, Western philosophy and Western knowledge." With the rise of European imperialism, however, "these cultures, peoples and their nation states were re-positioned as 'oriental,' or 'outsider' in order to legitimate the imposition of colonial rule."[134] Thus, as international law developed, states such as Turkey were sometimes classified as "semi-civilized" or "barbarian" rather than "savage," and recognized as having advanced to some degree on the scale of civilization, and thus acknowledged to have limited legal rights.[135]

Western historians have gone to extraordinary lengths to fit the history of the Other into a narrative that has a predetermined outcome—the triumph of the West—yet still feel obliged to maintain the appearance of objectivity and rationality. Despite their best efforts, however, the mere existence of once-flourishing civilizations that fall outside the genealogy of Europe, such as that of the Egyptians, Chinese, or Aztecs, poses a major problem. How are we to know that contemporary Euroderivative civilization is not just another in a long line of such powers, rising, perhaps, but destined also to fall?

The response generally seems to be that Western civilization is distinguished by virtue of its superior scientific and political achievements. Prior civilizations may have had, for their times, tremendous military strength and scientific or technological prowess, but their demise is attributed to causes from which the West believes it can exempt itself. Where concrete information is unavailable—perhaps because written records were destroyed or because Western historians do not consider local people's oral histories "reliable"—there is often speculation that disease or ecological disaster may have been the cause.[136] Contemporary science, of course, is presumed adequate to protect at least those who in live in the most "developed" countries from military threat, disease, or natural disaster.

In other cases the downfall of previous empires is often attributed to lack of viable forms of political organization.[137] That story goes something like this: there were societies that made considerable material progress, but they crumbled under their own weight because they were not sufficiently democratic; their leaders became corrupt, perhaps the people revolted, and either internecine warfare or conflict with a stronger power destroyed the civilization and it fell into barbarism. The West, in this narrative, will not fall prey to this fate because, in addition to its scientific accomplishments, it has evolved structures of representative government capable of responding to changing circumstances and is therefore of potentially indefinite duration. Thus even in contemporary analyses which posit the imminent rise of non-Western states such as China or India, the predictions are based on those societies' adaptation to the Western model.[138]

This brings us to the capstone of the presumptions about Western civilization: that its political institutions uniquely protect values, often framed in terms of freedom, democracy, and fundamental human rights, which are not only universally applicable but desired by all peoples. This is not only the reason why it represents the apex of human development and is indefinitely sustainable, but why it can and should be extended to the entire planet, with all its diverse cultures and peoples. As Fitzpatrick summarizes, "progression becomes a force of universal transformation. . . . Non-Western 'others' come to be known and possessed within that universality, the knowledge of which can only be acquired by those others if and to the extent that they can enter positively into this universality. . . . The very modes and possibilities of escape are contained in a Western progression, in the grandest of 'grand narratives'—the liberation of humanity."[139]

Fulfilling the "Civilizing Mission": American Exceptionalism and the War on Terror

Putting together the basic presumptions about the construct of civilization outlined above, it becomes clear why the United States is promoting the war on terror as an epochal struggle for civilization, and why it considers itself uniquely situated to lead that war. As the world's sole superpower in a post–Cold War world where Western civilization has been deemed triumphant, the United States has a claim to hegemony that is deeply embedded in a history rooted in many centuries of European consolidation and colonial expansion. This is reinforced, of course, by its rendition of its historical origins. Eric Wolf summarizes this familiar narrative:

> We have been taught, inside the classroom and outside of it, that there exists an entity called the West, and that one can think of this West as a society and civilization independent of and in opposition to other societies and civilizations. Many of us even grew up believing that this West has a genealogy, according to which ancient Greece begat Rome, Rome begat Christian Europe, Christian Europe begat the Renaissance, the Renaissance the Enlightenment, the Enlightenment political democracy and the industrial revolution. Industry, crossed with democracy, in turn yielded the United States, embodying the rights to life, liberty, and the pursuit of happiness.[140]

Those who resist incorporation into this history may simply be "backward" and in need of enlightenment. Those who refuse to assimilate despite having been given the opportunity, and who persist in opposing the spread of Western civilization, are the "enemies of freedom" and must be destroyed.

Richard Waswo points out a "central process of *transmission* that makes this picture of civilization uniquely western . . . and rather odd."[141]

> [It is] a narrative of displacement, exile, conquest, and reconstruction . . . structured as a journey, the search for a predestined and permanent home. The story thus presents civilization as that which comes from somewhere else. Specifically, it is borne by exiles from the east to the west. There, it is imposed by force on the indigenous population, who may or may not be given the opportunity to assimilate themselves to it. In any case, should they resist, they are wiped out.[142]

The caveat I would add to this analysis is that the classic Euroderivative response to those who do not, cannot, or will not assimilate is a bit more complex, given the construction of the "civilized" as the negation of the "uncivilized" or "savage." Because Western identity relies so heavily on the negation of the Other and is so embedded in a universalizing history of the "rise" of humanity from a state of nature, an uncivilized—or at least deficiently civilized—Other is a *necessary* component of this identity. Legal scholar Antony Anghie uses the phrase "dynamic of difference" to refer to an "endless process of creating a gap between two cultures, demarcating one as 'universal' and civilized and the other as 'particular' and uncivilized, and seeking to bridge the gap by developing techniques to normalize the aberrant society."[143] Peter Fitzpatrick extends the concept to his analysis of the development of Western law, noting that it "is imbued with this negative transcendence in its own myth of origin where it is imperiously set against certain 'others' who concentrate the qualities it opposes."[144] Simply put, without the Other, "we" would not know who we are.

This understanding of the "Other" is rooted in the work of the intellectual historian Edward Said, who explained the Orient as "the place of Europe's greatest and richest and oldest colonies, the source of its civilizations and languages, its cultural contestant, and one of its deepest and most recurring images of the Other," a construct that "has helped to define Europe (or the West) as its contrasting image, idea, personality, experience."[145] As Said explains further,

> It can be argued that the major component in European culture is precisely what made that culture hegemonic both in and outside Europe: the idea of European identity as a superior one in comparison with all the non-European peoples and cultures. There is in addition the hegemony of European ideas about the Orient . . . usually overriding the possibility that a more independent, or more skeptical, thinker might have had different views on the matter.[146]

This theme is revisited frequently in the history of the legal theories of Euroamerican colonial expansion that follows, for the invariant need for an uncivilized Other to justify a universalizing, assimilationist framework of law sheds much light on what otherwise appear to be contradictory policies and practices in international law.

Each of the premises about the war on terror and the construct of Western civilization set forth above could be described in much more nuanced detail, of course, but they briefly summarize the ideology underpinning European colonial expansion and its American extension.[147] As discussed in the following chapters, the Indigenous peoples inhabiting the lands claimed by European and Euroamerican colonizers were identified as "heathen" and, increasingly, "savage."[148] Not being civilized—not having conquered nature—these

Others were deemed to have made no "progress" in the Western scheme of development and therefore had no prior history worth acknowledging. Once colonized peoples were defined as less than fully human, it was a short leap to justifying the appropriation of their "unsettled" lands for "productive" use and for either eliminating the inhabitants or using them, much as domesticated animals, simply for their labor power.[149]

Many continue to contest the process of colonization, and in what has been termed the "Fourth World" of Indigenous nations[150] there continue to be numerous societies where people are presumed to be an integral part of a nonhierarchical natural world, with a nonlinear history. In various forms, most of these cultures have an understanding of human purpose that relates to a responsibility to the earth, rather than a destiny, ordained by an all-powerful God to tame the savage wilderness.[151] The genealogy of the West that Wolf outlines is not a reflection of historical fact but rather an ideological construct serving particular ends. As Seneca scholar John Mohawk reminds us, the "linear descendency of culture from the Greeks to the Romans to the Franks, to the French, to the English, to America, to now," is presented as if "there's no choice" but, in reality, all peoples have many ancestors, and many worldviews from which to choose.[152] Gustavo Esteva and Madhu Suri Prakash emphasize in their *Grassroots Post-Modernism* that rather than accepting a universalized and hierarchical notion of human identity and purpose, one could look to the "pluriverse" of peoples, histories, and worldviews for alternative understandings of human "good" not dependent on scientific or technological "advances."[153]

Within the dominant Western perspective, it generally has come to be accepted that all peoples are equally capable of becoming "civilized" and should be given the opportunity to do so. Nonetheless the "rights" that attend this concession remain, for the most part, deeply embedded in a framework that still accepts the precepts of a distinctly Euroderivative worldview. If one accepts the basic presumptions of this model, it is not difficult to make a case for the United States as representing, at least currently, the most evolved form of Western civilization. From there, it does not require much to accept its claims to exceptionalism, and to acquiesce in, perhaps even enthusiastically endorse, unilateral U.S. actions that it claims are for the greater good of humanity. Because we are now making political choices that will significantly affect the future of international law and world order, we would do well to consider not only the premises underlying our contemporary worldview but also the historical contexts from which these presumptions arose and in which they have been implemented.

Civilizing the Other

Colonial Origins of International Law

> When we Europeans felt we were barbarians, the Trojan legend
> told us we weren't; now that we know that we were barbarians
> but aren't any longer, we can drop the legend from our history,
> and use it henceforth to determine the history of the barbarians
> we've so lately discovered. The use of the legend . . . to deter-
> mine the fate of the indigenous populations in the new world
> is clearly visible in the formation of a special branch of law.
> This would eventually become international law, and was cre-
> ated expressly to deal with the accelerating conflicts among the
> major powers of Europe, due in large part to their competing
> claims over territory and trading privileges in the new world,
> and with the vexed question of the respective "rights" of the
> colonizers and the colonized.
> —Richard Waswo, *The Founding Legend of Western Civilization*

The U.S. assertion of a unilateral prerogative to conduct the current war on terror as it sees fit has many critics, but, nonetheless, its notion of a "new paradigm" of international law has met with little resistance. Some of this might be attributed to the United States' status as the world's sole superpower, but few would concede that this new paradigm is simply one of "might makes right." Instead, its acceptability to much of the American public and to U.S. allies rests on its incorporation of themes pervading the history of "Western civilization" and the international legal norms that have developed in conjunction with the consolidation of European power over many centuries.

As Richard Waswo points out, the legend of the noble Trojans who escape Greek attacks and flee west to establish Rome, a city destined to become the center of an "empire without end," is repeated in various forms throughout European history. In each iteration of the story, the hero, like Virgil's Aeneas, travels from East to West, bringing the arts and sciences with him, from the founding of Britain, to the *Reconquista* of the Iberian Peninsula, on to the "New World."[1] Or, in Peter Fitzpatrick's words, "Light travels, as Hegel helpfully reminds us, from East to West, coeval with 'the History of the World.'"[2] In each version the superiority of European civilization has been portrayed as "the redemptive source of the West's presumed mandate to impose its vision of truth on non-Western peoples."[3]

Conquest was always significant to this narrative, but the claim to be bringing the world to a higher stage of civilization could not be based solely on raw power. This would pose significant ideological problems, given the contrast the West has relied upon between the "order" characterizing its societies and the state of constant warfare it claims prevailed among those deemed savage.[4] The standard narrative of colonial expansion relies on the premise that

> Native society is simple, small and self-contained. It is characterized by uncertainty, stasis, inefficiency, and by a lawless or only incipiently legal condition. The colonists claim to bring a civilization which will provide many things, among them security and order, incorporation within a dynamic history, efficiency, law, and the opportunity for progress by means of social functions becoming differentiated.[5]

Thus law (accompanied by "order") has assumed a primary role in Western civilization, and European colonial expansion was conceived, from the beginning, as a legal project.[6]

Western conceptions of a unitary and hierarchical system of law fit very conveniently into the model of a world in which God ruled over "man" and man, in turn, was responsible for governing nature.[7] Once civilization had been defined in terms of distance from nature, the gradation of humanity into those more and less civilized justified the rule of the civilized over the barbarian or the savage, allowing law to become an instrument of either subordinating or "uplifting" the Other, depending upon one's perspective.[8] Furthermore, in practical terms, law became a means of governing relations between the "civilized" states aspiring to empire, enabling them to devote their resources to acquiring territories and developing trade rather than fighting one another.[9]

American exceptionalism, as articulated today and throughout U.S. history, has a great deal of resonance in what has been characterized as the "civilized" world because, even as the United States has claimed a prerogative to deviate from accepted international norms or shun transnational institutions, it has invoked foundational principles of the "law of nations" to support that claim. Because international law was designed not only to regulate relations between recognized states but also to rationalize their colonial ventures, it has always incorporated and relied upon the precepts of civilization outlined in the previous chapter. This has allowed the United States to invoke these presumptions, directly or indirectly, to argue that its distinctly American version of internationalism provides a superior path to implementing the underlying purposes and principles of international law. If our goal is to decolonize international law, and transform it into a global system of justice truly capable of universal application, we have to critically evaluate not only particular U.S. policies and practices but the presumptions of an international legal system designed to facilitate imperial expansion. This chapter briefly outlines the foundations of international law from this perspective, highlighting themes that continue to shape contemporary international relations.

Crusading Justice

On September 16, 2001, President Bush announced that "This is a new kind of . . . evil. . . . This crusade, this war on terrorism is going to take a while."[10] The use of the term "crusade" both by the president and by Vice President Dick Cheney evoked pained responses from U.S. allies, Arab leaders, and Arab Americans, among others, leading White House spokesperson Ari Fleischer to quickly, if somewhat ineptly, attempt to retract it by saying, "I think to the degree that that word has any connotations that would upset . . . anybody . . . the president would regret if anything like that was conveyed. But the purpose of his conveying it is in the traditional English sense of the word, it's a broad cause."[11] It is difficult to believe that both Bush and Cheney were unaware of the history or imagery the term "crusade" would evoke, but if it has come to mean a "broad cause" in ordinary English, that would attest to how deeply entrenched the notion of a crusade, or "just war," to extend and protect Western civilization has become in American ideology.[12]

Law, as promulgated by the Church of Rome, was the force legitimating Christian conquest, both before and after the Crusades of 1096–1271, and to a considerable extent the origins of contemporary international law can be found in the Church's struggle to answer what Robert A. Williams Jr. has termed the central question of the Crusades: "Under what circumstances might Christians legitimately dispossess pagan peoples?"[13] During this period, the existence of a unitary and hierarchical system of law, ordained by God, was presumed by Christians; their debates focused on the rights of non-Christians under natural law, and the relative supremacy of religious and secular rulers.

The legal foundation for the Crusades was laid in the mid-eleventh century by Pope Alexander II and his archdeacon Hildebrand, who extended St. Augustine's definition of "just wars" from only those waged in self-defense or to recover stolen property, to those approved by God.[14] At this time one of the most powerful tools of social control wielded by the Roman Church was its self-proclaimed monopoly on the forgiveness of sins, and this was utilized by Alexander II to give Christian warriors preemptive absolution for the killing of infidels as he sanctioned not only the attempted *Reconquista* of the Iberian Peninsula and the Norman invasion of England in 1066 but also sustained expansion into the "pagan" lands of Eastern Europe.[15] Hildebrand became the next pope and, as Gregory VII, he consolidated the position that the Church was both the embodiment and the arbiter of natural law. Any secular ruler who refused to acquiesce to papal rule was defying natural law, and therefore was an "evil prince" possessed by demonic "madness."[16] It was, of course, the responsibility of the Church to bring such rulers into compliance with natural law. "Difference mandating remediation thus emerged as a central category in Western legal and political thought and discourse."[17]

The "difference" at issue can, of course, be seen from several different perspectives. Even Lady Flora Louisa Shaw Lugard, "Colonial Editor" for *The Times* of London, described North Africa during the time of the Crusades in glowing terms:

> Throughout the dark period of the Middle Ages, when the Catholic Church was asserting its claim to dominate the conscience of the western world . . . all that was independent, all that was progressive, all that was persecuted for conscience's sake took refuge in the courts of Africa. Art, science, poetry, and wit found congenial homes in the orange-shaded arcades of the college of Hez, in the palaces of Morocco, and in the exquisite gardens of Tripoli and Tunis.[18]

These sites were all, of course, part of the same Islamic empire that was even then establishing large and prosperous cities, extensive agricultural development, science and industry, art and literature, public libraries, and universities on the Iberian Peninsula.[19]

The accomplishments of Islamic civilization were no secret, but this hardly prevented Christian leaders from painting Islamic leaders as barbaric. Pope

Urban II launched the First Crusade by announcing that "an alien people, a race completely foreign to God" had invaded Jerusalem and were there committing acts of barbarism and "defil[ing] the Holy Places with their filth."[20] As incentive, he extended the special benefits traditionally associated with spiritual pilgrimages to this military expedition.[21] The Pope was from France and deeply troubled by the constant battles being waged among the French, to whom he was speaking when he announced this Crusade. Anxious to divert their energies onto an Eastern enemy, he urged: "You, who have so often been the terror of your fellow men, go and fight against the barbarians. . . . If you must have blood, bathe in the blood of the infidels."[22] As characterized by Williams, Urban essentially attributed the strife within European societies to overcrowding and made "a *Lebensraum* argument in support of Eastern colonization, virtually identical in style and tone to the Discovery-era recruitment calls fashioned by later European promoters of colonization in the New World."[23]

Historian Janet Abu-Lughod notes that "by 1250 and particularly after Europe's 'discovery' of the Mongols, the benign hope of converting the world to Christianity began to fade as Europeans gained a better sense of the geographic size and population of the non-Christian world."[24] Within the European paradigm, this intensified questions concerning the legal rights of "infidels," especially in lands to which Christendom could not make a plausible prior claim. In the mid-thirteenth century Pope Innocent IV attempted to reconcile Aristotelian natural law with the notion of papal supremacy by declaring that non-Christian peoples were rational beings and thus subjects of natural law, but that those who rejected God's will were irrational and therefore in violation of that law.[25] The Church, of course, was responsible for ensuring the enforcement of this law. Within this universalizing vision of law intent on eliminating or assimilating all other perspectives, infidels possessed and had "dominion" over their lands, but if they insisted on acting "irrationally" by denying Christian supremacy, their property could be confiscated.[26]

Thus, "centuries prior to Columbus's transatlantic voyage, the thirteenth-century canon lawyer-pope Innocent IV had discovered for Christendom a new world of legal discourse, premised on the central orienting myth that the Christian European's vision of reason and truth entailed norms obligatory for all peoples."[27] Regardless of whether George W. Bush intended his characterization of the war on terror as a "crusade" to be interpreted literally, it is not surprising that those with some understanding of this history would see the parallels between the Crusades of the Middle Ages and Bush's proclamation of a war fought for the "convictions which bind [American and European] civilizations together . . . [and which] are universally true and right."[28]

Pope Innocent IV's formulation, which recognized that "infidels" had natural rights and simultaneously asserted "suprajurisdictional papal authority . . . where it was clearly necessary for the pope to intervene in order to protect the infidels' spiritual well-being,"[29] laid the foundation for the theories of international law later articulated to accommodate and regulate the colonial enterprise. In turn, these theories have been absorbed into contemporary transnational norms and structures and into the United States' rationale for its expansion, consolidation, and current international policies.

Unifying Europe

Europe, of course, is "both a region and an idea," as Robert Bartlett says in introducing *The Making of Europe*.[30] Before Europe could launch its so-called Age of Discovery and proceed to spread its version of civilization across the planet, the various peoples within the region had to be "Europeanized."[31] This process was taking place before, during, and after the Crusades and continued even as Portugal and Spain were "discovering" and colonizing Africa and the "New World." It involved not simply the expulsion of Islam but also the conquest and assimilation of many "pagan" peoples indigenous to the lands we now consider part of Europe, reminding us that many of the legal theories that evolved to justify the conquest and absorption of the Other were first used by Europeans on their immediate neighbors.[32] This history reminds us, as well, that although in its later phases the discourse of colonialism became increasingly racialized (as we now understand that term), the colonial project always emphasized perceived cultural and religious difference, whether or not these were described in racial terms, to justify political domination.[33]

In consolidating the power of the Roman Church in the mid-eleventh century, Pope Nicholas II countered Germanic imperial ambitions by entering into an alliance with the Normans and legitimating their conquest of southern Italy.[34] As noted above, shortly thereafter Pope Alexander II gave his blessing to both the reconquest of the Iberian Peninsula and the imposition of Norman feudalism in Britain.[35] Contemporaneously Christian forces were moving into territories occupied by the western Slavs, Prussians, Lithuanians, Latvians, Livonians, Estonians, and Finns described as the "arc of non-literate polytheism that stretched from the borders of Saxony to the Arctic Circle, . . . the most enduring bastion of European paganism."[36] The western Slavs were officially conquered in 1168, when the Danes invaded, destroyed their temples, and placed them under the rule of Christian bishoprics.[37] Conquering the remainder of the Baltics took much longer and was spearheaded initially by German missionaries and merchants. Beginning in the early 1200s the Teutonic Knights and other Germanic crusading orders extended their colonizing ventures into Eastern Europe, with the backing of Frederick II who, as head of the Holy Roman Empire, had assumed the mission of conquering all the barbarian nations of the world.[38]

As Robert Bartlett observes, one of the distinguishing features of Western Christianity was its "insistence on the dominance of one liturgical language and one cultic form," and its "goals were 'unity' (unitas) and 'harmony' (consonantia)" in its rituals.[39] As the construct of Latin Christendom evolved, this notion of "unity" expanded to form the basis of a perceived ethnic identity which unified diverse peoples across Western Europe. It also provided the rationale for extending colonial rule to Christian peoples who failed to conform sufficiently to Rome's dictates.[40]

Thus, for example, the Irish had been converted in the fifth century but maintained forms of social, political, and religious organization that diverged significantly from Roman practice. According to Bartlett,

> The absence of a territorial, tithe-funded church or unitary kingship, the very distinctive system of kinship and the non-feudal, uncommercialized economy struck Latin clergy and Frankish aristocrats as outlandish. When St. Bernard described the Irish in the early twelfth century, he wrote of their "barbarism" and their " beastlike ways," criticized their marriage customs . . . and concluded by condemning them as "Christians only in name, pagans in fact."[41]

Such characterizations justified Anglo-Saxon and Norman invasions of Ireland and established a precedent that would be relied on both in other portions of Europe and in the non-European world to rationalize the colonization of even those who had converted to Christianity.[42]

The contradictions inherent in this position, however, eventually instigated a rearticulation of the legal rationale of conquest from one relying solely on a religious mandate to one incorporating principles of natural law. The Baltics had been the site of a number of Christian campaigns in the twelfth and thirteenth centuries, which met with limited success.[43] Well into the latter half of the fourteenth century, the Germanic order of Teutonic Knights continued their attempts to conquer both Poland, a Christian state, and its ally, "pagan" Lithuania.[44] Eventually, to solidify the alliance, the

Lithuanian king agreed to Christianize his nation as well, but the Knights continued their holy wars, which consisted primarily of regular and profitable raids, arguing that neither Poland nor Lithuania was genuinely, or sufficiently, Christian.[45] The legitimacy of these claims eventually came before the 1414 Council of Constance. The Council, after much debate, condemned the activities of the Teutonic Knights, relying upon Pope Innocent IV's theory of the natural rights of infidels to dominion over their lands.[46]

This decision set the stage for the law that would apply to the colonization of the lands that were soon to be "discovered" by the European powers. The conquest of the Other would henceforth be justified within the framework of their "natural rights," which were, of course, determined by those who were invading their lands.[47] As discussed in the following sections, despite this shift in the legal theory undergirding colonial relations, the hegemonic vision of "unity" espoused by the Roman Church would continue to inform the West's understanding of natural law. As Robert Williams summarizes, the "conquest of infidel peoples and their lands could proceed according to a rule of law that recognized the right of non-Christian people either to act according to the European's totalizing normative vision of the world or to risk conquest and subjugation for violations of this Eurocentrically understood natural law."[48] Both the theory and practices accompanying this expansion were developed first with the Portuguese claims to the Canary Islands and their incursions into Africa as well as with the Spanish ventures into the Americas, and they were subsequently applied by the English in Ireland and in the New World.[49]

The "Age of Discovery"

Christian crusaders took Lisbon from the Moors in 1147, and by the end of the century Portugal was recognized by the Church as an independent kingdom.[50] As Immanuel Wallerstein explains, for the next several hundred years Portugal's relative stability, its geographic location, its continued contact with the Islamic world surrounding the Mediterranean, its commercial experience, and the financing of Genoese investors all positioned it to take the lead on Atlantic exploration and expansion.[51] By 1341 the Portuguese had laid claim to the Canary islands, and in 1415 they extended the *Reconquista* to the Moroccan side of the Strait of Gibralter, opening the door to further incursions into the west African coast and nearby islands.[52] Portuguese claims in these territories were contested by the neighboring kingdom of Castile, and the resulting violence led Pope Eugenius IV to ban all European Christians from the Canaries in 1434 for the protection of the islanders. This unusual prohibition on colonization was based on the recognition of "infidel" rights articulated by Innocent IV and confirmed by the more recent Council of Constance.[53] The ban, however, did not last long.

Upon their "discovery" the Canary islanders had been described by the Portuguese as friendly and welcoming, their leaders wearing colorful and well-sewn goatskin clothing. Several were immediately kidnapped and taken to Portugal, where they were described by Giovanni Boccaccio as "robust of limb, courageous, and very intelligent. When spoken to by signs they replied in the same manner. . . . They sang very sweetly, and danced almost as well as Frenchmen. They were gay and merry, and much more civilized than many Spaniards."[54] In contesting the papal ban a century later, however, King Duarte of Portugal argued the importance of bringing civilization to the "nearly wild" islanders who had neither houses nor clothing worthy of the name, and "are not united by a common religion, nor are they bound by the chains of law, they are lacking in normal social intercourse, living in the country like animals."[55]

Duarte also argued that by granting the Portuguese the exclusive right to Christianize the islanders, the Pope could prevent their exploitation by other European powers perhaps less friendly to Rome. The papal response, *Romanus Pontifex*, recognized Portugal's right to acquire the Canaries and, as reissued several times over the following decades, it opened up the African continent to Portuguese colonization, always in terms "emphasiz[ing] the more benign, paternalistic elements of papal suzerainty."[56] Conquest would bring civilization to the native inhabitants and, in return, Portugal received exclusive trading rights vís-à-vís other European colonial powers. The primary "commodity" of that trade would prove, of course, to be slaves.[57]

The Portuguese monopoly on African colonization left Spain looking for expansion in other directions. In 1492 the Moors were driven from Grenada, their final stronghold on the Iberian Peninsula; in an early instance of "ethnic cleansing," Muslim and Jewish residents were forced into exile unless they converted to Christianity.[58] The rulers of the newly united Spanish kingdom could now turn their attention to outward expansion, beginning with the request of Cristóbal Colón (Christopher Columbus) that they underwrite a voyage to find a western trade route to the Indies.[59] Queen Isabella obtained the approval of her ecclesiastical committees on the matter, and she authorized Columbus "to discover and acquire certain islands and mainland in the ocean sea" in exchange for which he would be appointed "our Admiral of the said islands and mainlands . . .[and] Viceroy and Governor therein."[60]

Columbus, of course, made his way to the opposite side of the planet, where he "discovered" and claimed Spanish title to a number of islands, beginning with the Taíno homeland of Guanahani, which he promptly renamed San Salvador. And we all lived happily ever after. Oops, wrong story. [61]

Columbus' "discoveries" and his subsequent actions as Viceroy and Governor raised a series of legal problems. The first related to the "natural rights" of the islands' inhabitants. Did they not, like the "pagans" of Lithuania or the Canary islanders, have legal dominion over their lands? Furthermore, Spain had not received papal sanction for the voyages, and Portugal was preparing to engage in its own exploration of the "New World." [62] Both these problems were resolved by Pope Alexander VI, of the Borgia family, who issued a series of papal bulls that first declared, to quote Robert Williams, that the Pope could "place non-Christian peoples under the tutelage and guardianship of the first Christian nation discovering their lands as long as these peoples were reported . . . to be 'well disposed to embrace the Christian faith.'" [63]

Alexander's best-known bull, *Inter caetera II*, clarified territorial claims by dividing the non-European world into eastern and western portions, with Portugal receiving "rights" to colonize Africa, and what is now Brazil and Spain granted exclusive access to the remainder of the North and South American continents. Any interference with these decrees would meet with the Church's ultimate legal sanction of excommunication. [64] The colonial enterprise was thus justified by the bringing of Christianity, that is, civilization, to the hitherto "undiscovered" peoples who had been placed by the Church under the "guardianship" of European sovereigns. The practices of colonialism, however, immediately generated more complex legal questions addressing the treatment of the peoples encountered.

Columbus returned to the Caribbean in 1493 with a larger military force and established himself on the island he named Española, which today is divided between Haiti and the Dominican Republic. His initial expectations of finding large quantities of gold were soon disappointed, and he quickly resorted to sending Indian captives to Spain as slaves. [65] Those who remained on the island faced conditions that have been described in numerous contemporaneous accounts, but perhaps most famously by the Dominican friar Bartolomé de las Casas:

> In this time, the greatest outrages and slaughterings of people were perpetrated, whole villages being depopulated. . . . The Indians saw that without any offense on their part they were despoiled of their kingdoms, their lands and liberties and of their lives, their wives, and homes. As they saw

themselves each day, perishing by the cruel and inhuman treatment of the Spaniards, crushed to earth by the horses, cut in pieces by swords, eaten and torn by dogs, many buried alive and suffering all kinds of exquisite tortures.[66]

As Kirkpatrick Sale notes, to obtain as much gold as possible, "every Taíno over the age of fourteen had to supply the rulers with a hawk's bell of gold every three months . . . those who did not were, as [Columbus' brother] Fernando says discreetly, "punished"—by having their hands cut off, as las Casas says less discreetly, and left to bleed to death."[67] Where the Spanish did find concentrations of gold, the Indians were forced to labor in the mines, where many thousands died.[68]

By 1496 it is estimated that the native Taíno population of Española had dropped from as many as eight million to three million, with perhaps one hundred thousand remaining by 1500, when Columbus was recalled to Spain to face criminal charges for his conduct.[69] By then, however, Columbus had established a "dynasty" in the islands, and the process he had initiated continued unabated.[70]

The governor sent to replace Columbus in 1501 had been instructed to abolish slavery on Española, but by that time the Spanish settler-colonists were becoming rich from the feudal system they had instituted and were resistant to any significant changes. The Crown, therefore, approved the *encomienda* system, which allowed enslavement for the alleged purpose of converting the Indigenous population. Articulating a theme that would be echoed throughout European colonies around the world, and by the U.S. government in its treatment of American Indians into the twentieth century,[71] King Ferdinand decreed: "Because of the excessive liberty the Indians have been permitted, they flee from Christians and do not work. Therefore they are to be compelled to work, so that the kingdom and the Spaniards may be enriched, and the Indians Christianized."[72]

As a result of the direct slaughter of civilians and the impressment or enslavement of the remainder, the population of the Caribbean islands plummeted, with the 1514 Spanish census of the Taíno population reporting only twenty-two thousand Indians. This number would drop to 200 by 1542, after which the Taíno were considered "extinct."[73] Las Casas ultimately estimated that twenty million Indians had been killed.[74] The genocidal policies of the Spanish colonizers and the decimation of the native populations throughout the Caribbean Basin generated yet another legal crisis. Not only were these policies clearly unsustainable for a colonial project that relied on Indian labor, but it was difficult to argue that Christian civilization and salvation were being brought to peoples who, quite literally, were being exterminated. Again, the debate focused on the rights and capacities of the Indigenous peoples at issue.

The first priests sent to the New World were the Franciscans, who generally avoided attempts to convert the Indians, instead considering their primary task to be ministering to the Spanish colonists.[75] In 1510, however, Dominicans arrived and soon began denouncing the atrocities they witnessed being committed against Española's Indigenous population.[76] King Ferdinand was forced to call a council, which met in Burgos in 1512, to consider whether Indians were rational beings and whether they had to be enslaved to be saved. This council determined that Indians had diminished capacity for reason and approved the *encomienda* system as a means of all-encompassing regulation of Indian life, the stated goal being their total assimilation to European norms.[77] In actuality:

> The institution known as the *encomienda* [was] a new variant of an old Castilian principle by which the governor [of a Spanish colony] could give, or "commend," certain Indians to various colonists (*encomenderos*) to use as they might choose (for tribute or forced labor), in return for which the masters' only obligation was to provide their charges with instructions on becoming good Christians. It was not *called* slavery, to be sure, and indeed the Indians were supposed to be paid pittances, but that was a provision no one much bothered to enforce, and the institution was essentially indistinguishable from outright slavery.[78]

As was "explained" at the time, subjugating Indians in this fashion was not only appropriate but necessary because "their marriages are not a sacrament but a sacrilege. They are idolatrous, libidinous, and commit sodomy. Their chief desire is to eat, drink, and worship heathen idols, and commit beastial obscenities."[79] Besides, they did not "know how to care for what they acquire [by] mining gold or tilling the soil . . . spending only for necessities, as a Castilian laborer would."[80] Hence, under the Laws of Burgos, "the Indians' normative divergence was [construed as] proof positive of an irrational incapacity [and] the Indians' consent to be governed was logically irrelevant to the drafters of the code."[81] This diminished legal status of Indigenous peoples would become a hallmark of European colonial rule around the world, persisting in the contemporary era.[82]

These debates laid the groundwork for the notorious *Requerimiento*, the Spaniards' legal charter for their colonial ventures. Because questions had been raised at Burgos concerning Spain's reliance on the papal bulls to claim territories in the Americas, Ferdinand commissioned two legal scholars, Matías de Paz and Juan López de Palacios Rubios, to delineate the Spanish rights of conquest.[83] Paz argued that the Pope's authorization gave the king the right to "govern these Indians politically and annex them forever . . . [and, after their conversion,] to require some services from them . . . to cover the travel costs and other expenses connected with the maintenance of peace and good administration of those distant provinces."[84] López, concerned about relying exclusively on the notion of the Pope's universal jurisdiction, added natural law arguments.

It was López who drafted the *Requerimiento*, which theoretically accepted the notion of the natural rights of "infidels" but, in reality, simply informed the Indigenous peoples of their legal obligation to abide by the conquistadors' version of historical and religious truth, including Spain's assertion of the right to rule their lands. Though the Indians' consent to allow missionaries was to be requested, it was an offer they were not allowed to refuse. In the event of such a refusal, the *Requerimiento* stated, "we shall take you and your wives and your children and shall make slaves of them, . . . and we shall take away your goods and shall do to you all the harm and damage that we can."[85] In fact, all this was irrelevant for, as Lewis Hanke observed, in practice it became a mere formality, read not only in a language that the Indians could not possibly understand but "to trees and empty huts . . . on the edge of sleeping Indian settlements, or even a league away before starting the formal attack," or to the Spanish soldiers rather than to the Indians they were about to slaughter.[86]

This legal formalism—or, perhaps more accurately, this magical incantation—was not abandoned until 1556, by which time Spain had decimated most of the peoples at issue.[87] In the meantime, however, despite the legal rationalizations provided both by the papal bulls and the *Requerimiento*, controversy over the practices employed to "civilize" the Indians persisted within the Spanish Church, much as today the U.S. practices of rendition and torture are debated, even among those who fundamentally agree on the goals of the war on terror. Most famously, las Casas debated Juan Ginés de Sepúlvida in Valladolid in 1550, where las Casas argued, based on his experiences in the Indies, that the native peoples had the rational capacity to become true Christians, ultimately overcoming Sepúlvida's arguments that the Indians lacked the rational capacity to comport with the law of nature, or *jus gentium*, and were therefore "natural slaves."[88] Although las Casas won that round, this debate would persist wherever chattel slavery was utilized by colonial forces.

Franciscus de Vitoria: "On the Indians Lately Discovered"

Within Spain the legal framework of colonialism also continued to be contested, spurring the evolution of what we now know as international law. The most influential scholar in that regard was Franciscus de Vitoria, who, in the course of applying the principles of Thomistic natural law to Spanish "discoveries" and settlement, laid the foundation in the early sixteenth century for an international jurisprudence designed to address relationships not only between the colonizers and the colonized but also between what Europeans recognized as independent sovereign states.[89] This move toward the universalization of law was, in Robert Williams' words, a "singular innovation" that "initiated the process by which the European state system's legal discourse was ultimately liberated from its stultifying, expressly theocentric, medievalized moorings and was adapted to the rationalizing demands of Renaissance Europe's secularized will to empire."[90]

Vitoria's legal framework was explicated in a series of lectures dealing with relations between the Spanish and the Indians of the New World, most famously *De Indis Noviter Inventis* ("On the Indians Lately Discovered") and *De Jure Bellis Hispanorum in Barbaros* ("On the Law of War Made by the Spaniards on the Barbarians").[91] Most fundamental, Vitoria replaced reliance upon divine law with a natural law whose origins can be traced to the teachings of Thomas Aquinas and the papal decrees of Innocent IV. He proceeded, however, to identify, or create, "universal" norms of natural law whose substantive content justified European conquest and colonialism. As a result, Vitoria has been characterized both as "the benign humanist who erected a basic defence of Indian *dominium* in the Americas" and as the architect of "a consummate legitimation for one of the more spectacularly rapacious imperial powers."[92]

Vitoria's argument can be broken down into several key points. First, he acknowledged that non-Christian peoples could both possess and exercise jurisdiction over their lands: "Unbelief does not destroy either natural law or human law; but ownership and dominion are based either on natural law or human law; therefore they are not destroyed by want of faith."[93] It followed logically that the Pope had neither an inherently universal jurisdiction, nor the authority, to convey such jurisdiction to secular rulers,[94] and therefore that the analysis would begin with a recognition of the rights of Indigenous peoples to dominion over their lands.

It is important to note that at this very preliminary stage of the evolution of our current system of international law, Vitoria clearly rejected the argument made by Columbus and other "explorers," as well as by American jurists to this day,[95] that they could claim title to property by virtue of its "discovery." Vitoria notes that *unoccupied* lands may be claimed by discovery– "the rule of the law of nations is that what belongs to nobody is granted to the first occupant"–but clearly distinguishes that situation from one in which Indigenous people occupy the land.[96] The doctrine of *territorium res nullius*, which would be heavily relied upon by the English settlers of the New World, was given short shrift by Vitoria. The notion of acquiring title by discovery, he says, "gives no support to a seizure of the aborigines any more than if it had been they who had discovered us."[97]

The key to Vitoria's argument is the proposition that Indians are rational human beings and therefore bound by *jus gentium*, the law applied by the Romans to all peoples.[98] Thus far, the argument would appear to be one in which Christians and non-Christians, or Europeans and Indigenous peoples, were on equal legal footing. The catch, of course, was in the substance of the norms Vitoria deemed universally applicable and, more fundamental, in the fact that they were being determined exclusively by Europeans, with no consideration given, even nominally, to alternative worldviews. For Vitoria, if the majority of nations agreed upon certain principles of law, the minority could be held to their dictates, over their objections.[99] Europeans were clearly assumed to be in this majority even though they were still "discovering" huge portions of the planet. The potential demographic problems involved in this framing were resolved by reference to the general practices of "civilized nations," language we see reflected in international law well into the twentieth century.[100]

Substantively the first essential right Vitoria accorded to the Spanish was to travel and "sojourn" in Indian lands. Moreover, a European right to proselytize, or send missionaries to the Indians, was found to be rooted in long-standing European recognition of the rights of diplomatic recognition and protection: "ambassadors are by the law of nations inviolable and the Spaniards are the ambassadors of the Christian peoples. Therefore, the native Indians are bound to give them, at least, a friendly hearing and not to repel them."[101] Thus,

> Victoria deemed that pagan princes were duty-bound to admit Christian missionaries and that resistance to the work of the missionaries, as well as any measure against Indians converted to Christianity, was a good cause of war which would entitle the Pope to depose Indian rulers in order to replace them with Christian princes.[102]

The rights of Christians to proselytize was not, however, reciprocal. Vitoria adhered to an argument used by Innocent IV in distinguishing the rights of Crusaders from those of Muslim missionaries on the basis that while the latter were "in error," "we are on the righteous path."[103]

The second core right of the colonizers was to engage in commerce and trade with native peoples. Thus, Vitoria found, "it is certain that the aborigines can no more keep off the Spaniards from trade than Christians can keep off other Christians."[104] According to Williams, "Not engaging in trade was seen as contrary to the mutual self-interests that all humankind shared. Therefore, such conduct was irrational and contrary to the Law of Nations, and could be punished."[105] Further, Vitoria, familiar with the many accounts describing the absence of the notion of private property among Indigenous peoples, decreed that "if there are among the Indians any things which are treated as common both to citizens and to strangers, the Indians may not prevent the Spaniards from a communication and participation in them."[106] Such "things," however, would come to encompass hunting, fishing, farming, and mining.

According to Vitoria, Indians were capable of rationality, but the extent of their potential for development was in question. They lived in a state perilously close to nature, and Vitoria noted the possibility, without directly endorsing it, that "although the aborigines in question are . . . not wholly unintelligent, yet they are little short of that condition, and so are unfit to found or administer a lawful State up to the standard required by human and civil claims."[107] There was one path toward progress, exemplified by European civilization, and the only issue was how far along that path the Indians might be brought. Their understandings of possession or dominion, or the fact that the Europeans might be violating the most sacred precepts of their world-views, were irrelevant.

This left the problem of the use of armed force against the peoples being encountered. In the course of his lectures, Vitoria established that war could be waged upon Indigenous peoples for denying the Spanish the rights guaranteed them by the "universal" principles of law he had enunciated. Most basically, resistance to European invasion or settlement was defined as an act of hostility justifying war: "to keep certain people out of the city or province as being enemies, or to expel them when already there, are acts of war."[108] Additionally, if cause was found for war, the Europeans "may enforce against [the Indians] all the rights of war, despoiling them of their goods, reducing them to captivity, deposing their former lords and setting up new ones," such "rights" being limited only by the rule of proportionality.[109]

Again, these were not reciprocal rights. As Peter Fitzpatrick puts it, Vitoria constructed an "imperial legality which could extend universally, naturally, to all 'men,' yet effect and rely on an exclusion of some in constituting this very universality. And it was the *barbari* . . . which carried the resulting contradiction 'in' imperial legality by being both utterly excluded yet always includable."[110] Indeed, as Anghie summarizes, war was, for Vitoria, "the means by which Indians and their territory are converted into Spaniards and Spanish territory, the agency by which the Indians thus achieve their full human potential."[111] In outlining the parameters of a "just" war, Vitoria notes that neither the Turks nor the Saracens could lawfully wage war against Christians, for essentially the same reasons that they could not send missionaries into Christian lands. This rationale, of course, would apply to Indians as well. "Since Indians are by definition incapable of waging a just war, they exist within the Vitorian framework only as violators of the law."[112] Anghie observes that the Indians' lack of capacity to wage a just war is then read backward by Vitoria to limit the sovereignty of Indian nations, for one who is sovereign is, by definition, capable of waging war, a twist of logic that would be later repeated in U.S. Supreme Court Justice John Marshall's denial of Indian title to land.[113]

Much like the current war on terror, war with the Indians might be perpetual, for Vitoria notes that, with respect to the "unbeliever," it may be "useless ever to hope for a just peace on any terms," leaving as "the only remedy" the destruction of all "who can bear arms against us, provided they have already been in fault."[114] Those who were not capable of bearing arms could, as noted above, be captured and enslaved. All this having been said, it was a short leap to the argument, which now appears rather beneficent, that those Indians who were not exterminated could be subjected to perpetual European "guardianship."[115] Williams summarizes, "Hierarchical subjugation of the Indian, so repugnant to Victoria and other Humanist theorists when presented in hierocratic papal discourse, was regarded as eminently acceptable when explained as necessitated by the totalizing vision of reason contained in a natural Law of Nations."[116]

Recurring Themes in Colonial Legal Discourse

The system of international law now being challenged and recast in the war on terror has evolved and expanded significantly since debates over the legal status of the Other emerged in the context of the Crusades and Europe's "Age of Discovery." Nonetheless, even as the natural law framing was challenged by positivist scholars, and the perceived source of law shifted to sovereign states much as it had earlier shifted from the Christian Church to secular or natural law sources, the presumption of the superiority of European civilization remained constant and the law was developed, albeit in somewhat different terms, to facilitate colonialism and legitimate the violence it entailed.

Hugo Grotius, often deemed the "father" of international law for influencing the shift in focus of international law to the sovereignty of states, relied upon the Eurocentric presumptions found in Vitoria, emphasizing, in Fitzpatrick's words, that "heathens and barbarians, even when civilized, were . . . much in need of conversion to standards typified by Europe."[117] Grotius characterized those who "excessively violate the law of nature or of nations" as barbarians and argued that "the most just war is against savage beasts, the next against men who are like beasts."[118] Rising to prominence in the mid-eighteenth century, Emmerich de Vattel anticipated the positivists' identification of a nation with particular geographic and demographic boundaries, "reinforcing . . . the opposition between a civilized territoriality and those not explicitly enough attached to the earth—those 'wandering tribes whose small numbers can not populate the whole country,' and whose 'uncertain occupancy' cannot be 'a real and lawful taking of possession,'"[119] a theme to which we return in chapters 3 and 4.

This distinction permeated the thought of positivist legal scholars such as John Westlake, who wrote in 1894 that,

> When people of European race come into contact with American or African tribes, the prime necessity is a government under the protection of which they have been accustomed in their homes, which may prevent that life from being disturbed by contests between different European powers for supremacy on the same soil, and which may protect the natives in the enjoyment of a security and well-being at least not less than they enjoyed before the arrival of the strangers. Can the natives furnish such a government, or can it be looked for from the Europeans alone? In the answer to that question lies, for international law, the difference between civilisation and the want of it.[120]

Westlake concludes that while the "Asiatic empires" have government sufficient to such purposes, the "native inhabitants" of Africa and the Americas do not, and because "the inflow of the white race cannot be stopped where there is land to cultivate, ore to be mined, commerce to be developed, sport to enjoy, curiosity to be satisfied," even a "fanatical admirer of savage life" would be forced to concede that "civilised states" must exercise sovereignty over such lands, if only to protect the "natives" from European incursions.[121]

As discussed in the following chapters, similar arguments have been made throughout the evolution of U.S. and international law. From the Crusades, through the emergence of a full-blown international law of colonial relations, to the mandate system of the League of Nations and the post–World War II era of decolonization, and into the current debates about the global war on terror, we see many of the issues referenced in this chapter reappearing.[122] One is the notion of formal equality, enunciated to some degree as early as the eleventh century in Innocent IV's formulation of "infidel" rights, and claimed by Vitoria as well. This concept took on added significance through the next several centuries and is a cornerstone of contemporary international norms, but even when stripped of its explicitly religious articulations, it remained undergirded by the presumptions about human nature and purpose embedded in the earliest constructions of European civilization. These presumptions continue to give substance to norms that are considered universally applicable, whether framed in terms of natural law or the positive law enacted by states. The substantive norms, in turn, have laid the legal foundation for a wide range of colonial practices, from the laws governing the use of force and the waging of war to the practices of slavery and forced labor, the forcing of colonized peoples into concentrated villages or urban settings, the imposition of colonial education (both religious and secular), and a wide-ranging set of assimilationist policies. They are also the norms that have given substance to and undergird the United States' self-proclaimed "manifest destiny" to continental and global hegemony discussed in the following chapters and to the exceptionalism it has claimed throughout its history.

"A City on a Hill"

America as Exception

> When the Heavenly City is brought to Earth, order becomes the first law of nature. Before then, the accepted histories have it, God was considered the supreme lawgiver. . . . Enlightenment replaces God with nature [and] the deific obstacle to humanity's progress in knowledge is eliminated, constraining superstition gives way to incandescent truth.
> —Peter Fitzpatrick, *The Mythology of Modern Law*

> America was targeted for attack because we're the brightest beacon for freedom and opportunity in the world.
> —George W. Bush, Presidential Address to the Nation, September 11, 2001

The notion that the United States uniquely embodies freedom and democracy undergirds the ideology of American exceptionalism. It gives the American public a comforting explanation for why others might oppose U.S. hegemony, reinforcing and resonating with the history most Americans are taught and neatly sidestepping any questioning of U.S. foreign policy. This self-proclaimed identity can be traced back to the earliest English settlers' understanding of what their new home would represent and runs consistently through to contemporary times. "Wee shall be as a city upon a hill," predicted Puritan minister John Winthrop in 1630, and more than 350 years later this imagery was invoked by President Ronald Reagan in his farewell address: "And how stands the city on this winter night? . . . [S]he's still a beacon, still a magnet for all who must have freedom."[1] Campaigning in 2008 as the Republican vice presidential nominee, Alaska Governor Sarah Palin also alluded to this vision, noting that the "world view that I share with John McCain . . . says that America is a nation of exceptionalism. And we are to be that shining city on a hill, as President Reagan so beautifully said, that we are a beacon of hope and that we are unapologetic here. We are not perfect as a nation. But together, we represent a perfect ideal."[2]

As discussed in chapter 1, a deeply rooted aspect of American identity is the belief that the United States represents the most advanced stage in the evolution of human civilization and therefore possesses a unique historical responsibility to bring its model of progress and development to the less fortunate. Reflecting themes consistent with European expansion since the Crusades and the early decades of Portuguese and Spanish colonialism, this characterization has defined Euroamerican history from the initial settling of North America by English colonists to its expansion across the continent and its reach for global hegemony. The sentiment was captured by Theodore Roosevelt's 1901 pronouncement:

> Of course our whole national history has been one of expansion. . . . That the barbarians recede or are conquered, with the attendant fact that peace follows their retrogression or conquest, is due solely to the power of the mighty civilized races which have not lost the fighting instinct, and which by their expansion are gradually bringing peace into the red wastes where the barbarian peoples of the world hold sway.[3]

This chapter focuses on the role played by this understanding of America's civilizing mission and its influence upon the legal framework employed both in the early years of English settlement and the establishment of what we now know as the United States. While the phrase "manifest destiny" was not coined until 1845[4] and is most often associated with the United States' expansion to the Pacific Coast, the concept represents a worldview that encompasses much more than a rationale for U.S. continental expansion, one that has been influential since the outset of English colonization in the New World. As summarized by historian Frederick Merk, its "postulates were that Anglo-Saxons are endowed as a race with innate superiority, that Protestant Christianity holds the keys to Heaven, that only republican forms of political organization are free, that the future—even the predestined future—can be hurried along by human hands, and that the means of hurrying it, if the end be good, need not be inquired into too closely."[5] These premises derive from the Protestant Reformation's reshaping of the ideology developed during the consolidation of Latin Christendom and are embodied perhaps most clearly in the worldviews of the Puritans.[6]

We begin, therefore, with a brief overview of the early Puritan settlements and the legal context within which their claims of bringing civilization to "New England" were framed, and then consider the founding of the American Republic and concomitant transformation of the Puritans' vision into a secularized yet nonetheless mission-driven state. The chapter concludes by tracing the colonists' rationale for independence to the United States' first exceptionalist argument, the notion that the new republic would represent a higher form of civilization and progress that justified the founders' violating the law of nations, as it was then recognized, while simultaneously invoking the core legal arguments of European colonialism to legitimize their occupation of American Indian lands.

The Emerging Law of English Colonial Encounters

Legal historian Christopher Tomlins points out,

> Curiously, much of the "colonial" era of American history . . . has been written of as a history not of colonizing at all, but of settlement. . . . One experiences a history of colonial encounter and colonizing process that disregards colonization as an interpretive perspective of relevance to this or any later period of American history, treating the arrival and presence of the English in America more or less as a given from which point history is written.[7]

Because the thesis of this book is that current U.S. approaches to international law are deeply rooted in the legal history of colonial encounters, the context of English "settlement" in North America provides an important backdrop.

Although the Spanish, French, and Dutch played a significant role in settling the North American continent, the English were much more concerned than were their European counterparts with acquiring territory and establishing settler colonial societies.[8] As a result, the United States has identified itself as a uniquely Anglo-Saxon creation, and the vision of the American mission to bring freedom and civilization to this continent and beyond is most clearly articulated in the first instance by the English colonists of "New England."[9] Both the Pilgrims and the much larger number of Puritans who followed shortly thereafter[10] brought with them a belief that the Anglo-Saxon "race" represented European civilization at its most advanced, thanks to having developed structures of political governance superior to those imposed by the Norman Conquest of 1066 and having led the movement that broke the bonds of domination imposed by the Roman Church.[11]

Until the Protestant Reformation, English colonial ventures were undertaken within the legal framework established by Rome and were generally careful to respect the claims of other European countries to territories occupied by "heathens" or "infidels."[12] When Henry VIII severed relations with the Catholic Church in 1529, he dramatically restructured economic and political relations within England, and this led to changes in English interpretations of international law as well. By claiming the extensive lands and resources of the Church, Henry was able to fund the expansion of the British Navy and accumulate the capital to underwrite the colonial enterprise.[13] Ultimate legal authority now rested with the state, rather than the pope, and commerce, rather than conversion, began to play a more significant role in the ideological justifications for territorial acquisition.[14]

By the mid-1550s England and France were challenging the monopoly on trade claimed by Portugal and Spain pursuant to the bulls issued by Alexander VI in the 1490s and asserting a right under the law of nations to travel freely on the high seas.[15] Unable to reach accord on this matter, Spain and France entered into a treaty concerning their rights within Europe, but leaving relations in the New World undefined. This inaugurated a new phase of international law in the Americas, allowing unfettered competition between "civilized" states. As Robert Williams observes, "America had become the first great experiment in laissez-faire market economics, without even a prohibition on predatory tactics. . . . As for the Indigenous inhabitants of the New World, as heathens and infidels they were regarded by Catholic and Protestant Christians alike as fit subjects for conquest, colonization, and Christianization."[16]

At this point England was not yet powerful enough to challenge Spain directly. Aside from investing in the African slave trade,[17] Queen Elizabeth I limited her imperial ventures to Ireland, where a peculiarly English form of privatized colonialism was refined.[18] The English had claimed dominion over Ireland since the twelfth century but had met with constant resistance, and the ideology and practices of English settlers in America were heavily influenced by the Irish experience. As would be the case for American Indians until well into the twentieth century, in the mid-fourteenth century the English described the Irish as "wild" and "savage" and attempted to impose English ways on them through law as well as force.[19] "Protection of life and property was guaranteed only to those of the Irish who spoke and lived like English people. Those who retained their tribal culture were regarded as outlaws. . . . The statutes also imposed strict penalties on any Englishman who adopted Irish customs or married into an Irish clan."[20] Under Queen Mary, English soldiers who participated in the wars to occupy Ireland were rewarded with tracts of land, much as British and American soldiers and settlers would later be paid for their services in Indian land.[21]

Elizabeth approved a system under which private companies established the equivalent of plantations in exchange for rights to the territories they occupied, and English settlers were given incentives to relocate to Ireland.[22] A striking parallel between the occupations of Ireland and North America can be found in the English argument that the Irish subsistence economy, which relied upon animal herding on communal lands, was wasteful and inefficient, and therefore irrational and uncivilized. Williams says, "Although the notion had not yet been elevated to a principle of natural law in English colonial discourse, a savage people's perceived underutilization of land was sufficient justification for an English colonial enterprise, obviating further discussion of its morality or legality."[23] Furthermore, when the Irish failed to cooperate, or to be restrained by "reason," the massacre even of noncombatants was deemed acceptable in the eyes of God, as well as English law.[24]

The English were able to begin seriously pursuing their North American ambitions only after they had destroyed the Spanish Armada at the end of the sixteenth century.[25] Much as the United States would later send seasoned "Indian fighters" to "pacify" the Philippines,[26] Elizabeth authorized Sir Humphrey Gilbert and Sir Walter Raleigh, both of whom had distinguished themselves in England's wars against the Irish, to establish permanent settlements in the New World.[27] In this effort they were guided by the instructions for colonial endeavors drafted by Richard Haklyut and his younger cousin of the same name. In 1578 the elder Haklyut wrote his *Notes on Colonization* to frame the project for Gilbert. In addition to cataloguing the practical tasks and a "wish list" of commodities the English hoped would result, Haklyut framed the underlying ideology as well. In Tomlins' words, it was "a portentious invocation of the kind of society required to facilitate such development, and the kind of statecraft required to give it ascendancy over the 'savages.' It was to be a permanent settlement. It was to aspire to dominion over its region. Above all it was to be a 'Citie'—a permanent settlement of brick and stone, of houses and roofs and walls, of all the 'thinges without which no . . . people [may] in civill sorte be kept together.'"[28] Similar advice was rendered by the younger Haklyut in his *Discourse of Western Planting*, written in 1584. The English goal, according to this document, was "the enlargement of the gospell of Christe" and it was to be accomplished "by plantinge colonies of our nation."[29] The overall objectives of "Christianity and commerce required planting as a pre-condition of their success," and successful planting in turn required both a concrete understanding of the land to be occupied and an appropriate body of law.[30]

The Haklyuts' perspective became the foundation for the 1606 charter granted Raleigh for colonizing Virginia, and for the approximately thirty charters granted by the English crown over the next seventy-five years.[31] These charters defined how governmental institutions would be established and power distributed, as well as how territory and the wealth acquired therefrom would be allocated. The peoples already living on the lands being "granted" under the charters were deemed "savage" both because they were not Christians and because they were presumed not to have developed agricultural settlements. As Tomlins notes,

> The [1606] charter offers an interesting contrast between its representation of the prospective population—transportable, interchangeable, but jurisdictionally organized and culturally "settled" in appropriate civic order— and the actual indigenous inhabitants, who were invoked as a preliminary only to establish that their want of civic personality rendered them unsettled, and therefore unfit to occupy what they, in fact, occupied.[32]

Although the efforts of both Gilbert and Raleigh to establish permanent settlements failed, they inspired the development of a Calvinist legal theory of conquest on which the Puritans and their American descendants would subsequently rely.

During this period Alberico Gentili, a Protestant Italian appointed to a professorship of law at Oxford, was influential in shifting the English approach from one in which religious differences were the primary justification for war to one that relied upon a more secular interpretation of natural law or, perhaps, human nature. In contrast to the Catholic natural law theoreticians who argued that rejection of the Christian God was a violation of natural law, Gentili focused on the peoples encountered. If they violated natural law by living "rather like beasts than men," they could be considered "the common foes of all mankind, as pirates are."[33] According to Gentili, the victors—presumed, of course, to be the colonizers—need not "tolerate" those who denied or doubted God's existence or those "whose religion impairs the security of victory and its laws."[34]

The result, of course, was a rationale for subordinating the Other remarkably similar to that advanced by Vitoria, but Gentili's argument was based not on the religious faith of the conquered per se but on his presumption that their failure to conform to the standards of the conquerors was evidence that they were less than fully human. Perhaps the conquerors could work with those who held divergent religious beliefs, but those who had no religion at all, as judged by European standards, were the equivalent of animals and could be treated as such: "Some kind of religion is natural, and therefore if there be any who are atheists, destitute of any religious belief, either good or bad, it would seem just to war upon them as we would brutes. For they do not deserve to be called men, who divest themselves of human nature."[35] The belief that Europeans had a monopoly on determining who was truly human and therefore did not have to comply with the rule of law when dealing with those they deemed mere "brutes" would become a staple of American law.

The Puritan Mission and Its Legal Framing

In 1607 Jamestown, the first successful English colony, was founded, and within twelve years African slaves were being imported as labor for Virginia's tobacco plantations.[36] A somewhat different model emerged in New England, where Pilgrims established a small colony in Plymouth in 1620, and Puritans founded the much larger Massachusetts colony a decade later.[37] The Puritans saw their journey to the New World as a "reenactment of the Exodus narrative revolv[ing] around a powerful theology of chosenness."[38] Central to their worldview was the concept of predestination, the belief in a divinely ordained "plan" for the world, and the notion that God had a particular "covenant" with humanity.[39] English Puritans could fulfill their part of this contract by bringing salvation to the New World, and, in return, they would be rewarded by God both in this life and the next. The "savages" of the Americas would benefit by receiving both Christianity and civilization, including "a well governed commonwealth" and education in the "mechanical occupations, arts, and liberal sciences."[40] Because Indian lands allegedly were underutilized the settlers could put them to productive use, thereby benefiting both the colonizers and the colonized.

Puritan ideology did not emphasize the notion of "overspreading" the entire continent, for, as Charles Segal and David Stineback have observed, "Puritan leaders . . . were opposed to the rapid expansion of their population into Indian territory, which they regarded as the realm of nature under Satan's control. Moreover, individual acquisitiveness for material possessions and land was an unintentional by-product of the ethic that Puritans brought to North America, not a human quality they admired."[41] According to Anders Stephanson, the territory was a "promised land" to the Puritans and therefore had a sacred quality, but acquiring land was simply the precursor to the establishment of the New Israel, or New Canaan, through which the world was to be regenerated and "God and humankind . . . reconciled at last."[42]

Claiming the Right to "Vacant" Lands

The desire for land would steadily expand until the entire continent had been claimed by one Euroderivative empire or another, but even in the earlier and more limited phases of English colonialism the settlers had to develop legal and moral justifications for their territorial claims. While invoking the rights articulated by Vitoria under natural law to "sojourn" to the New World and proselytize American Indians, the Puritans diverged significantly from the Spanish model in their reliance upon the doctrine of *territorium res nullius*, or the right to claim title to "unoccupied" lands.[43] As historian Anthony Pagden points out, this doctrine had been, for all practical purposes, irrelevant to the Spanish. First, as Vitoria had observed, the territories at issue were clearly occupied. More significant, the Spanish could rely on the papal grants of authority for their claimed right to seize and occupy land and to exercise jurisdiction over the Indigenous populations for the purpose of "saving" them. In addition, Vitoria's theories of "just war" could be invoked if the Spanish encountered resistance. Because the Spanish were more interested in utilizing Indian labor than in clearing the land for use by a large settler population, "the Castilian crown was as much concerned with its potential rights over the Indians themselves as with its rights over their property."[44] These "rights" to appropriate human labor would have been undermined rather than furthered by a *territorium res nullius* argument.

In contrast, the early English settlers, and the Puritans in particular, were primarily concerned with carving out space in North America for their "promised land." It was to be a place where they could create a society that focused on their own salvation and not that of the "savages," who were seen as an impediment to their goals rather than the purpose of their mission. Essentially the Puritans believed that they were creating a new model of civilization for the European world; the purported benefits they were bringing to Indigenous peoples in that process constituted something of a fallback argument. More charitably framed, the theory was that the Puritans would, by their example and by trading with the Indians, "breed civility" and convert them to Christianity.[45] Thus the settlers' prosperity—based, of course, on their industriousness—was intertwined, from the beginning, with their fulfillment of God's design.

Initially, at least, the English were also reluctant to rely on a theory of conquest by "just war" because of their commitment, framed within the context of the Norman Conquest, to "the 'continuity theory' of constitutional law in which the legal and political institutions of the conquered are deemed to survive a conquest."[46] The first and easiest, if least accurate, way to justify the establishment of English colonies was by declaring the land to be vacant and claiming title under the doctrine of *res nullius*. Thus, from their initial encounters with the Indigenous peoples of "New England," the English settlers began erasing them from history, both literally and figuratively. In the settlers' discourse, North American Indians were often deemed nonexistent; in other instances they were treated as part of nature—animals rather than humans—and therefore not "occupying" the land. The latter interpretation had the added benefit of allowing warfare and massacres to be characterized as the extermination of "wild beasts" rather than as the conquest of other human beings. When neither of those justifications sufficed, the theory invoked was that the Indians were not using the land "productively," and therefore it could be considered vacant.[47] To paraphrase Edmund Leach's description of anthropologists' beliefs about "primitive" peoples, the settlers' portrayals of Indigenous peoples demonstrated "an astonishing resilience in the face of adverse evidence."[48]

Even before the Pilgrims set sail John Smith had "proclaimed himself the true discoverer" of New England, and they arrived in 1620 with Smith's map, which had already identified the location of their colony as "Plymouth."[49] Smith described this land he had "discovered" as "so planted with Gardens and Corne fields, and so well inhabited with a goodly, strong and well proportioned people" that its suitability for colonization could not be contested.[50] Yet, virtually in the same breath, he described it as his favored place "of all the foure parts of the world that I have yet seene not inhabited."[51] In other words, he was invoking the doctrine of *res nullius* to claim title to the land by virtue of his "discovery" despite his own evidence to the contrary.

In the Puritans' dealings with American Indians we see foundations of the legal theories, or ideologies, of American occupation that persist to the present. They relied on a combination of often contradictory arguments incorporating the notions that the land was unoccupied, that conquest had in any case been justified because of the savage nature of the Indians, and sometimes that the Indians had consented to the takings. John Cotton, perhaps the best-known Puritan preacher, analogized their settlement to God's provision of a homeland for the people of Israel, noting that God had "espied" and "discovered" the land for them and had "carried them" to it over "all hindrances."[52] Once there, Cotton explained, God had made room for them in three ways—by casting out their enemies, by giving them "favor in the eyes of any native people" who thereafter sold or gave them the land, and by "mak[ing] a country though not altogether void of inhabitants, yet void in that place where they reside."[53]

Similarly struggling to justify the taking of American Indian lands, the founder of the Massachusetts Bay Colony, John Winthrop, incorporated these arguments and added to them Vitoria's notion that colonizers had an equal right to share in commonly held property. Winthrop thus asserted, "That which is common to all is proper to none. This savage people ruleth over many lands without title or property." He continued: "2dly, There is more than enough for them and us. 3dly, God hath consumed the natives with a miraculous plague, whereby the greater part of the country is left void of inhabitants. 4thly, We shall come in with good leave of the natives."[54]

Creating Terra Nullius through Disease and "Offensive Warr"

John Smith's counterfactual assertion that the land was "uninhabited" would soon become much closer to the truth, thanks to epidemics of small-pox and other diseases introduced by the colonizers, as well as through warfare and massacres.[55] When Juan Ponce de León first landed in Florida in 1513, there were approximately fifteen million people living in the terri-tory now claimed by the United States and Canada.[56] By 1900 the U.S. Cen-sus Bureau reported fewer than 250,000 native people living in the United States.[57] Much of this devastation was the result of diseases introduced by Europeans, with up to 90 percent of some peoples dying within two gen-erations of initial contact.[58] This was often celebrated by the early settlers as evidence that God was on their side. Thus Cotton Mather rejoiced in 1631 that "God ended the controversy [between the Massachusetts' Bay Colony and its Indian neighbors] by sending the smallpox amongst the Indians . . . who were before that time exceedingly numerous,"[59] and the governor of the Carolina Colony announced that "the hand of God was eminently seen in thin[n]ing the Indians, to make room for the English."[60]

To this day the notion that the Indigenous peoples of North America miraculously "disappeared," thereby making room for the colonial project that would become the United States, remains an essential element of the narrative of American exceptionalism. Like the assertion that civilization is a uniquely European accomplishment, this presumption must be scrutinized if we are to realistically assess American claims that the U.S. has achieved its hegemonic status by virtue of its superior "values." Although few Americans today would claim that the diseases that decimated Indian nations were the result of divine intervention on behalf of European colonists, most see this devastation as a "natural" and inadvertent consequence of intercontinental contact.[61]

It must be recognized, however, that although the very first Europeans to come into contact with Indigenous societies might have been unaware that they brought with them deadly pathogens, by "1550 at the latest, and probably earlier, it was common knowledge in Europe that there was a firm correlation between the arrival of 'explorers, settlers and military expeditions' on the one hand and massive die-offs of native peoples from [diseases such as smallpox, typhoid, diphtheria, measles, and various plagues] on the other."[62] Rather than halt or minimize contact as a result of this knowledge, European powers generally took advantage of the phenomenon. In addition to expanding as rapidly as possible, thereby exposing more Indigenous peoples to disease, they utilized slave labor, destroyed crops and induced famines, and dislocated and interned large population groups, often after arduous forced marches, creating conditions that they knew would worsen these epidemics based on their experience with plagues in Europe.[63]

In addition, in numerous instances the colonizers deliberately exposed Indigenous peoples to contagious diseases. As early as 1636 the Narragansetts tried and executed an officer of the Massachusetts Colony based on their conviction that he had deliberately infected them with smallpox three years earlier.[64] In 1763, during the last of the "French and Indian Wars," Lord Jeffrey Amherst suggested to a subordinate that peace talks be called with the Ottawas, who were aligned with the French, for the purpose of giving them gifts infected with smallpox. Amherst wrote, "You will do well to try to inoculate the Indians by means of blankets as well as to try every other method that can serve to extirpate this exorable [execrable] race."[65] Amherst's plan succeeded, spreading smallpox not only among the Ottawas but among numerous other peoples as well, killing thousands and clearing the way for the subsequent conquest of the Northwest Territories.[66]

The native peoples were not "disappearing" as a result of disease alone, of course. While the English colonists often found it expedient to have peaceful trade relations with the American Indian nations surrounding them, their insatiable desire for land inevitably generated Indigenous resistance. Resistance, in turn, was characterized as the "treachery" of savages, and any killing of Europeans became a "massacre." Many of the settlers already believed that "the way of conquering [the Indians] is much more easy than of civilizing them by fair means,"[67] and Indian resistance was used by the colonizers as an excuse for unrestrained warfare. Thus, for example, a 1622 attack by a confederation of Indian nations in the Tidewater area on English settlements, which had already extended more than sixty miles beyond Jamestown, led the Virginia Company to announce that "our hands which before were tied with gentleness and fair usage, are now set at liberty by the treacherous violence of the savages. . . . So that we . . . may now by right of war, and law of nations, invade the country and destroy them."[68]

Just as the "enemy" in the war on terror has been portrayed as evil, irrational, and uncivilized, early colonists frequently portrayed American Indians as irrational and irredeemable savages, agents of the devil, even cannibals. This is illustrated by the claim of William Bradford, Governor of the Plymouth Colony, that his neighbors were "savage people, who are cruel, barbarous, and most treacherous, being most furious in their rage and merciless where they overcome; not being content only to take away life, but delight to torment men in the most bloody manner that may be; flaying some alive . . . cutting off the member and joints of others . . . [and eating] the collops of their flesh in their sight whilst they live."[69] Although the Puritan leaders were well aware of their falsity, these portrayals provided the basis for English claims of a legal right to wage wars of conquest based on the nature and character of the enemy.[70]

Further, because that enemy was "uncivilized," the colonizers did not hold themselves to the laws of war to which they held "civilized" states. Thus, to give but one of many examples, in 1637 English settlers from Connecticut, armed with an explicit declaration of "offensive warr,"[71] set out to attack the Pequot Fort on the Mystic River, where they had "formerly concluded to destroy them by the Sword and save the Plunder."[72] There was no debate here about the "natural rights" of the Indians to dominion over their lands; instead, their status as "savages" rendered them natural enemies, against whom warfare was inevitable. According to one of the participants, "Many were burnt in the fort, both men, women, and children. Others forced out . . . which our soldiers received and entertained with the point of the sword. Down fell men, women, and children. . . . It is reported by themselves, that there were about four hundred souls in this fort, and not above five of them escaped out of our hands."[73]

The English ultimately claimed to have killed between eight hundred and nine hundred Pequots, leaving a few dozen known survivors,[74] and thus, according to Captain John Mason, "was God pleased to smite our enemies" and "give us their Land for an Inheritance."[75] It was not enough, however, to kill almost all the Pequots. As Richard Drinnon reports, "there would have been no known living members of that tribe had the colonizers had their way. They sought, as Mason said, 'to cut off the Remembrance of them from the Earth.'"[76] Not only the people but their very name was declared extinct by the General Assembly of Connecticut; the survivors could not be called "Pequots," the village of Pequot became "New London," and the Pequot River known as the "Thames."[77] Like Indigenous peoples more generally, their physical presence was to be destroyed and their history erased from memory.

Eliminating Discordant Perspectives

Chapter 1 discussed foundational presumptions of "the West," including the belief that its civilization represents the highest stage of human progress and that its worldview and understanding of human history is all-encompassing. One of the hallmarks of the colonizing process is the imposition of this "universal" perspective onto the Other and the judging, or ranking, of colonized subjects by their conformity to its dictates. Before this perspective could be projected onto the rest of the world, it had to be consolidated in Europe, a process briefly discussed in chapter 2, and it was still in progress at the time of the early English settlement of North America. As Tomlins notes, "seventeenth-century England was not singular but plural," and its colonizing ventures contributed to its "nation-building" process.[78] Thus the Puritans were concerned not only with clearing the prior inhabitants from the territory of their new "homeland" but also with confirming the righteousness of their own perspective by eliminating those peoples' divergent worldviews as well. In these settlers' narrative, the Indigenous peoples were agents of Satan; the challenge faced by the Puritans was to save them where possible— or convenient—and otherwise to eliminate them.[79] Expressing views we see articulated throughout U.S. history, including quite recently the justifications for the overthrow of "dictators" like Manuel Noriega or Saddam Hussein,[80] "Puritan writers constantly contended that ordinary Indians were tyrannized by their sachems (political leaders) and powwows (priests),"[81] and that the colonizers were there to "save" them from themselves.

In the seventeenth and even into the eighteenth century, according to Tomlins, the English colonization of North America was increasingly "a labour of transformation wrought by the English upon themselves," a means of Anglicization "expressed in processes of institution- and state-formation that challenged prevailing cultural affinities, rearranged hierarchies of rule and sought uniformities of practice where previously there had existed plurality and custom."[82] Thus intent on imposing a unitary and universalizing vision of "civilized" society, Puritan leaders were particularly harsh on settlers who diverged from their narrow reading of God's plan for humanity. This can be seen in their treatment of Thomas Morton, who rejected the Puritans' asceticism, and not only traded but socialized with his Indigenous neighbors. In 1627 Morton raised his famous "Maypole" in Merry Mount; the next year Merry Mount was invaded by Captain Miles Standish, and Morton was subjected to a series of arrests and trials for various offenses, including the selling of weapons and liquor to the Indians and offending "good order and government." He was sent into exile twice, and an order was issued to burn his house to the ground.[83] Richard Drinnon notes that despite this history of Morton's persecution, "the colonial authorities never once had compelling evidence that Morton had committed *any* punishable offense under English law."[84] His real crime was "going native" which, Drinnon points out, was not only about treating American Indians as human beings but "tantamount to 'going nature,'"[85] the ultimate undermining of the Euroderivative construction of civilization.

Similarly, in 1635, Roger Williams was condemned by a Massachusetts court for having "broached & divulged diverse new & dangerous opinions" and was banished from the colony.[86] One of Williams' primary offenses was to have lived among the Indians and purchased lands directly from them, vigorously contesting the notion that the colonists, by virtue of patents from the British king, could possess Indian lands without the consent of their Indigenous inhabitants and true owners. Williams denounced "the sinne of the Pattents, wherein Christian Kings (so called) are invested with Right by virtue of their Christianitie, to take and give away the Lands and Countries of other men."[87]

Although much of the mythology of early colonists centers around their flight from religious persecution and their quest for religious freedom, the cases of Thomas Morton and Roger Williams, among others, reflect that the Puritans were driven by a desire to be free to practice their religion, not a belief that others should be allowed to do likewise. Displaying an attitude still reflected in demands that those outside the "mainstream" assimilate, there was no room in the Puritans' world for divergent cultural practices or worldviews; their "God, in the end, demanded of every other culture the same allegiance that He demanded of His particular favorites. . . . No halfway measures were tolerated."[88] As Ernst Cassirer observed, Puritan leaders were "quite inimical to the conception of religious freedom of conscience," insisting upon the "severe persecution" and "merciless destruction of all dissidents."[89] Thus freedom was not a matter of individual or collective choice but a condition to be realized only within the framework of one particular understanding of salvation. Stephanson summarizes, "To be free was precisely to understand [their] destiny and conform to the direction of divine will, to 'make our destiny our choice,' as it was said at the time."[90]

With the formation of the American state, the framework of these early colonists was expanded to include various theological viewpoints, but a similar dynamic has persisted, with freedom defined to exist only within a limited understanding of "democracy" which, in turn, requires a particular form of civilization. [91] As Sacvan Bercovitch has said, the Puritans' ideology continues to influence our understandings of the "American Way," contributing "to the usurpation of American identity by the United States, and to the anthropomorphic nationalism that characterizes our literature. . . . American dream, manifest destiny, redeemer nation, and, fundamentally, the American self as representative of universal rebirth."[92]

Diverging Colonial Interests: The Foundation for Independence

Rapid or wide-ranging territorial expansion may not have been a focus of the first Puritan settlers, but it was an integral part of the plans of many English colonists who followed them, attracted by the vision of lands unencumbered by feudal claims. This soon led to conflicts not only with the American Indians whose territories were at issue but also between the colonists and the British government and among the Angloamerican colonies as well.

The Royal Proclamation of 1763

From London's perspective the purpose of colonies was to generate profit. This gave the central government incentive to maintain relatively peaceful relations with the Indians, both to enhance trade, particularly in furs, and to minimize the costs of maintaining a military presence. The latter was of particular concern after English expansion into Indian lands had triggered the so-called French and Indian War, which lasted from 1754 to 1763 and was fought at considerable expense to the British government.[93]

In order to limit the costs of maintaining the colonies, King George III issued the Proclamation of 1763 that prohibited English settlement without explicit permission from London in all lands west of the Allegheny and Appalachian mountains.[94] This document proclaimed British dominion over those lands, however, and promised to protect the Indians living there, saying that "the several nations or tribes of Indians with whom we are connected, and who live under our protection should not be molested or disturbed in the possession of such parts of *our* dominions and territories as, not having been ceded to or purchased by us, are reserved to them . . . as their hunting-grounds."[95] This assertion of lawful jurisdiction over territory that had not been ceded or purchased from the Indians reflects the British position that native land claims would only be recognized to the extent that Indigenous peoples remained in actual possession of the land. As Robert Williams notes, sovereignty, and therefore "lawful" title, could only rest with the "English king whose subjects had discovered and laid claim to that land, which was possessed not by Christian peoples but by infidels, who lacked all rights and status in English legal colonizing theory."[96]

The Proclamation of 1763 and the Stamp Act passed in 1765 to fund its implementation marked a turning point in relations between the Crown and the colonists. From the King's perspective, it was perfectly reasonable to reach an accommodation with the Indians that would assure maximum future profits for the colonial endeavor and to expect the colonies to bear some of the financial burden of their own protection. For the colonists, this was an unacceptable limitation on their expansionist visions, as well as the imposition of taxation without representation.[97] As articulated by Samuel Adams, Patrick Henry, and others who spoke on behalf of the colonists, both the 1763 Proclamation and the Stamp Act disregarded their right to self-government, established in the charters of the colonies, as well as "certain essential rights of the British Constitution of government, which are founded in the law of God and nature, and are the common rights of mankind."[98]

Claiming a Superior Anglo-Saxon Heritage

To make the case for independence, the American leaders relied heavily on English law, arguing that the Crown was invoking feudal powers in violation of rights guaranteed them under the British Constitution as well as the charters establishing the colonies. Thus the litany of complaints found in the Declaration of Independence focused on the king's failure to pass or uphold laws needed by the colonies, or to allow their legislatures to function, resulting in "a long train of abuses and usurpations" designed to subject the colonists to "absolute Despotism."[99]

The political theory of the emerging American Republic focused on the notion that the English system, which theoretically prevented despotism by dividing governmental powers between the king, the House of Lords, and the House of Commons, had broken down. As Merrill Peterson notes in his biography of Thomas Jefferson,

[Although] the Glorious Revolution established the supremacy of Parliament. . . . [the] King and ministry . . . corrupted the new balance of the constitution by wickedly employing favors, bribery, and intrigue in the debasement of Parliament. . . . If the King was the author of the system, Parliament had coalesced with him until the checks and balances of the constitution were meaningless or, as Thomas Paine bluntly said, "farcical."[100]

Furthermore, the colonies were not represented in Parliament and thus were entirely dependent on the King. The undemocratic nature of this relationship and the colonists' resulting grievances are reflected in the provisions of the Declaration of Independence which read as a bill of indictment against George III.[101]

Confronted with the failures of the English system but wishing to claim its ideals, the founders of the new republic looked to its antecedents. Jefferson apparently believed that the Romans had incorporated the best aspects of Greek democracy, which extended only to a narrow class of citizens, and remedied its most significant weakness with its *jus gentium*, a universal rule of law applicable to the entire Roman Empire.[102] In rejecting English feudalism, American legal and political theorists also looked to the Saxon roots of English constitutionalism, for the Saxons had "introduced into England an elective kingship, an annual assembly of tribal chiefs, the witenagemot—the true forerunner of Parliament—trial by jury, and the common law."[103] As they characterized this history, the advances of Saxons had been undermined by the Norman Conquest and its introduction of feudalism, then restored by the Magna Carta, and, finally, despite numerous popular struggles, lost again to more recent forms of governmental corruption and oppression.

The colonists traced the king's despotic rule to the Norman Conquest and claimed their true heritage to be that of the noble "race" of Saxons who had emigrated from Germany to the less-populated British Isles and, much like the American settlers, established freedom and democratic government in England. As Williams observes, Jefferson's argument that the people had a right under natural law to choose their own government "deployed the mythology of the restless, freedom-loving Saxons to dramatize the continuity of the Saxon struggle for natural rights now being played out on the American stage," depicting the king's abuse of his sovereign powers as "a wrongful continuation of the perversion of Saxon principles of right and justice, traceable to the first imposition of the Norman Yoke in 1066."[104]

Relying upon and Recasting International Law

In laying the legal foundation for their war of independence, the American colonists were making the radical claim that they, rather than the British Crown, possessed the right to colonize North America as they deemed appropriate. In three centuries of European expansion, the legal framing of colonialism had been considerably secularized, with sovereignty coming to be vested in the various European crowns rather than the pope, but in no case had the colonists themselves made the case that they independently possessed the right to exercise dominion over "infidel" lands. On its face, the American rebels were taking a position that violated international law as it was recognized by the "civilized" world for, under the law of nations of that time, colonies certainly had no right to rebel. Thomas Grey says bluntly, "The case for independence could not be made in legal terms."[105]

To justify their actions, the founders' Declaration of Independence accused the king of having "plundered our seas, ravaged our coasts, burnt our towns, and destroyed the lives of our people," bringing in mercenaries "to compleat the works of death, desolation, and tyranny, already begun with circumstances of Cruelty & Perfidy scarcely paralleled in the most barbarous ages, and totally unworthy the Head of a civilized nation."[106] As this passage indicates, the Angloamerican colonial leaders were invoking the law of nations, or international law, to lay the foundation for their claim to independence. The international law they invoked, however, explicitly privileged the rights of colonizing powers over Indigenous peoples, and in asserting a legal right to rebel under these conditions the colonial leaders certainly were not prepared to recognize a similar right of American Indians to self-determination.[107] Thus one of the points of contention raised by the Declaration was the colonists' claim that the king's actions were leaving them unprotected against "the merciless Indian Savages whose known rule of warfare, is an undistinguished destruction of all ages, sexes and conditions."[108] In essence, the "Founding Fathers" were asserting their superior rights *as* colonizers, claiming to be better representatives of the civilization being brought to the New World and denouncing Britain for treating them as colonial subjects rather than actors.

The impetus for independence had come, as noted above, from the limitations the Crown had placed on westward expansion. Thus, perhaps most fundamental, the colonists accused the British government of violating international law not only by denying their right to self-government but by prohibiting them from acquiring the lands they intended to put to "productive" use. In making this claim, the colonists were relying on an understanding of natural law articulated by John Locke in which the rights to life and liberty were inseparable from that of property, and property rights, in turn, derived from the labor humans put into improving nature. The Indians, in this construction, were idle, wandering savages. The colonists, through their labor, would increase the value of Indigenous "wastelands" many times over, and because such actions benefited all humanity, the settlers had not only a right but an affirmative duty to possess and improve the land.[109]

In international law this argument had also been made by Swiss legal theorist Emmerich de Vattel in his 1758 *Le Droit de gens ou principe de la loi naturelle*, in which he described the cultivation of the land as not merely a right but "an obligation imposed upon man by nature."[110] For Vattel, imposing civilization or Christianity was not sufficient justification for colonial conquest, but it was entirely lawful to appropriate the territory of those who "roamed" rather than inhabited land and put it to productive use.[111] Vattel's theory thus allowed British colonial practices to be distinguished from those of the Spanish and also provided grounds for the Americans to resist British attempts to restrain their settlement of western lands.

The characterization of American Indians as "wandering savages" was entirely inaccurate, of course. As John Smith noted before 1620, he had found well-tended gardens and fields of corn upon his arrival, and indigenous peoples had highly developed and extensive agricultural systems in place throughout the hemisphere prior to their "discovery."[112] According to legal scholar Vine Deloria, "the argument, therefore, that the Europeans brought the great conception of civilization, conceived as a sedentary agricultural enterprise, to the New World is absurd on its face."[113] Nonetheless the argument was essential to the colonists and remains central to American justifications for occupation, both historical and legal, to this day.[114]

Allocating Colonial Land "Rights"

As noted above, the conflicting interests of the British government and the American colonists came to a head with George III's Proclamation of 1763 forbidding English settlement on lands west of the Allegheny and Appalachian mountains in return for treaties ensuring the allegiance of various Indigenous nations. Rejection of the Crown's assertion of sovereign prerogatives, however, highlighted conflicts between the colonists over their respective "rights" to the western lands they claimed. Three competing interests were at work, generally represented by the colonies with indeterminate western boundaries, those with fixed limits, and the individual land speculators or private companies that had purchased lands independently from American Indians.[115]

At the heart of the debate was the ultimate colonial question: Who "owned" the western lands, and what was the source of their claimed rights to exercise dominion over them? In resisting the Proclamation of 1763, the colonists argued that the king's claim to exclusive jurisdiction over the western territories was an illegitimate extension of power deriving from the Norman Conquest. Many of the colonial leaders, including George Washington, had claims to thousands of acres beyond the boundary established by the Proclamation.[116] During the war for independence, the provisional government issued warrants for land in Indian territory in lieu of paying soldiers,[117] and in 1782 Washington presented the Continental Congress with a plan to expand U.S. territory by encouraging the settlement of western lands by veterans of the war. In the words of Allen Eckert: "These settlers, being largely veterans of the war and experienced soldiers, might tend to awe the Indians. Even if they did not . . . and the Indians rose up in arms, these settlers would then make excellent militia to protect United States claims in the Ohio country."[118] For all these reasons, western expansion was a given; what was lacking was agreement on the theory of land ownership that vested rights in the American colonizers.

One axis of the dispute focused upon the original colonial grants; some grants involved fixed boundaries, and others were unbounded to the west. This had not originally appeared to be a major issue, given the concentration of settlements along the eastern seaboard and the belief that the "South Sea"—the Pacific Ocean—was located not far to the west. However, as the extent of western lands came to be appreciated, the interests of the "landless" or territorially limited colonies such as Maryland and Pennsylvania came into sharp conflict with the "landed" colonies such as Georgia, North Carolina, and Virginia, all of which had undefined western boundaries.[119] Virginia's claims rested upon the vaguely worded charter granted the Virginia Company of London in 1609, and the other landed colonies made similar claims. The prospective states with fixed territorial limits argued that, with the Declaration of Independence, sovereignty had passed from the British Crown to the central government of the United States, which had an obligation to ensure that all the territory inured to the benefit of "the people" as a whole.[120] Both arguments relied, however, on recognizing the validity of the British claims that the colonists had just rejected.[121]

A logical alternative, advocated by the land speculators who had been purchasing tracts directly from the Indians, was to recognize that the Indigenous peoples of the continent had a right under natural law to both possession and dominion of their lands and therefore had the ability to transfer valid title to the settlers. Williams observes,

> Suddenly, even the most hardened land-market capitalist assumed the mantle of zealous advocate of the Indians' natural-law right to engage in unregulated real-estate transactions. Neither the king nor the landed colonies "owned" the lands on the frontier, argued these speculators. The Indian tribes occupied these lands as free and sovereign peoples. By natural law, the Indians could therefore sell their rights to the land to whomever they please, the Proclamation of 1763 and the landed colonies' charter claims notwithstanding.[122]

Though many of these land speculators were also influential political figures, they could not sufficiently counter the demands of the landed colonies, and for several years Virginia refused to surrender its claims to what was then considered the Northwest unless the Continental Congress declared void any purchases made directly from Indians in those territories by anyone other than Virginian companies.

Finally, a compromise was reached in 1784, and ratified by the 1787 Constitutional Convention, that undermined private land claims by recognizing a centralized federal power to trade and enter into treaties with American Indian nations but that did not explicitly divest the "landed" states of their claims until they were ceded to the United States.[123] Again, the natural law rights which the colonists claimed for themselves simply did not extend to the colonized. According to Williams, "The notion that under natural law and natural right, the Indians themselves . . . could sell to whomever they wished was denied by all white men of common sense in America. . . . Those who had won the war for America chose instead to explain their territorial rights . . . by the convenient Norman-derived fiction of a superior claim in European-derived governments to the lands of the Indians."[124] John Wunder concludes that, as a result, from the American Indian perspective, the Declaration of Independence was "perceived . . . as both a cruel myth and a dire geopolitical statement of purpose."[125]

Thus, as the settlers of the thirteen British colonies moved toward establishing an independent state, their political leaders rejected many of the specific provisions of the Puritans' theology while accepting their foundational belief in a national purpose, or mission, to spread Anglo-Saxon civilization. Like the earliest colonists, however, they, too, had to develop an ideology that encompassed the increased political rights and freedoms they envisioned for themselves and simultaneously legitimated their occupation of Indigenous territories. Like the Puritans, they accomplished this partly by defining their freedoms within the political parameters of their governing structures which, in turn, were cast in terms of civilization. Those who were deemed human enough to participate in that civilization would have the benefit of this freedom; those who resisted incorporation into those structures, or who were deemed unfit to participate—even by the counterfactual assertion that they were "wandering savages"—could be eliminated in good conscience for the greater good of human progress.

The establishment of the United States and the legal rationales its leaders developed to justify its appropriation of American Indian lands and resources thus reflect themes that have remained a constant part of American discourse and identity. Its very existence represented an American exception to the prevailing structures of international legal theory, rationalized by the American claim to more fully represent the principles of freedom and democracy within a "higher" and universally applicable law.[126] Thus it was central to American claims to legitimacy to be identified, in Supreme Court Justice John Marshall's words, as "a government of laws, not of men."[127] Nonetheless, while making what in many ways was a radical break from existing political and legal norms, the founders of the United States retreated to and reinforced a colonial worldview in which Western civilization was the norm to be imposed on all who were deemed Other.

Establishing the Republic

First Principles and American Identity

We hold these truths to be self-evident, that all men are created equal, that they are endowed by their Creator with certain
unalienable Rights, that among these are Life, Liberty and the
pursuit of Happiness.—That to secure these rights, Governments are instituted among Men, deriving their just powers
from the consent of the governed,—That whenever any Form
of Government becomes destructive of these ends, it is the
Right of the People to alter or to abolish it, and to institute new
government.

> —Declaration of Independence, In Congress, July 4, 1776

With this assertion of natural and inalienable rights, Angloamerican colonial leaders claimed for themselves the rights associated with British
imperial dominion in North America. The architects of the American rebellion were declaring the existence of an unprecedented entity, a settler colonial state claiming that it should be recognized as a member of the hitherto
exclusively European community of "civilized" nations because it represented
a more evolved, "progressive" phase of Western civilization. To justify this
expansion of the prevailing European paradigm, and its radical divergence
from international law as then framed, the American leaders called upon a
"higher" law, a natural law that recognized freedom, equality, and democracy
as inherent rights. Nonetheless, the United States was being created, literally,
by the appropriation of the land and labor of others, and its leaders needed
to rationalize the disparities between the rights they claimed for themselves
and those granted to their colonial subjects.

The justifications developed to explain why the United States should be
recognized as a legitimate colonial power in its own right are variants of the
arguments that have been proffered throughout U.S. history for its expan-

sion and domination not only of much of the North American continent but also for the hegemony it has exercised over its territorial "possessions" and what have been characterized as "client states." The same themes dominate its rationales for going to war, including its justifications of American exceptionalism in the current war on terror. In each of these cases, the core ideological dilemma has been, and remains, how to reconcile the values claimed as uniquely American—especially freedom and equality—with the United States' disparate treatment of those deemed Other. As discussed in the previous chapter, in the founding of the republic the colonial justifications for conquering others were not abandoned but incorporated into America's self-appointed "mission" of bringing Western civilization to a higher stage of development.

This chapter looks more closely at how the tension between democratic ideals and perceived colonial needs were reconciled within the framework of the U.S. Constitution and laws largely through the racialized portrayal of the "uncivilized" Other. It first provides a brief overview of the foundational principles and values that justified the establishment of the United States and formed the basis for its claims, past and present, to its territory and to an exceptional identity and status. It then addresses the new republic's justifications for continued appropriation of American Indian territories, focusing on the portrayal of Indigenous peoples as "savages" and the incorporation of this depiction into U.S. law. Finally, it turns to the question of slavery and its impact on determining the beneficiaries of American liberty and equality—in other words, who was an "American"—for it was by answering this question that the United States' claims to its "values" could be reconciled with the maintenance of colonial structures of domination and subordination.

A Government of the People

In the process of forming an independent state, American colonial leaders not only had to muster sufficient military force to break free of British rule, but they also had to agree on organizational principles that would accommodate both the aspirations to freedom, equality, and democracy articulated by Thomas Jefferson in the Declaration of Independence, and the material interests behind the push for independence. To justify their choices, as well as their legitimacy as a "civilized" player on the world stage, the colonists also had to develop a narrative that placed the new state solidly within the genealogy of the West.

Locating Sovereignty in the People

The principle that sovereignty resides with the people, not the state, was central to the colonists' rationale for breaking off from the British Empire. As stated in the 1776 Declaration, the rights of life, liberty, and equality could only be secured when "governments are instituted among men, deriving their just powers from the consent of the governed." This was one of the truly innovative aspects of the establishment of the American polity. As noted in earlier chapters, there were ongoing struggles within medieval European political theory as to how ultimate authority would be allocated between the papacy and secular governments. This struggle was framed within the Christian paradigm, a monotheistic tradition in which there could be no law, and hence no justice, without a supreme lawgiver. Initially this ultimate source of law was embodied in the monarch who, by divine right, wielded sovereign power. He was bound by divine or natural law but not the laws of the state.[1] As the Westphalian model of political organization emerged, the state itself, rather than its ruler, came to be seen as the repository of sovereignty.[2]

This trajectory of political thought culminated in Hegel's theory of the state as the apex of history as well as the manifestation of the divine. As stated in his 1821 *Philosophy of Right*, "The State is the spirit that dwells in the world and realizes itself in the world through *consciousness*. . . . When conceiving the State, one must not think of particular states, not of particular institutions, but one must much rather contemplate the *Idea*, God as actual on earth, alone."[3] In this construction, the people exist to serve the state, not vice versa. The American approach, at least as articulated by Jefferson, departed from the notion of the divine right of kings in essentially the opposite direction from that which would be taken by Hegel. For Jefferson, sovereignty was vested in the people, who gave the government specific powers to protect their freedom. In turn, these powers were carefully divided and delegated among the branches of government to ensure that the state would not usurp the people's rights or impair their freedoms. That the government exists to serve the people, and not vice versa, was emphatically affirmed by the statement in the Declaration of Independence that when a government ceases to fulfill its rightful purpose and instead becomes "destructive of these ends," it is the people's right to alter or abolish it.[4]

The Unacknowledged Influence of Indigenous Models

As Jefferson looked to ancient Saxon tribal governance for instruction on truly democratic forms of political organization, some of his contemporaries were pursuing a parallel path by looking to the political systems developed by their Indigenous neighbors.[5] Probably the most influential of these was the Covenant Chain of the Six Nations of the Haudenosaunee (Iroquois) Confederacy, a series of treaty agreements based on their Great Law of Peace.[6] This system had created a strong and peaceful union among the Senecas, Onondagas, Oneidas, Mohawks, and Cayugas since at least the 1400s, perhaps as early as 1000, and was joined by the Tuscaroras in the early 1700s. Among other things, the Great Law provided for a complex, consensus-based system of checks and balances among the constituent nations, election of leaders, delineation of their responsibilities, and provisions for their removal.[7]

In the 1730s and 1740s, when the English proposed consolidating their alliance with the Iroquois in order to drive out the French, the Iroquois had suggested that the northeastern colonies adopt their model of a strong and powerful confederation.[8] This led Benjamin Franklin, who was Jefferson's primary adviser in drafting the Declaration of Independence, to rely on the Great Law of Peace in drafting the Albany Plan for a federal union among the British colonies. In turn, the Articles of Confederation and the Constitution were heavily influenced by the Albany Plan.[9] Most attractive to the founders of the American Republic was the extent to which the Iroquoian and other Indigenous systems of government, as distinguished from extant European models, preserved individual freedom. Jefferson wrote in 1787, "I am convinced that those societies [such as the Indians] which live without government enjoy in their general mass an infinitely greater degree of happiness than those who live under European governments."[10] The point was not that American Indian nations lacked structures of governance but that they did not have governments as the Europeans conceived them. As the English explorer John Long said, "The Iroquois laugh when you talk to them about obedience to kings [because] they cannot reconcile the idea of submission with the dignity of man."[11]

In 1787 John Adams published his *Defence of the Constitutions of the Government of the United States,* a work that compared ancient and modern forms of governance and was widely discussed at the Constitutional Convention. According to historian Donald Grinde, in arguing for a bicameral legislature Adams urged leaders of the time to investigate the "government of . . . modern Indians," since the separation of powers in their government "is marked with a precision that excludes all controversy." Indeed, Adams remarked that the legislative branch in modern Indian governments is so democratic that the "real sovereignty resided in the body of the people."[12]

Charles Pinckney, a South Carolina delegate to the Constitutional Convention, recalled in 1788 that the delegates were looking to Indigenous

American models because "from the European world no precedents are to be drawn for a people who think they are capable of governing themselves."[13]

There was, of course, nothing inherently contradictory between the colonists' recognition that both the early Saxon tribal peoples and the Indigenous peoples of North America had developed democratic forms of governance, with sovereignty truly vested in the people, that could be used as complementary models for the new state. The founders' praise for the Iroquoian model and their actual history of cooperating with American Indian nations when it was expedient illustrate that they were well aware that the Indians were anything but "wandering savages" with no concept of government or law. Moreover, the realities of early colonial interactions with Indigenous nations also demonstrate that, had the early American leaders so desired, their neighbors in the Iroquois Confederacy were willing to allow them to participate in the system of international law that already existed in the northeast.[14] However, acknowledgment of the truly diverse heritage of the American constitutional model would have undermined American claims to be at the forefront of the linear trajectory of Western civilization and was incompatible with the notion of a uniquely American "destiny" to bring civilization to the continent as well as the expansionist intentions of the colonists.

Compromising Competing Interests

Notwithstanding the passionate phrasing of the Declaration of Independence, the founders did not agree on the reach of the democracy they were establishing. At the Constitutional Convention Alexander Hamilton argued brilliantly, if unsuccessfully, for a plan in which the president would be chosen for life, and senators for life or during good behavior, by electors meeting property qualifications. The president was to be able to veto any law enacted and to have the discretion to enforce or ignore existing laws. The sovereignty of the constituent states would be eliminated by having the president appoint governors with life tenure and the ability to overrule any act of the state legislatures. "Though his President, serving for life, was not called a king, he was to be armed with more arbitrary power than was possessed by the King of England. . . . '[W]hat he had in mind was the British Constitution as George III had tried hard to make it,' and failed because the English people would not tolerate it."[15]

The Convention rejected Hamilton's monarchical model, but the democratic ideals of those who prevailed were tempered, of course, by the fact that all the founders were intent on maintaining their colonial prerogatives. As

Charles Beard pointed out in *An Economic Interpretation of the Constitution*, a majority of those who drafted the constitution had significant investments in land, slaves, manufacturing, or shipping, half were lending money out at interest, and most held government bonds.[16] Thus, in Howard Zinn's words,

> [They] had some direct economic interest in establishing a strong federal government: the manufacturers needed protective tariffs; the moneylenders wanted to stop the use of paper money to pay off debts; the land speculators wanted protection as they invaded Indian lands; slaveowners needed federal security against slave revolts and runaways; bondholders wanted a government able to raise money by nationwide taxation, to pay off those bonds.[17]

This resulted in a constitution that, while incorporating guarantees of individual liberty, protected both manufacturing interests and the institution of slavery, and allowed for a strong, centralized government with the power to tax and the ability to create a standing army. To a large extent, the political power of the propertied class was protected by providing for popular elections only for the House of Representatives, with state legislators choosing their senators and the presidential electors, and the president appointing the Supreme Court.[18]

Countering these provisions were the limitations on the power of the government itself. The Constitution explicitly recognized that sovereignty rests with the people, who were establishing the Union for the purpose of "secur[ing] the Blessings of Liberty to ourselves and our Posterity." It created a government of limited powers and, as the final provision of the Bill of Rights clarifies, "The powers not delegated to the United States by the Constitution, nor prohibited by it to the States, are reserved to the States respectively, or to the people." Finally, following the Iroquoian model, the power of the federal government was distributed among the legislative, executive, and judicial branches to ensure that they would mutually constrain one another. Because each branch of government was thus limited to functions specified by the Constitution—which, in turn, derived its legitimacy from the will of the people—the government itself was not conceived as having any inherent rights.[19]

"A Government of Laws"

The founders were clear that if freedom (at least for some) was a preeminent and inalienable right, and democratic governance the primary means for its defense, the rule of law was critical to ensure that the powers entrusted to the government were used to preserve rather than crush liberty. They were also concerned, as their European colonial predecessors had been, with establishing a legal framework for their claims to dominion over lands and peoples, for law was essential to distinguishing civilization from a "state of nature." This was particularly important to the Americans because, as noted above, they had to justify their break from British rule as well as their own colonial practices. If the new United States was to become a member of the heretofore exclusively European "community of nations," it needed to be recognized as a "civilized" state according to the norms of that community.

The Rule of Law

Thus, although the term "rule of law" was not widely used until a century after American independence, the concept permeates the Constitution from its initial recognition of "We the People" to its explicit creation of a government of limited power, its complex system of checks and balances, and its specification of "the supreme Law of the land."[20] Although legal scholars have explained the rule of law in many different ways, the concept has certain common themes. Procedural guarantees are virtually always considered essential, perhaps because a primary purpose of the rule of law is to guard against arbitrary or capricious government action. Generally the lawmaking body must be the duly authorized arm of a legitimate government, acting within its mandate. The legislation it promulgates must be knowable—clear, publicly available, and promulgated in advance, not applied retroactively— and capable of being obeyed. It must be enforced consistently, equitably, and in good faith.[21] Provisions for ensuring compliance with these procedural requirements are found in the Bill of Rights which, largely owing to Jefferson's efforts, was drafted by James Madison and appended to the Constitution in 1791 in response to concerns that basic human rights were inadequately guaranteed by the document.[22]

The founders also recognized, however, that a narrow focus on procedural requirements could result in grossly unjust laws, even if applied in an equitable and consistent manner, and that this could undermine the founders' stated purpose to establish a government that would protect freedom. As expressed by law professor Berta Hernandez-Truyol, "the substantive conception of the rule of law is one of formal justice which promotes liberty."[23] According to legal philosopher Ronald Dworkin, this vision of the rule of law "assumes that citizens have moral rights and duties with respect to one another, and political rights against the state as a whole [and] . . . insists that these moral and political rights be recognized in positive law. . . . [I]t supposes that citizens have moral rights . . . other than and prior to those given by positive enactment.[24] Concerned that the first eight amendments might be interpreted as the sum total of individual rights guaranteed by the Constitution,[25] the drafters of the Bill of Rights explicitly stated in the Ninth Amendment that the enumeration of certain rights "shall not be construed to deny or disparage others retained by the people," and the Tenth Amendment reiterates that the government is one of limited powers. The judiciary was charged with the duty of ensuring that, in the words of Chief Justice John Marshall in his 1803 opinion in *Marbury v. Madison*, "this is a government of laws, not of men."[26] Consistent with the Jeffersonian notion that freedom itself is the ascendant value, and that the Constitution created a structure of government to preserve it, in this critical case Marshall clarified that the judiciary has an obligation to ensure that the Constitution remains paramount, overriding legislative or executive action when necessary.

The Centrality of International Law

The founders were well aware that recognition of the United States as part of the community of "civilized nations" rested upon their ability to demonstrate the legitimacy of the new republic under international law. As John Jay, the first chief justice of the U.S. Supreme Court observed in 1793, even before the Constitution had been ratified, "the United States had, by taking a place among the nations of the earth, become amenable to the laws of nations; and it was their interest as well as their duty to provide, that those laws should be respected and obeyed."[27] In the twenty-first century, when many Americans seem to consider international law to be optional,[28] it is difficult to grasp the extent to which the need for consistent compliance was presumed by early American leaders. Nonetheless, as legal scholar Jordan Paust has demonstrated through his painstakingly detailed research, the founders and framers stated repeatedly that the Congress, the executive branch, the states, the judiciary, and the people themselves were bound both by treaties and customary international law.[29]

Article III of the Constitution, which establishes and delineates the responsibilities of the federal courts, provides that "the judicial Power shall extend to all Cases, in Law and Equity, arising under this Constitution, the Laws of the United States, and Treaties made, or which shall be made, under their Authority."[30] The binding nature of treaty obligations is clearly spelled out in Article VI which states: "This Constitution, and the Laws of the United States which shall be made in Pursuance thereof; and all Treaties made, or which shall be made, under the Authority of the United States, shall be the supreme Law of the Land." This section continues by clarifying that not only the federal judiciary but "the Judges in every State shall be bound thereby, any Thing in the Constitution or Laws of any State to the Contrary notwithstanding."[31]

Thus, in his 1796 statement to the House of Representatives, President George Washington noted that all treaties, upon ratification by the Senate, "become obligatory."[32] As Paust observes, this understanding had earlier been affirmed by Congress in its unanimous acceptance of John Jay's 1786 report, which stated that a ratified treaty "immediately [became] binding on the whole nation, and superadded to the laws of the land."[33] It was also reflected in the early judicial rulings.[34] For example, interpreting a treaty with France in an 1801 case involving the seizure of ships as prize, Supreme Court Chief Justice John Marshall observed, "The constitution of the United States declares a treaty to be the supreme law of the land. Of consequence its obligation on the courts of the United States must be admitted."[35]

The fundamental obligation of the new country to comply with international law was not limited to treaties but also applied to customary international law, often referred to as the law of nations. In 1795 Supreme Court Justice James Iredell confirmed federal jurisdiction in another prize case, saying: "This is so palpable a violation of our own law (I mean the common law, of which the law of nations is a part, as it subsisted either before the act of Congress on the subject, or since that has provided a particular manner of enforcing it,) as well as of the law of nations generally; that I cannot entertain the slightest doubt, but that . . . the District Court had jurisdiction."[36] This understanding was perhaps most famously articulated by Justice Horace Gray in 1900 in *The Paquete Habana*, a case involving the exemption of fishing vessels from capture during hostilities. After tracing the history of this rule from decrees issued by King Henry IV of England in the early 1400s through the treaties, decrees, and practices of various European sovereigns as well as the U.S. in the 1700s and 1800s, Justice Gray observed: "International law is part of our law, and must be ascertained and administered by the courts of justice of appropriate jurisdiction as often as questions of right depending upon it are duly presented for their determination." With respect to customary law, he continued, "where there is no treaty and no controlling executive or legislative act or judicial decision, resort must be had to the customs and usages of civilized nations, and, as evidence of these, to the works of jurists and commentators."[37]

In light of the emphasis placed upon the law of nations by early leaders of the executive, legislative, and judicial branches of government, and their careful incorporation of structures of governance to ensure compliance with this body of law, how is it that the United States has managed to exempt itself from so much of international law over the years? Among the many examples Paust cites to support the founders' recognition of these principles, one quote from Peter Duponceau, a prominent attorney in the late eighteenth century, provides insight. According to Duponceau,

> The law of nations . . . may be said, indeed to be part of the law of every civilized nation; but it stands on other and higher grounds. . . . It is binding on every people and on every government. It is to be carried into effect at all times under the penalty of being thrown out of the pale of civilization, or involving the country into a war. . . . [T]his universal common law can never cease to be the rule of executive and judicial proceedings until mankind shall return to the savage state.[38]

The presumption reflected in this statement—that the rule of law is necessarily a product of Western civilization—has been employed to promote the belief that civilization constructs law and that, because civilization is ever evolving toward higher stages, law as it is known at one stage of the process can be overridden in the interest of the further development or expansion of civilization. In turn, this belief has facilitated U.S. deviations from accepted international law, for when the larger goals of U.S. growth have conflicted with law, law has been "trumped" fairly consistently by the benefits to civilization said to accrue from such expansion. This phenomenon is illustrated by the political and legal structures imposed by the United States upon American Indian nations.

American Indian and Land Rights: Myth Becomes Law

The relationship between Euroamerican colonists and American Indians was always fraught with contradiction as a result of the tensions between the colonists' need for assistance from and alliances with their Indigenous neighbors and their determination to extend their settlements with or without Indian consent, simultaneously imposing their vision of civilization upon native peoples. As the political and military power of the United States increased, American policies shifted from operating within a legal paradigm that recognized American Indian sovereignty to one in which Indigenous peoples were increasingly racialized as "savage" and therefore exempt from otherwise applicable protections of law.

Early Acknowledgment of Native Sovereignty

Having won its war for independence, the newly formed United States was anxious to gain international recognition as a legitimate state, particularly in the eyes of the European powers, which, anxious to expand their own empires, strongly condemned colonial revolts. Militarily weak, the United States needed to establish political relations with the Indigenous nations along its borders, nations whose sovereignty had been recognized by European states and whose military strength equaled or exceeded that of the emergent United States. As scholar Ward Churchill points out, "Indeed, what the Continental Congress needed more than anything at the time was for Indigenous nations, already recognized as respectable sovereignties in their treaties with the European states, to bestow a comparable recognition upon the fledgling U.S. by entering into treaties with *it*."[39]

To this end, the Northwest Ordinance of 1789 stated that "the utmost good faith shall always be observed towards the Indians; their land and property shall never be taken from them without their consent; and in their property, rights, and liberty, they shall never be disturbed . . . but laws founded in justice and humanity shall from time to time be made, for wrongs done to them, and for peace and friendship with them."[40] The Constitution explicitly limited relations with Indigenous nations to the federal government,[41] and by the time Congress officially suspended treaty making with American Indians in 1871, the United States had entered into approximately four hundred ratified treaties with Indian nations.[42]

The colonial law of nations recognized by the "civilized" world at the time of the founding of the United States was built on the framework established by Franciscus de Vitoria, Matías de Paz, Emmerich Vattel, and other international legal theorists.[43] Although these scholars disagreed on many points, certain principles had become fairly clearly established. As Vitoria had clarified, a European Crown only acquired outright title to "discovered" lands that were actually unpopulated (*territorium res nullius*).[44] If the land was inhabited, the rights attaching to "discovery" meant only that the right to trade with or acquire land from the Indigenous peoples rested solely with the "discovering power." Essentially this was a restraint of trade agreement among the European states to avoid unnecessary warfare between themselves.[45]

Occupied lands could only be acquired from their Indigenous inhabitants with their consent or, in a limited set of circumstances, through a "just war." Unless one was to revert to the arguments of the Crusades, or make the counterfactual assertion that the lands were "vacant," the conditions articulated by St. Augustine regarding a "just war" prevailed.[46] The use of armed force was lawful only if the native peoples initiated an unprovoked attack, arbitrarily refused to trade, or refused to admit missionaries among them—the latter, one might note, *not* extending to their subsequent refusal to convert. If one of these three conditions pertained, the discovering power had a legal right to use such force as was necessary to enforce the condition, and to impound native property as compensation for the cost of such action.[47] These requirements were acknowledged by Thomas Jefferson when he said, "We consider it as established by the usage of different nations into a kind of *Jus gentium* for America, that a white nation settling down and declaring that such and such are their limits, makes an invasion of those limits by any other white nation an act of war, but gives no right of soil against the native possessors."[48]

As a result, within their own paradigm, European colonial powers and the new American state obtained legally valid land title from American Indian nations by entering into formal treaties, agreements that, by definition, acknowledged the Indigenous peoples in question as fully sovereign and therefore capable of alienating their land.[49] Treaties of peace and friendship, trade agreements, and military alliances were also commonplace.[50] Attorney General William Wirt acknowledged in 1821, "So long as a tribe exists and remains in possession of its lands, its title and possession are sovereign and exclusive. . . . We treat with them as separate sovereignties; and while an Indian nation continues to exist within its acknowledged limits, we have no more right to enter upon their territory, without their consent, than we have to enter upon the territory of a foreign prince."[51] In the words of legal scholar Siegfried Wiessner, "There is no credible way to interpret out of existence the fact that the budding new player in the international arena of the 18th and 19th century, the United States, for whatever reason, did enter into treaties of friendship and alliance on a perfectly level playing field with the Indian nations. It treated them with the same respect, extending to them the same courtesies as to other nations of the then overwhelmingly European international legal order."[52]

The emergent United States needed to take this position both because of its relative military weakness and its desire to establish, vís-à-vís the European world, that it was not what we would now term a "rogue" state. The land it would claim was clearly inhabited—by more than four hundred Indigenous nations—so, absent the conditions recognized in international law for a "just war," legal title to land could only be transferred between sovereigns by virtue of a treaty. Initially American Indians in the northeast attempted to accommodate the settlers with limited land cessions, but it soon became clear to U.S. officials that the native inhabitants had no inclination to sell as much land as was desired. Indeed, for many Indigenous peoples, selling their lands was a concept at odds with their rights and responsibilities to the earth, namely, their highest law.[53]

The Portrayal of American Indians as "Savage"

Ultimately, despite the importance that the "Founding Fathers" placed on creating a "government of laws," the prospect of staying within the limits of legally acquired territory proved unacceptable; from the beginning, they had envisioned the United States as extending throughout the continent and beyond. Thus, as its relative military power grew, the U.S. government imposed its will on the hundreds of Indigenous nations it encountered with increasing frequency, violating both its own treaties and, more generally, applicable international law.[54] To justify this assertion of raw power, the settlers invoked the image of the Indian as "savage," for this opened up the possibility of declaring lands uninhabited by human beings, and therefore "vacant," or of rationalizing perpetual warfare as inevitable.

Treaty making was often regarded as a matter of expediency rather than compliance with law, as illustrated in a letter written by George Washington in 1783: "I am clear in my opinion, that policy and oeconomy [sic] point very strongly to the expediency of being upon good terms with the Indians, and the propriety of purchasing their lands in preference to attempting to drive them by force of arms out of their Country; which . . . is like driving the wild Beasts of ye forest."[55] For Washington, like so many colonial leaders before him, the Indigenous inhabitants could be treated as part of nature rather than as human beings when it was more convenient to do so. Thus he expressed his confidence that "the gradual extension of our settlements will as certainly cause the savage, as the wolf, to retire; both being beasts of prey, tho' they differ in shape."[56]

As this letter demonstrated, if Indigenous peoples could be portrayed as irredeemably savage, merely "wild Beasts of ye forest," Americans could feel justified in ignoring the laws of "civilized nations" in dealing with them.[57] This view was widely disseminated by public orators, "news" reports, and popular novels.[58] The latter genre, still reflected in "western" novels and movies today, was epitomized by Robert Montgomery Bird's *Nick of the Woods or the Jibbenainosay: A Tale of Kentucky*. Bird, a Philadelphia doctor, was fascinated by Daniel Boone who, with considerable literary license, appears to have been transformed into this novel's hero Nathan Slaughter, or Nick. Nick embodies the "good American," a pacifistic Quaker who, as a result of his encounters with the savage Shawnee, is inevitably, and therefore understandably, transformed into the ultimate Indian fighter. Bird describes Nick as a man of peace who hands over his hunting knife and rifle to a Shawnee chief, who immediately slaughters his family. "With my own knife he struck down my eldest boy! With my own gun he slew the mother of my children! . . . When thee has children that Injuns murder, as thee stands by,—a wife that clasps thee legs in the writing of death,—er blood, spouting up to thee bosom where she has slept,—an old mother calling thee to help her in the death-struggle;—then, friend, *then* . . . thee may call theeself wretched, for thee will be so!"[59] Nick thereupon embarks on a vividly described life of revenge, rescuing white captives and, with a "hideous grin of delight," slaughtering, mutilating, and scalping all the Indians he can find.

Published in 1837, *Nick of the Woods* "enjoyed immediate and lasting public favor," appearing in twenty-nine editions, and was still available in the 1970s.[60] Richard Drinnon summarizes the import of this tale:

> Through a Quaker man of peace [Bird] demonstrated the horrifying consequences that would have awaited other Anglo-Americans had they acted on such principles of nonviolence and goodwill. As it was, what Nathan Slaughter had suffered personally, in extreme form, the whole country had suffered collectively. . . . In return, the United States might expropriate and kill and even scalp them. . . . Bird's allegory helped citizens believe they might proceed in good conscience with "emptying"—in the elegant euphemism of a modern historian—the Eastern states of those merciless savages still ambulatory.[61]

This was, in many respects, a return to the position Vitoria had articulated when he stated that, in conflict with infidels, it might be "useless ever to hope for a just peace on any terms," leaving as "the only remedy . . . to destroy all of them who can bear arms against us, provided they have already been in fault."[62]

Again, this was a classically colonial framing. As Peter Fitzpatrick explains, Western civilization defined itself not so much in positive terms but as the negation of that which was deemed "uncivilized," and therefore the international law that emerged to justify colonization depended on the existence of an Other who purportedly lacked settled agrarian communities, the recognition of property, law, and thus sovereignty.[63] According to Fitzpatrick, in colonial settings, "the savage was the carrier of the irresolution in occidental identity and the constituent negation of its civilization and, so, had to be maintained as intractably apart from that identity and that civilization."[64]

Conforming Law to Conquest

This construction of the "savage" Other was reflected not only in popular American novels and political pronouncements, but it was also incorporated into the framework of domestic law. It was, perhaps, most famously articulated by Supreme Court Chief Justice John Marshall—himself the beneficiary of western land claims[65]—in a series of cases addressing issues of title to and jurisdiction over the territory being claimed by the United States. The foundation for federal hegemony over American Indian lands and ultimately the nations themselves was laid in the 1810 case of *Fletcher v. Peck*.[66] There the Court recognized the validity of a 1795 sale by Georgia of lands on its western frontier, thus asserting that Georgia's claims had not been extinguished by the Proclamation of 1763 and upholding the compromise effected between "landed" and "landless" states at the Constitutional Convention.[67] In so doing, Marshall framed the question as concerning whether the "vacant lands" of the west belonged to the individual states or the Union, invoking the right of the colonizers to consider land that was not cultivated as "wasteland" that could rightfully be appropriated by those who would put it to "productive" use.[68] Any claims the Indians may have had to those lands under natural law were simply irrelevant to the discussion.

Native legal rights were more directly and explicitly denied in a trilogy of Supreme Court opinions authored by Marshall in the 1820s and 1830s. The first, *Johnson & Graham's Lessee v. McIntosh*, decided in 1823, was a title dispute between two settlers, one of whom claimed to have purchased the land in question directly from its Indigenous owners. In order to justify his conclusion that individuals could only obtain valid title from the United States government, not from the Indians, Marshall turned the doctrine of discovery "on its head," to use Churchill's framing.[69] The Chief Justice asserted that because the European nations had agreed among themselves that only the "discovering" power could enter into treaties for land with the Indigenous inhabitants, the Indians' capacity to sell the land to whomever they chose was correspondingly restricted and consequently they could not have truly "owned" it.[70] Recognizing the problems with this reasoning, Marshall invoked the Indigenous peoples' alleged lack of civilization to support his conclusions:

> Although we do not mean to engage in the defence of those principles which Europeans have applied to Indian title, they may, we think, find some excuse, if not justification, in the character and habits of the people whose rights have been wrested from them. . . . Most usually, [the conquered] are incorporated with the victorious nation, and become subjects or citizens. . . . But the tribes of Indians inhabiting this country were fierce savages, whose occupation was war, and whose subsistence was drawn chiefly from the forest. To leave them in possession of their country, was to leave the country a wilderness.[71]

According to Justice Marshall, the settlers were reduced to choosing between "abandoning the country," "enforcing [their] claims by the sword," or living alongside American Indians, thereby "exposing themselves and their families to the perpetual hazard of being massacred."[72] In other words, civilization—particularly the great American experiment in democracy—could not proceed without exterminating Indians. As summarized by historian Francis Jennings, Justice Marshall "argued with impeccable logic from a false assumption to a conclusion that he admitted would be criminal if not for the assumption."[73]

It is not that a more realistic view of American Indian cultures and perspectives—one that did not invoke the spectre of savage butchery—was inaccessible. From the beginning, the Puritans had made explicit their plans to wipe out extensive Indigenous agricultural settlements, thus acknowledging that the local inhabitants were anything but "wandering savages."[74] As noted above, Benjamin Franklin and others influential in the drafting of the Constitution were influenced by the political organization of the Haudenosaunee, or Six Nations Iroquois Confederacy.[75] By the time Bird and Marshall were writing, the Cherokee were well known for their assimilation to Western ways, including the formation of a government and promulgation of a constitution based on the U.S. model.[76] Legal scholar Rennard Strickland reports that in attempting to resist removal from their treaty-guaranteed homelands in Georgia, "the Cherokees toured and lectured along the Eastern seaboard seeking Congressional support, attempted direct negotiations with the President and the federal Indian bureaucracy, and even pushed for some kind of compromise with Georgia's state officials."[77]

These, however, were not—and still are not—convenient facts for set-tlers unwilling to question their fundamental right to be on someone else's land. If the Indigenous peoples would not simply disappear, or "retire" with the wolves, it was necessary to define them as less than human and "extirpate" them from the grand narrative of progress.[78] Marshall as much as conceded in *Johnson v. McIntosh* that he was abandoning justice in favor of raw power: "Conquest gives a title which the Courts of the conqueror cannot deny, whatever the private and speculative opinions of individuals may be, respecting the original justice of the claim which has been successfully asserted."[79] This exercise of power was in turn justified by the same arguments that had always been applied to colonial appro-priation. As legal scholar James Gathii summarizes, "although [Marshall] had spoken eloquently against the rights of belligerents insofar as they undermined free commerce in the United States' international relations with its European counterparts, for Indians, war was the solution for their subjugation."[80]

Georgia, in the meantime, continued to pass laws asserting jurisdiction over Cherokee peoples and lands. Asserting its criminal jurisdiction, the state accused Corn Tassell of the murder of another member of the Chero-kee Nation, and prohibited both the defendant and his Cherokee witnesses from testifying at trial. Not surprisingly Corn Tassell was convicted, and in December 1830 Georgia executed him in defiance of a writ of error issued by Justice Marshall.[81] With respect to the territory, "new Georgia laws declared the Cherokee lands to be 'Cherokee County' within the State of Georgia, and designated this as 'surplus' land to be opened to Georgia citizens for settle-ment by lottery. Indians were denied the right to appear in court under this legislation, and non-Indians living within this Cherokee area were required to obtain a permit from officials of the State of Georgia."[82]

These laws were challenged by the Cherokee Nation, with the assistance of former U.S. attorney general William Wirt. As a result, in the 1831 case of *Cherokee Nation v. Georgia* the Court considered whether the state of Geor-gia could exercise jurisdiction over Cherokee lands. That question, however, was not decided. Despite the fact that the United States had by then entered into numerous treaties with American Indian nations, including the Chero-kees, thereby recognizing their sovereignty—and, indeed, depended upon those treaties to justify its claims to much of its territory—Marshall held that the Cherokee Nation did not constitute a "foreign state" and therefore did not have standing to sue the state of Georgia. Based on that reasoning, the Court dismissed the case for lack of jurisdiction.[83] This was vigorously contested by

Justice Smith Thompson who, in dissent, cited extensively to Emmerich de Vattel to argue that Marshall's conclusion that American Indian nations were not separate states was clearly at odds with international law.[84] As Churchill concludes, "in practical effect, Marshall cast Indigenous nations as entities inherently imbued with a sufficient measure of sovereignty to alienate their territory by treaty when and wherever the U.S. desired they do so, but never with enough to refuse."[85]

Despite holding that the Court lacked jurisdiction to hear the case, Marshall proceeded to elaborate on the status of American Indian nations, unilaterally assigning them a unique and lesser status relative to "foreign states." "They may," he declared, "more correctly, perhaps, be denominated domestic dependent nations. They occupy a territory to which we assert a title independent of their will. . . . Their relation to the United States resembles that of a ward to his guardian."[86] As will be addressed in chapter 5, this formulation became, and remains, the foundation of the legal relationship between the federal government and American Indian peoples.[87] Of particular note in the context of colonial law is Marshall's extension of this holding not simply to the Cherokee nation but to *all* Indigenous nations in territories claimed by the United States, even those peoples who had never encountered the United States. If the United States claimed their lands, they were, by definition, "domestic" and "dependent."

The following year, in *Worcester v. Georgia*, the final case of the "Marshall trilogy," the Chief Justice returned to the question initially presented in *Cherokee Nation* to clarify that a state could not exercise jurisdiction on Indian lands because that power was reserved to the federal government.[88] There was no jurisdictional issue in *Worcester*, for the appellant was a missionary and a citizen of Vermont living on Cherokee land with the permission of the Cherokee Nation but in violation of Georgia legislation requiring white people living on Indian land to obtain a license from, and swear allegiance to, the state. Sentenced to four years at hard labor, Samuel Worcester challenged the constitutionality of the statute, and the Supreme Court held the Georgia statute in question to be in violation of the Constitution, treaties, and laws of the United States.[89]

Worcester was, however, a pyrrhic victory for the Cherokee Nation. President Andrew Jackson simply disregarded the treaty rights confirmed by the Supreme Court and proceeded to enforce an 1830 Act requiring the "removal" of all Indians to points west of the Mississippi River. As a result, the Cherokees were forced onto the infamous "Trail of Tears," losing one-quarter of their population during their forced march to Oklahoma.[90] Moreover, although Justice Marshall acknowledged that the Cherokees did constitute a "nation" recognized by the United States, he relied upon the doctrine of discovery for his holding that the federal, rather than state, government had an exclusive right to negotiate with the Cherokees. Marshall acknowledged that although "discovery" alone did not transfer the property rights of all the inhabitants of the "discovered" territory, "power, war, conquest, give rights, which, after possession, are conceded by the world; and which can never be controverted by those on whom they descend."[91] Ultimately this opinion merely confirmed the self-appointed "right" of the U.S. to exercise jurisdiction over not just the Cherokee Nation but all American Indian peoples within its claimed boundaries.

Addressing the question most central to the legitimacy of the United States' claims to the land it occupied, Marshall was asserting a jurisprudential version of American exceptionalism. International law was clearly acknowledged to be at the heart of the dispute in *Johnson, Cherokee Nation,* and even *Worcester,* but it was applied in an extremely inconsistent manner. Marshall relied on the doctrine of discovery, yet ignored the distinction Vitoria made between occupied and unoccupied lands and his articulation of the rights of Indigenous peoples under natural law. In justifying U.S. hegemony in terms of "conquest," Marshall similarly disregarded the parameters of just warfare well established in the law of nations.

In each of these cases the Supreme Court could have chosen to acknowledge that Indians, like all other human beings, had rights universally cognizable under natural law. It could have held that a country that based its claim to independence on overturning feudal law in favor of a natural law which ensured freedom and democracy had an obligation to abide by that higher law. Instead, writing for the majority, Justice Marshall reverted to arguments based upon the inherent superiority of Western civilization, describing American Indians as "an anomaly unknown to the books that treat of states, and which the law of nations would regard as nothing more than wandering hordes, held together only by ties of blood and habit, and having neither laws or government, beyond what is required in a savage state."[92] Even as Marshall acknowledged that his reasoning might appear "extravagant," he invoked a version of the colonial powers' doctrine of discovery that had been repudiated even by Vitoria, and made arguments premised on the entirely counterfactual assertion that even those Indian peoples who had never encountered the United States, much less been defeated in war, were "wards" of the U.S. government by virtue of "conquest." The result was the entrenchment of another variant of American exceptionalism in the jurisprudence which continues to inform federal law governing Indians well into the twenty-first century.[93]

Defining "The People": Slavery and Race

The founders of the American Republic thus relied upon the rationale of bringing civilization to the "new world" to develop a legal—as well as religious and political—framework for their appropriation of American Indian lands and concomitant decimation of Indigenous peoples. In the process of consolidating their political independence on the basis of bringing Western civilization to a higher state of democratic governance and the protection of individual liberties, these early American leaders were faced with the contradictions involved not only in their treatment of American Indians but of the increasing numbers of enslaved Africans they were importing to make the occupied lands more profitable. As can be seen in Justice Marshall's rationale in the *Cherokee Nation* case, in the settlers' framing native peoples were, by definition, the Other, mythologized "wandering savages" in opposition to whom "We the People" could be defined.

Peter Fitzpatrick observes that "myth precedes and is negated by modernity. Modernity is what myth is not."[94] As discussed above, the early Angloamerican settlers' depiction of American Indians as uncivilized both helped justify the imposition of occupation and colonial rule upon the Indians and precluded the settlers from acknowledging the realities of Indigenous histories, cultures, and political structures, illustrating Fitzpatrick's point that the "primitive" Other, depicted as

> uncontrolled, fickle, irresponsible, of nature, and so on . . . does not exist primarily or initially apart from its relation to a West which encompasses it. . . . The other, in its uncivilized or pre-modern state, is a construct of the West. . . . The closure is, in a Western perspective, impregnable in that the other cannot speak against it because of the West's arrogation to itself truth as singular yet universal.[95]

Like the Indigenous peoples of North America, peoples of African descent were regarded by Angloamerican colonists as "uncivilized" Others, a construction utilized to justify their enslavement and long-term subordination. In turn, this colonial framework helped to consolidate a racialized dividing line against which "real" Americans could define themselves.

The Racial Discourse of Early European Colonization

As discussed in earlier chapters, the English colonists who established the United States were following in the footsteps of the Spanish who initially colonized much of the Americas in the name of Christian Empire. The Spanish, in turn, began their expansion shortly after expelling the Moors—and subsequently the Jews—from Southwestern Europe in the late 1400s.[96] These North African Arabs, whose institutions and culture had brought Europe out of the Dark Ages, were from slaveholding societies, and their association of slavery with blackness, as well as the justification advanced by some Arab authors for slavery based on Noah's curse of his son Ham, had remained a current of European thought long after the Moors were driven out.[97] The Spanish characterized their conquest of the New World as a mission from God. Bartolomé de las Casas found particular significance in Cristóbal Colon (Christopher Columbus)'s name, noting that Cristóbal "means bearer or carrier of Christ. . . . For in truth it was he who was the first to open the gates of the Ocean Sea, through which he entered bringing our Saviour Jesus Christ and his blessed name to remote land and hitherto unknown realms."[98] In addition, "colon" is the root of "colony" and "colonizer." Yet, despite his glowing characterization, las Casas was certainly aware of the wholesale slaughter and enslavement of Indigenous people wrought by Columbus during his seven-year tenure as governor of Hispaniola.[99]

This reflects the conflict faced by the *conquistadors*, as well as by colonial settlers in North America, of how to reconcile the devastation, dehumanization, and dispossession wrought by conquest with the "civilizing" mission it was supposed to embody. Much of the Spanish justification of the 1500s relied on the Aristotelian notion of "natural slaves"[100]—some people were simply inferior, and it was their lot in life to serve others. Las Casas argued for decades against the notion that Indians fell into this category, successfully obtaining an ordinance, promulgated by King Philip II in 1573, that limited, at least in law, the harshness with which the Indians could be treated and changed the terminology describing the Spanish occupation from "conquest" to "pacification."[101] Yet las Casas accepted the necessity of forced labor, proposing that Indigenous labor be replaced by imported African slaves. For las Casas, the Indians of the Americas had souls that should be "saved" through more humane methods, a proposition he did not extend to Africans until much later in his life.[102]

Las Casas spent half a century agitating against the most brutal practices of Spanish colonization, but he did not question the superiority of Christianity nor its imposition on the peoples of the Americas. The debates over "natural slavery" reflected the presumption that Christian Europeans were inherently superior, leaving only two options: those being eliminated, colonized, or enslaved could be considered inferior as a result of their culture or environment, and therefore capable of becoming "civilized" under European tutelage, or they were simply inherently doomed to a subordinated status in any civilized society. Jefferson's position on the slavery question seems to have vacillated between these options. Sometimes he seemed to be saying that all men may have been *created* equal, a rejection of the Aristotelian notion of "natural slaves," but that they were not *in fact* equal—merely capable of becoming so. On the other hand, he also asserted that the "improvement of the blacks in body and mind, in the first instance of their mixture with the whites, has been observed by everyone, and proves that their inferiority is not the effect merely of their condition of life. . . . This unfortunate difference of color, and perhaps of faculty, is a powerful obstacle to the emancipation of these people."[103]

Throughout U.S. history, "mainstream" debates over the treatment of the racialized Other have been framed by these options. Peoples of color, or those otherwise divergent from Euroderivative norms, are either inherently and therefore immutably inferior to those of European descent, or they are in fact "less than" but retain a capacity for improvement. Depending upon the perceived needs of those making the determination, characterizations of the Other have often slipped readily from one classification to the other. However, the possibility that the divergent qualities of non-European cultures and peoples could be superior to European models has never been seriously entertained.

Slavery and the Construction of Race in Colonial America

The African slave trade initiated by the Portuguese in the 1400s was well established in Spanish and Portuguese settlements in the Americas by 1550.[104] Englishmen soon discovered its profitability, and by the mid-1600s many British colonies in the Caribbean had more African slaves than English settlers.[105] In 1619, the year before the Pilgrims landed at Plymouth, John Rolfe, Secretary of the Virginia Colony, reported that a Dutchman had sold twenty Africans to the colonists.[106] The initial status of these Africans in the American colonies is unclear; some seem to have been treated similarly to European indentured servants, and others appear to have been enslaved.[107] During this period the institution of chattel slavery—as distinguished from the enslavement of those captured in war—was just beginning to emerge, as was the notion of "race" as a distinct human grouping based on biology or genetics rather than religion or national origin.

In the early years of the colonies, the distinction between those who could be enslaved and those who could not was often expressed in religious rather than racial terms. Under the English law governing the colonies, a captive who had been converted to Christianity was deemed free, and in 1624 a Virginia court freed a black man because he had been baptized in England in 1612.[108] But "Christian" was more often used as a racial signifier. As historian Winthrop Jordan points out, "the term *Christian* seems to have conveyed much of the idea and feeling of *we* as against *they*: to be Christian was to be civilized rather than barbarous, English rather than African, white rather than black."[109]

In 1667 the Virginia legislature acknowledged this conflation and attempted to clarify the racial dimensions of slavery by passing an act that stated:

> Whereas some doubts have arisen whether children that are slaves by birth, and by the charity and pity of their owners made partakers of the blessed sacrament of baptism, should by virtue of their baptism be made free, it is enacted that *baptism does not alter the condition of the person as to his bondage [or] freedom; masters freed from this doubt may more carefully propagate Christianity by permitting slaves to be admitted to that sacrament.*[110]

Similarly South Carolina's Fundamental Constitution of 1669 provided that "Every Freeman of Carolina shall have absolute power and authority over Negro slaves, of what opinion or Religion soever."[111] In other words, enslavement originally justified on religious grounds was becoming legally entrenched on the basis of an emerging notion of race, yet the rationalization could be maintained that the enslaved were benefiting from their captivity by virtue of becoming Christians, a step, presumably, toward "civilization."

Laws regulating slaves began to be enacted in the colonies in the mid-1600s. A 1641 act ironically titled "Body of Liberties" made the Massachusetts Bay and Plymouth colonies the first to authorize slavery through legislation and provided that colonists could enslave "lawful captives taken in juste warres, and such strangers as willfully sell themselves or are sold to us."[112] In reality, of course, this fairly elaborate definition allowed the enslavement of virtually any American Indian or African, for both were prototypical "strangers" and inevitably had been reduced to slavery by armed force or "sale." This logic is illustrated by Georgia's "early colonial regulation granting to her citizens the right to exterminate 'Indians at war' without even a declaration of war."[113]

Most of the Angloamerican colonies consolidated their slave laws into unified codes between 1660 and 1682.[114] These codes generally created a legal presumption that all black persons and sometimes all "non-Christians," that is, Africans or American Indians, brought into their jurisdiction were slaves. The law clarified the distinction between chattel slavery and indentured servitude, providing that the slave's loss of freedom was complete and that slavery was a lifelong and eventually hereditary condition. With each succeeding generation, the slaves' actions were more minutely regulated and slaveholders' privileges expanded. Thus, for example, South Carolina slave codes enacted in the early 1700s restricted gatherings of slaves, prohibited travel without a pass, outlawed the possession of anything that could be used as a weapon, and provided severe penalties for any infraction. A 1669 Virginia statute, on the other hand, notified slave owners that they would not be criminally liable for the "casual" killing of slaves.[115]

For various reasons, including the need of the early colonies to recognize the sovereignty of American Indian nations in order to survive at all, the extensive social organization and military capacity of the native peoples, and the genocidal campaigns waged against them by the colonists, American Indians were considered less suitable for wholesale enslavement than Africans were. South Carolina, which had the largest number of Indian slaves, used them primarily to generate revenue by "exporting" them to the West Indies, but those who remained in the colony were regulated by the statutes applicable to African slaves.[116]

With the consolidation of race-based slavery, and the proliferation of laws that dictated conduct and provided for punishment on the basis of race, the notion of distinct races also emerged, for it became increasingly important to identify just who would be enslaved or otherwise subjected to such laws. Initially people identified themselves by ethnicity, nationality, or religion, not by race; racialized identity only became central as it became associated with particular privileges or burdens. As James Baldwin reflected,

> [Black Americans'] first sight of America was this marketplace and our legal existence, here, begins with the signature on the bill of sale. Of course, it is true that many White people . . . entered the country on similar terms . . . but these all managed, and speedily enough, after all, to become

White. They knew, at a glance, what would happen to them if they did *not* become White, and by no means metaphorically, on which side such bread as they might hope to find would be buttered. I say, to "become" White, for they had not been White before their arrival, any more than I, in Africa, had been Black.[117]

Eventually American orthodoxy would hold that, as the trial judge said in 1959 in the celebrated anti-miscegenation case of *Loving v. Virginia*, "Almighty God created the races white, black, yellow, malay and red, and he placed them on separate continents."[118] But they were now on the same continent, where anti-miscegenation laws were as ineffective in the seventeenth and eighteenth centuries as they were to be in the twentieth.

In an increasingly "mixed" society, who was to be assigned the benefits of whiteness or the disabilities of blackness? Initially children with parents of two different races were not considered to be of either race. Were they to be enslaved or otherwise subject to the social and legal disabilities of blackness? In 1770 Thomas Jefferson represented an enslaved man before a Virginia court, advocating—unsuccessfully—that he should be freed because his grandmother had been white and, under Virginia law, a child was supposed to inherit the status of the mother. Virginia, like other slaveholding colonies, had reversed the presumption of English law under which the child would inherit the status of the father. Instead, the law mandated that children would inherit the status of their mothers, a provision that added to the workforce children born to enslaved women raped by white men.[119]

For a combination of reasons, including the economic benefits of having more people enslaved and the ideological justifications of racial subordination based on the superiority of a "pure" Anglo-Saxon race, "white" was defined in increasingly exclusive ways and "black" in a correspondingly inclusive manner. Eventually only those without discernable non-European ancestry would be identified as white and, conversely, people of one-fourth, one-eighth, or even one sixty-fourth African descent became black. In most slaveholding jurisdictions, this also meant that they were presumed to be slaves. Ultimately this practice devolved into the hypodescent or "one drop" rule, which labeled as black or "colored" a person with *any* discernable African ancestry.[120]

With respect to other racial groups, classification systems developed in American law in a variety of ways, with specific criteria often dependent upon the economic or social interest at stake.[121] However, several patterns were established by these early colonial laws that have remained consistent throughout American history. Justifications for the differential treatment of human beings evolved from what had initially been cultural factors, such as religion or level of civilization, to distinctions based on hereditary, and therefore immutable, characteristics. Remaining intact was the notion of a unitary and hierarchical structure or measure of value, with Europeans or, more specifically, Anglo-Saxons, at the apex. Not only did the colonizers determine the relative "place" of different "races" in this system, but they also assumed the prerogative of defining each individual's racial identity; how individuals or communities might identify themselves was deemed irrelevant.[122]

As this construct of racialization emerged, it did more than ensure a particular structure of domination and subordination in the United States. It also reinforced the ideology of American exceptionalism in two ways. First, it ensured in very concrete and personal terms that humanity would not be viewed as a "pluriverse" of identities and societies[123] but rather as a fixed hierarchy in which those who represented Western civilization in its "purest" form were the ideal type. This then rationalized a legal order in which those at the top of the hierarchy could claim exceptional privileges, and impose differential burdens, upon those of lower status. This was a classically colonial legal regime, as described by Peter Fitzpatrick, in which

> the colonist took on the "burden" of pervasive powers in the cause of an inclusive civilization, only to use them to exclude, dissipate and generally "hold down" the savage as incorrigibly deviant. Comprehensive and draconian legal regimes sought to separate out and stultify not only the colonized but the traditional or customary institutions and process imputed to them.[124]

Thus it should come as no surprise that as the United States began the process of expanding and consolidating its territorial base and its political hegemony over diverse peoples, its racialized justifications facilitated not only internal disparities but external ones as well.

Slavery and the Constitution

By the time the American colonies declared their independence the institution of African chattel slavery and the ideology of white supremacy had thus been an integral part of their existence and identity for well over a century. The inconsistency between slavery and the principles enunciated in the Declaration of Independence, as well as the growing international movement to ban the slave trade, ensured that the question of slavery would be hotly debated at the Constitutional Convention of 1787. Nonetheless it soon became apparent that the Union would only be formed if slaveholding interests were well protected, for northern shipping interests as well as southern planters were adamant on the issue.[125]

The result was a Constitution that, without ever using the word "slave" or "slavery," ensured that the power of the newly organized federal government would protect the interests of those who owned or traded in slaves in numerous ways, prompting William Lloyd Garrison to call it "a covenant with death, and an agreement with hell."[126] In one of the only constitutional provisions that could not be amended, Congress was forbidden to ban the slave trade before the year 1808, and it had no obligation to do so then. The provision that slaves were to be counted as three-fifths of a person for purposes of taxation and representation did not mean, as is often assumed, that slaves had fewer rights than white citizens. In fact, they had no rights at all, and the purpose of the clause was to guarantee slaveholding states a disproportionate influence in the House of Representatives. States could ban slavery, but they were nonetheless obliged by the fugitive slave clause to use their resources to capture and return persons claimed as slaves, and the power granted Congress to call forth the militia to "suppress Insurrections" embodied a commitment to use federal resources to quell slave rebellions.[127]

Slavery was, in fact, well protected. When independence was declared, there were approximately seven hundred thousand slaves in the thirteen colonies; by the Civil War this number had grown to four million, approximately 10 percent of the U.S. population.[128] But enslaved persons were not the only ones excluded from "We the People" of the Constitution. Both slaveholding and non-slaveholding states and territories had numerous laws specifically regulating or excluding "free" black persons as well as other persons of color, compounding the social and legal presumption that all persons of African descent were slaves.[129] Supreme Court Justice Roger B. Taney articulated this most clearly in 1857 in *Scott v. Sandford*. Dred Scott had sued for his freedom in federal court, arguing, among other things, that the time he had spent in territory where slavery was forbidden had rendered him a free man. Scott was suing his purported owner, a citizen of New York, under federal diversity jurisdiction. Much as Justice Marshall had refused to grant the Cherokee Nation standing because he deemed them to be a "domestic, dependent nation" rather than a foreign state, Justice Taney held that the federal court had no jurisdiction because Scott could not be considered a citizen of Missouri. Taney did not stop there, however, going on to elaborate that black people were not citizens of the United States, or therefore of any particular state, nor even "persons" under the law. He reinforced this notion of the colonized Other by stating that *all* those of African descent, whether enslaved or not, had been regarded by the founders as "beings of an inferior order, and altogether unfit to associate with the white race, either in social or political relations; and so far inferior, that they had no rights which the white man was bound to respect."[130]

"We the People": Emergence of an American Identity

The presumption of the superiority of Western civilization rests on the central ideological premise that it protects and promotes the universal values of freedom and equality through democratic structures of government to a degree achieved by no other cultures or civilizations. As articulated in the Declaration of Independence, "life, liberty and the pursuit of Happiness" are recognized as natural and therefore inalienable rights, applicable equally to "all men," and the United States has claimed to represent the highest form of such civilization from this initial declaration through its consolidation and expansion to its current assertions of global superpower status. It was this history that President George W. Bush was invoking when he proclaimed, shortly after the attacks of September 11, 2001, that "the advance of human freedom— the great achievement of our time, and the great hope of every time—now depends on us,"[131] adding soon thereafter that "anyone who sets out to destroy freedom must eventually attack America, because we're freedom's home."[132]

Reconciling this ideological claim with the realities of a settler colonial state has always been at the heart of American claims to exceptionalism. In 1770, six years before drafting the Declaration of Independence, Thomas Jefferson had boldly argued on behalf of an enslaved man that, "under the law of nature, all men are born free, and every one comes into the world with a right to his own person, which includes the liberty of moving and using it at his own will."[133] Jefferson himself, however, was a slave owner who just the previous year had offered a reward for the capture of a runaway slave and subsequently sold the man after he was captured.[134] Jefferson thus embodied one of the most fundamental conflicts of the new republic. How was a country founded on the assertion of the rights of all people under natural law to freedom, equality, and a government whose legitimacy derived from their consent to reconcile these principles with its policies of Indian extermination and African chattel slavery?

American leaders and political theorists would take a wide range of often conflicting positions on this question, but essentially it was resolved by limiting the understanding of "people," at least those deserving of full rights and recognition, to those who embodied the "highest" form of human progress. As the history summarized above illustrates, American Indians and people of African descent clearly did not fit this description. In 1857, when the Supreme Court considered whether Dred Scott was a citizen for purposes of federal jurisdiction, Justice Taney wrote:

> The question is simply this: Can a negro whose ancestors were imported into this country, and sold as slaves, become a member of the political community formed and brought into existence by the Constitution of the United States, and as such become entitled to all the rights, and privileges, and immunities, guarantied by the instrument to the citizen?[135]

Taney's answer was, of course, a resounding no; for the Court, even "free negroes" were not part of "this people" as contemplated by the Constitution.[136] Even after birthright citizenship was incorporated into the Constitution by virtue of the Fourteenth Amendment,[137] the U.S. found legalized apartheid to be constitutional and did not consider American Indians to be eligible for citizenship.[138] The founders' vision of American identity is perhaps best summarized by John Jay, the first Chief Justice of the Supreme Court, who wrote in 1787 that "Providence has been pleased to give this one connected country, to one united people—a people descended from the same ancestors, speaking the same language, professing the same religion, attached to the same principles of government, very similar in their manners and customs."[139]

As would become clear in the law governing naturalized citizenship enacted by the First Congress in 1790[140] and in later immigration legislation, only "white" persons, preferably of British or northwestern European descent, were eligible to become Americans.[141] This is illustrated by the Supreme Court's opinion in a 1923 case in which an immigrant from India argued that he was "Caucasian" and therefore should be eligible for naturalization. The Court, retreating from earlier cases in which it had equated "white" with "Caucasian," concluded:

> The words of familiar speech, which were used by the original framers of the law, were intended to include only the type of man whom they knew as white. The immigration of the day was almost exclusively from the British Isles and Northwestern Europe, whence they and their forebears had come. When they extended the privilege of American citizenship to "any alien being a free white person" it was these immigrants—bone of their

bone and flesh of their flesh—and their kind whom they must have had affirmatively in mind.[142]

Eventually the legal framing of human freedom and equality would shift dramatically, but for the United States, in most of its first century and in some respects even into the present day, the construction of the Other was, and continues to be, deeply embedded in the presumptions of Euroderivative civilization outlined in chapter 1. The most important of these are that humans are, by definition, separate and distinct from nature; that human history is most accurately understood as a linear progression toward higher forms of civilization; and that the West represents the pinnacle of human development to date. These precepts, considered so obvious as to be "common sense" in the American worldview, have allowed the United States to maintain its claim to be upholding "universal" human values while relegating the Other to a lesser legal, political, and social status. Sometimes this has been accomplished by deeming those subjected to colonialism as subhuman, so "uncivilized" as to be more akin to nature than humanity. In other instances, the Other is simply at a lower stage of human development, perhaps theoretically entitled to certain rights under natural law but incapable of fully exercising them without becoming more "civilized." In both cases the focus is on difference and on the "ranking" that can be assigned to individuals and peoples, as a result of that difference, on the universal scale of Western development or, as often put, "human progress."[143]

Across this spectrum the representatives of civilization are fulfilling their moral and legal responsibilities either by eliminating those deemed "savage" for the greater good of humanity, or by uplifting those who are characterized as having the potential to become civilized. In the latter case, the exercise of sovereignty over Others, regardless of their consent, is more than justified. Or, to quote Fitzpatrick again, "the progressive and evolutionary assumptions of imperial rule placed the colonist in a position which enveloped all lesser conditions of existence. From this exalted position, therefore, the colonist could know and speak for the natives better than they could themselves—and thence decide to act with an appropriate force."[144] Just as the Puritans believed that they were creating a society that would serve as an example to the infidels, limiting the privileges of democratic self-governance to those considered "real" Americans was not viewed as discriminatory but rather as providing a model to which the less civilized could aspire. As discussed in the following chapters, this perspective characterized U.S. expansion across the continent and overseas, and still influences its implementation of international law today.

Establishing the Republic | 105

A Manifest Destiny

Colonizing the Continent

Away, away with all these cobweb tissues of rights of discovery, exploration, settlement, contiguity, etc. . . . [The American claim] is by the right of our manifest destiny to overspread and to possess the whole of the continent which Providence has given us for the development of the great experiment of liberty and federative self government entrusted to us.
— John L. O'Sullivan, *New York Morning News,*
December 27, 1845

The phrase "manifest destiny," coined in 1845 by American lawyer, author, and adventurer John O'Sullivan, quickly assumed widespread popularity in mainstream discourse, for it evoked the earliest English settlers' vision of a "new Canaan" and captured the essence of the United States' claim to the legitimacy not only of its independent existence but its constant expansion.[1] The expropriation of native land and the concomitant decimation of Indigenous peoples within the claimed territory of the United States, discussed in chapters 3 and 4, provided the material base for the extension of U.S. hegemony over other peoples, and the rationale used to accomplish this consolidation "at home" has been extended subsequently to justify the global reach of U.S. power. More recently, the legacy of this peculiarly American vision of "manifest destiny" was reflected in George W. Bush's 2002 statement that the war on terror "is our calling. This is our nation's time to lead the world, and we're going to do that."[2]

Early visions of American expansion were not limited to the territories contiguous to the original colonies. In 1783 Washington described the United States as a "rising empire," and in 1786 Thomas Jefferson wrote that "our confederacy must be viewed as the next from which all America, North and South, is to be peopled."[3] Between 1803 and 1853, as a result of the Louisiana

Purchase, the acquisition of Florida, the annexation of about half of Mexico, and the occupation of the Oregon territory, the United States extended its territorial claims to encompass all of what is now known as its "lower forty-eight" states. In 1867 it also claimed possession of Alaska by virtue of its "purchase" from Russia.[4] There was, of course, continued resistance from Indigenous peoples in these territories, but in 1890, following the Wounded Knee Massacre, the United States declared the "internal frontier" to be closed.[5]

This chapter provides a brief overview of this century of continental expansion, which involved numerous acquisitions of territory from both Indigenous nations and from countries acknowledged to be fully independent sovereign states. Although force was generally used, in each case the United States was anxious to justify its expansion as a lawful, or at least legitimate, exercise of power under international law. It was unwilling, however, to limit itself to the bounds of that law, and therefore throughout the process we see numerous examples of the sort of American exceptionalism that is the focus of this book. Quite consistently, where the law obstructed U.S. purposes, the United States exempted itself from its application by claiming, as European colonial powers had for centuries, that the rules of "civilized" warfare did not apply to uncivilized peoples or by invoking the "higher good" of bringing civilization to new lands and peoples.

In turn, this required the constant reinforcement of the racialized differentiation of the Others being encountered and the presumption, embodied in the Constitution and the earliest U.S. laws, that to be American was to be "white." As Thomas Jefferson wrote to James Monroe in 1801 in the course of advocating the resettlement of freed blacks to a location beyond the hemisphere:

> However our present interests may restrain us within our own limits, it is impossible not to look forward to distant times when our rapid multiplication will expand itself beyond those limits, and cover the whole northern, if not the southern continent, with a people speaking the same language, governed in similar forms, and by similar laws; nor can we contemplate with satisfaction either blot or mixture on that surface.[6]

This chapter focuses on the interplay between the presumption of the superiority of a universalizing Western civilization, and its manifestation in a peculiarly American "destiny" to extend this civilization across the continent, and the United States' claim to be extending the rule of law as part of its civilization in that process.

The Occupation of Native North America

The notion that the United States embodied freedom and democracy in their highest known forms not only legitimated the colonies' break from British rule but, more generally, reinforced the belief that America was at the forefront of the movement of Anglo-Saxon civilization across the planet. Whereas the Indigenous nations encountered by European settlers were initially acknowledged, at least in principle, to be fully sovereign, American Indians, like those of African descent, were assumed to be inferior to Euroamericans. As such, the question was presented as a choice of whether they were capable of being redeemed by Anglo-Saxon institutions or incapable of civilization and therefore destined for extinction; in fact, however, both assertions may have been simultaneously necessary to rationalize the colonial enterprise while maintaining an Other against whom the "civilized" could define themselves and measure their "progress."[7] Both these perspectives were reflected in U.S. attitudes and actions, often leading to pronouncements and policies that appear contradictory but are bound together into a coherent whole by the underlying presumption of white supremacy and the certitude that all things native must yield to the relentless march of Euroamerican progress.

A "Disappearing Race"?

One of the most frequently articulated assertions underpinning the notion of American manifest destiny—one that is still at least implicitly relied upon to justify the fact that American Indians even nominally retain only 2.5 percent of their original land base—is that native cultures and peoples simply "disappeared" in the face of contact with a superior civilization. As noted earlier, by 1900 the U.S. Census Bureau reported fewer than 250,000 native people living in the United States, a population decline that, perhaps not coincidentally, matched the decline in their ownership of land.[8] The process by which Indigenous peoples "disappeared" and American settlers occupied their lands is thus the first question that must be addressed in examining the nature of this "destiny."

Much of the decimation of native peoples was caused by the introduction of contagious diseases, sometimes inadvertently but, as discussed in chapters 2 and 3, often deliberately. This was compounded by policies encouraging the massacres of Indian communities, sometimes in the name of warfare and sometimes as a matter of private enterprise.[9] For many settlers the means mattered little, as long as the result was accomplished, as illustrated by an 1853 California newspaper report which stated, as a simple fact, that the incoming white settlers were "ready to knife [the Indians], shoot them, or innoculate them with smallpox—all of which have been done."[10] As this news report indicates, the native peoples were not simply "disappearing."

Reliance upon "conquest" is problematic as well, for there were few if any documented instances in which American Indians engaged in unprovoked attacks that would have allowed for a "just war" within the European legal paradigm.[11] However, even if, for purposes of argument, one accepts that the United States' "Indian wars" conveyed legitimate title by conquest, one must still confront the fact that, according to the U.S. Census Bureau, about forty such wars had been fought as of 1890; a number that clearly cannot justify the occupation of the territory of approximately four hundred Indigenous nations.[12] It is true, nonetheless, that armed force was essential to quell native resistance to Euroamerican colonization.

The military actions engaged in by the early colonists and later the United States government are far too numerous even to list here, so a few representative examples must suffice. We can begin with the orders given by George Washington in 1779 to Major General John Sullivan to engage in a "preemptory" strike against the Senecas and other members of the Haudenosaunee (Six Nations Iroquois Confederacy), orders that forbade Sullivan to "listen to any overture of peace before the total ruin of their settlements is effected."[13] Before returning home with the scalps and tanned skins of the Indians they encountered,[14] Sullivan's troops destroyed hundreds of homes as well as extensive acreage of corn and beans, "with axe and torch soon transform[ing] the whole of that beautiful region from the character of a garden to a scene of drear and sickening desolation."[15]

Having suffered similar incursions in 1780 and 1794,[16] the Shawnees of the Ohio River Valley were defeated and subsequently mutilated by U.S. troops under the command of the future president William Henry Harrison.[17] The Muscogee Red Sticks met a comparable fate at Horseshoe Bend in Alabama, where in 1814 General Andrew Jackson, another future president, "supervised the mutilation of 800 or more Indian corpses—cutting of their noses to count and preserve a record of the dead, slicing long strips of flesh from their bodies to tan and turn into bridle reins."[18] In 1833 General, and future president, Zachary Taylor led a similar massacre of three hundred Sacs and Foxes on the Bad Axe River in what is now known as Wisconsin; serving under his command at the time was Abraham Lincoln.[19]

That so many prominent political leaders engaged in these barbaric actions is evidence of an apparent consensus among the settler population that such measures were not only legally permissible but were to be commended when employed to eliminate those deemed "uncivilized." This attitude persisted well into the nineteenth century. In 1851 U.S. commissioners met with California Indians and obtained cession of much of the state under treaty terms that would have left the Indians about 8.5 million acres in reservations. However, because the white Californians resisted even that accommodation, the Senate refused to ratify the treaties and left the Indians at the mercy of the settlers. Eventually, in the 1850s, smaller reservations were worked out, but meanwhile the prophecy uttered by California Governor Peter H. Burnett in his annual message of 1851 rapidly became reality: "That a war of extermination will continue to be waged between the two races until the Indian race becomes extinct, must be expected; while we cannot anticipate this result with but painful regret, the inevitable destiny of the race is beyond the power and wisdom of man to avert."[20]

Again, we see the pattern underlying so many instances of American exceptionalism. When the lawful means of obtaining land by treaty proved inconvenient, or less than adequate to meet the desired ends of the settler colonial population, warfare was resorted to and justified by the nature of the "enemy." The California governor's claim of "destinies" defined by racial difference is an invocation of the opposition between savagery and civilization and, with it, the implication that wars of extermination were inevitable and hence justifiable. As Antony Anghie points out, some version of this argument has consistently undergirded the Euroderivative international law developed to accommodate colonial and imperial expansion. Vitoria, he points out, emphasized that "extension of empire is not a just cause of war"[21] but went on to argue that the Spanish had a right to enter Indian territory and, once there, could justify "the complete conquest of the Indians and their territory, as it was only in this way that the Spanish could ensure their own safety."[22] Immanuel Kant, despite his critiques of European colonialism, similarly argued that although people living in "a legal civil state" could not take "hostile action" against others unless they had already been injured by them, one who exists "in a mere state of nature . . . may not have injured me actively (*facto*) but he does injure me by the very lawlessness of his state (*statu injusto*), for he is a permanent threat to me."[23]

Thus, by attributing "lawlessness" to American Indians, the settler society could "lawfully" employ any means it desired to remove or eliminate them. This prerogative was not limited to the government, but extended to government-sanctioned "individual affairs" as well—the killing of American

Indians by individual white settlers. Small groups and even entire villages were regularly decimated by local raiding parties, a practice that was primarily responsible for the decline of the Indigenous populations of California and Oregon from about 250,000 in 1800 to less than 20,000 by 1870.[24] This process was encouraged by the lucrative scalp bounties offered by local governments and, later, by private business associations. Typical of such bounties, which at one time or another were offered in every state or territory of the Union, was that of Texas, which "placed a bounty upon the scalp of any Indian brought in to a government office—man, woman, or child, no matter what 'tribe'—no questions asked."[25]

According to demographer Russell Thornton, American Indian deaths resulting this kind of "direct violence" may have reached a half-million by 1890, when the frontier was officially declared closed.[26] That year Frank L. Baum, author of the much beloved *Wizard of Oz*, would celebrate the Wounded Knee Massacre with these words:

> The nobility of the Redskin is extinguished. . . . The Whites, by law of conquest, by justice of civilization, are masters of the American continent, and the best safety of the frontier settlements will be secured by the total annihilation of the few remaining Indians. Why not annihilation? Their glory has fled, their spirit broken, their manhood effaced; better that they should die than live the miserable wretches that they are.[27]

Thus even a brief summary of the encounters of white settlers with the native peoples of this continent illustrates that American Indians did not "fade away" in the face of a superior civilization but were systematically driven off their land, hunted down, imprisoned, and often systematically murdered. Nonetheless the outright slaughter of all American Indians was neither militarily feasible nor easily reconcilable with American visions of occupying the entire continent for the stated purpose of extending the benefits of Western civilization to those peoples. As a result, much of the occupation of native North America was accomplished by the perhaps equally destructive but more palatable means of forced displacement and mass internment.

Removals and Internments

After passage of the Indian Removal Act in 1830[28]—a time, it should be noted, when there were no hostilities occurring with the nations being displaced—the military was used to forcibly relocate virtually all American Indians who remained in the eastern third of what was to become the continental United States. This policy primarily affected the "Five Civilized Tribes"—the Cherokee, Creek, Chickasaw, Choctaw, and Seminole nations—who were rounded up and held in concentration camps and then force-marched across the country, often in mid-winter, with inadequate food, shelter, or medical attention and with attendant death rates of up to 50 percent.[29] In 1829 Andrew Jackson had assured the Creeks, "Your father has provided a country large enough for all of you, and he advises you to remove to it. There your white brothers will not trouble you; they will have no claim to the land, and you can live upon it, you and all your children, as long as the grass grows or the water runs, in peace and plenty. It will be yours forever."[30] However, once in the west, the Creeks and all the other eastern nations were to discover each of Jackson's promises to be false.

Eventually, pursuant to the Indian Intercourse Act of 1834, the peoples of sixty-seven separate nations, only six of whom were actually indigenous to that land, were forced into an "Indian Territory" encompassing what is now Oklahoma.[31] With the establishment of the Missouri, Arkansas, and Iowa territories and the annexation of Texas in 1845, the Oregon territory in 1846, and the northern half of Mexico (including present-day Arizona, New Mexico, Nevada, and California) in 1848, white settlers moved in from all sides. As a result, instead of having lands on which they could live in peace, American Indians—both those who had been relocated and those native to the western territories—were increasingly subjected to harsh internments as well as campaigns of extermination. As was the case with the Trail of Tears, removals and internments were generally supervised by the military, and Indians were treated as prisoners of war regardless of the fact that, for the most part, they were not at war against the United States and most of those interned were noncombatant women, children, and elders.

Thus, for example, in the aftermath of the 1862 "Little Crow's War" in Minnesota, virtually the entire Santee Sioux population was interned at Fort Snelling for several months under conditions that left about one-quarter of them dead. As a deterrent to escape, a scalp bounty of $200 was proclaimed on all Santees found outside the concentration camp. Relocated to an even harsher facility at Crow Creek in the Dakota Territory, a comparable proportion died during the first year.[32] Similarly, beginning in 1863, the Navajo (Diné) people were forced on a three-hundred-mile "Long Walk" from their homelands in Arizona to the Bosque Redondo, near Fort Sumner, New Mexico, where, without adequate food or shelter, about half of them died during their four-year internment as "prisoners of war."[33]

Attempts to follow government orders did not protect the Indians from wholesale slaughter. In 1864 about seven hundred Cheyennes, mostly women, children, and elders, were assembled on the banks of the Sand Creek, Colorado, on the order of the territorial governor where, disarmed and dismounted, their safety had been "guaranteed" by the U.S. Army. Their leader, Black Kettle, a member of the Cheyenne "peace faction," prominently displayed both an American flag given to him by Abraham Lincoln and a white flag of surrender. Nonetheless, these Cheyennes were brutally attacked by a regiment of U.S. volunteer cavalry, led by Colonel John M. Chivington, a Methodist minister, who directed his troops to "kill and scalp all, big and little."[34] As one veteran scout reported, the soldiers "used their knives, ripped open women, clubbed little children, knocked them in the head with their guns, beat their brains out, mutilated their bodies in every sense of the word. . . . [C]hildren two or three months old; all lying there; from sucking infants up to [the elderly]."[35]

The brutality of these campaigns was not hidden from the public but celebrated. Thus, for example, upon their return Chivington's troops proudly paraded through downtown Denver, "displaying bloody body parts of their victims to more than a thousand wildly cheering people."[36] By 1877 the remaining Cheyennes had been interned in Oklahoma, where they were issued only three pounds of food per day and were soon wracked with malaria, dysentery, and other illnesses. When a small group composed primarily of women and children desperately attempted to escape, fifteen thousand troops were sent in pursuit. Most of these Cheyennes, even children as young as three, were ultimately massacred, and many of the dead were scalped or otherwise mutilated.[37]

At about the same time the Apaches were concentrated and held as prisoners of war at the San Carlos Reservation in present day Arizona, a malaria-infested area without grass or game.[38] When Geronimo attempted to escape with his band of Chiricahuas, full military force was employed to hunt him down, and, after his surrender in 1886, the government retaliated by sending the entire Chiricahua population—including elders, women, children and even those men who had fought *for* the United States—to military prisons in the east, where they were all held as "prisoners of war" for twenty-seven years.[39] By that time the Chiricahua population had dropped from approximately three thousand to five hundred within one generation, and would be reduced by another 40 percent during their first eight years of imprisonment.[40]

Not until 1879 did the presumption begin to be questioned that Indians could be treated as prisoners of war simply because they were Indians.

That year, a group of Poncas led by Standing Bear left the Indian territory in Oklahoma, to which they had been forcibly relocated, and returned to their traditional lands because, as Standing Bear testified, in Oklahoma 158 of the 581 Poncas had died within the first year and most of the others were ill or disabled.[41] The U.S. government sent troops under the command of General Crook to capture, imprison, and return the Poncas to Oklahoma, despite the fact that they had been welcomed and given land on which to live with their relatives on the Omaha reservation. Standing Bear petitioned the Nebraska circuit court for a writ of habeas corpus and obtained a ruling, apparently the first of its kind, that Indians were "persons" capable of suing for habeas corpus.[42] The circuit court judge then found that General Crook had the statutory authority to remove the Poncas from the Omaha reservation, but that "without some specific authority found in an act of congress, or in a treaty with the [Poncas], he could not lawfully force the relators back to the Indian territory, to remain and die in that country, against their will."[43] This, the judge reasoned, was a power that might be used against enemy aliens in times of war, but the Poncas were not at war and they had to be treated in accordance with civil law.[44]

The Supreme Court held in 1900 that an Indian on a reservation could not be arrested where there was no evidence that he had violated any law, rule, or regulation[45] and, citing to this precedent, it was held by the Arizona Supreme Court in 1909 that American Indians could not be classified and treated as "prisoners of war" simply because they were Indian. In this case, Ex parte *Bi-a-lil-le,* the court noted that the Secretary of War, at the request of the Secretary of the Interior, had sent two troops of cavalry into the Navajo reservation where they had "captured" eight Navajos who were subsequently "confined for an indefinite period at hard labor," to be released at the discretion of the War Department.[46] Countering the U.S. attorney's assertion that Bi-a-lil-le and his companions were prisoners of war, the court noted that no state of war existed, and that such imprisonment was "characteristic of the punishment of criminals, and not, under the code of modern civilized warfare, an incident of the detention of prisoners of war."[47] Again reflecting the federal government's position that any means were acceptable if used for the purpose of "civilizing" the Other, the Arizona court noted that the prisoners' confinement was being underwritten by the Interior Department "as an object lesson to the rest of their tribe" and because they had, according to the Secretary of the Interior, "defied the government and its authorities" and "impeded the progress of the other Indians in their efforts to improve and better their conditions."[48]

Although these cases recognized some tentative limits on clearly illegal exercises of governmental authority over American Indians, they only constrained federal power to that which might be authorized by Congress or a treaty. Thus the order preventing the army from returning Standing Bear's group to Oklahoma was limited by the court's emphasis on the fact that these individuals had purportedly severed their relationship with the "tribe."[49] Essentially the court held that to be free from such restraints Indians had to relinquish their ties to their cultures and families, "cut loose from the government, go to work, become self-sustaining, and adopt the habits and customs of a higher civilization."[50] As a result, it did nothing to prevent the government from forcing other Poncas, or members of other nations, to remain within whatever boundaries might be assigned them, subject to whatever regulations might be imposed upon them.

The Evisceration of Treaties

Even where the United States had entered into treaties clearly guaranteeing certain territorial and other rights to American Indian nations, treating Indians as military threats or criminals when they tried to enforce these rights was commonplace. Thus, for example, in what is often termed the last of the "Indian Wars," more than three hundred unarmed Minneconjou Lakotas were surrounded and slaughtered with Hotchkiss guns on the Wounded Knee Creek in South Dakota. Often overlooked is that their "offense" was an attempt to flee their assigned agency, where they were starving, and seek refuge with their Oglala relatives at the Pine Ridge Agency at Standing Rock, both agencies located within the boundaries of the "Great Sioux Reservation," all of which the U.S. officially acknowledged to be Lakota territory.[51] As the Wounded Knee Massacre indicates, compliance with treaties was increasingly regarded as "optional"—not only by the U.S. government but also by the Supreme Court.

The Court's move away from the recognition of the necessity—constitutional and otherwise—of respecting treaties can be seen clearly in the case of Race Horse, a member of the Bannock nation. Race Horse, arrested in 1895 by a Wyoming sheriff for hunting elk allegedly in violation of a state law, filed a petition for a writ of habeas corpus, arguing that his right to hunt on the land in question was guaranteed under the U.S. Constitution as a consequence of a treaty entered into between the United States and the Shoshone and Bannock nations in 1868. Under the terms of that treaty, the Indians agreed to "make said reservations their permanent home, and they will make no permanent settlement elsewhere; but they shall have the right to hunt on the unoccupied lands of the United States so long as game may be found thereon, and so long as peace subsists among the whites and Indians on the borders of the hunting districts."[52]

In a clear exposition of applicable constitutional and international law, the Wyoming District Court first noted that the terms of the treaty had been complied with; indeed, the judge took pains to point out that peace prevailed, and the location where the elk were killed was far from any settlement, in a region "30 miles wide by 36 miles long" within which "a very few settlers, not to exceed seven in number" had established ranches.[53] As a result he concluded that, under Article VI of the Constitution, the federal court had not only a right but a duty to issue the writ and to find that "the state law being in conflict with the provisions of the treaty, it cannot be enforced against these Indians."[54] In his analysis, the district judge relied extensively upon Chief Justice Marshall's opinion in *Worcester v. Georgia*, noting that "the language used in treaties with the Indians should never be construed to their prejudice," and finding in such cases "the treaty provisions are binding alike, both upon the government and the Indians, to the same extent that they would be in [the] case of a treaty made with one of the civilized nations."[55] To support this, the judge in the *Race Horse* case again quoted *Worcester*:

> The constitution, by declaring treaties . . . to be the supreme law of the land, has adopted and sanctioned the previous treaties with the Indian nations, and consequently admits their rank among those powers who are capable of making treaties. The words "treaty" and "nation" are words of our own language, selected in our diplomatic and legislative proceedings by ourselves, having each a definite and well-understood meaning. We have applied them to the Indians, as we have applied them to the other nations of the earth. They are applied to all in the same sense.[56]

The Supreme Court, however, chose to retreat from its own explication of international law and the Supremacy Clause of the Constitution, holding that for all practical purposes the Indians' treaty rights had evaporated when Congress passed a "superseding" law admitting Wyoming as a state.[57]

It is the Court's reasoning that is particularly interesting for our purposes, and worth quoting at some length. Justice Henry Brown, in his dissent, pointed out that the "treaty was entered into at the close of a war between the two contracting parties" and that, for the Indians, the right to hunt "was not one secured to them for sporting purposes" but a matter of subsistence and therefore "of supreme importance to them" in agreeing to the treaty,[58] Nonetheless Justice Edward White wrote for the majority:

> When, in 1868, the treaty was framed, the progress of white settlements westward had hardly . . . reached the confines of the places selected for Indian reservation. While this was true, the march of advancing civilization foreshadowed the fact that the wilderness . . . was destined to be occupied and settled by the white man, hence interfering with the hitherto untrammeled right of occupancy of the Indian. For this reason, to protect his rights, and to preserve for him a home where his tribal relations might be enjoyed under the shelter of the authority of the United States, the reservation was created. While confining him to the reservation, and in order to give him the privilege of hunting in the designated districts, so long as the necessities of civilization did not require otherwise, the provision in question was doubtless adopted, care being, however, taken to make the whole enjoyment in this regard dependent absolutely upon the will of congress.[59]

Contained within this statement is the fundamental premise of American exceptionalism that the primary purpose of international law—here, in the form of treaties—was to smooth the way for "the march of advancing civilization," and that when its specific provisions proved inconvenient to colonial expansion, they could be disregarded in favor of the "greater good" of that civilization. This "march" is presumed inevitable; law must conform to its demands.

Thus, as previously asserted by Justice Marshall in the *Cherokee Cases*, Indians did not actually own their lands but merely had a "right of occupancy" that the federal government was "protecting" for them by reserving certain lands from settler encroachment. There was no question in Justice White's mind of the legality of "confining" the Indians to these reservations; their rights to continue hunting for the purpose of survival was deemed a "privilege" granted by the federal government. This privilege would be recognized only so long as it did not interfere with the expansion of civilization, and this, according to Justice White, was the reason it was made "dependent absolutely on the will of congress." The "very object" of the treaty was to smooth the path for settler expansion, keeping the peace where possible. In other words, the treaty was not a mutual pact between nations, as had been so often articulated by the founders and recognized even by Justice Marshall in *Worcester*, but simply a unilateral act of the United States, designed to further its manifest destiny.[60]

Just five years later Justice Brown, who had dissented in *Race Horse*, would use this logic to make the counterfactual assertion in *Montoya v. United States*, that "the North American Indians do not, and never have, constituted 'nations' as that word is used by writers upon international law."[61] The term "nation," according to Brown, implies "independence of any other sovereign power . . . , an organized government, recognized officials, a system of laws, definite boundaries, and the power to enter into negotiations with other nations."[62] For Brown, the inability of American Indians, by 1901, to exercise such sovereign powers was not due to colonial occupation and expropriation but "to the natural infirmities of the Indian character, their fiery tempers, impatience of restraint, their mutual jealousies and animosities, their nomadic habits, and lack of mental training."[63] In making this assertion, Justice Brown not only presumed that all Indians had the same "character" as had been assigned to those deemed "savage" the world over, but he entirely disregarded the historical record as recognized by, among others, the drafters of the Constitution.[64]

Felix S. Cohen, the "unrivaled authority" of federal law pertaining to American Indians, would observe in 1939:

> The history of Indian constitutions goes back at least to the Gayaneshagowa (Great Binding Law) of the Iroquois Confederacy, which probably dates from the 15th Century. We have the wampum records and transcripts of the traditional recitations expounding the provisions of this constitution—the rule of unanimity, the federal structure of government, the provisions for initiative, referendum, and recall. . . . So too, we have the written constitutions of the Creek, Cherokee, Choctaw, Chickasaw, and Osage nations, printed usually on tribal printing presses, constitutions which were in force during the decades from 1830 to 1900. . . . The rules concerning council procedures, selection of officers, and official responsibilities, which have been followed by the Creek towns, or by the Rio Grande Pueblos, without substantial alteration across four centuries, certainly deserve to be called constitutions.[65]

Nonetheless, at the dawn of the twentieth century, the Supreme Court characterized all American Indian governments as "nothing more than a temporary submission to an intellectual or physical superior" with "no established laws, no recognized method of choosing their sovereigns by inheritance or election, no officers with defined powers."[66] In the *Montoya* opinion—which has been distinguished but never overruled—Justice Brown concludes, "in short, the word 'nation' as applied to the uncivilized Indians is so much of a misnomer as to be little more than a compliment."[67]

Forced Assimilation

Systematic decimation of Indigenous societies and the forced relocation and internment of their remaining members may have been the most effective means to fulfill the founders' visions of a country that stretched from coast to coast, but it also stood in direct contrast to their proclaimed principles of freedom, democracy, and equality, their stated commitment to the rule of law, and the explicit promises made, both verbally and in treaties, to the original inhabitants of the land. A central means by which Euroamerican society has attempted to avoid the fact that its expansion and consolidation have been achieved not only at the expense of the Indigenous population but in violation of its own legal strictures has been to construct a racialized identity of American Indians as uncivilized, and then use this depiction to develop a special body of law that applies to American Indians but not to the settler population.

As noted with respect to the earliest Puritan colonists, one of the most consistently used "exemptions" from otherwise applicable laws governing the acquisition of territory was to claim that the lands at issue were effectively "vacant," and therefore available for those who would put it to productive use.[68] This was essentially the reasoning employed by Supreme Court Chief Justice John Marshall in the 1810 case of *Fletcher v. Peck* to belatedly justify the redemption of vouchers for land issued to American troops in lieu of cash during the war of independence.[69] It was also the premise of the 1862 Homestead Act, under which any U.S. citizen could claim 160 acres of "undeveloped" land by paying a nominal patent fee and subsequently obtain title to the land if they "improved" it within a specified number of years.[70]

The theory that American Indians simply did not exist for purposes of occupying the land could only stretch so far, however. The most fundamental undermining of native legal rights came in the trilogy of the Supreme Court opinions authored by Chief Justice Marshall in the 1820s and 1830s. As noted in chapter 4, *Johnson v. McIntosh*, decided in 1823, was a title dispute between two settlers, one of whom claimed to have purchased the land in question directly from its Indigenous owners. In order to establish that individuals could only obtain land from the state, Marshall completely inverted the discovery doctrine, arguing that because the doctrine restricted the right of competing European powers to negotiate with the native inhabitants for purchase of the land, it also restricted those inhabitants from being able to sell it to anyone other than the "discovering" power. On that basis, Marshall concluded that Indigenous peoples did not have absolute (and therefore alienable) title, but only a "right of possession."[71] In the 1831 case of *Cherokee Nation v. Georgia*, Justice Marshall unilaterally assigned not only the Cherokees but all Indigenous nations the unique status of "domestic dependent nations" and "wards" of the U.S. government.[72] And the following year, in *Worcester v. Georgia*, Marshall gave the federal government the exclusive ability to exercise jurisdiction over Indian lands.[73] Legal scholars Vine Deloria Jr. and David Wilkins point out the long-term implications of these three cases:

> The original assumption is that the federal government is authorized and empowered to protect the Indians in the enjoyment of their lands. Once it is implied that this power also involves the ability of the federal government by itself to force a purchase of the lands, there is no way the implied power can be limited. If the government can force the disposal of lands, why can it not determine how the lands are to be used? And if it can determine how the lands are to be used, why can it not tell the Indians how to live? And if it can tell Indians how to live, why can it not tell them how to behave and what to believe?[74]

This was, in fact, what the U.S. government proceeded to do after native resistance to U.S. expansion had been all but crushed in the late 1800s. In 1871 Congress simply declared that American Indian "tribes" would no longer be recognized as capable of entering into treaties with the United States.[75] Recognizing its need to claim the benefits of existing treaties, it promised to honor them, and, in fact, over the next four decades it proceeded to enter into more than one hundred agreements that, in Deloria's words, "resembled treaties. Indeed, at the negotiating table Indians were told they *were* treaties, and federal district courts later acknowledged that these agreements stood on a par with treaties as legal documents. But the congressional attitude was that treaties could be violated at whim because Congress in its wisdom would act in the best interest of the Indians."[76]

The unilateral suspension of treaty making by Congress was followed by a series of laws designed to achieve "the quick and permanent assimilation of Indians into the American social fabric."[77] In 1883 the Supreme Court overturned the conviction of Crow Dog, accused of killing another Lakota, on the grounds that the applicable federal statute excluded from U.S. jurisdiction cases of crimes committed in "Indian country" by one Indian against another.[78] The Court explained that it could not, without explicit congressional authorization, allow Indians to be tried "not by their peers, nor by the customs of their people, nor the law of their land, but by superiors of a different race, according to the law of a social state of which they have an imperfect conception, and which is opposed to the traditions of their history, the habits of their lives, to the strongest prejudices of their savage nature; one which measures the red man's revenge by the maxims of the white man's morality."[79]

As this illustrates, it was clear to the justices that the Lakotas in question had their own legal system—which had, in fact, been applied in this case[80]— but it was presumed, without any factual analysis, to be inherently savage and therefore inferior. Not surprisingly, the newspapers of the time depicted this as a decision furthering "lawlessness" in Indian country, and, in response to the ensuing public outcry, in 1885 Congress passed the Major Crimes Act, giving federal courts jurisdiction over most serious criminal offenses committed on reservations.[81] This was upheld in *United States v. Kagama* where, relying on the logic of the Marshall cases, the Supreme Court announced that Indigenous nations were "semi-independent" with limited authority over their "internal and social relations."[82] Acknowledging that the Constitution did not delegate authority over American Indians to the federal government, the Court fell back on the notion that such power must be inherent, drawing on an earlier pronouncement by Marshall that "the right to govern may be the inevitable consequence of the right to acquire territory."[83] In reality, as Deloria notes, the result was increased lawlessness on reservations, as the assertion of settler colonial jurisdiction "undercut Indian reliance on their own institutions as a means of resolving disputes" and Indians "were discouraged from using known, traditional codes of conduct."[84]

Having thus turned U.S. military power over American Indians into purportedly civilian police powers, Congress soon passed the General Allotment Act of 1887.[85] Touted as a measure that would turn American Indians into citizen farmers owning and working individual plots, it was quite aptly described in 1901 by President Theodore Roosevelt as "a mighty pulverizing engine to break up the tribal mass."[86] The Allotment Act divided up collective landholdings, assigning individual sections of reservation lands to "qualified" Indians and allowing the "surplus" to be claimed by the government or sold to white settlers, a process that resulted in the loss of two-thirds of all Indian-held lands between 1887 and 1934.[87] Assigning land parcels required a determination of which individuals would receive them. Rather than respecting each nation's understanding of citizenship, the federal government gave a commission, headed by Senator Henry Dawes, the prerogative of creating "tribal rolls" for purposes of allotment.[88] In the process, a system of "blood quantum" rules was created that imposed a "race"-based federal definition of identity on the peoples involved and which, in many variations, continues to be used to "define" Indians to this day.[89]

The allotment policy occasioned yet another major development in the legal rationale for the exercise of colonial powers. In *Lone Wolf v. Hitchcock* a Kiowa band chief challenged the Allotment Act on the grounds that it violated both the 1867 Treaty of Medicine Lodge and the Fifth Amendment's guarantee of due process. In its 1903 ruling the Supreme Court upheld the Act by making the entirely counterfactual claim that "plenary authority over the tribal relations of the Indians has been exercised by Congress from the beginning, and the power has always been deemed a political one, not subject to be controlled by the judicial department of the government."[90] In other words, the Supreme Court abdicated its responsibility to uphold the Constitution and gave the government an absolute power completely unconstrained by either the Constitution or international law. Since then, this "plenary power" doctrine has became of cornerstone of what is known as "federal Indian law," and it continues to be used to allow the government unlimited and arbitrary power over American Indian affairs.[91]

By 1894 Indigenous spiritual practices had been outlawed, "a measure expressly intended to eradicate all vestiges of the traditions that afforded cohesion and continuity to native cultures."[92] Federal officials had begun forcibly removing American Indian children from their families, sending them to remote boarding schools whose express purpose was, as articulated by Captain Richard Henry Pratt, founder of the system, to "kill the Indian, save the man."[93] At these institutions, which resembled prisons more than schools, the children were stripped of all vestiges of their culture, forbidden to speak their language and taught that all things Indian were unworthy. From about 1890 to 1970, approximately half the native children in each generation were subjected to these "schools."[94] They were often taken at age four or five and not allowed to return home for ten years—should they survive so long, the children were subjected to harsh corporal punishment, sexual abuse, slave labor, and high rates of malnutrition and communicable disease, all in the name of making them "civilized" enough to participate in a white culture which, of course, had no intention of regarding them as equals, regardless of their education.[95] In many institutions up to half the children died; most of those who survived suffered—and continue to suffer—all the predictable effects of long-term traumatic abuse.[96]

Many other examples of the failures of the government's policies of forced assimilation could be given. In addressing the "problem" of the Indians who remained after their lands had been occupied, legal scholar Robert Odawi Porter observes that the architects of U.S. Indian policy, although not necessarily acting out of malice, were "limited greatly by their own cultural myopia, which prevented them from formulating other policy options, such as simply leaving the Indians alone."[97] Instead, Porter notes, they attempted to "civilize" Indigenous peoples through what he terms "a kind of Four Horsemen of the Indian Apocalypse"—the imposition of Christianity and Western education, the individualized allotment of commonly held land, and the unilateral imposition of U.S. citizenship upon them.[98]

The disastrous consequences of the "allotment era" policies were documented in what is often referred to as the 1928 Meriam Report, summarizing a study which concluded that American Indians, for the most part, were living in dire poverty, without access to decent health care or education, and suffering exceedingly high rates of mortality, often owing to preventable diseases.[99] In the decades since then, federal policies have fluctuated greatly but have always clung to the notion, first articulated by Justice Marshall, that American Indians could be characterized as "wards" of the U.S. government and expanded into a system of "permanent trusteeship" during the nineteenth century.[100] As Cohen concluded:

> [Wardship] soon became a magic word in the mouths and proclamations of [federal] Indian agents and Indian Commissioners. Over the years, any order or command or sale or lease for which no justification could be found in any treaty or act of Congress came to be justified by such officials as an act of "guardianship," and every denial of civil, political, or economic rights to Indians came to be blamed on their alleged "wardship." Under the reign of these magic words nothing Indian was safe. The Indian's hair was cut, his dances forbidden, his oil lands, his timber lands, and grazing lands were disposed of, by Indian agents and Indian Commissioners for whom the magic word "wardship" always made up for any lack of statutory authority.[101]

Meaningful exercise of American Indian sovereignty was apparently beyond the scope of what could be envisioned by U.S. officials who had accepted the parameters established by the universalizing presumptions of Western civilization.[102]

The Taking of Spanish Florida: A Black and Indian War

The means used to consolidate the territorial base of the United States—as well as the rhetoric of manifest destiny employed to justify its "growth"—became the blueprint for U.S. expansion into lands, both contiguous and far-flung. They were employed not only against American Indians, unilaterally defined by the 1830s as "domestic dependent" nations, but also against powers recognized by the United States as fully sovereign. The taking of Florida, where the U.S. extended its "Indian Wars" to territory already under the jurisdiction of another colonizing power, Spain, is an instructive example.

As early as 1803 Thomas Jefferson had drafted a constitutional amendment in connection with the Louisiana Purchase,[103] which would apply to Florida "whenever it may be rightfully obtained."[104] In 1811 Congress agreed in secret session to the taking of Florida. With President James Madison's approval—which he denied when Spain protested—and in violation of a treaty of friendship with Spain, troops from Georgia attempted to invade Florida in 1811, 1812, and 1813.[105] When these efforts failed, white settlers and adventurers simply occupied land in northern Florida and declared themselves to be a "republic" which they hoped the United States would recognize and defend.[106] Their uprisings, too, were defeated and their project disavowed by the U.S. government but, as discussed in chapter 6, this strategy would later prove successful in Texas and Hawai'i.

Americans, particularly southerners, had long been bothered by the fact that since 1693 the Spanish in Florida had protected persons of African descent, providing a refuge for runaway slaves from Georgia and the Carolinas.[107] The Seminole nation, which had been formed in the mid-1700s by native peoples and by escaped African slaves and their descendants,[108] vigorously defended against U.S. incursions. The most spectacular of many U.S. raids against them was an unprovoked attack ordered by Andrew Jackson in 1816 on a fort on the Apalachicola River occupied by the Seminoles. American troops and gunships attacked and burned the fort, killing 270 and wounding virtually all the remaining 334 Seminoles, mostly women and children, who were inside. Two warriors, designated by the Americans as "chiefs," were gruesomely tortured and killed, and the survivors were sold into slavery.[109] When the Spanish governor of Florida protested, the commander of the U.S. gunboats responded that the "property" taken—namely, slaves—belonged not to Spain but to the Seminoles, from whom "it" had been taken by "conquest."[110] Writing in 1858, Ohio Congressman Joshua Giddings noted that "perhaps no portion of our national history exhibits such disregard of international law, as this unprovoked invasion of Florida," going on to ask what law or constitutional power allowed officers of the United States to "dictate to the crown of Spain in what part of his territory he should, or should not, erect fortresses" or to "invade the territory of a nation at peace with the United States, destroy a fort, and consign its occupants to slavery."[111]

Shortly after Jackson's incursion, the Seminoles launched a retaliatory attack on a U.S. vessel, an incident that was used—without mention of the burning of the fort—to convince Congress to allocate funds for what became the First Seminole War. Thus began a series of three protracted wars, fought until 1858 in the United States' effort, first, to acquire Florida and, then, to remove the Seminoles to western territories.[112] In the meantime, while Secretary of State John Quincy Adams was negotiating to acquire Florida from Spain, Andrew Jackson simply invaded, crushing the black and Indian resistance he encountered. Although the president and all the other members of the Cabinet believed that Jackson had engaged in an unauthorized and illegal act of war, Adams strenuously argued that Jackson's actions were a necessary response to the misconduct of Spanish officials in Florida and justifiable as "*defensive* acts of hostility." Invoking a long-standing justification for abandoning the rules of war when force is used against "uncivilized" peoples, he also argued that it was acceptable under international law to commit genocidal acts against "a ferocious nation which observes no rules."[113]

By this time the Spanish treasury had been drained by the Napoleonic Wars and, unable to effectively counter rising U.S. military power, Spain agreed to cede its claims to Florida for five million dollars.[114] This was, on its face, a blatant example of the United States' use of raw military power to overwhelm another colonial power and take one of its "possessions" in violation of international law. Although Spain itself could not be cast as "uncivilized" to justify this action, its inability—or failure, according to the United States—to control the "savagery" of the Indigenous peoples and their allies of African descent under its rule was proffered as justification for the United States' appropriation of this territory. Having consolidated U.S. control of the eastern seaboard, American leaders now turned their attention to northern Mexico.

Annexing Northern Mexico

Americans had long had their eyes on Mexico, among other places in the hemisphere.[115] As early as 1767 Benjamin Franklin expressed the belief that both Mexico and Cuba would one day be part of the—as yet unformed—United States, and Thomas Jefferson had claimed, unsuccessfully, that the southern border of the 1803 Louisiana Purchase was the Rio Grande.[116] Through what became known as the Monroe Doctrine, the United States announced, in 1823, that the Americas were no longer open to colonization by Europe, but it did not similarly constrain itself.[117] Under the terms of the 1819 Transcontinental Treaty, Spain ceded Florida to the United States, which in turn renounced its claim to Mexico and, shortly thereafter, in 1822, Mexico won its independence from Spain. However, this did not stop U.S. citizens from moving into Texas, where, by 1830, about twenty thousand American settlers and two thousand of their slaves lived.[118]

The Angloamerican colonists were reluctant to comply with Mexican laws, especially after Mexico abolished slavery in 1829,[119] and they began militating for Texas to be recognized as an independent republic. Emulating an earlier and equally unsuccessful uprising by James Long,[120] Hayden Edwards seized the town of Nacogdoches in 1826 and announced the creation of the Republic of Fredonia. When the Mexican government suppressed the revolt, U.S. newspapers described the insurgents as "apostles of democracy crushed by an alien civilization."[121] Worried by these developments and having just rejected an offer from President John Quincy Adams to buy Texas for $1 million, the Mexican government sent a boundary commission led by Manuel Mier y Terán to Texas to study the situation.

The report of Mexico's Terán Commission is worth quoting at length, for it outlines a strategy for colonial expansion that has been repeated frequently in U.S. history:

> They commence by introducing themselves into the territory which they covet, upon pretence of commercial negotiations, or of the establishment of colonies, with or without the assent of the Government to which it belongs. These colonies grow, multiply, become the predominant party in the population. . . . These pioneers, excite, by degrees, movements which disturb the political state of the country. . . . When things have come to this pass . . . the diplomatic management commences: the inquietude they have excited . . . the interests of the colonists . . . the insurrections of adventurers, and savages instigated by them, and the pertinacity with which the opinion is set up as to their right of possession, become the subjects of [diplomatic] notes, full of expressions of justice and moderation, until, with the aid of other incidents, which are never wanting in the course of diplomatic relations, the desired end is attained. . . . Sometimes more direct means are resorted to; and taking advantage of the enfeebled state . . . of the possessor of the soil, they proceed, upon the most extraordinary pretexts, to make

themselves masters of the country, as was the case in the Floridas; leaving the question to be decided afterwards as to the legality of the possession, which force alone could take from them.[122]

In response to this report Mexico banned further immigration to Texas in 1830, but this, too, failed to stem the tide of U.S. settlers who were now "illegal aliens."[123]

The following year Sam Houston, protégé of Andrew Jackson, led a "war party" that rioted over customs duties at Anáhuac, and in 1832 he launched an unsuccessful attack on a Mexican military garrison.[124] By the time of Stephen Austin's September 1835 call for yet another armed uprising, "the Texans saw themselves in danger of becoming the alien subjects of a people to whom they believed themselves morally, intellectually, and politically superior."[125] Although initially routed at the Alamo and Goliad, in April 1826 Houston captured Mexican General Antonio López de Santa Anna, forcing him to sign an agreement relinquishing the territory. The Mexican government repudiated the treaty and protested the United States' role in providing troops and arms to the Texans, but Andrew Jackson made it clear that, regardless of Mexican approval, the U.S. would support the Republic of Texas and its newly elected president Sam Houston.[126]

Texas was, of course, only part of a larger plan, for by the 1840s Americans were actively debating the acquisition of both Oregon and the rest of Mexico. John O'Sullivan was addressing the Oregon question in his 1845 editorial which popularized the term "manifest destiny," but earlier that year he had used it to criticize other countries, particularly Mexico, for interfering in U.S. affairs with "the avowed object of thwarting our policy and hampering our power, limiting our greatness and checking the fulfillment of our manifest destiny to overspread the continent allotted by Providence for the free development of our yearly multiplying millions."[127]

Because this understanding of manifest destiny was inextricably intertwined with notions of racial superiority, American approaches to Mexico and Oregon were quite different. Reginald Horsman observes that "in discussing Texas and Mexican rule Congressmen drew few distinctions between Mexicans and their government. It was argued that the instability and ineffectiveness of the Mexican government stemmed from the inadequacies of an inferior population."[128] By contrast, the "English were respected as fellow Anglo-Saxons who were not to be swept out of Oregon as an inferior breed; and those who opposed war with England frequently discussed the disastrous effects of a clash between the two great branches of the Anglo-Saxon race.[129] The Americans, Horsman continues, "thought as little of clashing with the Mexicans as they did of clashing with the Indians."[130]

The election of James K. Polk was widely interpreted as a mandate for continuing national expansion, and in December 1845, shortly before his inauguration, Texas was incorporated into the Union. In response, the Mexican government broke off diplomatic relations with the U.S., and Polk ordered General Zachary Taylor to Texas to "protect the border." The troops were sent, however, into the 150-mile-wide strip between the Río Grande and Nueces rivers, which the U.S. claimed was part of Texas but had historically been understood as part of Mexico proper. With U.S. military force thus in place, Polk sent John Sidell to negotiate for the disputed area; the Mexican government refused to recognize Sidell, and Polk began drafting his declaration of war. In the meantime, Mexican troops fired on U.S. troops within the contested zone, and Polk, declaring that Mexico had "invaded American territory and shed American blood upon the American soil," went to war.[131] According to Horsman, "The sentiment that the United States' flag would be the flag of the world when tyranny had perished was a common one, and many united in conceiving of the invasion as a war of liberation. . . . A New York poet in May 1846 conjured up an image of Mexicans joyously shouting 'The Saxons are coming, our freedom is nigh.'"[132]

Although often portrayed as an easy victory for the Americans with their vastly superior military power, it was, in fact, a brutal war in which Mexican forces fiercely contested their "liberation" and thousands of civilians were killed. Huge areas of several cities, including Matamoros, Vera Cruz, and Mexico City, were leveled by indiscriminate shelling; prisoners of war were executed, houses and fields burned, civilians terrorized.[133] One American described to his parents an action taken to "avenge the death" of an officer slain in battle: "Grog shops were broken open first, and then, maddened with liquor, every species of outrage was committed. Old women and girls were stripped of their clothing—and many suffered still greater outrages. Men were shot by dozens . . . their property, churches, stores and dwelling houses ransacked."[134] While many Americans in positions of responsibility recognized that this was an unlawful invasion, few did anything about it.[135]

Colonel Ethan Allen Hitchcock said of the bombing of Vera Cruz, "I shall never forget the horrible fire of our mortars . . . going with dreadful certainty and bursting with sepulchral tones often in the centre of private dwellings—it was awful." Nonetheless he proceeded to draft a widely disseminated statement, issued by General Winfield Scott, assuring the Mexican people that "we have not a particle of ill-will towards you—we treat you with all civility—we are not in fact your enemies; we do not plunder your people or insult your women or your religion."[136] Ulysses S. Grant later wrote that he believed Polk had provoked the war and that the annexation of Texas had been an act of aggression, adding, "I had a horror of the Mexican War . . . only I had not moral courage enough to resign."[137] And Abraham Lincoln, elected to Congress in 1846, believed the war was "unnecessarily and unconstitutionally commenced by the President" but nonetheless voted to continue its funding.[138]

Again, the recognition that U.S. actions were in violation of both the Constitution and international law was overridden by the notion so deeply ingrained in the construction of American identity that its "mandate" to extend its civilization allowed self-exemption from the rule of law. As put crudely by an 1846 Cincinnati newspaper editorial, "Though the barbarians fall thick as hail, still, as their disposition is warlike and as the slaughter of their armies by the superiority of scientific warfare and the unflinching bravery of men disposed to peace, would teach them helpful lessons, the loss of a few thousand of them would not be so deplorable. The Mexicans will be led by this war to think of their weakness and inferiority."[139]

As American victory became imminent, the debate within the United States turned to whether all or only part of Mexico should be annexed. Most Americans wanted just the sparsely populated northern provinces; others wanted it all but were reluctant to incorporate so many people of color presumed incapable of measuring up to the standards of Anglo-Saxon civilization. Florida Senator James D. Westcott shuddered at the thought of being "compelled to receive not merely the white citizens of California and New Mexico, but the peons, negroes, and Indians . . . and other half-monkey savages . . . as *equal citizens of the United States.*"[140] Reflecting this view, the *Richmond Whig* said, "We have far more to dread from the acquisition of the debased population . . . than to hope from the extension of our territorial limits,"[141] and the *Cincinnati Herald* asked what America would do with eight million Mexicans "with their idol worship, heathen superstition, and degraded mongrel races."[142] Those who argued for the annexation of large portions of Mexico largely based their arguments, in Horsman's words, "on the twin assumptions that the largely Indian Mexicans would fade away, and that the American Anglo-Saxons were destined to outbreed the whole world."[143]

The debate was put to rest by the 1848 Treaty of Guadalupe Hidalgo, under which Mexico ceded "only" the northern third of its territory.[144] The United States government paid Mexico $15 million indemnity, allowing the *Whig Intelligencer* to make the self-righteous assertion that "we take nothing by conquest. . . . Thank God."[145] Under the treaty, the approximately one hundred thousand Mexicans in the conquered territories had the right to remain and were given their choice of Mexican or U.S. citizenship; those who did not specify their preference within a year would be deemed U.S. citizens. This was a citizenship limited, however, by race, for they were not guaranteed the rights of *white* citizens,[146] nor given state citizenship, "the source of political representation and potential voting rights."[147] The lands and peoples were to be fully incorporated into the Union not, as the Louisiana Purchase agreement had stipulated, "as soon as possible" but "at the proper time (to be judged of by the Congress of the United States)."[148]

Meanwhile discrimination against Mexicans extended not only to formal rights but more generally to their treatment at the hands of white settlers, who engaged in "lynchings, murders, kangaroo trials, riots and robberies" for decades thereafter.[149] The Treaty of Guadalupe Hidalgo as initially drafted had provided that "all grants of land made by the Mexican government . . . shall be respected as valid, to the same extent [as] if the said territories had remained within the limits of Mexico," and that, pending full incorporation, those Mexicans who became U.S. citizens "shall be maintained and protected in the enjoyment of their liberty, their property, and the civil rights now vested in them according to the Mexican laws."[150] The Senate, however, acting on President Polk's recommendation, limited the protection of individual rights to "the free enjoyment of their liberty and property" and "free exercise of their religion," and deleted the provision promising to honor land grants, instead issuing a "Statement of Protocol" under which holders of Mexican land grants "may cause their legitimate [titles] to be acknowledged before the American tribunals."[151] In other words, to obtain title to lands that they had occupied for generations, Mexicans had to affirmatively prove their claims in American courts, a process involving costly litigation often lasting decades and frequently proving futile, for the U.S. tribunals required documentation of a kind that generally did not exist in the Mexican legal system.[152] In many cases Anglo settlers simply ran Mexicans off their land; in other cases, they filed preemptory claims that were given priority by American courts. Most significant, huge tracts of land were lost as a result of a U.S. Supreme Court decision which held, contrary to both Spanish and Mexican law, that land owned under community grants was not titled in the community but in the government and had therefore passed directly to the United States under the treaty.[153] In California alone this resulted in the loss of thirty-three of the thirty-six million acres claimed under original Mexican or Spanish grants.[154]

The war to obtain Mexico, the subsequent denial of rights to Mexican citizens in the territory claimed by the United States, and the procedures used to rob those citizens of their land were all illegal under the applicable treaty and customary international law. This problem was resolved, not surprisingly, by portraying Mexicans as savage, or barbaric, and then claiming that such law simply did not apply to uncivilized peoples. A *New York Morning News* editorial of October 1845 summarized this position succinctly:

> We are contiguous to a vast portion of the globe, untrodden save by the savage and the beast, and we are conscious of our power to render it tributary to man. This is a position which must give existence to a public law, the axioms of which a Pufendorf or Vattel had no occasion to discuss. So far as the disposition to disregard mere conventional claims is taken into account, the acquisition of Texas, commencing with the earliest settlements under Austin down to the last conclusive act, may be admitted at once, to be aggressive. But what then? It has been laid down and acted upon, that the solitudes of America are the property of the immigrant children of Europe and their offspring. Not only has this been said and reiterated, but it is actually, although perhaps, not heretofore dwelt upon with sufficient distinctness, the basis of public law in America.[155]

Violations of law were thus deemed acceptable, perhaps inevitable, in furthering what was presumed to be the greater good; the effects of these violations were rarely considered significant, even by those who criticized U.S. policies. As Horsman notes, "In the mid-nineteenth century opponents of aggressive expansionism for the most part did not object when other races were condemned to permanent inferiority. They were far more concerned with what was to happen to the United States than with what was to happen to the rest of the world."[156]

This chapter has considered the rationale used by the United States to exempt itself from the strictures of international law, as well as the U.S. Constitution, in the course of its nineteenth-century expansion from the lands east of the Allegheny and Appalachian mountains to the Pacific Ocean. The arguments used by the earliest English settlers to justify the taking of American Indian lands for the purpose of establishing a "beacon" of freedom and enlightenment were expanded by the articulation of a unique "manifest destiny" to overspread the continent in furtherance of that purpose. Just as the American colonists had argued in declaring their independence that international law had to be violated to take human progress to a new and higher stage, the United States insisted that it was a "government of laws" while repeatedly exempting itself from the application of international law by invoking the European colonial mission of expanding Western civilization. Summarizing this perspective, the 1845 *New York Morning News* editorial, quoted above, concluded, "We take from no man; the reverse rather—we give to man. This national policy, necessity or destiny, we know to be just and beneficent, and we can, therefore, afford to scorn the invective and imputations of rival nations. With the valleys of the Rocky Mountains converted into pastures and sheep-folds, we may with propriety turn to the world and ask, whom have we injured?"[157]

6

American Imperial Expansion

After the Mexican War it was clear that if American expansion
was to continue into populous areas it either had to be through
colonial rule or economic penetration. The American republican government was not a government for all races and all col-
ors. . . . A search for personal and national wealth was put in
terms of world progress under the leadership of a supreme race.
In thrusting into the Pacific, Americans revived arguments that
the American advance would bring freedom and civilization to
all peoples; but the reality of attitudes toward neighboring peoples . . . made nonsense of the claims that the American penetration of Asia was intimately connected with the regeneration
of other races.

—Reginald Horsman, *Race and Manifest Destiny*

With the Union consolidated following the Civil War, Indigenous
resistance effectively crushed by the late 1800s, and domestic markets reaching saturation, further expansion was seen as the key to the United States'
continued success in the twentieth century. Increasingly this was framed
not in terms of extending its borders but rather its economic, political, and
military reach. American visions had shifted from the creation of a state with
indefinitely expanding territory to the domination of much of the rest of the
world through colonial ventures that would undergird indefinite economic
growth. The ideological framing, however, remained remarkably consistent
with that of the Puritan's beacon on the hill and the mid-nineteenth century
articulation of a unique and manifest destiny. As Albert J. Beveridge, aspiring to a seat in the Senate, would say in 1898,

American factories are making more than the American people can use;
American soil is producing more than they can consume. Fate has writ-
ten our policy for us; the trade of the world must and shall be ours. . . .
Great colonies governing themselves, flying our flag and trading with us,

will grow about our posts of trade. Our institutions will follow our flag on the wings of commerce. And American law, American order, American civilization, and the American flag will plant themselves on shores hitherto bloody and benighted but by those agencies of God henceforth to be made beautiful and bright.[1]

This shift in self-identification from a country that had liberated itself from colonial rule to one that would control colonies of its own can be traced most directly to the decision not to annex all of Mexico because of the perceived problems of incorporating its largely nonwhite population. The theory that the "inferior" races would fade away in the face of "superior" civilization had been undermined, and in the post–Civil War era those who had always understood "American" to mean "white" had to grapple with the reality that not only had slavery been abolished, but a constitutional amendment passed that mandated equal protection under the law and provided birthright citizenship to almost all persons—except American Indians—born in the United States.[2]

The founders' hope of expanding to encompass the hemisphere—"continentalism"—had been replaced by a more explicitly imperialist vision of political, military, and economic control over territories that would be administered by, but not incorporated into, the United States. According to Merk, this was so primarily because of "a national reluctance to add peoples of mixed blood to a blood that was pure. . . . Only those people should be admitted to the temple who would qualify someday for equal statehood in the Union, and this requirement the colored and mixed races to the south could not meet. . . . These are the principal reasons why continentalism was allowed to die, and why, later, another concept had to be devised to take its place."[3]

Accompanying this transition was a change in emphasis from the purported superiority of Anglo-Saxon civilization that, in theory, could be extended to all peoples to the association of this civilization with an Anglo-Saxon "race." The most salient dividing line was still between the "civilized" and the "uncivilized," but the "savage" nature of those deemed Other was attributed less to cultural or environmental factors and increasingly to intractable racial difference. The emerging scientific paradigm of the nineteenth century was used to develop a "science" of racial differentiation and hierarchy, providing a purportedly objective basis for the political and legal exclusion of the Other. This chapter briefly outlines the emergence of this theory of "scientific" racism that played a critical ideological role in the expansion of U.S. imperialism, particularly its acquisition of overseas "possessions." It then considers how economic pressures for expansion fueled the acquisitions of empire at the turn of the century, focusing on the exceptionalist claims undergirding the incorporation of imperialism into the United States' interpretations of international and constitutional law.

Eugenics and the Vision of an "American" Race

The "uniquely American" values and structures of democratic government embodied in the Declaration of Independence and the U.S. Constitution— and touted today as *the* model for the rest of the world—were seen by the founders as a return not only to the best of English constitutionalism, which had been corrupted by the king and parliament, but to a Saxon tradition predating the Norman conquest. As structures of racial classification and subordination were consolidated in the United States, Euroamerican settlers came to see the power of their Anglo-Saxon heritage, real or imagined, as rooted in racial rather than political character.[4]

Since the 1530s the English had emphasized their Saxon heritage, initially to justify Henry VIII's rejection of the Roman Catholic Church as a return to a purer religious tradition. The break with Rome also encouraged an emphasis on the Germanic—rather than Roman—colonization of England and fueled the development of a theory that Anglo-Saxons represented the purest and most highly developed branch of the Germanic race, one that had translated their innate love for freedom into effective systems of political organization.[5] This, in turn, was tied to the belief that the Germanic peoples were the most advanced of the Indo-Europeans, later referred to as Aryans, who had emerged from the Caucasus, spreading freedom and civilization as they moved westward, following the sun.[6] In the last few decades of the eighteenth century, the German Romantic movement exerted great influence in England and, by extension, in the American colonies. Historian Reginald Horsman notes that the Romantic emphasis on the "idea of a nation's possessing its own *Volkgeist*, its own special national spirit, fell on fertile ground among English-speaking peoples who had long traced their institutions to a glorious Anglo-Saxon past and were seeking to explain their success in the modern era."[7]

As discussed earlier, the American colonists initially justified their break from England—just as England had its separation from Rome—by emphasizing that they were returning to an earlier and purer form of Anglo-Saxon political organization. The Americans, however, had to rationalize not only their independence but their destruction of American Indian nations and their failure to extend their vaunted rights and freedoms to African slaves and their descendants or to immigrants of color. These developments were more easily explained by attributing the glories of their Anglo-Saxon heritage—not only their political organization but their civilization as a whole—to be the result of a superior racial character. This process was greatly aided, and in turn fueled, by the emergence of nineteenth century scientists and philosophers who countered the predominant eighteenth century belief that human differences arose primarily from environmental causes with the tenets of scientific racism, provoking debates reminiscent of those presided over by Pope Innocent IV and King Ferdinand about the humanity of Indigenous peoples.[8]

Until this time, English and American thinking had been influenced primarily by the Enlightenment view that although there was a hierarchy of human societies—with Europeans at the pinnacle—the differences between them were the result of history and geography; they were not immutable, and therefore all peoples had the capacity to "progress" and become "civilized."[9] Rooted in the biblical notion of human descent from a common origin, this approach, referred to as monogenism, saw races as having declined to different degrees from the perfection of the original Adam and Eve. Not surprisingly, the darker races were inevitably portrayed as having degenerated the most dramatically, with climate commonly considered the primary cause.[10] By the early 1800s, however, European and Euroamerican historians, philosophers, naturalists, and physicians had begun to focus on what made human populations distinct, rather than on what they had in common.[11] These theorists identified "races" in differing ways, but all posited some variant of the black/red/yellow/brown/white schema still prevalent today.[12]

Monogenism was soon supplanted in the United States by the doctrine of polygenism, which posited multiple origins of humanity, thereby rationalizing theories of immutable racial difference. Its most prominent proponents were the Swiss naturalist Louis Agassiz, who emigrated to the United States in the 1840s and became a professor at Harvard, and prominent scientist-physicians such as Charles Caldwell and George Morton. Based on his studies of the geographic distribution of plants and animals, Agassiz developed a theory of "centers of creation," which he extended to human beings, and, after coming to the U.S., he concluded that the human races had been created as separate species. Caldwell was the first major American phrenologist, and his theories were furthered by Morton, who focused on proving the separate species theory by analyzing the size, and therefore presumably the brain capacity, of human skulls, and using his results to rank races.[13] By the time of his death in 1851, Morton had collected more than one thousand human skulls for this purpose. Stephen Jay Gould, who re-analyzed Morton's data, concludes that Morton's findings represented "a patchwork of fudging and finagling in the clear interest of controlling a priori convictions," but they were nonetheless accepted as the kind of scientific truth that only Western civilization was capable of producing.[14]

The "sciences" of physiognomy, craniology, and phrenology became very popular in the mid-1800s, as doctors and scientists compared skull size, bone structure, skin color, and hair texture and then, using the distinctions they claimed to find, attributed what they saw as the relative successes or failures of each race to these differences. They were using completely circular logic, of course, for it was presumed that Euroamerican society represented the highest form of human civilization and that the Anglo-Saxon race was the most intelligent, capable, and beautiful. The inferiority of other races, evidenced by the fact that so many had been subjugated by Anglo-Saxons, was attributed to physiological, and hence relatively immutable, distinctions. Some scholars concluded that humanity was divided into distinct races with inherently different capacities; others questioned whether some groupings, particularly Africans and American Indians, were even of the human species.[15]

It is instructive to consider phrenology, which asserted that the brain was divided into separate faculties, the power and size of which could be determined by examining the head or skull. This new field was taken very seriously in the scientific community during the 1820s and 1830s and, although discredited by the 1840s, continued to have a widespread popular following. Not surprisingly, there was widespread agreement among English and American phrenologists that "the Anglo-Saxons had the most perfect cerebral organization, an organization that placed them above other Caucasians as well as far above the non-Caucasians of the world."[16] This, in turn, was said to explain the success of European colonization. As the *Phrenological Journal* concluded in 1846, "among nations, as among individuals, force of character is determined by the average size of head; and that the larger-headed nations manifest their superior power, by subjecting and ruling their smaller-headed brethren—as the British in Asia, for example."[17]

With Charles Darwin's publication of the *Origin of the Species* in 1859, "evolutionary theory swept away the creationist rug that had supported the intense debate between monogenists and polygenists, but it satisfied both sides by presenting an even better rationale for their shared racism."[18] Evolution combined with the emerging conviction that objective truth could be established by numerical data, laying the foundation for the new science of eugenics. Darwin's cousin, the premier statistician Francis Galton, believed that everything could be quantified and that human characteristics such as intelligence, beauty, and personality were not only quantifiable but hereditary.[19] In 1883 he coined the term "eugenics" by combining the Greek words for "well" and "born" and subsequently developed a theory that through "germ plasm" humans inherited the qualities of their ancestors in precise mathematical fractions—one-half each from their parents, one-quarter each from their grandparents, and so on.[20] According to Galton, when eugenically preferred people mated with each other, their children were improved; their mating with inferior persons would "promote a downward biological spiral," and "two people of bad blood would only create progressively more defective offspring."[21]

Throughout the nineteenth century, all the emerging Western sciences contributed to the general development of scientific racism, which was used not only to justify the global reach of European colonization but to portray it as the inevitable march of human progress. Horsman summarizes this ideological trajectory:

> By 1850 a clear pattern was emerging. From their own successful past as Puritan colonists, Revolutionary patriots, conquerors of a wilderness, and creators of an immense material prosperity, the Americans had evidence plain before them that they were a chosen people; from the English they had learned that the Anglo-Saxons had always been peculiarly gifted in the arts of government; from the scientists and ethnologists they were learning that they were of a distinct Caucasian race, innately endowed with abilities that placed them above other races; from the philologists, often through literary sources, they were learning that they were the descendants of those Aryans who followed the sun to carry civilization to the whole world.[22]

As the theory of evolution took center stage, it was eagerly embraced by those seeking to justify their history of genocide and slavery as well as ongoing race-based segregation and exclusion. Indeed, it set the stage for the American eugenics movement whose goal was, in Galton's words, to give "the more suitable races or strains of blood a better chance of prevailing speedily over the less suitable."[23] Although the specific findings of such nineteenth-century thinkers have long been discredited, it is important to remember that they were *the* scholars and scientists of the day. As journalist and scholar Edwin Black observes, "The racial purity and white supremacy doctrines embraced by America's pioneer eugenicists were not the ramblings of ignorant, unsophisticated men. They were the carefully considered ideals of some of the nation's most respected and educated figures, each an expert in his scientific or cultural field, each revered for his erudition."[24] As a result their theories, which conveniently promoted white supremacy as both natural and inevitable, were readily absorbed into both popular culture and the American legal system.

Following the Sun: The Economic Potential of the Pacific

By the latter half of the nineteenth century the promotion of U.S. economic interests—and their protection by armed force—had become the focus of American foreign policy. The territory taken from Mexico, especially California, was considered particularly significant as the gateway to Asia, with its tremendous commercial potential. As early as 1784 an American merchant ship, *Empress of China*, had sailed to Canton, and explorations of the Pacific were commissioned in the 1820s and 1830s.[25] In 1853–1854 the U.S. sent warships to force the "opening of Japan," and in 1859 troops were dispatched to protect American interests, particularly the "Open Door" policy, in Shanghai.[26]

In the 1850s the United States began its practice of acquiring territory neither contiguous to nor incorporated into the Union but "appurtenant" thereto.[27] In 1867 Secretary of State William Seward acquired Alaska from Russia[28] and took the Midway Islands "for the price of sailing in."[29] The Kingdom of Hawai'i was occupied and annexed, and following the 1898 war with Spain, the United States occupied Cuba, ensuring it had a "friendly" government, and took possession of Puerto Rico, the Philippines, and Guam as external colonies. These developments, discussed in the remainder of this chapter, each required extensions of the doctrine that the United States had the prerogative to exempt itself from otherwise applicable international law in the name of furthering Anglo-Saxon civilization.

The Discovery and Occupation of the "Guano Islands"

In the mid-1800s most Americans lived on farms, and agriculture accounted for about three-quarters of U.S. economic production. As their agricultural practices drained the soil of its nutrients, farmers became increasingly dependent on commercial fertilizer made from guano, bird droppings generally found on small barren islands.[30] This led to an interesting extension of the doctrine of discovery and the acquisition by the United States of dozens of small but economically and, ultimately, militarily significant territories. Pressured by businessmen anticipating great profits from the trade, Congress passed the 1856 Guano Islands Act, which provided that "when any citizen or citizens of the United States may have discovered . . . a deposit of guano on any island, rock or key not within the lawful jurisdiction of any other government, and not occupied by the citizens of any other government," the president had the discretion to consider it "as appertaining to the United States" and the "discoverers" would "be allowed, at the pleasure of Congress, the exclusive right of occupying said islands" to obtain the guano. The president was authorized to use U.S. military forces "to protect the rights of the said discoverer or discoverers," but had no obligation to do so.[31]

In other words, the United States was relying on the so-called doctrine of discovery to unilaterally claim ownership of unoccupied islands that it wished to exploit economically, regardless of their location or other countries' claims to them.[32] In the 1890 case of *Jones v. United States* the Supreme Court upheld the constitutionality of the Guano Islands Act.[33] This case involved black workers brought to mine guano on the Caribbean island of Navassa and forced to work under horrific conditions tantamount to slavery. Following a rebellion in which five white supervisors were killed, numerous workers were brought back to the U.S. and several were convicted of murder in federal court. Three were sentenced to death and appealed to the Supreme Court. The question in *Jones*, therefore, was whether Congress had the power to extend federal criminal jurisdiction to Navassa.[34] In turn, this hinged on the legality of U.S. claims to Navassa, for if it was legitimately a U.S. territory, the jurisdiction provided under the 1856 Act was consonant with the provision of the Constitution giving Congress the "Power to dispose of and make all needful Rules and Regulations respecting the Territory or other Property belonging to the United States."[35]

The Supreme Court found "ample warrant for the legislation of congress concerning guano islands" because,

> by the law of nations, recognized by all civilized states, dominion of new territory may be acquired by discovery and occupation as well as by cession or conquest; and when citizens or subjects of one nation, in its name, . . . take and hold actual, continuous, and useful possession . . . of territory unoccupied by any other government or its citizens, the nation to which they belong may exercise such jurisdiction and for such period as it sees fit over territory so acquired.[36]

The Court continued, "Who is the sovereign, *de jure* or *de facto*, of a territory, is not a judicial, but a political, question, the determination of which by the legislative and executive departments of any government conclusively binds the judges, as well as all other . . . subjects of that government."[37]

The Haitian government had, since 1858, protested U.S. claims to Navassa, arguing that the island had been the property of Spain, subsequently ceded to France, and then included in the "dependencies" that became part of Haiti upon its independence in 1825.[38] It would seem that the status of Haiti's claim under international law would be of significance to the Court in this case. However, on this issue Justice Gray, writing for a unanimous Court, simply deferred to the executive branch:

> If the executive, in his correspondence with the government of Hayti, has denied the jurisdiction which it claimed over the island of Navassa, the fact must be taken and acted on by this court as thus asserted and maintained; it is not material to inquire, nor is it the province of the court to determine, whether the executive be right or wrong; it is enough to know that in the exercise of his constitutional functions he has decided the question.[39]

In other words, rather than considering and enforcing international law as part of the supreme law of the land, Justice Gray declared that the dispute with Haiti was a political, rather than legal, question.

This unwillingness to ensure that the United States actually complied with international law is a continuation, in many respects, of the position articulated by Chief Justice Marshall in *Johnson v. McIntosh* that, "however extravagant the pretension of converting the discovery of an inhabited country into conquest may appear," if it has been successfully asserted and sustained, it "cannot be questioned," and "however opposed to natural right, and to the usages of civilized nations" the "concomitant principle, that the Indian inhabitants are to be considered merely as occupants" may seem, "if it be indispensable to that system under which the country has been settled . . . [it] certainly cannot be rejected by Courts of justice."[40] Practically speaking, the *Jones* holding meant that the federal courts, though unwilling to step in to protect the human or constitutional rights of the workers on a guano island, would uphold, without further inquiry, congressional assertions of authority over territories claimed as "appurtenances" to the United States. As we will see, this assertion of jurisdiction without concomitant rights would become even more explicit in the governing not only of American Indian nations but also of unincorporated colonial territories such as Puerto Rico and the Philippines.

In the meantime, under the Guano Islands Act, the United States had claimed sixty-six territories scattered throughout the Pacific and the Caribbean by 1884,[41] leading economic historian Jimmy Skaggs to observe that "in the United States, flag follows enterprise."[42] As commercial fertilizer production diversified in the early 1900s and guano became less profitable, the U.S. government began using many of these possessions for both military and commercial purposes, installing weather stations, naval facilities, and airstrips; as of 1994 nine erstwhile guano islands were still claimed as U.S. possessions.[43] The legacy of *Jones v. United States* also persists, cited as recently as 2008 to support the position, in connection with the United States' control of the Naval Base at Guantánamo Bay, Cuba, that "questions of sovereignty are for the political branches to decide."[44]

Hawai'i: Stepping Stone to Asia

The pursuit of expanding economic interests was a bit more complicated in occupied territories than it was in the guano islands. Trade with China was a prime impetus behind the transcontinental railroad, the "new highway to the commerce of Asia"—ironically completed in 1869 largely by imported Chinese labor under conditions approximated only by slavery[45]—for it would allow efficient transport of goods from manufacturing centers and markets on the East Coast to U.S. ports on the Pacific. With a view toward encouraging Chinese investment in the U.S. and promoting trade with China, the Burlingame Treaty was signed in 1868, recognizing, among other things, "the inherent and inalienable right of man to change his home and allegiance" and "the mutual advantage of . . . free migration."[46] Although these provisions would soon be overridden by the Chinese Exclusion Act of 1882,[47] trade with China remained a centerpiece of the American vision of economic expansion, and, in that context, the islands of Hawai'i became a prime target in the next phase of U.S. expansion.

As early as 1810 there had been considerable American interest in Hawai'i's sandalwood forests and its potential as a base for whaling operations.[48] In classic colonial fashion, Congregationalist missionaries arrived in 1820, followed in 1826, 1829, and 1831 by American warships that anchored at Pearl Harbor to emphasize that the U.S. would tolerate no interference with its policy of "free trade."[49] Despite the fact that, to quote the U.S. Congress, "between 1826 and 1893 the United States recognized the independence of the Kingdom of Hawaii, extended full and complete recognition of the Hawaiian Government, and entered into treaties and conventions with the Hawaiian monarchs,"[50] Americans in Hawai'i followed the pattern described by the Terán Commission with regard to Texas—increasing numbers of settlers moved in, displacing the native peoples, restructuring the economy, appropriating political power, and eventually creating an uprising or "incident" that would be used to justify deployment of the U.S. military and, ultimately, annexation of the territory.[51]

Playing upon the destruction wrought on the Kanaka Maoli (Native Hawaiians), not only by the ecological disasters triggered by the destruction of the islands' sandalwood forests but also by the tremendous population decline that resulted from diseases the colonists introduced,[52] the missionaries' influence grew rapidly, and they soon became the Hawaiian monarchy's closest political and economic advisers. By the early 1840s they had gained enormous economic interests of their own, and they constituted the most powerful political force in the archipelago.[53] Like their Puritan forebears, the settlers attributed the decimation of the Native Hawaiian people to divine Providence. As one businessman and former missionary said in 1851: "Diseases are fast numbering the people with the dead, and many more are slow to take advantage of the times and of the privileges granted to them by the king and Government. . . . The Lord seems to be allowing such things to take place that the Islands may gradually pass into other hands."[54]

In what may have been their most significant blow to the economic and cultural independence of the Kanaka Maoli, these settlers undermined the existing communal system of land tenure by pressuring King Kamehameha III into allowing the 1848 "Great *Mahele*" (Division of Lands). This allowed land to be purchased by the *haole* (white settlers), mostly missionary descendants, with the result that by 1886 they held title to two-thirds of the Kingdom.[55] On these lands they created enormous sugar plantations, and the Kanaks, who had been forced from their traditional taro root production into wage labor in the cane fields, were soon all but completely displaced by hundreds of thousands of Chinese, Japanese, and Filipino workers imported by the planters.[56]

Angloamerican business interests were facilitated by the U.S. government, which, in 1826, imposed a treaty on the Kingdom opening it to economic penetration. In 1842 the U.S. announced a corollary to the Monroe Doctrine "in which Hawai'i, while recognized as constituting an 'independent state,' was proclaimed part of the U.S. sphere of 'intercourse,' and a 'decided remonstrance'—i.e., use of military force—threatened against any third power 'interfering' with America's commercial hegemony there."[57] These actions were followed in 1849, 1875, and 1884 by treaties, negotiated for all practical purposes between the U.S. government and American business interests in Hawai'i, which gave the United States even greater influence, including an exclusive right to establish naval facilities at Pearl Harbor.[58] Meanwhile Kanak resistance was growing. In 1873 King Lunalilo died, and when it became clear that the *haole* elite was planning to install their protégé, David Kalakaua, rather than Lunalilo's wife, the popular Queen Emma, a Kanak rebellion broke out. It was quelled, and Kalakaua was crowned after a show of force by U.S. sailors and Marines deployed from warships stationed at Pearl Harbor.[59] Kalakaua was succeeded in 1891 by his sister Lili'uokalani, who shortly thereafter announced her intention to promulgate a new constitution designed to limit the planters' influence and restore political power to the Kanaka Maoli.

By late 1892 John L. Stevens, U.S. Minister to the Kingdom, had announced to Secretary of State John Foster that, regardless of the legal implications, because the "value of the Hawaiian Islands to the United States for commercial and naval purposes has been well understood . . . for more than half-a-century," the "golden hour is at hand" to completely "Americanize the islands" and "assume control over 'crown lands.'"[60] He also supported U.S. intervention by claiming that "the monarchy now is only an impediment to good government—an obstruction to the prosperity and progress of the islands," an argument that is still proffered in foreign policy debates today.[61] On January 15, 1893, a well-armed group of about one hundred U.S. citizens calling themselves the "Committee for Public Safety" took over government buildings in Honolulu and installed a "provisional government." They were backed by a "citizens' militia" composed of *haole* settlers as well as a contingent of Marines deployed to "assist in preserving public order," and Queen Lili'uokalani had little choice but to step down.[62]

As with the annexation of Mexican lands, the popular and congressional debate on what should be done about Hawai'i devolved not upon consideration of the United States' legal obligations but on how to relate to a territory in which so many people of color resided.[63] Carl Schurz, a European immigrant, wrote the following in *Harper's Magazine* in 1893: "Their population, according to the census of 1890, consists of 34,436 natives, 6,186 half castes, 7,495 born in Hawaii of foreign parents, 15,301 Chinese, 12,360 Japanese, 8,602 Portuguese, 1,982 Americans . . . and other foreigners. If there ever was a population unfit to constitute a State of the American Union, it is this."[64] In the course of the debate over annexation, Senator Richard F. Pettigrew of South Dakota invoked the principles underlying the establishment of the United States:

The founders of this government—recognizing the difficulty of maintaining as a unit a republic of extensive proportions—inaugurated the Federal system . . . hoping thereby to extend self government over vast areas and to maintain therein the purity of republican principles—each State . . . of necessity containing a population . . . of men capable of governing themselves. Therefore the founders . . . made it an unwritten law that no areas should be brought within the bounds of the Republic which did not, and could not, sustain a race equipped in all essentials for the maintenance of free civilization . . . . Therefore, if we adopt the policy of acquiring tropical countries, where republics cannot live, we overturn the theory upon which this Government is established.[65]

On the other side of the debate, Theodore Roosevelt called the failure of the U.S. to immediately annex Hawai'i "a crime against white civilization."[66] Finally, spurred by the outbreak of war with Spain, Congress, "acceding to a desire expressed by the government of Hawaii," resolved in July 1898 to annex the so-called Republic of Hawaii as a "permanent trust territory of the United States."[67] According to the congressional resolution, the U.S. acquired "absolute fee and ownership of all public, government, or Crown lands, public buildings or edifices, ports, harbors, military equipment, and all other property . . . belonging to the government of the Hawaiian islands" as a result of "the government of the Republic of Hawaii having, in due form, signified its consent, in the manner provided by its Constitution."[68]

An Organic Act signed into law by President William McKinley in 1900 established a territorial government, extinguished its treaties with other governments, nullified all traditional laws, and claimed U.S. title to all lands not deeded to individuals or corporations—more than 40 percent of Hawai'i's landbase.[69] This led to an economic boom in which the "Big Five" sugar companies regularly realized annual profits of as much as 30 percent, Hawai'i became completely dependent on trade with the U.S., and the cost of living soared as wages were driven down by a combination of U.S.-imposed labor laws and antiunion actions by police and National Guard units.[70] By 1940 "almost half the total land area in Hawaii was in the hands of 80 private owners," and most of the native Hawaiian population, which had dropped to less than twenty-five thousand, had been rendered landless.[71] In the meantime the U.S. government proceeded to construct forty-six major military installations on the islands.[72]

The actions undertaken by the United States in the "acquisition" of Hawai'i were recognized, consistently and contemporaneously, as violations of international law. President Grover Cleveland subsequently acknowledged that the 1893 coup had been an "unprovoked act of war" and a gross violation of "international morality," but he nonetheless refused Queen Lili'uokalani's repeated requests to reinstate her and restore the rule of law, choosing instead to recognize the new "Republic of Hawaii" as a "lawful State."[73] Again, the United States exempted itself from complying with the law governing relations between independent sovereign states by invoking the greater good of "white civilization" and turning the discussion to the means by which Hawai'i's "less civilized" peoples would be governed.

To this day the United States relies significantly on the logic of "conquest" articulated by Justice Marshall in the *Cherokee Cases*. In 1958, faced with the United Nations (UN) mandate for decolonization, the U.S. held a referendum in which the voters—who, in violation of UN procedures, included not only the Kanaka Maoli but *haole* settlers—were given a choice only between statehood or continued "trust" status.[74] Not surprisingly statehood won, and in 1959 Hawai'i became the fiftieth state of the Union. In 1993 the U.S. Congress passed a joint resolution officially acknowledging "the illegal overthrow of the Kingdom of Hawaii on January 17, 1893," spelled out the history of U.S. involvement, and apologized for the "participation of agents and citizens of the United States" in the overthrow and the "deprivation of the rights of Native Hawaiians to self-determination."[75] Despite this official admission that Hawai'i was acquired in blatant violation of international law, the United States has yet to take any concrete steps to right this wrong.

Extensions of Empire into the Caribbean and Asia

Between February 15, 1898, when an explosion of unidentified origin sank the *U.S.S. Maine* in Havana Harbor, and December 10, 1898, when the Treaty of Paris was signed, the United States fought a brief war with Spain, emerging with possession of Cuba, Puerto Rico, Guam, and the Philippines. Contemporary debates over the U.S. obligation to uphold international law with respect to Puerto Rico, as well as at its naval base at Guantánamo Bay, Cuba, are part of the legacy of its decision at that time to become an explicitly colonial power, exercising complete political, military, legal, and economic power over territories it had no intention of incorporating.

Cuba

The Caribbean had always been of particular interest to American leaders. As early as 1823 John Quincy Adams had claimed that Cuba was "indispensable to the continuance and integrity of the Union itself" but he did not advocate an outright invasion, arguing instead that "there are laws of political as well as of physical gravitation; and if an apple severed by the tempest from its native tree cannot choose but fall to the ground, Cuba, forcibly disjoined from its own unnatural connection with Spain, and incapable of self support, can gravitate only toward the North American Union, which by the same law of nature cannot cast her off from its bosom."[76] Thomas Jefferson agreed that the U.S. should not immediately go to war for Cuba, because "the first war on other accounts will give it to us, the Island will give itself to us, when able to do so."[77]

As Merk notes, however, "ripening is a time-consuming process. It cannot be waited for in some cases. A gentle shaking of the tree becomes necessary."[78] The first such "shake" involved a U.S. attempt in the late 1840s to buy Cuba from Spain for $100 million.[79] This failed but triggered a debate—similar to those we have seen in the contexts of Mexico and Hawai'i—over what would be done with its predominantly black population should Cuba be acquired. As President Millard Fillmore put it in his annual message of December 1852, "Were this Island comparatively destitute of inhabitants, or occupied by a kindred race, I should regard it, if voluntarily ceded by Spain, as a most desirable acquisition. But, under existing circumstances, I should look upon its incorporation into our Union as a very hazardous measure."[80] By 1898, however, as we have seen with respect to Hawai'i, Americans were beginning to conclude that territory could be acquired or controlled without necessarily being brought into the U.S. itself.

A severe depression that began in 1893 had rekindled the desire to expand overseas markets, and many Americans agreed with the sentiment, bluntly expressed by Theodore Roosevelt in a letter written in 1897: "In strict confidence . . . I should welcome almost any war, for I think this country needs one."[81] Cuba was of significant commercial interest, for U.S. trade with the island had reached $103 million by 1893, and, according to President Grover Cleveland, by 1896 Americans had invested between $30 and $50 million in, among other things, plantations and mines.[82] By 1898 Cuban rebels had been engaged for three years in a fierce struggle for independence from Spain, and U.S. financial stakes compounded political concern that, should the ongoing rebellion against Spain succeed, Cuba would become "another black republic" like Haiti.[83] Thus, according to historian Philip Foner, President William McKinley hurried into war, bringing intense pressure on Spain in the wake of the sinking of the *Maine*, because he feared that "if the United States waited too long, the Cuban revolutionary forces would emerge victorious, replacing the collapsing Spanish regime."[84]

McKinley announced that Spain's inability to protect the *Maine* had moved him "to secure in the island the establishment of a stable government, capable of maintaining order and observing its international obligations, insuring peace and tranquillity and the security of its citizens as well as our own."[85] On April 10 McKinley received word from the American minister in Madrid that the Spanish government had all but capitulated to American demands, but McKinley's mind was made up, and the following day he requested and received congressional authority to use the army and navy to "end hostilities" in the island.[86] Richard Drinnon notes the parallels between McKinley's War Message of 1898 and John Quincy Adams' 1818 defense of Andrew Jackson's invasion of Florida:

> As with the "derelict province" of Florida, Spanish officials had allowed revolutionary Cuba to become a colony of "barbarities, bloodshed, starvation, and horrible miseries." In both colonies there had been the same "wanton destruction of property," the same chaotic conditions that invoked the "necessities of self-defence" for the United States; or, as McKinley put it, "the present condition of affairs in Cuba is a constant menace to our peace." . . . [Both McKinley and Adams] spoke and acted "in the name of humanity, in the name of civilization, [and] in behalf of endangered American interests," all of which came down to the same goal of protecting, in [Secretary of State John] Hay's words, the "sacred mission of liberty and progress" the United States represented.[87]

Spain put up little resistance and by July 26 was asking to negotiate a peace treaty. No Cuban (or Puerto Rican or Filipino or Chamorro) was allowed to participate in the negotiations concerning the surrender or the terms of the treaty, under which Spain relinquished sovereignty over Cuba, and ceded Puerto Rico, the Philippines, and Guam to the United States.[88] In return the U.S. paid Spain $20 million, approximately the same amount paid to Mexico in 1848. Motivated partly by sympathy for the Cuban struggle for independence and partly by the fear of incorporating a predominantly black and brown population, shortly after declaring war in April 1898 Congress passed what was known as the Teller Amendment disclaiming any intention to annex Cuba. As a result, instead of directly taking possession of Cuba, the U.S. occupied the island, using its troops to ensure "stability" and protect the approximately $30 million of American capital invested during the occupation.[89]

A Cuban constitutional convention was informed that the United States would only withdraw its military if the new Cuban Constitution incorporated the terms of the Platt Amendment, passed by Congress in February 1901. It stipulated that Cuba could enter no treaty with another power that might impair Cuban independence; that it was to lease coaling or naval stations to U.S.; and that the U.S. had a right to intervene at its discretion to "maintain orderly government."[90] The convention rejected these terms several times as an "obnoxious and inadmissible" effort to annul Cuban sovereignty, but the U.S. refused to leave under any other terms and eventually the Cubans acquiesced.[91] In 1934, in accordance with Franklin Roosevelt's "Good Neighbor" policy, these conditions were replaced by a treaty canceling all of the United States' special rights except the lease of the naval base at Guantánamo Bay, which, of course, it still occupies.[92]

Puerto Rico

In Puerto Rico, following Spain's surrender, the United States first established a military government and then, under the Foraker Act of 1900, a colonial civil government.[93] The governor was appointed by the U.S. president, as were the members of the Executive Council. A second legislative body consisted of representatives elected in Puerto Rico, but their ability to determine local law was always subject to being overridden by the U.S. Congress.[94] The legal status of Puerto Rico was a subject of much debate, often framed in terms of whether the "Constitution follows the flag."[95] The Supreme Court addressed this issue in a series of decisions known as the *Insular Cases*, beginning with *Downes v. Bidwell* in 1901,[96] in which it extended the arguments used by Justice Marshall in the 1820s and 1830s from American Indians to the United States' newly acquired overseas possessions. Legal scholar Efrén Rivera Ramos summarizes Justice Brown's opinion:

> "The power to acquire territory by treaty," [Brown] affirmed, "implies not only the power to govern such territory, but to prescribe upon what terms the United States will receive its inhabitants, and what their status shall be in what Chief Justice Marshall termed the 'American Empire.'" . . .
> The Constitution applied to the territories only to the degree that it was extended to them by Congress. As to the probability of despotism resulting from such plenary power, the inhabitants of the new territories should not fear: "there are certain principles of natural justice inherent in the Anglo-

Saxon character which need no expression in constitutions or statutes to give them effect or to secure dependencies against legislation manifestly hostile to their real interests."[97]

Justice Harlan warned, "It will be an evil day for American liberty if the theory of a government outside of the supreme law of the land finds lodgement in our constitutional jurisprudence. No higher duty rests upon this court than to exert its full authority to prevent all violations of the principles of the Constitution." But this was, in fact, the essence of the principle established with respect to American Indians in the Marshall cases and now extended to external U.S. colonies.[98]

In 1917 Congress passed the Jones Act, unilaterally making Puerto Ricans U.S. citizens rather than "nationals."[99] The Act, however, did not confer all the rights of citizenship.[100] To this day Puerto Ricans have no representation in Congress and, more significant, no right to determine their political relationship to the United States, for they are still fully subject to congressional plenary power.[101] Under circumstances similar to those discussed in the context of Hawaiian statehood, in 1952 Puerto Ricans voted to accept "commonwealth" status rather than continuing in "trust status." They have not, however, ever been allowed to vote in a binding referendum on either independence or incorporation in the Union and thus remain a colony of the United States.[102]

U.S. policies of colonial administration in Puerto Rico were initially justified on the basis that Puerto Ricans were not "civilized" enough to be self-governing, yet under Spanish rule in 1898 Puerto Ricans were Spanish citizens with full constitutional rights; they had an elected parliament, equal representation as a province in the Spanish legislature, the ability to enter into treaties or to approve those made on their behalf, and control over monetary policy. The charter governing its relationship with Spain could only be changed with Puerto Rico's consent. Ironically, as Spanish subjects in 1898, Puerto Ricans had more political power than they have in their U.S.-imposed "commonwealth" status today.[103] Article IX of the 1898 treaty with Spain provided that the "civil rights and political status of the native inhabitants of the territories hereby ceded to the United States shall be determined by the Congress."[104] "Inoffensively and inconspicuously," Merk says, "a principle was thus adopted, new to the Constitution and revolutionary—the principle that peoples not candidates for equal statehood in the Union were annexed and their status as colonial subjects left to Congress. This was imperialism."[105] It is also the principle that continues to determine Puerto Rico's status today.

The Philippines

On April 11, 1898, the day after Spain sued for peace, future secretary of state John Hay promptly declared the conflict to have been a "splendid little war."[106] He failed to foresee, however, that, unlike its relatively effortless occupation of Cuba and Puerto Rico, the United States would be engaged in a lengthy war, neither little nor splendid, to "pacify" the Philippines. As Indiana Senator Albert Beveridge noted in supporting a congressional resolution to take possession of the Philippines, the islands were considered a significant source of agricultural products such as rice, coffee, sugar, and tobacco, as well as wood, coal, and mineral wealth. In addition, it was believed that the Philippines was critical in trading with the rest of Asia, particularly "China's illimitable markets."[107] President McKinley later claimed that he had not wanted the Philippines "when they came to us as a gift from the gods,"[108] but even before the explosion aboard the *Maine*, McKinley had ordered Commodore George Dewey to destroy the Spanish fleet in the Far East as soon as hostilities with Spain commenced, and even before receiving confirmation of Dewey's victory at Manila Bay in May 1898 he had decided to send supporting troops.[109]

McKinley also asserted that only after pacing the floor and praying "night after night" did he receive the word from "Almighty God . . . [t]hat there was nothing left for us to do but to take them all, and to educate the Filipinos, and uplift and civilize and Christianize them."[110] However, as Howard Zinn says, "the Filipinos did not get the same message from God."[111] After three centuries of intermittent revolts against Spanish rule, a war for independence had begun in earnest in 1896. Just as Dewey sailed into Manila Bay, the Filipinos, led by General Emilio Aguinaldo, "by their own military efforts broke the back of Spanish rule in the Philippines and established an independent and republican form of government for themselves."[112] This, of course, did not prevent Spain from "ceding" the Philippines as part of the December 1898 peace treaty, and U.S. forces were sent to occupy Manila. On February 4, 1899, detecting the presence of Filipinos on a U.S. base, a sentry shouted, "Line up, fellows, the n***s are in here," shooting several Filipinos and setting off what the U.S. referred to as the Philippine "insurrection." Aguinaldo requested a truce, but General Ewell Otis refused, saying that the fighting would go on "to the grim end."[113]

U.S. troops began moving beyond Manila, determined to conquer the rest of the country and instigating a war that would last officially for three years and unofficially for at least twice that long.[114] By the time Roosevelt prematurely declared the war over on July 4, 1902, more than 120,000 U.S. soldiers had fought and more than 4,000 had died.[115] The Filipino death toll was far higher. As in its earlier wars against those deemed "uncivilized," in April 1899 U.S. General William Shafter predicted, "It may be necessary to kill half the Filipinos in order that the remaining half of the population may be advanced to a higher plane of life than their present semi-barbarous state affords."[116] As Filipino resistance grew stronger in 1900, "Secretary of War Elihu Root announced that the Army must resort to the 'methods which have proved successful in our Indian campaigns in the West.'"[117] This resort to the familiar strategy of the "Indian Wars" was not simply a figure of speech, for the military commanders assigned to the Philippines were experienced "Indian fighters," and, as with American Indians, Filipinos were simply killed or forcibly removed to internment camps.[118] Tellingly the islands had been placed under the jurisdiction of the War Department's Division of Insular Affairs which, under the Organic Act of 1902, became the Bureau of Insular Affairs, modeled directly after the Bureau of Indian Affairs.[119]

In this war the United States felt no compulsion to respect long-standing rules of warfare distinguishing between civilians and combatants; all Filipinos were the enemy. In the first battle Dewey fired five-hundred-pound shells into the Filipino trenches, and "dead Filipinos were piled so high that the Americans used their bodies for breastworks. A British witness said: 'This is not war; it is simply massacre and murderous butchery.'"[120] After McKinley was safely reelected in 1900, all pretense of civil government in the Philippines was abandoned and martial law was declared. Under the overall command of General Arthur MacArthur, coastal villages in southern Luzon were shelled and all fifty-one thousand residents of Marinduque Island were ordered into concentration camps. A "depopulation campaign" was waged in northern Luzon, where entire villages were burned and all food supplies destroyed.[121] A visiting American congressman subsequently reported, "You never hear of any disturbances in Northern Luzon because there isn't anybody there to rebel."[122] In Samar General Jacob H. "Howlin' Jake" Smith, who had participated in the Wounded Knee Massacre,[123] told his troops not to take prisoners, but to "kill and burn, kill and burn, the more you kill and the more you burn the more you please me." When asked about the age limit on such killing he responded, "Everything over ten." All the survivors among the island's 266,000 inhabitants were sent to the camps.[124]

Similar campaigns were carried out throughout the country. Historians Daniel Schirmer and Stephen Rosskam Shalom summarize the carnage:

How many Filipinos died resisting American aggression? . . . The figure of 250,000 crops up in various works; one suspects it is chosen and repeated in ignorance. . . . Records of the killing were not kept and the Americans were anxious to suppress true awareness of the extent of the slaughter. . . . [Major General Franklin J.] Bell, who, one imagines might be in as good a position to judge such matters as anyone, estimated in a [May 1901] *New York Times* interview that over 600,000 people in Luzon alone had been killed or had died of disease as a result of the war. . . . A million deaths? . . . Such an estimate . . . might conceivably err on the side of understatement.[125]

Despite efforts to censor the press, the American public was aware that atrocities were being committed in their name, even if not informed of the actual numbers of the casualties. There was daily coverage of the war, and no shortage of reporting on how it was being conducted. For example, in November 1890 front-page headlines in the *Boston Herald* announced "Will Show No Mercy . . . Kitchener Plan Adopted," a readily recognized reference to the British strategy, employed against the Boers in South Africa, of mass executions and internments.[126] In April 1901 the *Philadelphia Ledger* reported,

The present war is no bloodless, opera bouffe engagement; our men have been relentless, have killed to exterminate men, women, children, prisoners and captives, active insurgents and suspected people from lads of ten up, the idea prevailing that the Filipino as such was little better than a dog. . . . Our soldiers have pumped salt water into men to make them talk, and have taken prisoners people who held up their hands and peacefully surrendered, and an hour later . . . stood them on a bridge and shot them down one by one, to drop into the water below and float down, as examples to those who found their bullet-loaded corpses.[127]

Many of these atrocities were read into the Congressional Record in 1902 by Massachusetts Senator George Hoar, who described "the torture of prisoners and of unarmed and peaceful citizens," including "hanging men up by the thumbs."[128]

Apparently the bulk of the American populace regarded this as simply another "Indian war" in which wholesale slaughter of civilians was acceptable, even to be lauded. Attempting in 1900 to convince Congress to prosecute the war more vigorously, Senator Beveridge had made this analogy by arguing that "our Indian wars would have been shortened, the lives of soldiers and settlers saved, and the Indians themselves benefited had we made continuous and decisive war; and any other kind of war is criminal because ineffective."[129] According to Beveridge, the Filipinos were "a barbarous race, modified by three centuries of contact with a decadent race," namely, the Spanish.[130] Senator Hoar countered by citing an 1898 report of two U.S. naval officers that on the island of Luzon they found "everywhere courts, municipal government, peace and order, the Spanish prisoners kindly treated, schools and churches; that they were received with elegance and hospitality."[131] Nonetheless, for Beveridge race simply trumped such evidence. Beveridge opined that the Filipinos

> are not capable of self-government. How could they be? They are not of a self-governing race. . . . What alchemy will change the oriental quality of their blood and set the self-governing currents of the American pouring through their Malay veins? How shall they, in the twinkling of an eye, be exalted to the heights of self-governing peoples which required a thousand years for us to reach, Anglo-Saxon though we are?[132]

This view was supported by scholars such as Dean Conant Worcester, a university professor who had studied in and written extensively about the Philippines, and served on both the first and second Philippine Commissions before being appointed Secretary of the Interior of the Philippines. He had strongly opposed U.S. withdrawal in 1898, arguing that the "civilized" natives (i.e., those who had been converted to Catholicism by the Spanish) could not be left alone, for "their utter unfitness for self-government at the present time is self-evident."[133] Worcester claimed that the seven million people of the Philippines were a collection of savage tribes, one sector of whom he described as "little, wooly headed, black, dwarf savages," "not far above the anthropoid apes" and "absolutely incapable of civilization."[134] The clear implication was that the Filipinos did not constitute a "people," and therefore the United States was moving into "unpeopled" territory.[135] Moreover, otherwise illegal actions, such as deliberate starvation, could be justified by Worcester's observation that the laziness of these indolent savages "might be remedied by increasing their necessities."[136]

Again, the portrayal of those being colonized as less than human allowed the United States, in fulfilling its self-appointed task of bringing civilization to the planet, to justify the most uncivilized of conduct, not only morally but legally as well. The U.S. maintained the view, proclaimed by President

McKinley in 1898, that its "paramount aim" was "to win the confidence, respect, and affection of the inhabitants of the Philippines by assuring them in every possible way that full measure of individual rights and liberties which is the heritage of free peoples, and by proving to them that the mission of the United States is one of BENEVOLENT ASSIMILATION substituting the mild sway of justice and right for arbitrary rule."[137] Root, a prominent lawyer as well as Secretary of War, claimed that "the war in the Philippines has been conducted by the American army with scrupulous regard for the rules of civilized warfare . . . with self-restraint and with humanity never surpassed,"[138] but the McKinley administration felt compelled to address accusations that it had violated international law.

Yale professor and international law expert Thomas Woolsey was enlisted to address the fact that Filipino General Aguinaldo had been captured by Americans who dressed in Filipino uniforms and infiltrated his headquarters, a clear violation of the laws of war. According to Stuart Miller,

> Woolsey had to resort to the reasoning that since the United States was not at war "with a civilized power," and "since the Aguinaldo party was not a signatory of the Hague Convention . . . there was no obligation on the part of the United States Army to refrain from using the enemy's uniforms for the enemy's deception." On the other hand . . . the Filipinos were obligated to follow the rules of the Hague Convention since they were fighting a civilized power and signatory of that agreement. . . . [Woolsey] asked his readers to "contrast the good likely to flow from the hastening of the end of the insurrection by means of it, with the offense of the use of enemy uniforms—a stratagem illegal in war only with a lawful belligerent—and you have the measure of the justice of the criticism."[139]

The same logic of the ends justifying the means, at least when "savages" were at issue, was applied when a Senate investigation into the much more serious atrocities of the Philippine War was convened in 1902.[140] As a result of this investigation the War Department was pressured into charging ten junior officers with "cruelties" including murder; although convicted, none ultimately faced penalties any more severe than a loss of pay or rank or both. In one case, a major acknowledged overseeing several massacres, but he was exonerated on the ground that he was simply following orders. Those orders had come from "Howlin' Jake" Smith who was tried not for war crimes or murder but for conduct prejudicial to "good order and military discipline." Found guilty of this minor offence, he was "punished" with early retirement on a full pension. General Adna Chaffee, who had instructed Smith and Bell to use "any means" to accomplish their objectives, was not even symbolically reprimanded but was rewarded with an appointment as Theodore Roosevelt's Army Chief of Staff.[141] Apparently General MacArthur was not the only one who believed, as he testified to the Senate, that the process by which the United States conquered the Philippines was simply a "fulfillment of the destiny of our Aryan ancestors."[142]

Eventually Filipino resistance was crushed and the colonial occupation consolidated. In 1904 the Supreme Court, following the *Insular Cases*, held that the Philippines, like Puerto Rico, was an "unincorporated territory" in which U.S. governmental actions were not constrained by otherwise applicable constitutional guarantees.[143] With the overarching aim of maintaining enough political control to promote American economic interests and preserve a military presence in south Asia,[144] a colonial government with limited self-rule was established. In 1916 the Jones Act gave "dominion status" to the Philippines, proclaiming an intent to withdraw "as soon as a stable government can be established therein."[145] The Tydings-McDuffie Act of 1934 promised Philippine independence after a ten-year transition period during which it was to have commonwealth status. The Second World War intervened, however, and after a brutal three-year Japanese occupation General MacArthur's son Douglas, also a general, reconquered the Philippines and installed a "friendly" government.

On July 4, 1946, the Philippines was declared an independent republic but, as had been the case in Cuba, its independence was highly circumscribed. Economic relations were governed by the Bell Trade Act, passed two days before the Philippines' independence, which "tied the Philippine economy to that of the U.S. by establishing a system of preferential tariffs between the two countries; it placed various restrictions on Philippine government control of its own economy and required the Filipinos to amend their constitution to give a special position to U.S. capital."[146] Under a 1947 Military Bases Agreement, the United States obtained exclusive rights to vast tracts of land for military bases, secured by ninety-nine-year rent-free leases, and the right to recruit Filipino volunteers into the U.S. Army.[147] After the ouster of U.S.-supported dictator Ferdinand Marcos, the Philippine Senate voted in 1991 not to extend the 1947 treaty and U.S. troops were withdrawn in 1992. However, the following year they returned to participate in joint military exercises, and since 2001 the U.S. has been involved in extensive "counterterrorism" activities in cooperation with the Filipino government.[148]

In 1852 Commodore Robert F. Stockton had predicted that within fifty years the United States would "acquire more wealth and power than any sovereign potentate or dominion which now sways or ever before swayed any portion of the destiny of mankind."[149] During this period the notion that the "uncivilized" Other would fade away with the advance of civilization—"retire with the wolves," as George Washington had put it—was recast in increasingly Darwinian terms.

As an 1852 article in *De Bow's Review* stated, "Wherever they go, this inferior native population, as a result of amalgamation, and that great law of contact between a higher and lower race, by which the latter gives way to the former, must be gradually supplanted, and its place occupied by this highest of races."[150] Eventually, it was believed, wars of conquest would be replaced by the workings of "natural selection," and the United States in all probability would "occupy the entire extent of America, the rich and fertile plains of Asia, together with the intermediate isles of the sea, in fulfillment of the great purpose of heaven, of the ultimate enlightenment of the whole earth, and the gradual elevation of man to the dignity and glory of the promised millennial day."[151] According to Horsman, "This, of course, was not the regeneration of the peoples of the world, but the creation of a better world by the replacement of a variety of other races by a superior race."[152]

This approach had been rooted to a considerable extent in the belief that those of the Anglo-Saxon race, by virtue of their superior physical characteristics, would reproduce more quickly than those of inferior or "mongrel" stock. By the late nineteenth century, however, as the economic incentives to control far-flung territories mounted, it was becoming clear that the United States was reaching the limits of its ability to directly incorporate territory and that the "lesser" peoples of the Americas, Asia, and the Pacific Islands would long outnumber any white American colonists. Furthermore, in order to maintain its economic growth, American businesses demanded access to natural resources and markets in parts of the world where the U.S. would have to directly confront well-established European colonial powers if it were to attempt direct territorial control. Thus, as the United States entered the twentieth century, a new approach was required.

Quoting an 1855 *Merchant's Magazine* article, Horsman records the belief that "wars of extermination were not needed . . . because superior races simply had the commercial power to secure for themselves the largest share of the means of subsistence. This would bring about 'the extinction in future times of all the barbarous races.'"[153] However, as illustrated above, securing this disproportionate share of the means of subsistence entailed concerted and often extremely brutal warfare. Such warfare, however, was recast as a necessary and indeed positive corollary of the spread of civilization. Addressing the Senate in 1900, Albert Beveridge articulated the leitmotif of American exceptionalism, with its echoes of puritanical mission and manifest destiny:

> It is elemental. It is racial. God has not been preparing the English-speaking and Teutonic peoples for a thousand years for nothing but vain and idle self-contemplation and self-administration. No! He has made us the master organizers of the world to establish system where chaos reigns. He has given us the spirit of progress to overwhelm the forces of reaction throughout the earth. He has made us adepts [sic] in government that we may administer government among savage and senile peoples. Were it not for such a force as this the world would relapse into barbarism and night. And of all our race He has marked the American people as His chosen nation to finally lead in the regeneration of the world. This is the divine mission of America, and it holds for us all the profit, all the glory, all the happiness possible to man. We are trustees of the world's progress, guardians of its righteous peace.[154]

Describing the role of propaganda in justifying the nineteenth-century strategy of territorial acquisition, Merk notes the importance of "surround[ing] the taking with an aura of reasonableness and good conscience, as well as the benefits of assigning a teleological purpose to the taking.[155] Illustrating this point, he adds,

> Propaganda designed to prepare for a seizure of territory has a characteristic language. . . . The stereotypes of the [eighteen] forties were "wars of liberation," "protection of the better classes," "regeneration of the downtrodden," "better use of the gifts of Providence," "superior rights of God's elect." . . . Another characteristic of the language was that it was upside down. Old and familiar words and phrases took on meanings opposite to those they had once had. Thus a term frequently used—"extending the area of freedom"—came to mean "extending the areas of slavery." "A war of liberation" came to mean "a war of acquisition."[156]

This strategy, which can be traced back to the earliest of colonial ventures, would prove equally useful in justifying the new forms of global domination that were to replace direct colonial control in the twentieth century.

As Theodore Roosevelt put it in his 1901 autobiography,

[O]ur whole national history has been one of expansion. . . . That the barbarians recede or are conquered, with the attendant fact that peace follows
their retrogression or conquest, is due solely to the power of the mighty
civilized races which have not lost the fighting instinct, and which by their
expansion are gradually bringing peace into the red wastes where the barbarian peoples of the world hold sway.[157]

By the early 1900s the U.S. had indeed consolidated its control of what
are now the "lower forty-eight" states, exercised jurisdiction over Alaska,
Hawai'i, and numerous "unincorporated" territories, and controlled the
lives of more than ten million native peoples held as "subjects" rather than
citizens.[158] This expansion of imperial power continued for the next several
decades. As Howard Zinn summarizes, in furtherance of its "Closed Door"
policy the United States

engineered a revolution against Colombia [1901–1903] and created the
"independent" state of Panama in order to build and control the Canal.
It sent five thousand marines to Nicaragua in 1926 to counter a revolu-
tion, and kept a force there for seven years. It intervened in the Dominican
Republic for the fourth time in 1916 and kept troops there for eight years.
It intervened for the second time in Haiti in 1915 and kept troops there
for nineteen years. Between 1900 and 1933, the United States intervened in
Cuba four times, in Nicaragua twice, in Panama six times, in Guatemala
once, in Honduras seven times. By 1924 the finances of half of the twenty
Latin American states were being directed to some extent by the United
States.[159]

During this period U.S. troops were also deployed in—among other places—
Mexico, to promote "regional stability"; in Abyssinia, to "assist" in the negotiation of a treaty of commerce; in Seoul, Korea, to reinforce the U.S. "open
door" trade policy; in several Chinese cities in conjunction with the nationalist revolution; and in Vladivostok, to support counterrevolutionary Russian forces.[160]

The United States was engaging in what Merk termed the "remodeling of
empire," in which territories desired for military purposes were kept under
direct control and those of primarily commercial value left nominally independent but always subject to intervention.[161] The overt language of manifest

destiny, framed in terms of the god-given mission of the Anglo-Saxon race to literally supplant all other peoples, began to be replaced by a framework of "international cooperation" through which the dominant colonial powers would continue to bring civilization and progress to "underdeveloped," that is, "backward" or "savage," nations. As discussed in the following chapter, a notion of "world order" emerged in which the United States and the most powerful European colonial powers would be able to retain the benefits of their wars of conquest while ostensibly repudiating the means by which they had acquired the material basis of their power.

Making the World
Safe for Democracy

> We have bought some islands from a party who did not own them . . . we are as indisputably in possession of a wide-spreading archipelago [the Philippines] as if it were our property; we have pacified some thousands of the islanders and buried them; destroyed their fields; burned their villages, and turned their widows and orphans out-of-doors; furnished heartbreak by exile to some dozens of disagreeable patriots; subjugated the remaining ten millions by Benevolent Assimilation, which is the pious new name of the musket. . . . And so, by these Providences of God—and the phrase is the government's, not mine—we are a World Power.
>
> —Mark Twain, 1902

The twentieth century is often regarded as a period in which the United States, having become a dominant world power, first retreated into an "isolationist" phase and then, having been drawn into both major world wars, played an influential role in establishing international institutions designed to ensure a relatively orderly transition to a global world order in which democratic governance and economic progress would be increasingly available to all peoples. To describe U.S. foreign policy as alternating between isolationism and internationalism is somewhat misleading, however. As the history recounted in earlier chapters demonstrates, the United States has never limited its activities to the confines of its own borders or cut itself off from interaction with other countries. As a result, it may be more helpful to consider the United States' relationship to international law and institutions in terms of its emphasis on unilateral or multilateral action, as its sphere of influence, or action, expanded across the globe.[1]

This chapter examines the "world order" that emerged in the twentieth century from this perspective, with the transition from the direct control of colonies by the dominant powers[2] to a system perhaps better characterized as imperialist, in which dominion was exercised over the "less civilized" by a combination of military, economic, political, and social means.[3] It looks, in particular, at the role the United States played in the development of international institutions and law, from the early years of the twentieth century through the League of Nations and the United Nations, focusing specifically on the "mission" of these entities to ensure peaceful world governance while moving from an explicitly colonial model to one in which "less developed" peoples were purportedly being assisted in their transition to modernity.

The Dawning of a New Century of International Law

The United States' foreign policy during the first few decades of the twentieth century is often described as isolationist, and the League of Nations, along with the courts, organizations, and treaties promulgated under its auspices, depicted as a visionary but futile endeavor to ensure peace and stability through the globalization of the rule of law. In fact, however, the United States was extraordinarily active during this period, playing a formative role in the development of international institutions that continue to have pervasive political, legal, and economic influence today. One of the most significant developments of the twentieth century, and a primary focus of this chapter, was the political transformation of the world from one in which about fifty states were recognized, and claimed much of the rest of the world as their colonial possessions, to one in which virtually all the planet's territory was divided among nearly two hundred at least nominally independent states.[4]

This transition had a significant impact on international law, generally defined in terms of the formal agreements made between and enforced by sovereign states, as well as their consistent or customary practices, to the extent they are considered legally obligatory.[5] In this context a state can be defined, to quote geographer Bernard Nietschmann, as "a centralized political system within international legal boundaries recognized by other states" which "uses a civilian-military bureaucracy to establish one government and to enforce one set of institutions and law."[6] In understanding the decolonization dynamics of the twentieth century, it is helpful to distinguish states from the more than five thousand nations of the world; "nation" being used here to refer to the "geographically bounded territory of a common people as well as to the people themselves . . . [who identify] as 'one people' on the basis of common ancestry, history, society, institutions, ideology, language, territory, and, often, religion."[7]

The contemporary emphasis on states as the almost exclusive source of law, both domestic and international, is in many respects a legacy of nineteenth-century positivism, with its emphasis on law as an abstract, scientific discipline. As summarized by the prominent British jurist John Westlake, the foundation of international law was the existence of a "society of states,"[8] and, for states to be recognized within this legal system, not only did they need defined territories, fixed populations, and effective government but they also required a sufficient level of "civilization."[9] As jurist Henry Wheaton put it in 1866, "The public law, with slight exceptions, has always been, and still is, limited to the civilized and Christian people of Europe or to those of European origin."[10] Exhibiting what James Crawford terms "a formal incoherence," the predominant view of legal scholars of the time was that there were no fixed rules for determining statehood; instead, "the matter was within the discretion of existing recognized States."[11]

Generally states and sovereignty were, and continue to be, defined in circular fashion; sovereignty is the power exercised by states, and, for an entity to be a state, it must possess sovereign power over a defined territory and identifiable population.[12] To ensure that only the progeny of European civilization qualified as sovereign states, positivists first associated sovereignty with control over territory, allowing them to exclude Indigenous societies that could be depicted as "wandering" or "nomadic," as U.S. Supreme Court opinions had described American Indians, regardless of actual forms of socioeconomic organization.[13] The numerous Asian and African states that clearly had effective political control over fixed territories were, in turn, excluded by virtue of their cultural and social "distance" from European civilization.[14]

As we have seen, some of the most fundamental principles of Euroderivative international law emerged to provide a unitary legal framework for, and accounting of, European colonial and imperialist expansion from its inception in the canon law of the Crusades and its elaboration during the fourteenth and fifteenth centuries. Generally this law was designed to minimize confrontations between colonial powers and to regulate, and hence justify, the relationship between colonizer and colonized. From this perspective, one of the most significant legal developments of the nineteenth century was the recasting of international law as a system that purported to be universal, yet recognized only "civilized" states as participants.[15] It is this process, reflective of the broader pattern of universalizing European civilization and then attempting to eliminate or absorb all Others into it, that characterizes the global institutions created during the twentieth century.

Colonial "Responsibility" and the Conference of Berlin

As the eminent international legal scholar and political scientist Quincy Wright observed in 1930, well before World War I "nationalism or its antecedent, government by consent of the governed," had rendered a shift in the rationale for the possession and administration of colonies "to conform to the theory of protectorates and to an American suggestion at the Berlin conference of 1885 [that] the authority of the protector was based on treaties with the native chiefs."[16] This approach is in many respects a legacy of Justice Marshall's theory, articulated in the *Cherokee Nation* case, that American Indians should be considered "wards" of the U.S. government, and it reflects a significant shift in international law that echoes the transition represented by the "Marshall trilogy" in U.S. law.[17]

As discussed in previous chapters, in the early years of the republic U.S. lawmakers were quite clear, despite their many actions to the contrary, that American Indian nations were sovereign entities and that treaties made with them fell squarely within the rubric of international law. Or, as Antony Anghie puts it, "the existence of a treaty . . . presupposed a legal universe to which both parties adhered."[18] However, by asserting that Indigenous peoples were "domestic, dependent nations" and "wards" of the government, the Marshall opinions of the 1820s and 1830s made a dramatic break from the prior legal framing and laid the foundation for the U.S. claim to absolute, plenary power over these nations.[19] Marshall's framing was subsequently incorporated into the theories of legal experts such as James Lorimer, who noted in 1883 that the "right of undeveloped races, like the right of undeveloped individuals, is a right not to recognition as what they are not, but to guardianship—that is, to guidance—in becoming that of which they are capable."[20] In this construction, international law provided "protection" to Indigenous peoples, but did not recognize them as state actors.

This perspective dominated the 1884–85 Berlin Conference, at which European colonial powers attempted to regulate their "possessions" in Africa. Africans were entirely excluded from the process, as they were deemed too primitive, or uncivilized, to participate.[21] Although numerous African nations had long since been organized in forms that met European criteria for state recognition and had highly advanced civilizations, as legal scholar Makau Mutua observes, "without much knowledge about the continent, early European jurists and publicists had decided that much of Africa was a no-man's land that could be brought under legal occupation."[22] Taking colonial domination as a given, the "civilized" powers focused on formulating a more "humanitarian" approach, consistent with Justice Marshall's theory in which treaties with Indigenous peoples were interpreted not as mutually beneficial and binding legal instruments but instead as justifications for occupation accompanied by commitments to "protect" the "natives" from undue exploitation.

Thus, while the General Act promulgated by the Berlin Conference participants, including the United States, focused primarily on the uniform regulation of trade and navigation, it also reflected the newer emphasis on "trusteeship." The parties committed themselves "to watch over the preservation of the native tribes, and to care for the improvements of the conditions of their moral and material well-being, and to help in suppressing slavery," and to develop institutions "which aim at instructing the natives and bringing home to them the blessings of civilization."[23] This perspective was also reflected in a subsequent resolution of the Institute of International Law, which emphasized "the duty of colonizing powers to avoid useless severities, to respect native [rights to] . . . property, to education and [to] improve their moral and material conditions, to respect liberty of conscience, to prepare for the abolition of slavery, and to prohibit slave and liquor trade."[24]

Wright notes that "humanitarianism was strengthened by a new appreciation of economic expediency" as the industrialized states increasingly desired natural resources and markets outside their colonies.[25] German Chancellor Otto von Bismarck said of the Berlin Conference, "all the Governments invited share the wish to bring the natives of Africa within the pale of civilization by opening up the interior of the continent to commerce."[26] This conflation of the moral and material "well-being" of colonized peoples, and the regulation of the internal life of their societies that accompanied it, took on increasing significance under the mandate system of the League of Nations and the trusteeship system of the United Nations and continues to be influential in the regulatory processes accompanying contemporary "globalization." To understand the role of the United States in these developments, it is important to consider the active part it played in the establishment of an increasingly centralized international legal system.

U.S. Influence on Early Global Institutions

Although it had only declared the American frontier "closed" as of 1890, by the end of its war in the Philippines the United States was, as Mark Twain noted, an imperial world power. Lagging far behind Europe in terms of its colonies in Asia and Africa, the U.S. played a critical role in the transformation of the world from one in which a small number of recognized "civilized" states occupied and claimed to possess vast areas of other continents, to one in which those same states, by and large, would exercise effective political, military, and economic hegemony over former colonies. Framing its colonial "responsibilities" in terms of an inevitable transition to independence, President McKinley described Filipinos as "the wards of the nation" and U.S. occupation of the Philippines as "an unsought trust which should be unselfishly discharged."[27] In 1901 the Supreme Court stated that Cuba was "territory held in trust for the inhabitants of Cuba . . . to whose exclusive control it will be surrendered when a stable government shall have been established."[28] In the same vein President Theodore Roosevelt emphasized that American policy "endeavor[s] to develop the natives themselves so that they shall take an ever-increasing share in their own government."[29]

Advocacy of some have termed a "neo-colonial U.S. foreign policy"[30] had been articulated as early as 1823, when President James Monroe proffered what has come to be known as the Monroe Doctrine. Monroe declared "that the American continents, by the free and independent condition which they have assumed and maintain, are henceforth not to be considered as subjects for future colonization by any European powers."[31] He emphasized that any such activity would be considered "dangerous to our peace and safety," and that while the United States had no intention of interfering with "the existing colonies or dependencies of any European power," it could not "view any interposition for the purpose of oppressing them, or controlling in any other manner their destiny, by any European power in any other light than as the manifestation of an unfriendly disposition toward the United States."[32]

President James Polk added a caveat that European states could not cede territories in the Americas to other European powers,[33] and this policy was significantly expanded by President Theodore Roosevelt in 1904. Announcing what has come to be known as the Roosevelt Corollary to the Monroe Doctrine, the president announced a policy that has since been followed not only in Latin America but in other parts of the world as well:

> If a nation shows that it knows how to act with reasonable efficiency and decency in social and political matters, if it keeps order and pays its obligations, it need fear no interference from the United States. Chronic wrongdoing, or an impotence which results in a general loosening of the ties of civilized society, may in America, as elsewhere, ultimately require intervention by some civilized nation, and in the Western Hemisphere the adherence of the United States to the Monroe Doctrine may force the United States . . . to the exercise of an international police power.[34]

Thus, by the dawn of the twentieth century, the United States had assumed the mantle of policing the western hemisphere to ensure "civilized" conduct, including the enforcement of international debts, a concern precipitated by threats of European intervention in Venezuela and the Dominican Republic for defaulting on loans.[35]

American leaders during this period saw the development of an effective international legal system that would promote political stability and pave the way for economic expansion as very much in its national interest, and U.S. lawyers, operating solidly in the positivist tradition, played a significant role in ensuring its consolidation. The importance of law is reflected, if anecdotally, in President McKinley's insistence on appointing Elihu Root as Secretary of War in 1899 on the grounds that he needed a lawyer in the position, overriding Root's objection that as a corporate lawyer he knew virtually nothing about military affairs.[36] In 1905 Root became Secretary of State, a post that was continuously occupied by lawyers from 1899 to 1945.[37] Recruiting one of the country's most prominent corporate lawyers to serve in these positions reflects the political significance of the need to reconcile the imperialist course the U.S. had chosen, exemplified by the Spanish-American War and its aftermath, with its insistence on the primacy of the rule of law and its self-proclaimed identity of democratic exemplar.[38]

Attempting to address this dilemma in the Philippines, Root—while in the process of overseeing the genocidal war being waged there—established the Philippine Commission and appointed Sixth Circuit Judge and future president William Howard Taft to lead it.[39] The Commission, which was charged with establishing the structures of colonial administration in the Philippines, initiated economic development projects, created a Filipino militia to counter the "insurgents," and promoted a political party loyal to American rule. In many respects this would become the template for the global transition from colonialism to neocolonialism developed in large measure by the United States and adopted by the "civilized" states of the world in the twentieth century.

Legal scholar Francis Boyle describes the legalist approach taken by U.S. international policy makers between 1898 and 1922 as characterized by five objectives: establishment of an obligatory dispute arbitration mechanism, creation of an international court, expanded codification of customary law into treaties, mutual arms reduction, and regularly convened international peace conferences.[40] In the western hemisphere, the United States had already initiated a series of international conferences of American states; the first was held in Washington, D.C., in 1889, with subsequent gatherings in 1901, 1906, and 1910 in Mexico City, Rio de Janeiro, and Buenos Aires, respectively. This began a process of inter-American negotiations to establish arbitral tribunals and draft conventions regulating political, diplomatic, and commercial relations which laid the groundwork for the post–World War II formation of the Organization of American States. A Central American Court, established at the urging of the United States, functioned from 1908 to 1918.[41]

In U.S. relations with Latin America we see again the tensions emerging between the United States' promotion of the rule of law, particularly international law, and its reservation of a unilateral "right" to intervene in the affairs of other peoples, that is, to exempt itself from the strictures of law as it deemed necessary. Thus, on the one hand, the United States was intimately involved in establishing an American Institute of International Law which, in 1916, promulgated a Declaration of the Rights and Duties of Nations acknowledging states' rights to independence, equality, and exclusive sovereignty over their territory, and confirming that international law was part of each country's national law. This declaration was later described by Secretary of State Charles Evans Hughes as supported by U.S. Supreme Court decisions and reflective of U.S. foreign policy in Latin America.[42] Ironically Hughes was speaking at a 1923 event commemorating the hundredth anniversary of the Monroe Doctrine which, especially with its Roosevelt Corollary, was quite antithetical to the principles enunciated.

In the broader international arena, the United States accepted Czar Nicholas II's invitation to the 1899 Hague Peace Conference on the condition that its ongoing war with Spain would not be addressed. Secretary of State John Hay endorsed a Russian suggestion that optional arbitration to avoid armed conflict be agreed upon at the conference, and the U.S. delegation was prepared to propose that such arbitration be made obligatory. Ultimately the conference participants accepted a more limited plan for voluntary mediation, but the U.S. vision of a permanent—though not obligatory—international arbitral tribunal was adopted in principle at the next Hague Peace Conference in 1907.[43] In the meantime the Permanent Court of Arbitration—not actually a court but a process for selecting arbitrators[44]—was established at the Hague, and the 1899 Convention for the Pacific Settlement of International Disputes entered into force.[45] At the 1907 Hague Peace Conference the Convention was strengthened, a declaration supporting the principle of obligatory arbitration was unanimously adopted, and the Senate subsequently ratified twenty-two arbitral treaties based on the Convention.[46]

In 1902 the United States also helped consolidate the Permanent Court of Arbitration by submitting to the tribunal its first case, a dispute concerning funds donated to spread Catholicism in California prior to the 1848 Treaty of Guadalupe Hidalgo.[47] Before the outbreak of World War I, the court decided thirteen additional cases, several of which continue to be influential.[48] Although U.S. efforts at the 1907 Hague Conference to transform the Permanent Court of Arbitration into something more closely resembling a standing court did not reach fruition, U.S. representatives were instrumental in developing a Draft Convention Relative to the Institution of a Court of Arbitral Justice, which laid the structural foundation for the Permanent Court of International Justice, created in 1921, and its successor, the current International Court of Justice.[49]

In addition to these efforts to develop standing international judicial forums, the United States played a key role in attempts by both Hague Conferences to codify the laws of war. The primary body of rules governing land warfare during both World War I and II are found in the 1899 and 1907 Hague Conventions addressing the Laws and Customs of War on Land.[50] In turn,

> these Hague codifications of the laws of war on land traced their origins back directly to the Instructions for the Government of Armies of the United States in the Field prepared by Dr. Francis Lieber, a professor at Columbia College in New York during the American Civil War, that were promulgated by President Lincoln on April 24, 1863, as General Orders Number 100.[51]

Lieber's Code, as it is known, was the first comprehensive compilation of the rules governing modern land warfare, and one finds that the laws recognized by the United States in 1863 contain many provisions often assumed to be of more recent vintage.[52] Thus, for example, Lieber notes that enemy subjects cannot be forced into the service of the victors; that the property of churches, hospitals, schools, and museums cannot be seized; and that works of art, scientific collections, libraries, and hospitals "must be secured against all avoidable injury, even when they are contained in fortified places whilst besieged or bombarded."[53] Unarmed civilians are "to be spared in person, property, and honor as much as the exigencies of war will admit" and, in contrast to "barbarous armies," in "modern regular wars of the Europeans, and their descendants in other portions of the globe, protection of the inoffensive citizen of the hostile country is the rule."[54] Disabled enemy soldiers and prisoners of war may not be killed but must be treated with humanity, and "the modern law of war permits no longer the use of any violence against prisoners in order to extort the desired information or to punish them for having given false information."[55]

In this code, and the attempts to develop multilateral treaties explicating the laws of war which followed, leaders of the United States and the participating European powers clearly recognized the existence of an underlying body of customary international law. Thus, as was stated in the preamble to the Hague Convention of 1907, "In cases not included in the Regulations adopted . . . the inhabitants and the belligerents remain under the protection and the rule of the principles of the laws of nations, derived from the usage, established among civilized peoples, from the laws of humanity, and the dictates of the public conscience."[56] The drafters' primary focus at this stage was the formation of international treaties and mechanisms to enforce this customary law. As illustrated by these examples, in the decades leading up to World War I the United States not only acknowledged the importance of international law but played a prominent role in its codification, implementation, and expansion.[57] It would continue this role, in a somewhat more circumscribed manner, in the aftermath of the Great War.

The Inter-War Years

Creation of the League and the Permanent Court of International Justice

The Third Hague Peace Conference, scheduled for 1915 and then 1916, was preempted by the outbreak of war in Europe.[58] Until this point, much of the U.S. effort to construct systems of world order had focused on the creation of arbitral bodies for the pacific settlement of disputes and treaties designed to encourage states to remain neutral when armed conflict did ensue. Thus, under President William Howard Taft, Secretary of State Philander Knox negotiated treaties—not ultimately ratified by the Senate—which obliged the parties to arbitrate most disputes, and President Woodrow Wilson's first Secretary of State, William Jennings Bryan, negotiated a series of treaties and treaty renewals, many of which were ratified, that he believed would "make armed conflict between the contracting nations almost, if not entirely, impossible."[59] This bilateral approach would change significantly as a result of World War I, with the emphasis shifting to international institutions charged with collectively enforcing the peace.

Initially, of course, the United States insisted on remaining neutral during World War I. The laws of neutrality allowed trade with belligerent parties, however, and the United States made loans to and engaged in extensive trade with the Allies and, as a result, had significant financial interest in their victory.[60] In 1915, following the German attack on the British passenger ship *Lusitania,* a measure intended to counter a British blockade on food,

President Wilson disregarded Bryan's proposal for an international investigative commission, prompting Bryan's resignation.[61] The Allies' reliance upon trade with the United States was a significant factor in Germany's decision to engage in unrestricted submarine warfare, and this, in turn, provided the impetus for Wilson's decision to enter the war in 1917.[62] Notable, however, is the effort Wilson made to frame the rationale for going to war in legal terms, rather than simply invoking American interests more generally.

In Wilson's words, it was a war fought "to make the world safe for democracy"; put another way, it was an opportunity to extend the American vision of its manifest destiny across the planet even as thousands of American were being imprisoned at home under decidedly undemocratic wartime measures such as the Espionage Act.[63] Wilson, in asking Congress to declare war, had emphasized that the German people were not to be blamed, for the war was "determined upon as wars used to be determined upon in the old, unhappy days when peoples were nowhere consulted by their rulers." He continued, "Self-governed nations do not . . . set the course of intrigue to bring about some critical posture of affairs which will give them an opportunity to strike and make conquest. Such designs can be successfully worked out only under cover and where no one has the right to ask questions."[64] In other words, democratic governance was the key to a peaceful world, a theme reiterated throughout the twentieth century.

This view was expanded upon in Wilson's 1918 "Fourteen Points" speech to Congress in which he proclaimed: "We entered this war because violations of right had occurred. . . . What we demand . . . is that the world be made fit and safe to live in; and particularly that it be made safe for every peace-loving nation which, like our own, wishes to live its own life, determine its own institutions, be assured of justice and fair dealing by the other peoples of the world as against force and selfish aggression.[65] The president laid out what he described as the "programme of the world's peace," also characterizing it as "our programme" and "the only possible programme, as we see it."[66] In addition to making specific recommendations concerning the reorganization of European states, Wilson called for transparent peace agreements, absolute freedom of navigation upon the seas, the removal of trade barriers, arms reductions, an "absolutely impartial adjustment of all colonial claims, based upon a strict observance of the principle that in determining all such questions of sovereignty the interests of the populations concerned must have equal weight with the equitable claims of the government whose title is to be determined," and the establishment of a "general association of nations" to ensure "political independence and territorial integrity to great and small states alike."[67]

By the end of the war the Allies were much indebted to the United States, and, convinced that the League of Nations was the only hope for a lasting global order, Wilson used all the powers at his disposal to ensure its establishment as a means of implementing his vision of a postwar global order.[68] According to historian Richard Hofstadter, Wilson's plan was based on three key elements:

> National self-determination, the international equivalent of democracy in domestic politics, would embody the principle of consent of the governed. Free trade would soften national rivalries and broaden prosperity. The League was to give security to the whole system through mutual guarantees of territorial integrity and common actions against an aggressor.[69]

Although Wilson's draft of the League Covenant proposed that future territorial adjustments could be made "pursuant to the principle of self-determination," this language was dropped and the final version did not explicitly mention self-determination at all. Most of the territorial divisions incorporated into the Treaty of Versailles were based on secret agreements between the Allies and rarely involved plebiscites or referenda to consider the desires of the peoples involved.[70]

The establishment of the League of Nations marked a significant transition from an international legal system in which individual states were the only recognized subjects, or actors, to one in which those states had come together to create a supranational actor. Through its founding Covenant, League members agreed that the Covenant was to supersede all other treaties or agreements inconsistent with it and that all future treaties entered into by any member would be registered with and published by the Secretariat of the League.[71] They further committed themselves to the obligatory arbitration of justiciable disputes, to the creation of a Permanent Court of International Justice (PCIJ), and to the submission of other significant disputes to the League Council. Members who resorted to war in defiance of League decisions could be subject to collective sanctions imposed by the League, including the severance of trade, financial, or personal relations and, ultimately, intervention by an armed force to which members would "severally contribute."[72]

Another significant development was embodied in Article 10 of the Covenant—included at Wilson's insistence—that member states would be collectively committed to protecting all other members from external acts of aggression against their political independence or territorial integrity. This was buttressed by an article, which stated that "any war or threat of war, whether immediately affecting any of the Members of the League or not, is hereby declared a matter of concern to the whole League, and the League shall take any action that may be deemed wise and effectual to safeguard the peace of nations."[73] This meant, in effect, that in cases of international armed conflict, the default position of member states would no longer be neutrality but belligerency. Ironically it was this provision that ultimately precluded the United States from joining the League. Key U.S. senators were reluctant to concede any of their power to an international body, even though the League was, in large measure, the product of U.S. diplomatic efforts.[74] Under pressure from these senators, Wilson had the draft Covenant amended to allow for withdrawal, to reserve the right to resolve disputes under domestic jurisdiction, and to explicitly accept "regional understandings, like the Monroe Doctrine."[75] However, he remained adamant about including Article 10, and the Senate refused to ratify the Covenant or the Treaty of Versailles.[76]

Although the United States never joined the League or the Permanent Court of International Justice, it continued to be active and influential in international affairs. Following World War I the United States formed a temporary alliance with Britain and France in an unsuccessful attempt to overthrow the Russian government established by the Bolshevik Revolution of 1917.[77] In 1921, at the Washington Conference called by the U.S. Secretary of State, three treaties were concluded. In one, the United States, Great Britain, France, and Japan agreed to mutually respect their Pacific island "possessions"; in another those powers and Italy agreed to limit their naval power; and, in a third, nine countries lent their approval to an "open door" policy in China, where the U.S. military was sent on numerous occasions to handle "emergencies" deemed threatening to American interests.[78] Perhaps most notable, in what is known as the 1928 Kellogg-Briand Pact, the United States, France, and fifteen other signatories renounced war and agreed to settle all difference by peaceful means.[79] In addition, the impact of U.S. policymakers continued to be felt not only in the international institutions that emerged in the aftermath of the Second World War, modeled in large measure on the League and the PCIJ, but in the Mandate System of the League which initiated the global transition from colonialism to forms of "trusteeship" very much along the lines implemented by the United States in its dealings with American Indian nations.

Colonialism and the Mandate System

The Monroe Doctrine, especially with its Roosevelt Corollary, was consistently invoked by the United States to justify military as well as political and economic interventions in Latin America, often in the name of advancing civilization.[80] In explaining away the apparent contradiction between the structures of world governance embodied in the Covenant of the League of Nations and the Kellogg-Briand Pact and the United States' reliance upon the Monroe Doctrine, historian Page Smith notes that Wilson insisted that the doctrine "was simply an early statement of the basic principle of the League itself: that strong nations should not impose by force of arms their will on weak ones."[81] Nonetheless, during this period, in addition to "purchasing" the Virgin Islands from Denmark in 1917,[82] the United States initiated numerous unilateral interventions in Latin America, where the United States maintained troops in Nicaragua, Haiti, and the Dominican Republic and intervened militarily in Mexico, Panama, Guatemala, Honduras, and Cuba.[83] With the exception of Puerto Rico, however, the United States did not directly colonize the peoples of Latin America, instead pursuing a policy that purported to assist and defend their "development" into fully sovereign states while simultaneously undermining the exclusive control exerted by European colonial powers in the region.[84]

The ultimately successful extension of this approach to most of the rest of the world can be traced in significant measure to the Mandate System established by the League of Nations. Rather than dividing up the colonies of Germany and the Ottoman Empire in the wake of their defeat in World War I, or actually implementing their claimed commitment to self-determination, the Allies developed a prototype for the transition from colonialism to neocolonialism over the course of the twentieth century. Jan Smuts, Afrikaaner general and future prime minister of South Africa, initially proposed the system for the European peoples of the former empires of Russia, Turkey, and Austria-Hungary, whom he characterized as "incapable of or deficient in power of self-government."[85] Wilson endorsed the framework proposed by Smuts, but he transformed it to apply only to the Middle Eastern territories of the Ottoman Turkish Empire and the colonies held by Germany.[86] The European territories would be incorporated into sovereign states through a complex redrawing of borders and a system of treaties guaranteeing the rights of national minorities.[87]

Article 22 of the League's Covenant began with a formulation reminiscent of Justice John Marshall's characterization of the United States as the "guardian" of American Indians:

To those colonies and territories which as a consequence of the late war have ceased to be under the sovereignty of the States which formerly governed them and which are inhabited by peoples not yet able to stand by themselves under the strenuous conditions of the modern world, there should be applied the principle that the well-being and development of such peoples form a sacred trust of civilisation.[88]

The Article continued by asserting that "the best method of giving practical effect to this principle is that the tutelage of such peoples should be entrusted to advanced nations."[89] Three classifications of mandate territories were established, based on their perceived degree of "civilization." The "A" mandates consisted of the non-European territories of the Turkish Empire, recognized as having "reached a stage of development where their existence as independent nations can be provisionally recognized subject to the rendering of administrative advice and assistance by a Mandatory until such time as they are able to stand alone." Former German colonies in Central Africa became the "B" mandates, "at such a stage that the Mandatory must be responsible for the administration of the territory," subject to certain guarantees protecting their peoples and securing "equal opportunities for the trade and commerce of other Members of the League." The "C" mandates, which included South-West Africa and islands in the South Pacific, were deemed "best administered under the laws of the Mandatory as integral portions of its territory," again subject to certain safeguards for their Indigenous populations.[90]

The power to govern the mandates was divided up among the Allies, who continued to hold their own colonies.[91] In many ways, therefore, this system functioned simply as a redistribution of colonial possessions, except that under the terms of Article 22, the mandatory powers, as they were known, were responsible to the League which was, of course, composed only of "civilized" states.[92] Disputes concerning administration of mandate territories were to be handled by the Permanent Mandates Commission, which advised the League Council, and could ultimately be referred to the Permanent Court of International Justice. The peoples of the mandates had no direct input into the process, other than an ineffectual right to submit petitions to the Mandates Commission.[93] After noting that under the Mandate System the British, French, Japanese, and Italian empires grew considerably, Page Smith observes that nonetheless, "the days of the mandates were numbered; the seeds of independence had been sown, and the ideal officially recognized. The new landlords would, in the main, find they had rebellious tenants and short leases.[94]

Of great significance, however, was the template for "development" created during this tenure, for it would have lasting effects on the decolonization movement and on the contemporary world order, in which purportedly equal and sovereign states must function within structures that increasingly use measures of "progress" and "development" to assess their competency and degree of "civilization." Antony Anghie's incisive analysis, building upon Quincy Wright's detailed exposition of the internal workings of the Mandate System, explains how much of this structure was put in place in the decades following World War I. At its heart was an ideological commitment to the notion that it was "a system of a progressive, enlightened colonialism, as opposed to the bad, exploitative colonialism of the nineteenth century."[95] The Allies, of course, needed to justify the apparent disparity between establishing mandates for the German and non-European Ottoman Turkish colonies and maintaining their own African and Asian empires which, in Anghie's words, "naturally fell into the category of 'good colonialism.'"[96]

Having already rejected attempts by the Japanese representative to include a statement on racial equality in the League Covenant,[97] the Western powers and their lawyers relied upon the legal theories of Franciscus de Vitoria as well as U.S. Supreme Court Justice John Marshall that colonial, or mandatory, powers served as guardians or trustees of their "native" wards.[98] Thus, for example, in a classic text published during this period, British colonial administrator Frederick Lugard, a member of the League's Permanent Mandate Commission, emphasized the "dual mandate" of the British to bring the benefits of civilization to African peoples while opening their territories to international commerce.[99]

What might otherwise have been perceived as tension between the humanitarian goals of the Mandate System and its commitment to economic development was reconciled by the presumption that economic "advancement" was a prerequisite of civilization. Thus the Covenant emphasized that "the well-being and development" of those not adequately prepared to cope with "the strenuous conditions" of modernity constituted "a sacred trust of civilization,"[100] and explicitly provided that League members were to "endeavour to secure and maintain fair and human conditions of labour" and to "undertake to secure just treatment of the native inhabitants of territories under their control."[101] The well-being of the Indigenous peoples at issue was largely measured by their economic productivity which, in turn, required the maintenance of certain levels of health, hygiene, and education. While the Permanent Mandates Commission (PMC) discussed labor conditions extensively, often measuring them by mortality and morbidity statistics, at least some of its members believed that certain "races" were simply unsuited to economic survival in the modern world.[102]

Subsistence economies that did not produce a marketable surplus were, by definition, backward, and reluctance to engage in wage labor or indifference to the accumulation of wealth were deemed cultural impediments to progress for, according to the PMC, "the law of labor is a law of nature, which no one should be allowed to evade."[103] Traditional forms of governance were eviscerated and Indigenous leaders rendered impotent under the theory that, "scarcely aware of the fact that their little sovereignty has been transferred to a higher group, they will assist in the work of the mandatory government and will be content with the empty title and the modest stipend."[104] Employing what was termed the "science of colonial administration,"[105] every aspect of native society was studied and the PMC collected volumes of data on issues such as governmental structure and functioning, taxation, land use, labor conditions, health care, and educational facilities, relying heavily on complex questionnaires to be completed by the mandatory powers.[106] This information was then used to develop increasingly detailed means of regulating all aspects of Indigenous societies. "Progress" was measured by the development of infrastructure—roads, railroads, and telegraph systems—which, in turn, allowed the mandatory powers to penetrate the interior of the territory and, once there, not only to transform the economy but each society's political, education, health, legal, and policing systems as well.[107]

Underlying this international effort was the belief that eventually the mandate territories would be sufficiently "developed" to be recognized as independent sovereigns, but the entire process of transforming former colonies into self-governing states was so deeply infused with the ideological presumptions of Western civilization that the notion of "self-determination" was stripped of any real meaning. Only by conforming to Western understandings of civilization could "backward" societies be deemed eligible to be independent, for, as noted above, sovereignty was defined as requiring recognition by the community of already recognized "civilized" states. Despite the League of Nations having expanded this "community" to include not only European countries and the United States but a number of Latin American states and Japan,[108] the prevalent belief was that fundamentally divergent understandings, worldviews, and value systems were simply impediments to progress.[109]

In the positivist international legal framework that emerged in the nineteenth century, "sovereignty, in the case of non-European societies, does not arise 'naturally'; rather, it has to be bestowed,"[110] and the Mandate System made it clear that it would be bestowed only when the colonial powers deemed that the purportedly objective and scientific criteria they had established had been met.[111] In other words, peoples would be recognized as having the capacity to be self-determining only after abandoning any under-standings of their own histories, cultures, or worldviews that conflicted with Western values, thereby effectively conceding to the "inevitability" that genuine self-determination was no longer an option.[112]

Internal Colonialism and American Indian "Reorganization"

Despite the United States' proclamations of a postwar world in which freedom, democracy, and self-determination would be governing principles, in the early years of the twentieth century these were not envisioned as applying to *all* peoples, any more than were the rights to liberty and equality articulated in the Declaration of Independence. The Supreme Court had nullified the Reconstruction Congress' Civil Rights Act in the 1883 *Civil Rights Cases* and sanctioned apartheid in its 1896 decision in *Plessy v. Ferguson*.[113] Upon assuming office, Wilson had removed numerous prominent African Americans from federal positions and segregated employees in the departments of the treasury and post office.[114] With respect to Wilson's emphasis on self-determination, his Secretary of State, Robert Lansing, said that the more he thought about it, "the more convinced I am of the danger of putting such ideas into the minds of certain races. . . . Will it not breed discontent, disorder, and rebellion?"[115]

The primary concern of U.S. representatives at the Versailles negotiations was not the liberation of colonized peoples but economic access to the colonies or mandate territories held by other powers. As the American ambassador to Britain stated in May 1920, when negotiating the Versailles Treaty, the United States

> consistently took the position that the future peace of the world required that, as a general principle, any alien territory which should be acquired pursuant to the Treaties of Peace with the Central Powers, must be held and governed in such a way as *to assure equal treatment in law, and in fact to the commerce of all nations.* It was on account of, and subject to, this understanding that the United States felt itself able and willing to agree that the acquisition of certain enemy territory by the victorious Powers would be consistent with the best interests of the world.[116]

When the League failed to provide for "open door" policies in the mandates in a manner sufficient to satisfy U.S. interests, American diplomats delayed confirmation of the specific allocations of mandates while they negotiated bilateral treaties giving the U.S. access to the territories.[117]

Nonetheless, in considering the ideological history of American exceptionalism with respect to international law, and the role played by the construction of the Other in this history, it is critical to appreciate the tremendously influential role played by the United States in the establishment of the League of Nations and the functioning of its Mandate System. Given the extent to which international law developed in conjunction with European colonialism, it is not surprising that U.S. attitudes toward international law have also been heavily influenced by American colonial encounters, and thus we turn briefly to U.S. Indian policy in the era following World War I.

As noted in previous chapters, despite the racist imagery often used by the founders of the republic to depict American Indians, their nations were acknowledged to be sovereign political entities, and the U.S. consistently relied on treaties with them to legitimate the occupation of their lands. As the United States grew more powerful, however, it began to develop theories of colonial law under which American Indian sovereignty was denied and Indian nations transformed under U.S. law into "domestic, dependent nations," purportedly because of their lack of "civilization."[118] Thus, by 1872, Commissioner of Indian Affairs Francis Walker could respond to a question about national honor and the treatment of American Indians by retorting, "There is no question of national dignity, be it remembered, involved in the treatment of savages by a civilized power."[119] A year earlier Congress had declared that it would no longer enter into treaties with American Indian nations, and in the 1903 case of *Lone Wolf v. Hitchcock* the Supreme Court asserted that Congress possessed, and always had, the "plenary power" to abrogate extant treaties.[120] The outcome may perhaps most accurately be described as the consolidation of a process of internal colonialism, explained by Ward Churchill as "the result of an especially virulent and totalizing socioeconomic and political penetration whereby the colonizing power quite literally swallows up contiguous areas and peoples, incorporating them directly into itself."[121]

Unlike the "classic" European colonial model in which far-flung territories were claimed as possessions, exploited for their land, labor, and resources, and ultimately administered from a distant center, the United States was established as a settler state, with England "export[ing] a sufficient portion of its own population ('settlers'), to supplant rather than simply subordinate the indigenous people(s) of the colony."[122] After the Angloamerican settlers were recognized as possessing independent sovereignty, they proceeded to "swallow up" American Indian nations, claiming a legal right to exercise unfettered political control over their affairs as they were forcibly incorporated into the United States. Having so prominently promoted the notion of self-determination, in the years following World War I the federal government once again reconsidered its approach to "the Indian problem."

The policies of what is often termed the Allotment era had been disastrous, stripping American Indians of two-thirds of the land they had held as of 1890, and leaving communities decimated and in dire poverty.[123] In 1923 the Secretary of the Interior convened a national committee to make policy recommendations, one result of which was the Indian Citizenship Act of 1924, a law that unilaterally conferred U.S. citizenship on American Indians.[124] This, of course, was in many respects a continuation of the assimilationist policies of the Allotment era and met with significant Indigenous resistance.[125] In 1928 "The Problem of Indian Administration," more commonly referred to as the Meriam Report, "document[ed] the massive white expropriation of Indian resources as well as the catastrophic economic and social collapse" that had followed implementation of the Allotment Act.[126] At the urging of Indian Commissioner John Collier, Congress passed the Indian Reorganization Act (IRA) of 1934.[127]

Instead of functioning as "a mighty pulverizing engine to break up the tribal mass," as President Theodore Roosevelt had described the Allotment Act,[128] the IRA purported "to grant to Indians living under Federal tutelage the freedom to organize for purposes of local self-government and economic enterprise."[129] Paralleling in many respects the Mandate System's vision of assisting "backwards" peoples toward self-government, the bill proposed that "the functions of government now exercised over Indian reservations by the Federal Government . . . shall be gradually relinquished and transferred to the Indians of such reservations."[130] Or, as President Franklin Roosevelt told Congress, extending "to the Indian the fundamental rights of political liberty and local self-government and the opportunities of education and assistance that they require . . . is but the obligation of honor of a powerful nation toward a people living among us and dependent upon our protection."[131]

Though often portrayed as a dramatic reversal in the federal government's policy toward American Indians, the IRA did not limit the plenary power exercised by the U.S. government but simply used it to make its colonial administration more efficient.[132] Just as the mandates established by the League of Nations had to "develop" in ways prescribed by their more "civilized" mandatory powers before they were eligible to be recognized as sovereign, the federal government made the limited powers of self-government available under the IRA contingent upon conformity to changes in internal governance dictated, in essence, by the Department of the Interior, through its Bureau of Indian Affairs (BIA). To receive the "benefits" of federal recognition, which included limited powers of internal governance and access to federal funds for social and economic programs, the "tribes"[133] had to vote within a two-year window to accept the provisions of the IRA and then adopt constitutions and bylaws approved by the Secretary of the Interior.[134] Ultimately 358 elections were held, with 181 tribes accepting the IRA and 77 rejecting recognition under its terms.[135] In this purportedly democratic process, the BIA determined who was eligible to vote and the rules governing elections, with the result that recognition could be "approved" by as few as 16 percent of potential voters.[136]

Indigenous nations, of course, not only had traditional means of determining membership very different from those imposed by the Bureau of Indian Affairs,[137] but they also had their own traditional forms of government, decimated though they had been by centuries of colonial occupation. Although varying greatly, many were characterized by complex and multilayered processes that maintained decentralized lines of authority and generally ensured a significant role for community consensus.[138] For many peoples, the very act of voting in an IRA referendum was "antithetical to the traditionally consensus-based modes of governance they were seeking to preserve," but such principled abstention could result in "approval" of the IRA.[139] Thus, for example, about 85 percent of the Hopis boycotted their referendum "only to have Collier falsify the tribal census as a means of casting the impression that reorganization had been decisively approved."[140]

Rejection of recognition under the IRA was interpreted as reflecting the "backwardness" of the peoples involved.[141] Acceptance meant that all subsequent decisions of any significance were conditioned upon approval by the Department of the Interior,[142] leading Robert A. Williams Jr. to describe it as "a congressionally sanctioned scheme to streamline and decentralize the administration of the United States' Indian colonies" which encouraged "tribes to adopt Anglo-style constitutions and bylaws in a mimetic effort toward civilized 'self-government.'"[143] In 2004 President George W. Bush defined contemporary American Indian "tribal sovereignty" by saying that it means "you have been given sovereignty and you're viewed as a sovereign entity."[144] Although the president's response was the subject of considerable parody, the core of his definition—that sovereignty was something "given" to American Indian nations—conveyed quite accurately the United States' position on the issue. It also closely parallels the presumption of the Mandate

System that non-European societies must have sovereignty "bestowed" upon them by "civilized" states of European derivation and reflects the extent to which this view became entrenched in federal law and policy in the decades following World War I.

World War II and the Postwar Vision of Global Order

World War II was in many respects a watershed in the history of American exceptionalism, for by the mid-twentieth century the United States had become "the principal source of order in the world, both as a great power and as an advocate of increased respect for juridical arrangements."[145] This section looks at the new world order that emerged in the second half of the twentieth century, focusing particularly on the tremendous influence of American leaders in the establishment of the United Nations as well as the International Court of Justice, on the evolution of international law in the postwar period, and the changes in international relations resulting from the global movement for decolonization. The result of this process, in very general terms, was a world in which nominally sovereign and independent states governed virtually all lands and peoples, and a network of global institutions had been established with the potential to resolve conflicts between them in a peaceful, or at least orderly, manner. It was a world, however, in which the legacies of colonialism could not be ignored, and the familiar struggles for control of resources simply took on new forms.

The Creation of the United Nations

In recent decades the United Nations has often been portrayed in the American media and by U.S. politicians as an ineffective, bureaucratic organization unworthy of American support, sometimes even as an international conspiracy to undermine American democracy by forcing the United States to comply with "foreign" law.[146] Since 1980 the United States has routinely withheld significant portions of its UN dues,[147] and it remains one of the few major powers refusing to ratify some of the most significant multilateral conventions promulgated under the auspices of the UN, including the Rome Treaty establishing the International Criminal Court, the Law of the Sea Treaty, the Kyoto Protocols on global warming, the convention banning landmines, the Convention on the Elimination of Discrimination against Women, and the Convention on the Rights of the Child.[148] Although these failures to participate are often attributed to isolationism, this approach fails to take into account the leading role played by the United States in the establishment of the United Nations and in the creation of each of the treaty regimes mentioned. This often contradictory history, in which the U.S. has exerted tremendous influence over the development of international institutions and simultaneously prevented them from fulfilling their potential, reflects the long-standing tension between multilateralism and unilateralism in U.S. policy that undergirds American exceptionalism and is the source of much of the international community's frustrations with American policies and practices.

Franklin D. Roosevelt, a key figure in the establishment of the United Nations, had initially been a strong supporter of the League of Nations, but he abandoned that position in his 1932 presidential campaign in exchange for the support of media magnate William Randolph Hearst.[149] By the late 1930s, however, Roosevelt was again emphasizing the need for American leadership in global affairs as he laid the groundwork for U.S. entry into World War II, supporting, for example, an amendment modifying the Neutrality Act and convincing Congress to revive the military draft.[150] In his January 1941 annual address the president prepared the country for war, emphasizing that this was a matter of preserving democracy and assuring the United States' place at the forefront of Western civilization. In what may be his most often cited speech, Roosevelt discredited isolationism by asserting that "the historic truth is that the United States . . . has at all times maintained clear, definite opposition to any attempt to lock us behind an ancient Chinese wall while the procession of civilization went past."[151]

Roosevelt then framed the war as a battle for democracy, noting that "the democratic way of life is at this moment being directly assailed in every part of the world," that "the future and the safety of our country and of our democracy are overwhelmingly involved in events far beyond our borders," and that "armed defense of democratic existence is now being gallantly waged in four continents." Eleven months before the Japanese attack on Pearl Harbor, the president noted the possibility of "the invasion of this Hemisphere" and asked Congress to authorize and fund the "wartime production of implements of war," including munitions, aircraft, and warships for use by both the United States and "those nations which are now in actual war with aggressor nations." He preempted charges that this could be regarded "as a breach of international law or as an act of war" by asserting that such claims would come from "dictators" whose "only interest is in a new one-way international law, which lacks mutuality in its observance, and, therefore, becomes an instrument of oppression."[152]

Finally, Roosevelt laid the groundwork for what would be a new global order by "look[ing] forward to a world founded upon four essential human freedoms," freedom of speech and expression and of religion, freedom from want and freedom from fear, each to be established "everywhere in the world" and "in our own time and generation." Having invoked a "world order . . . of free countries, working together in a friendly, civilized society," as well as "the guidance of God," the president concluded: "Freedom means the supremacy of human rights everywhere. . . . To that high concept there can be no end save victory."[153] In the words of the influential *Emporia* newspaper editor William Allen White: "the people of the United States through their President have given the world a new Magna Carta of Democracy."[154]

Shortly thereafter a new division was created within the State Department "to study plans for a world assembly or, as [Secretary of State Cordell] Hull put it, 'a future world order.'"[155] In August 1941, Roosevelt and British Prime Minister Winston Churchill made a joint declaration, known as the Atlantic Charter, in which Churchill proposed the eventual establishment of an "effective international organization" to ensure global peace and security, language that was changed at Roosevelt's request to a proposal for "the establishment of a wider and permanent system of general security."[156] Having temporarily suspended its earlier anticommunist crusade to ally itself with the Soviet Union, in January 1942 the United States joined the United Kingdom, the Soviet Union, China, and twenty-two smaller powers in issuing a declaration supporting the principles of the Atlantic Charter in the name of "the United Nations."[157] This was followed in late 1943 by the Moscow Declaration, drafted by Hull, in which the major allied powers recognized "the necessity of establishing at the earliest practicable date a general international organization, based on the principle of the sovereign equality of all peace-loving States, and open membership by all such States large and small, for the maintenance of international peace and security."[158]

In the meantime, with Roosevelt's approval, the Undersecretary of State had written a full draft for a proposed United Nations that became the basis of the plan adopted by the "big four" at Dumbarton Oaks in August 1944 and ultimately the basis of the Charter adopted at the 1945 founding of the United Nations.[159] To ensure that this initiative would not meet the fate of the League of Nations, Secretary of State Hull, in 1943, negotiated the passage of resolutions in both the Senate and the House of Representatives authorizing the creation of international organizations to counter aggression and maintain the peace, and he met consistently with the Senate Foreign Relations Committee to keep its members apprised of the status of the draft Charter.[160]

By 1944 the State Department had launched an unprecedented national campaign to promote the United Nations, creating and distributing public information, sending speakers around the country, enlisting the support of various religious and political organizations, and utilizing the newspapers, radio, and even the movie industry.[161]

To smooth the path of ratification in the Senate, Roosevelt appointed powerful senators and congressmen, both Democrats and Republicans, to the U.S. delegation to the founding conference of the United Nations.[162] In addition to generating support within the country, American leaders went to great lengths to ensure that the international community would reach agreement on a plan acceptable to the U.S. By hosting the conference in San Francisco and providing a location in New York for the UN headquarters, U.S. representatives were able to exert decisive influence over the organization and succeeded in "imbuing the conference with U.S. values and goals."[163] Ultimately the delegates to the founding conference agreed upon—and the U.S. Senate ratified—the UN Charter, creating the institutional framework for the contemporary world order.

Meeting in San Francisco while the war was still in progress, the Allied Powers agreed on the importance of creating a strong international organization to maintain the peace they believed would soon be achieved, but they spent many weeks grappling with difficult issues. A central goal of the "big four" was the creation of a monopoly on the use of force, and the overarching question was how this could be achieved in a manner that maintained their power while ensuring the cooperation of the smaller states. The U.S. still wanted to establish an international court with compulsory jurisdiction, and there was the outstanding question of what would be done about colonies and mandate territories. The compromises reached on these issues are reflected in the UN Charter which established the institutions that remain central to world order in the twenty-first century.

Implementation of the Vision

The United Nations was established by its Charter, a treaty which by its terms "trumps" all other international accords and commits its members to collective action. To the extent that member states are parties to treaties that conflict with the Charter, their obligations under the Charter prevail. States parties agree to register and publish all their international agreements through the UN Secretariat, thus ensuring against any secret pacts.[164] Balancing these internationalist commitments, the Charter explicitly provides for the recognition and protection of state sovereignty, prohibits "the threat or use of force against the territorial integrity or political independence of any state," and precludes the United Nations from "interven[ing] in matters which are essentially within the domestic jurisdiction of any state."[165]

Key to obtaining the consent of both large and small states to participate in an overarching international organization was, of course, the balance struck between ensuring that the most powerful states would retain their dominant positions while reassuring the less powerful that their interests would not be arbitrarily overridden. This was accomplished by dividing UN functions between the General Assembly, governed by a one-state, one-vote rule, and the Security Council, whose substantive decisions require not only the approval of a super-majority but also the concurrence of its permanent members (the United States, Britain, the Soviet Union, China, and France), giving them an effective veto.[166]

Under the Charter, all members agree to refrain from using force against other members, with the exception that a member that has suffered an armed attack has a right to "individual or collective self-defense" but *only* "until the Security Council has taken measures necessary to maintain international peace and security."[167] Thus the power to use force lawfully, other than in limited cases of self-defense, is concentrated exclusively in the Security Council, which is empowered to investigate any dispute likely to "lead to international friction" or to endanger international peace and security, and to call upon members to settle such disputes through some form of arbitration or mediation. Should it find a threat to the peace, breach of the peace, or act of aggression, it can impose sanctions including the interruption of economic relations, communications, and diplomatic relations, and, should these prove insufficient, it can enforce blockades and sanction military interventions.[168] All members are responsible for providing the "mutual assistance" required to implement measures decided upon by the Security Council."[169] Thus a structure was established which, in theory, can address and authorize preemptive or responsive action in all situations likely to lead to war.

While the primary concern of the Allied Powers was the development of a mechanism for effectively maintaining the peace, they recognized that this required not only a commitment to what was essentially a collective mutual defense pact but also to a world order in which the underlying social and economic conditions that so often led to war were alleviated. Thus the first purpose articulated in the Charter is the maintenance of international peace and security through collective action against threats to the peace and acts of aggression, and an agreement to settle international disputes "in conformity with the principles of justice and international law." This is supplemented by provisions for fostering friendly international relations based on "respect for the principle of equal rights and self-determination of peoples," encouraging cooperation in "solving international problems of an economic, social, cultural, or humanitarian character," and promoting "human rights and fundamental freedoms."[170]

The General Assembly's mandate extends to political, economic, social, cultural, educational and health-related matters, and to the development and codification of international law.[171] Although General Assembly resolutions are not legally enforceable, they are significant indicators of international political opinion and, especially when passed by an overwhelming majority, have been taken as evidence of binding customary international law.[172] The studies and reports commissioned by the General Assembly often result in declarations which, in turn, form the basis of binding multilateral treaties.[173] As a result, although enforcement powers were concentrated in the hands of the major powers, the United Nations structure nonetheless provides a global structure through which all the peoples of the world have a voice, at least in theory. This has resulted in some significant changes in international law, including the expansion of individual criminal liability which, in turn, has spurred the development of human rights law.

International Courts and Accountability for War Crimes

The establishment of the United Nations and the tribunals created for the prosecution of war criminals following World War II had a dramatic effect on both the substance of international law and the judicial venues available for its implementation. Prior to this time much of international law was embodied in the practices that "civilized" states acknowledged as legally obligatory, otherwise known as customary international law. One purpose of the United Nations was to centralize this body of law by a process for codifying customary law and articulating new law, creating a repository for all treaties, and establishing a world court with jurisdiction to resolve legal disputes.

Although the United States had never ratified the treaty creating the Permanent Court of International Justice, U.S. diplomats had been influential in its creation, and its home, the Peace Palace in the Hague, had been financed by Andrew Carnegie.[174] The "new" court created by the UN Charter, the International Court of Justice (ICJ), was in many respects a continuation of the PCIJ, "in doctrine, procedures, acceptance and application of precedent, facilities, and most staff personnel, even a few judges-to-be."[175] One significant difference was that the ICJ was created as the "principal judicial organ" of the United Nations, with each UN member automatically becoming a party to the Statute of the ICJ and agreeing to comply with its decisions in cases to which it was a party.[176] In negotiations over the structure of the League, the United States had supported the compulsory jurisdiction of the PCIJ, and initially President Harry S. Truman took the same position with respect to the ICJ. However, he was soon convinced that the Senate would not ratify the UN Charter under those terms and, along with the Soviet Union, the United States insisted that the ICJ Statute make the compulsory jurisdiction of the court an option but not a requirement.[177]

The International Court of Justice did not, and still does not, have the power to prosecute individuals for criminal violations of international law. By the time it was inaugurated in April 1946, however, the Allies were already using international tribunals to prosecute war crimes. Even before the United Nations was founded, officials within the U.S. Departments of State and War were envisioning what emerged as the International Military Tribunal (IMT), more commonly known as the Nuremberg Tribunal. As early as January 1942, representatives of nine governments in exile met in London as the "Inter-Allied Commission on the Punishment of War Crimes" and, while condemning the execution of "innocent hostages" and other horrors in German-occupied territories, they repudiated acts of vengeance and issued a joint declaration that the "sense of justice of the civilized world" required that they "place among their principal war aims the punishment, through the channel of organized justice, of those guilty of or responsible for these crimes."[178]

A few months later both Churchill and Roosevelt approved trials for war crimes, with Joseph Stalin expressing a preference for "a special international tribunal."[179] After Roosevelt's sudden death in April 1945, just before the San Francisco conference, President Truman asked Supreme Court Justice Jackson to present a plan for the prosecution of Axis leaders to the UN organizing conference.[180] Under U.S. pressure, by August the governments of the United Kingdom, the Soviet Union, and France had joined the United States in creating the Charter of the IMT, also called the London Charter, authorizing by treaty the tribunal that would try German war criminals.[181]

The plan used to prosecute not only German but also Italian and Japanese leaders was developed primarily by American lawyers, and it dramatically expanded the notion of individual criminal accountability for war crimes.[182] Although war crimes had long been recognized under international law, they were generally considered to be limited to acts conducted either by members of a military force or by armed non-members engaged in hostilities. Beyond this, international law was widely regarded as regulating the conduct of states, not individuals, making the prosecution of individual Nazi leaders not in the armed forces problematic.[183] The London Charter filled this gap by giving the IMT jurisdiction over individuals responsible for crimes against the peace, war crimes, and crimes against humanity.[184] Of these, the category of war crimes, defined as "violations of the laws or customs of war," was the least controversial, for there was a fairly well-established body of law on the subject.[185]

Crimes against the peace were defined by the Charter as encompassing the preparation for, initiation of, or waging of a war of aggression and, at U.S. insistence, included "participation in a common plan or conspiracy" to do so as a means of extending criminal liability under international law to individual civilian leaders.[186] Concerned about the undemocratic implications of convictions based on guilt by association, IMT judge and U.S. Attorney General Francis Biddle proposed that "each organization declared criminal be defined to include persons 'who became or remained members of the organization with knowledge that it was being used for the commissions of acts declared criminal by . . . the Charter," thereby "restor[ing] the necessity of proving individual guilt."[187] The concern that prosecuting aggressive warfare would be perceived as the imposition of ex post facto law was countered by the assertion that wars of aggression had long been prohibited by customary law and were outlawed by the 1928 Kellogg-Briand Pact, ratified by both Italy and Germany, which had renounced any "recourse to war" as "an instrument of national policy."[188] Although these were admittedly thin legal arguments, the concept was overwhelmingly supported, in the words of Nuremberg prosecutor Telford Taylor, by " peoples whose nations had been attacked and dismembered without warning."[189]

The third category, crimes against humanity, was defined by the London Charter to include "murder, extermination, enslavement, deportation, other inhumane acts committed against any civilian population, before or during the war, or persecutions on political, racial or religious grounds" in connection with any crime over which the Tribunal had jurisdiction, regardless of whether such acts violated the domestic law of the perpetrator's country. This was a novel concept insofar as it provided for international jurisdiction over a government's treatment of its own citizens.[190] Nonetheless the parties ultimately agreed that some version of the concept was necessary and, as a result, international law was again extended by invoking the construction of Western civilization. [191]

Although only twenty-one defendants were tried and eighteen convicted in the initial Nuremberg proceeding,[192] the Tribunal established a significant precedent for the numerous trials of Axis leaders that followed and also became a model for the multilateral enforcement of international law.[193] One of the first resolutions of the UN General Assembly "affirmed the principles of international law recognized by the Charter of the Nuremberg Tribunal and the judgment of the Tribunal,"[194] setting the stage for the creation of a permanent International Criminal Court.[195]

The Nuremberg process is also noteworthy for its highlighting of two themes that have continued to shape international law and, more specifically, the tensions reflected in American exceptionalism since the end of World War II. One was the importance of the global rule of law in the newly emerging world order, law that would be applicable to all. As Justice Jackson had emphasized, the United States was "not prepared to lay down a rule of criminal conduct against others which we would not be willing to have invoked against us."[196] A second theme was the framing of the purposes of not only the tribunal but the war itself as the preservation and expansion of Western civilization, thus setting the stage for the universal application of a body of law framed within the Western worldview.[197]

The Nuremberg prosecutors sharply contrasted their understandings of freedom, democracy, and human rights to Nazi practice, with French prosecutor François de Menthon inverting the history of European colonial encounters and their racialization of the Other by asserting that with Nazi racialism, "We are brought back . . . to the most primitive idea of the savage tribes. All the values of civilization accumulated in the course of centuries are rejected, all traditional ideas of morality, justice, and law give way to the primacy of race. . . . The individual, his liberty, his rights and aspirations, no longer have any real existence of their own."[198] Somewhat ironically, then, the world order that emerged from the defeat of the Nazis was framed as a triumph of Western civilization, and the postwar structures of world governance hailed by Allied leaders as the next stage in the implementation of Western ideals. There still remained, however, the thorny problem of colonialism.

Decolonization

The twentieth century saw a remarkable transformation of political jurisdiction, from its opening years when European powers recognized only a handful of non-European states as sufficiently "civilized" to participate in a proposed world government, to the creation of the United Nations with approximately fifty founding states, to its closing decade in which nearly two hundred independent states were recognized. In 1945 the UN founders anticipated some additional members, but they did not envision a wholesale transformation of colonies or "dependencies" into "civilized states," as illustrated by the instructions given the architects of the UN Headquarters building to create a hall for the General Assembly which could eventually house delegations from seventy countries, a number far short of its current membership.[199] According to the United Nations' "Decolonization Unit," almost one-third of the world's population was "non–self-governing" in 1945, but by 2002 eighty former colonial territories had been recognized as independent.[200] These political changes were accompanied by dramatic transformations of international law and legal institutions in the postwar period. The question to be explored, however, is the extent to which these structural changes reflect continuities or discontinuities in colonial relations.

As the Allies initially formulated their vision of the new world order it was not obvious that colonialism, even in its most explicit forms, would be dismantled. Thus, for example, international law scholar Nathaniel Berman points out that when Germany surrendered on May 8, 1945, the French took to the streets to celebrate the triumph of democracy and "the right to be free men." On the same day, however, when celebrations of the Allied victory in the French colony of Algeria included calls for decolonization, the French military "respond[ed] ferociously and massively. Thousands of Algerians [fell] to urban massacre and rural bombardment."[201] Initially the British and French were adamant about retaining their colonial possessions, while the Americans pushed for a "trusteeship" system, modeled on the League's Mandate System, that would give the United States greater access to the markets and resources of former European colonies, while "lay[ing] hands chastely on the Japanese islands in the Pacific."[202] Ultimately American leaders proposed placing Allied territories in "trust" only with the agreement of their governing power, emphasizing the notion of "self-government" rather than "independence" to ensure British and French support.[203]

The U.S. proposals generally prevailed and the Charter described colonies and mandated areas as "territories whose peoples have not yet attained a full measure of self-government." Reflecting the rhetoric of long-standing U.S. policies toward American Indians, the British conception of its colonial "dual mandate," and the structure of the League of Nations' Mandate System, the UN Charter declared that colonial powers were endowed with "a sacred trust" to promote the political, economic, social and educational well-being of "non–self-governing territories," including a commitment "to develop self-government, to take due account of the political aspirations of the peoples, and to assist them in the progressive development of their free political institutions, according to the particular circumstances of each territory and its peoples and their varying stages of advancement."[204] Only eleven territories were placed under the supervision of the Trusteeship Council, with Palau, "administered" by the United States, the last to be recognized as independent.[205] However, the establishment of the system, in conjunction with the UN's emphasis on the right to self-determination, lent considerable moral, political, and legal currency to the movements for independence that had always existed but developed increasing momentum during the postwar years.[206]

While those drafting the UN Charter had consciously distinguished "self-government" from independence, many colonized nations had contributed troops to the war the Allies claimed was being fought for freedom and democracy, and their peoples had been extensively exposed to both Allied and Axis propaganda denouncing the evils of imperialism. During the subsequent Cold War, Western imperialist powers were also spurred to make concessions to their colonies to counter the aid that the Soviet Union was giving to decolonization movements.[207] The genie of decolonization had been let out of the bottle, and the formal structures of international governance irrevocably changed. Although the United Nations played a significant role in the decolonization process,[208] it must be recognized that neither the UN nor the colonial powers themselves "granted" independence to "dependent" territories; independence was hard won by colonized peoples, and usually only reluctantly acknowledged after the fact by their colonizers.[209] As Argentine journalist Adolfo Gilly observed, in his 1965 introduction to political philosopher Frantz Fanon's *Studies in a Dying Colonialism*, "The whole of humanity has erupted violently, tumultuously onto the state of history, taking its own destiny in its hands. . . . Liberation does not come as a gift from anybody."[210]

In 1960 alone the independence of eighteen African states was acknowledged by the United Nations.[211] By the end of that year the General Assembly had passed its groundbreaking Resolution 1514 on the Granting of Independence to Colonial Countries and Peoples, which stated that colonialism (described as "the subjection of peoples to alien subjugation, domination and exploitation") constituted a denial of fundamental human rights; that all peoples have a right to self-determination; that lack of "political, economic, social or educational preparedness should never serve as a pretext for delaying independence;" that "all armed action or repressive measures . . . directed at dependent peoples" should immediately cease; and that power should be unconditionally transferred to the peoples of non–self-governing territories "in accordance with their freely expressed will and desire."[212] Although the resolution passed by an overwhelming vote of 89 to 0, the U.S. joined the major colonial powers in abstaining, citing concerns about "the maintenance of law and order" if independence were to be granted immediately.[213]

The right to self-determination had been recognized in the UN Charter and was affirmed not only by the 1960 Declaration but also by common Article 1 of the 1966 International Covenants on Civil and Political Rights and on Economic, Social and Cultural Rights, other human rights treaties,[214] and by subsequent decisions of the International Court of Justice.[215] Nonetheless, from the beginning, it was narrowly conceived and effectively limited to conform to Western understandings of international law and human rights. Although the number of new states recognized and admitted to UN membership was dramatic, this did not result in a reconstruction of international law but instead an expansion of its Euroderivative structures to acknowledge the newly independent entities as sufficiently "civilized," in Western terms, to be considered sovereign states. In addition to the issues attending this construction of sovereignty, the legacy of colonialism was reflected in the fact that, for the most part, the new states were defined by territorial boundaries that had been arbitrarily imposed upon them by European powers. [216]

As legal scholar Makau Mutua summarizes, "the right to self-determination was exercised not by the victims of colonization but by their victimizers, the elites who control the international state system."[217] This control is reflected in the two final provisions of the 1960 Declaration, which protected "the national unity and the territorial integrity" of extant states. The day after passing Resolution 1514 the General Assembly, under pressure from the United States and the Soviet Union, passed Resolution 1541, which identified three possible routes to self-government: independence, free association, and integration with an independent state. Although it clarified that the latter two options were only acceptable if freely and voluntarily chosen by the subordinated peoples, this caveat was, for all practical purposes, ignored by the United States in its subsequent incorporation of Hawaiʻi and its continued governance of Puerto Rico and its Pacific "possessions."[218] More significant, it spelled out principles for determining whether a territory should be considered non–self-governing under the UN Charter, including an initial presumption that such territories need to be "geographically separate."[219] This ensured that neither the Indigenous peoples of settler states nor any contiguous territories that had been acquired by force would be subject to scrutiny by the trusteeship council.

A core problem with the paradigm of decolonization established by the United Nations and strongly supported by the United States was its unswerving dedication to transforming colonized territories into states that would assimilate into the international order already constructed by the colonial powers. To the extent that these new states attempted to change extant legal rules or institutions, or contested the "civilizing mission" of international law, they were marginalized. [220] As a result, in the postwar period, colonial structures were replicated in many instances by the new states. As legal scholar Joel Ngugi observes, using the UN's emphasis on territorial integrity and its limited definition of "non–self-governing" people, "the concept of 'internal sovereignty' would be employed by the new states to 'incorporate and assimilate' those whom the classical colonizers had 'forgotten' to 'modernize' . . . . [justifying] the incorporation and assimilation of the communities that remained deeply indigenous after the colonial encounter."[221] Addressing the legacy of colonialism became the problem of the formerly colonized, now relegated to being "less developed" states or "minorities" within developed countries.

With the formation of the United Nations, the structures of world order had been dramatically refashioned to accommodate the new presumptions that all people were or would eventually be full citizens of sovereign states and that international relations and law would be determined by the collaborative efforts of and agreements between those states. Within the space of a few decades the "problem" of colonialism had been defined away, the explicitly imperial world order transformed into a system in which all peoples were to be self-governing and all states formally equal. Although the European states that had been major colonial powers collaborated with the new "superpowers," the United States and the Soviet Union, to maintain military and economic domination in this new world order, international policies and institutions capable of promoting global security, the rule of law, and dramatically improved social well-being now existed. Although the United States had singular influence over the establishment of these institutions, as it gained political, economic, and military "superpower" status in the following decades American leaders were also influential in undermining their potential, invoking the familiar themes of American exceptionalism to consolidate hegemonic power. This dynamic is the subject of the following chapter.

8

The New World Order and
American Hegemony

The peoples of the earth . . . look to the United States as never
before for good will, strength, and wise leadership. . . . [W]e
must embark on a bold new program for making the benefits
of our scientific advances and industrial progress available for
the improvement and growth of underdeveloped areas. . . . All
countries, including our own, will greatly benefit from a constructive program for the better use of the world's human and
natural resources. . . . Slowly but surely we are weaving a world
fabric of international security and growing prosperity.
—President Harry S. Truman, Inaugural Address,
January 20, 1949

The United States is the world's only superpower, combining
preeminent military power, global technological leadership, and
the world's largest economy. Moreover, America stands at the
head of a system of alliances which includes the world's other
leading democratic powers. At present the United States faces
no global rival. America's grand strategy should aim to preserve
and extend this advantageous position as far into the future as
possible.
—Project for a New American Century,
"Rebuilding America's Defenses," September 2000

    The half-century following World War II was an extraordinary
epoch accompanied by tremendous hopes for a world of true peace and security. Structures were created, most notably the United Nations and its related
organizations, with the potential for containing the use of armed force to
limited and collectively agreed upon situations and for furthering the right
of all peoples to self-determination. Economic, social, civil, and political

195

rights and responsibilities were recognized as critical to long-term security and stability, and it appeared that the material effects of centuries of colonial exploitation might be acknowledged and redressed, at least in some measure. In assessing the apparent failure of these institutions to realize this potential, two significant historical trends bear consideration. The first is the transfer of responsibility for addressing the consequences of colonialism from international political organizations such as the UN General Assembly, in which all states—if not all peoples—had a voice, to international financial institutions such as the International Monetary Fund and the World Bank, institutions controlled by an elite group of already powerful countries. The second is the failure of the United States to participate meaningfully in the structures of global governance which it had gone to such lengths to establish and shape, thereby rendering them largely ineffectual.

This chapter begins with the paradigm of "development" that emerged during the second half of the twentieth century, as former colonial powers were pressured to recognize newly independent states as sufficiently "civilized" to participate in international political institutions, and the ways in which this framing served to perpetuate inequities within the global order. It then addresses in some detail the mixed messages the U.S. has sent the international community since the end of World War II by both relying upon and participating in international institutions and multilateral treaties and initiatives, and simultaneously claiming that many aspects of this system should not apply to the U.S. The final section considers whether this approach has succeeded in creating a viable status quo for the world or even the United States, examining some of the indices that need to be accounted for in assessing the success of the structures of world governance and "development" that have been implemented by the Western powers. The chapter concludes with the recognition that even a cursory overview of these contemporary realities suggests the need to take a far more critical approach not only to particular U.S. or multinational policies but also to the ideology underlying American exceptionalism.

The New World Order and Its Doctrine of Development

In his January 1949 Inaugural Address, President Harry Truman described the struggle being waged against communism by Western forces of freedom and democracy and pledged that the United States would continue its "unfaltering support" for the United Nations, maintain programs for "world economic recovery," "strengthen freedom-loving nations against the dangers of aggression" through collective security agreements, and make "our scientific advances and industrial progress available for the improvement and growth of underdeveloped areas."[1] Truman thus inaugurated the "era of development,"[2] simultaneously pushing the issue of poverty to center stage by emphasizing that "more than half the people of the world are living in conditions approaching misery."[3]

Completely erasing the history of colonial exploitation, he described the problem as one that was natural and inevitable to "underdeveloped" areas but capable of being remedied by Western science and technology.[4] This depiction of both the problem and the solution quite accurately summarized the philosophy of modernization and development that would dominate international relations for the next half-century.[5] This framing contained, of course, all the presumptions of the classic colonial model in which the Other lags behind on the inexorable, linear, and universal path of modernization and progress. In 1948 the World Bank began quantifying development in strictly monetary terms, equating per capita income with "underdevelopment" and disempowering alternative understandings of social well-being or internally generated, culturally rooted methods of ensuring collective survival.[6]

This approach began to be institutionalized in 1960 when, at President John F. Kennedy's request, the UN General Assembly announced the first Development Decade. The program's goal was for each "underdeveloped" country to achieve at least 5 percent annual growth in national income by the end of the decade, aided by contributions of capital and aid of approximately 1 percent of the national income of each "developed" country.[7] The first decade's goals were not met, but rather than questioning the project itself, the UN simply gave the three subsequent "development decades" somewhat less ambitious goals.[8] Even when the United Nations Educational, Scientific and Cultural Organization (UNESCO) decided that "endogenous development" was the solution, it presumed that economic growth was necessarily the goal rather than recognizing that, in the words of Mexican scholar Gustavo Esteva, "if the impulse is truly endogenous, that is, if the initiatives really come out of the diverse cultures and their different systems of values, nothing would lead us to believe that from these would necessarily arise development—no matter how it is defined—or even an impulse leading in that direction."[9]

Having thus defined the problem as one of poverty, and the solution as development, the focus of international institutions now turned to control over the economic resources.

Contesting Control over Economic Resources

The paradigm that emerged in the postwar decades not only presumed "development" as a universal goal but attempted to erase the role played by the international institutions of imperialism in the impoverishment or "underdevelopment" of colonized peoples. The "progress" of former colonies was to be measured strictly in Western economic terms, yet the extent to which they had been stripped of their wealth (as measured in the same terms) was disregarded; similarly ignored was the extent to which the Western powers had relied upon the exploitation of the resources of these colonies for their own development.[10] It was as if the historical slate had been wiped clean at the moment the former colonies were recognized as new states; they were now simply "backward" or "less developed," and those who had become powerful at their expense would create institutions to "aid" in their development.[11]

The historical record had been erased, that is, except to the extent that the colonial powers insisted that new states abide by the leases and concession agreements entered into, often under duress, prior to their independence.[12] The 1941 Atlantic Charter had described a world order in which all states would have equal access "to the trade, and to the raw materials of the world," thus "characteriz[ing] the resources of the mandate territories as somehow belonging to humanity as a whole."[13] Former colonies would be recognized as legitimate states only if they agreed to abide by established international law. This was, of course, the law that had legitimated the appropriation of their resources and now, under its doctrine of state succession, insisted that they comply with agreements entered into by their former colonial rulers. Nationalization of resources was permissible only upon payment of "just" compensation, determined by standards established when colonized territories had no say in the legal system.[14]

The newly independent states recognized that their ability to survive and prosper depended on controlling their own resources. They used their power in the General Assembly to contest what they perceived as predatory legal rules, ensuring that the General Assembly's 1960 Resolution 1514 on Decolonization "affirmed" that "peoples may . . . freely dispose of their natural wealth and resources."[15] A 1962 resolution declared that the "right of peoples and nations to permanent sovereignty over their natural wealth must be exercised in the interest of their national development and the well-being of the people concerned."[16] Its provision for nationalization was ambiguous, however, providing that "appropriate compensation" was to be paid "in accordance with the rules in force in the State taking such measures in the exercise of its sovereignty and in accordance with international law," the latter phrase having been insisted upon by the United States and Britain.[17] Just as American Indians had been deemed sovereign enough to alienate their lands through treaties, but not sovereign enough to insist that the United States adhere to those treaties,[18] the colonies becoming independent in the post–World War II era had not been recognized as sovereign enough to prevent colonial occupation and expropriation but were now deemed to have had just enough sovereignty to have alienated their natural resources.[19]

In the early 1970s a number of Third World leaders associated with the "Non-Aligned Movement" attempted to rectify this contradiction by launching a New International Economic Order (NIEO).[20] They succeeded in getting the General Assembly to declare the existence of the NIEO and to pass a related program of action and a Charter of Economic Rights and Duties of States.[21] Among other things, the Charter removed reference to international standards of compensation for the nationalization of foreign property, providing instead that in the absence of other agreement, national law would be applied.[22] The United States was one of just six states voting against the Charter, which otherwise received overwhelming support in the General Assembly, particularly among smaller and newly recognized countries.[23]

The world's most economically powerful countries refused to acknowledge that this attempt to restructure economic relations between the "developed" and "developing" areas—often termed North and South—had any binding effect. The United States and its allies relied upon the international law previously developed by the exclusive club of "civilized" states to argue that developing countries could not be treated more preferentially than developed ones, that the NIEO Charter's concept of collective economic security was without legal basis, and that settled law required full and prompt compensation for foreign property that was nationalized. Further, they maintained that nonbinding resolutions of the General Assembly could not change customary law without their consent.[24]

As Antony Anghie explains, however, the Northern states went beyond enforcing extant law to develop new rules intended to undermine attempts by recently recognized states to exercise sovereignty over their natural resources. Traditionally contracts with private entities had been governed by the laws of the country in which they were doing business.[25] In the mid-1970s, as disputes arose over oil contracts with Arab states, international arbitral tribunals began announcing a "new" international law of contracts privileging Western notions of private property. This law essentially gave the private corporations doing business in "foreign" countries a quasi-sovereign status by declaring that the agreements they had entered into were not simply contracts subject to the host country's domestic law but, instead, international agreements subject to an amalgamation of private contract law and international law governing treaties.[26]

In many respects this legal shift represented the importation of the construct of civilization into contemporary economic policies and institutions, as illustrated not only by the development of the new international commercial law but also by the evolution of the international financial institutions that have come to dominate relations between the global North and South. By the late 1970s, the global economic growth that had been promised since the end of World War II had not materialized, the most powerful states had successfully blocked any fundamental legal or structural change that might have at least narrowed the gap between the richest and poorest states, and, with the debt crisis of the 1980s, "many Third World governments were now pleading for sufficient funds to stay afloat rather than demanding economic and political concessions."[27] At this point effective control over development shifted away from the political venues of UN organs to the financial institutions conceived at the United Nations Monetary and Financial Conference held at Bretton Woods, New Hampshire, in 1944, and revitalized in the mid-1970s.[28]

The Expanding Influence of International Financial Institutions

The most significant of the Bretton Woods institutions were the International Monetary Fund (IMF) and the International Bank for Reconstruction and Development (IBRD), also known as the World Bank. The IMF had been established to encourage global economic growth and trade by stabilizing currency exchange rates and providing short-term financing;[29] the World Bank was to facilitate economic rebuilding in Europe after World War II by providing the capital needed for reconstruction, relief, and economic recovery.[30] Shortly after the war the United States implemented its "Marshall Plan" for financing European reconstruction, leaving the IBRD to focus on the "less developed" countries.[31] Because the IBRD was designed to make long-term loans at near-market rates for which the poorest countries failed to qualify, in 1960 the International Development Association (IDA) and various regional development banks were created to provide "soft loans" at lower rates.[32] A third Bretton Woods institution, the proposed International Trade Organization, did not materialize, although attempts to create it did result in the General Agreement on Tariffs and Trade (GATT) which eventually led to the creation of the World Trade Organization.[33]

The transfer of "development" functions from UN organs to the IMF and the World Bank signaled a significant shift in political as well as economic power. The United Nations, with its commitment to the equality of states and its "one nation, one vote" policy, is formally structured as a democratic institution. Although most states are members of the IMF and the World Bank, these entities lack democratic constraints, as their voting power is determined by the member state's contribution or capital subscription which, in turn, depends on the country's relative economic size—a structure that was unsuccessfully challenged by the UN General Assembly.[34] When the IMF and IBRD were established, the U.S. controlled about one-third of the voting power in each,[35] and although this share has dropped to about 17 percent,[36] the United States effectively has veto power over any policy changes, for the Articles of Agreement of either organization can only be changed by agreement of three-fifths of the members, who must collectively control 85 percent of the voting power.[37] Unlike most treaty-based international institutions, each organization preserves the right to interpret its Articles of Agreement without appeal to any outside court, tribunal, or arbitral process.[38]

This very rigid governance structure of the world's primary financial institutions was justified initially on the grounds that they were to be involved only in economic, not political, activity. Thus, for example, the charter of the IBRD, which is almost identical to that of the IDA, provides that loans are to be granted with "due attention to considerations of economy and efficiency and without regard to political or other non-economic influences or considerations," and that the Bank is not to "interfere in the political affairs of any member" nor "be influenced in their decisions by the political character" of the member(s).[39] Lending decisions have, however, always been politicized. During the 1960s the World Bank invoked the prohibition on political involvement to ignore UN resolutions requesting that it refrain from making loans to South Africa and Portugal because of their policies of apartheid and continued colonialism,[40] but during this same period loans were used strategically to support regimes perceived to be anticommunist. Thus, for example, Nicaragua received ten loans during the 1950s when its government worked closely with the U.S. military, whereas Guatemala, which had a much larger population, received none at all until its supposedly communist leaders were ousted.[41]

Over the next several decades IMF and World Bank policies and practices began to overlap as they focused increasingly on "less developed" countries unable to obtain loans from more conventional sources.[42] Simultaneously both institutions began to impose conditions on borrower states reminiscent of those employed by the Mandate System to require economic and, eventually, social and political restructuring. In the mid-1970s the IMF began making medium-term loans to poorer countries, and by the 1980s it was lending almost exclusively to Third World states.[43] By then the Bank, which had previously concentrated on project-specific, long-term loans, was also offering medium-term "structural adjustment" loans conditioned on the implementation of changes purportedly necessary to address the underlying causes of the recipient state's economic deficit.[44] These conditions often entailed devastating cutbacks in government spending, and therefore in health, education, employment, and welfare programs.[45]

Even though the loan programs of the international financial institutions have been no more successful than the "development decades" of the United Nations in eliminating malnutrition and unemployment or otherwise closing the gap between "developed" and "developing" countries, their power has continued to grow. In fact, the failure of IMF and World Bank policies to achieve their stated goals has been used to extend their influence more intrusively into all sectors of society.[46] Their working definition of "economic considerations" has grown to include political and social factors, and now incorporates assessments of environmental policies, human rights, and "governance."[47] Law professor and former IMF counsel John Head notes that "today it is common to find these institutions requiring their borrowing member countries to accept and adhere to prescribed policies on environmental protection, indigenous peoples, involuntary resettlement, governance, corruption, public participation, the role of women in development, and poverty reduction."[48] As a result of "mission creep," he concludes that the multilateral development banks "should be regarded as having been transformed from financial institutions into regulatory agencies."[49] This regulatory function is particularly significant because, by the end of the twentieth century, two-thirds of all states, representing about half the world's population, were indebted to international financial institutions.[50]

By the 1990s the World Bank, IMF, and their regional variants were framing their development policies in terms of "democratization" and "good governance," based on the theory that deficiencies in these areas—rather than, say, neocolonialism and its attendant economic exploitation—were the cause of underdevelopment. The failure of the previous decades' development initiatives to reduce poverty or improve living conditions did not lead to questioning of the project, or to structural adjustment of the international economic system itself, but rather to intensified efforts to "modernize" the global South.[51] In many ways the development paradigm currently shaping international political and economic policy can be understood as an extension of the mandate system in which colonized territories could only hope to be recognized as independent by allowing intense micro-management of their social and political institutions by the Western mandatories.[52] Although now formally recognized as self-governing, these newer states (much like American Indian nations) can often survive only by surrendering any real sovereignty they might have to the institutions that control their economic survival and, often, their political leadership.[53] The alternative, in many cases, is to be deemed a "failed state," susceptible to political and military, as well as financial, intervention.[54]

Human Rights and Development

The institutional focus on good governance has merged into—and exercises considerable influence over—the international human rights law that took center stage in the era immediately following World War II. The contemporary "age of rights," as Louis Henkin has termed it,[55] can be traced, in some respects, to the Nuremberg Tribunal with its articulation of "crimes against humanity" and its insistence that certain critical human rights can and will be enforced by the international community, regardless of a state's domestic laws.[56] More fundamental, as the world was shifting away from an explicitly colonial order, the liberatory potential of decolonization was channeled into what now falls under the rubric of human rights, and it was incumbent upon the former colonial powers to respond to the reality that much of the decolonization movement was framed in terms of civil and political rights, social and racial equality, access to education and health care and, most important, the right to self-determination.[57]

From the beginning, the form and substance of the rights at issue have been contested, with the industrialized, capitalist states of the First World emphasizing civil and political rights, and the Second World of purportedly communist or socialist states arguing for the primacy of economic and social rights.[58] More significant than the particular rights at issue, however, has been the struggle over the framework itself. During the Cold War both sides claimed to support self-determination for the Third World,[59] but each emphasized that the rights at issue were those "granted" to peoples by the centralized power of the modern state. Neither the statist model nor the construct of development were challenged by the great powers, leaving "self-determination" a hollow promise, especially for the Indigenous peoples of the "Fourth World."[60]

For formerly—and still—colonized peoples, the human rights framework has succeeded in shifting the terms of the discourse and occasionally improving their conditions of life in limited ways. Human rights advocates of the 1970s emphasized that all peoples had not only "needs" but "rights," and that development programs which focused solely on economic indices were inadequate.[61] As noted above, it is now undisputed that at least in theory "all peoples have the right to self-determination."[62] Treaties prohibit genocide, slavery, apartheid, and torture, and these principles have come to be accepted as *jus cogens* or preemptory norms of customary international law.[63] It is recognized that all persons are entitled to fundamental human rights "without discrimination of any kind, such as race, colour, sex, language, religion, political or other opinion, national or social origin, property, birth or status."[64] Multilateral conventions protect the rights of women, children, and racial and ethnic groups,[65] and more specific treaty regimes have been or are being developed to protect the rights of immigrants, stateless persons, and prisoners, and to prohibit disappearances, sex trafficking, and the use of child soldiers.[66] And after a quarter-century of pressure from a broad alliance of Indigenous groups, in September 2007 the UN General Assembly finally approved the Declaration on the Rights of Indigenous Peoples.[67]

Yet one only has to read the daily paper to know that this rapidly evolving body of law and the organizations that monitor, enforce, and promote it have not eliminated widespread and persistent violations of human rights. Nonetheless the expectations of much of the world's people have changed dramatically, and the visions articulated through international institutions contain a liberatory potential that had been denied, at least to non-European peoples, in the explicitly colonial world order that prevailed a few decades ago. Under the mantle of "human rights," however, the battles continue between those who frame these rights within a trajectory of human progress represented by Western civilization, and those who would use the space created by expanded understandings of human rights to contest the linear, Euroderivative model of "modernization" and "development" that is thrust upon them.

Human rights are purportedly integrated into the programs of the international financial institutions, but because economic development is presumed to require a "free market" and the sacrifice of current benefits for long-term gain, those in the "less developed" world are informed that some hardships must be accepted in the interest of their future economic and social well-being.[68] Thus these institutions tend to follow the United States' lead in emphasizing what are sometimes termed "negative" rights—for example, the right of individuals to be free from undue interference in either their personal liberties or their property rights; "rights" as envisioned in this context certainly do not extend to social movements that seek to implement visions at odds with neoliberal Western understandings of political democracy or market economies.[69]

Given the United States' predominating influence in both UN organizations and international financial institutions, and its recently acquired status of the world's sole remaining superpower, it is not surprising that both the framework of rights emphasized in major human rights treaties and the rights considered essential to "development" are those "core" civil and political rights long recognized in Angloamerican jurisprudence. As Makau Mutua notes, both the Universal Declaration of Human Rights and the International Covenant on Civil and Political Rights—where these rights are most prominently articulated—are considered universally applicable, but in fact they are "derived from bodies of domestic jurisprudence developed over several centuries in the West" and represent "attempts to universalize civil and political rights accepted or aspired to in Western democracies."[70]

This emphasis has led many in the global South and, in particular, many Indigenous peoples to view the contemporary human rights regime as a "Trojan horse," to borrow the phrasing of Gustavo Esteva and Madhu Suri Prakash, designed to impose Western cultural and political values upon their societies, thereby denying them the opportunity for meaningful exercise of their rights to self-determination.[71] These issues are embedded in most contemporary debates over the appropriate role of international law and institutions, bringing to a head the tensions between those peoples who have been excluded from, or colonized by, the international legal system for centuries and those who have molded its laws and institutions in the name of expanding "civilization." This sets the stage for a discussion of American exceptionalism in the contemporary era, where U.S. foreign policy has been framed in terms of its support for democracy and the rule of law.

Mixed Messages: American Unilateralism and Multilateralism in Tension

In 1950 a highly influential report to the National Security Council commonly known as NSC 68 stated that the United States' "overall policy at the present time may be described as one designed to foster a world environment in which the American system can survive and flourish. It therefore rejects the concept of isolation and affirms the necessity of our positive participation in the world community." It continued by noting that it was this goal which "gave rise to our vigorous sponsorship of the United Nations."[72] Since that time, however, the United States has developed a reputation, even among its allies, for acting unilaterally, and often hypocritically, with respect to international law, a reality it was forced to confront rather abruptly in 2001 when it lost its seat on the UN Human Rights Commission for the first time since 1947.[73] Even as American leaders have continued to emphasize the importance of bringing democracy and the rule of law to all peoples, they have exempted the United States quite regularly from the international legal regimes they played an instrumental role in creating. Thus, for example, U.S. officials have repudiated the International Criminal Court; announced a new doctrine of "preemptive" war which, to all appearances, violates the UN Charter;[74] and opined that the Geneva Conventions are "obsolete" and can be considered optional.[75] Since the attacks of September 11, 2001, U.S. officials have "disappeared" and arbitrarily detained U.S. citizens, permanent residents, and foreign nationals alike in violation of American obligations under both treaties and customary international law, and subjected prisoners to practices condemned internationally and domestically as torture.[76] In light of the dominant role played by the United States in establishing the financial, political, and military structures through which global power is now exercised and international law defined, the question becomes why it would put such effort into creating a legal regime only to reject it in so many respects.

U.S. representatives have cited the exigencies of a newly identified threat of global terrorism to explain away these particular deviations from international law, invoking the familiar argument that extant rules are inadequate to preserve the United States and, more generally, Western civilization from the ravages of barbarism.[77] As many observers pointed out, however, these actions are quite consistent with U.S. practice through much of the twentieth century, when terrorism was not considered a major threat. One could go back, of course, to the efforts of the Wilson administration to shape the terms of the Versailles Treaty and establish the League of Nations, and the Senate's refusal to ratify that treaty, thereby precluding American participation in the League or the Permanent Court of International Justice.[78] In the era following World War II, with the establishment of so many more global institutions and multilateral treaty regimes, the pattern of intense U.S. involvement in the formative stages followed by inconsistent participation in the result has emerged with much greater clarity. This section considers these practices in the arenas of international courts, treaties, and military engagements.

Acceptance and Rejection of International Courts

The International Court of Justice

As noted in chapter 7, as World War II drew to a close the United States lobbied vigorously for the creation of a new international court with compulsory jurisdiction. Having ratified the UN Charter, the United States was, by its terms, a party to the Statute of the International Court of Justice.[79] However, almost immediately moves were made by American officials to limit the Court's jurisdiction over the United States. The ICJ Statute gives the Court jurisdiction over certain disputes involving international law over matters not within the domestic jurisdiction of a state and makes the Court the final arbiter of disagreements concerning its jurisdiction.[80] It further provides that states parties to the Statute may recognize the Court's jurisdiction as compulsory in relation to other states that have made a similar commitment, an option ratified by the U.S. Senate. In so doing, however, the senators added a proviso reserving for the United States the right to decide whether a matter was within its domestic jurisdiction, thereby directly contravening the jurisdictional provision of the Statute and, as Senator Claude Pepper argued, disregarding the principle "fundamental in law that no one can judge his own case."[81] Ultimately, however, this proved to be a moot point, as the United States withdrew its accession to this proviso when it appeared likely to lose a case before the ICJ.

In 1984 Nicaragua filed claims with the ICJ charging the United States with supporting mercenaries (the "contras") engaged in armed attacks intended to overthrow the Nicaraguan government in violation of the UN Charter, the Charter of the Organization of American States, and customary international law.[82] Faced with a case it was likely to lose, the Reagan administration questioned the integrity of the Court, unsuccessfully contesting its jurisdiction and refusing to participate in hearings on the merits of Nicaragua's claims. The United States then withdrew its agreement to submit to the compulsory jurisdiction of the ICJ, but the withdrawal did not take effect before the Court had concluded that the United States had violated international law by financing, supplying, and training the contras and by using its Central Intelligence Agency to mine Nicaraguan waters and attack Nicaraguan ports and oil facilities.[83] Since then, the United States has only acknowledged ICJ jurisdiction on a case-by-case basis.

The International Criminal Court

In addition to being the primary moving force behind the International Court of Justice, American representatives were also key to the establishment of the Nuremberg Tribunals, insisting that the Axis war criminals be tried rather than summarily executed.[84] Anxious to legitimate the principles established at Nuremberg, the UN General Assembly asked its newly appointed International Law Commission to draft an international criminal code and a statute to establish an international criminal court.[85] After fifty years of work, the 1998 Rome Statute of the International Criminal Court (ICC) was signed by the representatives of 120 states; by 2002 it had been ratified by the requisite minimum of 60 states and the ICC officially came into existence.[86] The United States was intimately involved in negotiations at the Rome Conference, intent on ensuring that U.S. consent would be required before U.S. nationals could be prosecuted. This provision was rejected by the drafters, and the United States initially voted against the Rome Statute in 1998 but continued to lobby—unsuccessfully—for special protections. President Bill Clinton finally signed the treaty on December 31, 2000, the last day it remained open for signature, but soon after taking office President George W. Bush "unsigned," thereby clarifying that the United States had no intention of acknowledging the jurisdiction of the criminal court.[87]

As Lynn Sellers Bickley notes, coming upon the heels of U.S. support for the ad hoc criminal tribunals established by the UN with regard to Rwanda and the former Yugoslavia, and its advocacy of a permanent court to prosecute "mass killings, mass rapes and other atrocities," the United States' refusal to become a party to the Rome Statute "represented a stunning setback" for its allies, leaving it "in the company of strange bedfellows with questionable human rights records such as Cuba, Libya, Iraq, China, Qatar, and Israel."[88] Undersecretary of State John Bolton, who was later appointed U.S. Ambassador to the United Nations, illustrated how far the United States had departed from its earlier advocacy of the court when he stated, "Whether the ICC survives and flourishes depends in large measure on the United States. We should therefore ignore it in our official posture, and attempt to isolate it through our diplomacy, in order to prevent it from acquiring any further legitimacy or resources."[89] Subsequently the U.S. began implementing this proposal by passing domestic legislation declaring that no U.S. officials or military personnel would be subject to ICC jurisdiction and negotiating numerous bilateral treaties in which the other states parties agree not to refer any U.S. citizen to the ICC for prosecution.[90]

Summarizing the history of the United States' relationship to international criminal courts, legal scholar John Cerone concludes that the U.S. has "tended to support" these courts "where the U.S. government has (or is perceived by U.S. officials to have) a significant degree of control over the court, or where the possibility of prosecution of U.S. nationals is either expressly precluded or otherwise remote," and that when assured that prosecution of Americans is unlikely, "it will engage in a balancing of interests to determine its level of support or opposition."[91] In analyzing the range of factors that influence U.S. decisions in this context, Cerone notes that two factors underlying American resistance to such courts are a "belief in the superiority of the US justice system, and U.S. governance generally," and a "belief that the U.S., in light of its global pre-eminence, activities and responsibilities, is not similarly situated to other states, and that therefore its agents should not be subject to the same constraints and legal liabilities as those of other states."[92] These, of course, are foundational premises of the ideology of American exceptionalism.

U.S. Participation in Treaty Regimes

The pattern of strong American participation in the drafting of treaties and the creation of international institutions followed by withdrawal from or significant restriction of support for such entities has not been limited to international courts, or to the administrations of Ronald Reagan and George W. Bush. Since World War II the United States has promoted itself as the bastion of human rights while contemporaneously refusing to ratify basic human rights treaties, or doing so subject to numerous reservations, a practice often denounced as hypocritical. The standard American response has often been that it is reasonable to exempt itself from obligations to which it holds others because it has a higher or more evolved domestic legal and political system which provides adequate, even superior, protection of these rights.

The Genocide Convention

The most striking case of the push-pull dynamic of U.S. participation in a human rights treaty regime may be that of the Genocide Convention, a treaty that the UN, upon its establishment, considered a top priority.[93] The term "genocide" was coined by Polish legal scholar Raphael Lemkin in the 1930s to describe the practices engaged in by the Third Reich that went beyond mass murder to the political, economic, social, cultural, and biological destruction of groups defined by race, religion, or other characteristics, and to criminalize "preparatory" acts, including propaganda intended to incite genocide, as well as directly genocidal conduct.[94] Even as Lemkin began drafting the treaty at the request of the UN's Economic and Social Council the United States lobbied to narrow its scope, obtaining, among other concessions, the elimination of "cultural genocide" from its terms in exchange for the limitation of socioeconomic factors deemed problematic by the Soviet Union.[95] Ultimately, largely as a result of U.S. pressure, the convention's definition of genocide was constrained to "any of the following acts committed to destroy, in whole or in part, a national, ethnical, racial, or religious group, as such:

(a) Killing members of the group;
(b) Causing serious bodily or mental harm to members of the group;
(c) Deliberately inflicting on members of the group conditions of life calculated to bring about its physical destruction in whole or in part;
(d) Imposing measures intended to prevent births within the group;
(e) Forcibly transferring children of the group to another group."[96]

In addition to genocide itself, the convention made punishable conspiracy, direct and public incitement, and attempts to commit genocide, as well as complicity in genocide.[97]

The Genocide Convention was adopted in December 1948 and entered into force just over two years later.[98] Although President Truman signed the convention in 1949,[99] it was effectively quashed by the Senate Committee on Foreign Relations, which failed to present it to the full Senate for ratification. In 1970, faced with growing criticism of the United States' war in Vietnam, President Richard Nixon resubmitted the Genocide Convention to the Senate, but again it was stalled.[100] The convention's ultimate ratification in 1988—forty years after it was finalized—was conditioned by a package of two reservations, five "understandings," and a declaration which, in the eyes of many legal scholars, were incompatible with the object and purpose of the treaty, and therefore invalid under international law.[101] Why was the United States, which had insisted on the prosecution of Nazi leaders for their crimes against humanity, so reluctant to commit itself to a treaty which, in the words of the International Court of Justice, had been "manifestly adopted for a purely humanitarian and civilizing purpose" and was intended to codify a norm of customary law acknowledged as universally binding?[102] A brief exploration of this question sheds considerable light on subsequent U.S. practice.

During this period there was much talk among elected officials about the need to protect American sovereignty from communist-dominated instruments of world government, a discourse often framed in terms casting the

United States as the world's exemplar of civilization. As Georgia Senator Walter F. George said, "I don't think the peoples of the earth are in any position where they can tell this great people on morals, politics and religion, how they should live. I still feel that we are ahead of them in that respect, and I would hate to bind ourselves."[103] Striking closer to home than the thought of Bolsheviks overrunning the country was the concern that international scrutiny would undermine another significant aspect of the American status quo, its racial hierarchy.[104] As one representative of the American Bar Association (ABA) said during hearings on the Genocide Convention, "I leave it to your imagination as to what would happen . . . if subversive elements should teach minorities that the field of civil rights and laws had been removed to the field of international law."[105]

"Minorities," of course, did not need to be "taught" this lesson. Just as Haudenosaunee leader Deskaheh had attempted to present Iroquois claims to the League of Nations, those targeted by U.S. policies of internal colonialism, genocide, and slavery had always recognized their illegality.[106] The only question was whether the new forum embodied in the United Nations would be available to those who now contested these practices in their twentieth-century forms, including legalized apartheid and widespread lynchings. African American scholar and activist W. E. B. DuBois drafted petitions submitted to the UN by the National Negro Congress and the National Association for the Advancement of Colored People in 1946 and 1947, and in 1951 Paul Robeson and William L. Patterson of the Civil Rights Congress presented a third titled "We Charge Genocide: The Crime of Government Against the Negro People."[107] Although the UN took no action, the petitions proved to be a significant embarrassment to the United States, strengthening resistance in the U.S. to ratification of the Genocide Convention while simultaneously providing momentum to the growing movement for civil rights.[108]

Human Rights Conventions and the Bricker Amendment

Other human rights treaties have faced similar opposition from U.S. lawmakers. Soon after the UN Economic and Social Council was created, it established a Human Rights Commission, initially chaired by Eleanor Roosevelt and charged with drafting a declaration of human rights, a treaty codifying those rights, and a program for their implementation.[109] Its first product was the Universal Declaration of Human Rights, adopted by the General Assembly in 1948. Prior to identifying specific rights it states that "recognition of the inherent dignity and equal and inalienable rights of all members of the human family is the foundation of freedom, justice and peace in the world" and proclaims it "essential, if man is not compelled to have recourse, as a last resort, to rebellion against tyranny and oppression, that human rights should be protected by the rule of law."[110] U.S. leaders generally supported passage of the Declaration, perhaps because they did not believe it to be legally binding, but they were much more resistant to the Covenant on Human Rights which was to codify its principles.[111]

U.S. representatives were successful in getting most of their proposals included in the draft Covenant on Human Rights, but the proposed treaty generated even more anxiety among U.S. lawmakers than the Genocide Convention had. ABA president Frank Holman lobbied tirelessly against the Covenant, citing it as the foundation for a communist-inspired world government that would undermine American freedom.[112] William Fleming wrote articles for the *ABA Journal* claiming that the Covenant would destroy the basic rights of Americans by, among other things, its promotion of "extreme egalitarianism." One of Fleming's arguments illustrates the extent to which American exceptionalism undergirded these debates, allowing its advocates to participate in multilateral initiatives while refusing to be bound by their results: "The efforts of the United States to bestow the blessings of liberty on the world as a whole have boomeranged. The crusading missionary returning home from abroad finds himself converted to the creed of the nonbelievers to whom he was supposed to teach the gospel! What a spectacle, ludicrous and tragic at once."[113]

Although the General Assembly had declared that economic and social rights were "interconnected and interdependent" with civil and political rights, under U.S. pressure the Commission ultimately agreed to split the Covenant into two separate treaties, one addressing civil and political rights, the other economic, social, and cultural rights.[114] Even so, the U.S. took only belated and partial action on these treaties.

Attempting to prevent the U.S. from becoming a party to any human rights treaty, in the early 1950s Ohio Senator John Bricker introduced several proposals to amend the U.S. Constitution. Among other things, his proposed amendments would have required Congress to pass implementing legislation before any treaty provision could be domestically enforced, thus ensuring that no treaty would be considered self-executing under the Supremacy Clause of Article VI. The effect would have been to subordinate treaties to federal law, strengthen states' rights, and transfer significant foreign affairs powers from the executive to the legislature.[115] Ultimately the amendment was defeated, but only after Secretary of State John Foster Dulles promised that the Eisenhower administration would not ask the Senate to ratify any human rights treaty, a policy that was to have a lasting effect on American foreign policy.[116]

Ratifications Contingent on Exceptionalist Reservations

In 1963 President John F. Kennedy sent three treaties to the Senate for ratification: a supplement to the 1926 Slavery Convention, to which the U.S. was already a party; a treaty on the political rights of women; and a convention on the abolition of forced labor. His intent, apparently, was to ease into a reintroduction of the Genocide Convention and the two major human rights covenants.[117] However, none of the treaties was even considered by the Senate until 1967 when it ratified the Supplementary Slavery Convention. The Convention on the Political Rights of Women was not ratified until 1975, and the ILO Convention on the Abolition of Forced Labour in 1991.[118]

As noted above, President Richard Nixon sent the Genocide Convention to the Senate for its advice and consent, where it was debated periodically until finally ratified in 1988.[119] In 1977 President Jimmy Carter signed the American Convention on Human Rights, as well as the International Covenant on Civil and Political Rights (ICCPR) and the International Covenant on Economic, Social and Cultural Rights (ICESCR). The following year these were transmitted to the Senate, along with the International Convention on the Elimination of All Forms of Racial Discrimination (ICERD), which had been signed by President Lyndon Johnson in 1966. Ratification again met with significant resistance, and the Bricker Amendment was reintroduced. Ultimately two of these conventions were ratified, the ICCPR in 1992 and the ICERD in 1994, but, as of 2009, neither the American Convention on Human Rights nor the ICESCR has been ratified. The U.S. has signed and ratified the Conventional Against Torture and Other Cruel, Inhuman or Degrading Treatment or Punishment, but still is not a party to the Convention on the Elimination of All Forms of Discrimination against Women or the Convention on the Rights of the Child. The latter, notably, has been ratified by all UN member states with the exception of the United States and Somalia which, for most of its recent history, has not had an effective government.[120]

Perhaps most significant, all the submissions and ratifications have been accompanied by numerous reservations, declarations, and understandings limiting the reach or interpretation of the treaties. Professor Louis Henkin has summarized the "principles" underlying these qualifications to the United States' commitments as follows:

1. The United States will not undertake any treaty obligation that it will not be able to carry out because it is inconsistent with the United States Constitution.

2. United States adherence to an international human rights treaty should not effect—or promise—change in existing U.S. law or practice.

3. The United States will not submit to the jurisdiction of the International Court of Justice to decide disputes as to the interpretation or application of human rights conventions.

4. Every human rights treaty to which the United States adheres should be subject to a "federalism clause" so that the United States could leave implementation of the convention largely to the states.

5. Every international human rights agreement should be "non-self-executing."[121]

According to Henkin, Senator Bricker may have lost the battle but won the war, for the reservations, understandings, and declarations that now accompany U.S. ratification of any human rights treaty "achieve[d] virtually what the Bricker Amendment sought, and more."[122]

This insistence on qualifying the United States' obligations with respect to human rights law has done much to diminish its reputation internationally. As law professor Johan van der Vyver observes, U.S. policies are perceived as a form of schizophrenia, "fluctuat[ing] between the seemingly contradictory forces of engagement and isolationism," creating a sharp contrast between its domestic constitutionalism and its international relations, in which "the United States belies those very same principles of justice and equity to which it owes the acclaim and the envy of the international human rights community."[123] Although the United States has clearly exempted itself from international human rights regimes, as van der Vyver notes, it nonetheless has participated actively in the drafting of multinational human rights treaties and has enthusiastically promoted and participated in other types of multilateral treaties. Thus "isolationism" does not appear to be the appropriate descriptor of U.S. policy and practice. The United States' approach is perhaps more accurately described in terms of the tension between unilateralism and multilateralism, and its apparently contradictory positions may be reconciled when viewed through the lens of perceived American "interests," as illustrated by its approach to treaties governing economic relations.

Economic Treaties: A Different Path

Consideration of the United States' accession to, or compliance with, human rights agreements could lead one to believe that it is simply unwilling to participate meaningfully in multilateral treaty regimes. With respect to arms limitations treaties and environmental agreements, the U.S. pattern of leveraging its influence in the drafting and negotiation phases, but then refusing to sign or ratify treaties, has been replicated. Thus, for example, the United States played a strong role in negotiations over the Comprehensive Test Ban Treaty and the Kyoto Protocol to the UN Framework Convention on Climate Change and signed the resulting agreements, but it has failed to ratify them.[124] Similarly the U.S. has ratified but done little to comply with the Nuclear Nonproliferation Treaty and the Chemical Weapons Convention, withdrawn from the Anti-Ballistic Missile Treaty, and refused to become a party to the treaty banning anti-personnel mines.[125]

However, in assessing U.S. participation in and compliance with international legal regimes, it is useful to contrast what van der Vyver termed the United States' "schizophrenic" approach to some types of multilateral conventions with its attitudes toward treaties addressing economic issues. The United States' strong endorsement of and participation in these regimes illustrate that it is not averse to multilateral agreements, and that where there is the political will, the process of ratification by the Senate can simply be avoided. As noted above, the U.S. was highly influential in the creation of the World Bank and International Monetary Fund. Since that time, it has participated in the establishment of numerous other multilateral treaty regimes designed to facilitate international trade, finance, and property rights, most notably the 1947 General Agreement on Tariffs and Trade (GATT), which was modified in 1994 by the Marrakesh Agreement Establishing the World Trade Organization (WTO), the General Agreement on Trade in Services, the Agreement on Trade-Related Aspects of Intellectual Property Rights (TRIPS), and a number of related agreements implemented under the "umbrella" of the WTO.[126] During what has been termed the Clinton era of "aggressive multilateralism," the U.S. also advocated for and joined the 1994 North America Free Trade Agreement (NAFTA), which superseded a free-trade agreement with Canada.[127] According to the Office of the U.S. Trade Representative, total trade among the U.S., Canada, and Mexico more than doubled between 1993 and 2002.[128]

In contrast to the long delays that have accompanied the ratification of human rights treaties, as a general rule the United States has rapidly become a party to these economic agreements. As law professor Connie de la Vega points out, one reason for this disparity is that human rights treaties and economic agreements are often implemented through different domestic mechanisms. Whereas human rights conventions, if they are signed at all, are sent to the Senate for ratification, a process has emerged whereby economic or trade-related treaties are adopted by agreement between Congress and the executive. Because such agreements require the approval of a simple majority in Congress, they tend to pass more quickly and are not usually burdened by the reservations, understandings, and declarations that attend Senate ratifications.[129]

There are also significant disparities in the effective domestic enforcement of international commitments. Human rights treaties that have been ratified are often accompanied by declarations that the treaties, or salient articles thereof, will not be considered self-executing.[130] This means that Congress must pass implementing legislation before the courts will enforce the treaties, and often this legislation is either not enacted or includes provisions limiting the effectiveness or enforceability of the treaties in significant ways.[131] On the other hand, treaties entered into through agreements between Congress and the executive are the direct product of legislation, and therefore their enforceability is not subject to further hurdles.

Although this explains the mechanism by which trade or economic agreements have been "fast-tracked" while human rights treaties often linger in limbo, it does not address why these disparate approaches have been adopted. If the United States was actually averse to committing itself to multilateral treaty regimes, it would seem unlikely that a means for avoiding the ratification process would have been developed. Instead, it may be that the United States has promoted international economic regimes because these agreements and institutions have been structured to provide concrete material benefits to the U.S. and other "developed" countries, and because the decision-making processes within these institutions tend to protect the economically powerful.[132] There is, of course, a domestic balance to be struck between the desire of U.S. businesses to access markets globally and to protect them at home. As James Gathii observes:

> In the debate running up to the Trade Act of 2002, this tension was perhaps best demonstrated by the desire to empower the President to enter into new free trade agreements, while at the same time a growing sense that domestic labor and the environment ought to be protected from foreign investors in the United States. Yet, there was a simultaneous desire to ensure that U.S. investors would not have to be encumbered by similar limitations abroad.[133]

Generally, however, the U.S. government has enthusiastically participated in the economic treaty regimes that it has helped institute over the past several decades, a pattern that stands in sharp contrast to its reluctance to comply with human rights, arms limitation, or environmental treaty regimes. If one views the United States' choice to act unilaterally or multilaterally in any given situation as a function of the perceived benefit to relatively immediate American interests, then the contrast in these positions is not so much hypocritical as it is consistent with an agenda that focuses on advancing American hegemony.

U.S. Military Engagements

The history of U.S. military engagements since the end of World War II is far beyond the scope of this chapter, but it bears noting that the U.S. military's direct and indirect use of armed force during this period also reflects the contradictions permeating American attitudes toward international law more generally. During this period the United States has wielded its influence where it could to obtain UN support for its positions, but when it could not get that support it has not hesitated to act in defiance of international opinion. Thus, for example, throughout the Cold War era, the United States voted against dozens of General Assembly resolutions condemning apartheid in southern Africa;[134] vetoed dozens of Security Council resolutions critical of Israel, supporting only those lacking provisions for effective enforcement; and voted against some two hundred General Assembly resolutions supporting Palestinian rights or condemning Israeli actions as illegal.[135] On several occasions, when the United States could obtain UN Security Council resolutions to support its actions—as it did with respect to Korea in 1950 and Kuwait in 1990—it relied on this evidence of multilateral support to justify what were, for the most part, unilateral military ventures.[136]

Until 1990 effective Security Council action was preempted by the exercise of the permanent members' veto powers. The United States obtained UN approval of the "police action"—that is, war—in Korea only because the Soviet Union was boycotting Security Council meetings in an attempt to force UN recognition of the People's Republic of China. Even then, Security Council action was prohibited by the terms of the Charter, but the U.S. managed to get the General Assembly to adopt a "United for Peace" resolution authorizing the deployment of troops in Korea under a unified American command.[137] Throughout the next several decades, the United States engaged in numerous military interventions, generally in the name of fighting communism and almost always unilaterally and in violation of the UN Charter's provisions for the protection of the territorial integrity of states and their right to self-determination.

Thus, for example, in the 1950s Central Intelligence Agency (CIA) operatives were deployed to ensure the overthrow of the Mossadegh government in Iran and install Shah Mohammed Reza Pahlavi;[138] to support a coup in Guatemala replacing democratically elected president Jacobo Arbenz with military leaders more sympathetic to the interests of U.S. corporations;[139] and to coordinate "counterinsurgency" actions from Costa Rica and Cuba to Southeast Asia, Morocco, Egypt, and Lebanon.[140] This was followed in the 1960s with the United States' exacerbation of conflict in the recently independent "Belgian" Congo and the consequent assassination of Patrice Lumumba; the employment of counterinsurgency forces in Peru, Uruguay, and Bolivia; support for military coups d'état in Brazil, the Dominican Republic, Indonesia, and Ghana; attempts to overthrow the government of Fidel Castro in Cuba; and the deployment of U.S. troops in numerous countries.[141]

Similarly, in the 1970s, the U.S. supported attempts to overthrow the democratically elected government of Jose Figueres in Costa Rica, backed Augusto Pinochet's coup and subsequent reign of terror in Chile, as well as the dictatorial regime of Anastasio Somoza in Nicaragua, and intervened in Jamaica to undermine the government of Michael Manley.[142] Using some combination of U.S. troops, CIA operatives, and mercenaries, the U.S. subverted democratic political processes in Zaire, Angola, and the Seychelle Islands, among other locations.[143] During the following decade, similar tactics were used throughout Latin America, perhaps most visibly in Nicaragua and El Salvador, as well as in the direct U.S. invasions of Grenada and Panama.[144] U.S. troops were sent to Lebanon to support an Israeli incursion and to the Sinai to ensure Israel's control of the Gaza Strip. Libyan cities were bombed and a Libyan airliner was shot down by U.S. forces, perhaps provoking the attack on a Pan American Airlines flight over Scotland.[145] CIA and military personnel were also sent to support the *mujahedin* fighting the Soviet Union in Afghanistan, thus strengthening the Taliban forces against whom the United States remains at war at the time of this writing.[146]

The U.S. war in Southeast Asia was its largest and most controversial military engagement during the second half of the twentieth century. Beginning in the early 1950s, with the dispatching of military "advisers" to support French efforts to maintain their colonial regime in Vietnam, the United States engaged in a protracted war to "contain communism" in Asia that would ultimately result in several million deaths in Vietnam, Laos, and Cambodia. Throughout this conflict, the American officials who promoted the U.S. military involvement in Southeast Asia,[147] with its many parallels to earlier U.S. wars to "liberate" or pacify other territories,[148] consistently invoked exceptionalist arguments for what was increasingly accepted as a war being fought in violation of international law.[149] Repeatedly the Vietnam War was justified as an effort to defend freedom and democracy in the face of communist aggression, but the broader notion of bringing "civilization" to Asia was never far behind.[150] Stanley Karnow observes that Americans in Vietnam often "considered it their duty to educate the 'natives'—just as, in their day, French administrators were committed to the *mission civilisatrice*."[151] When this mission met with staunch resistance, a U.S. military officer in Vietnam would explain the devastation of the Ben Tre provincial capital by saying, "It became necessary to destroy the town to save it," just as General Shafter had said in 1899 about the war in the Philippines.[152]

As Neil Sheehan says about this era in U.S. history, "Americans perceived their order as a new and benevolent form of international guidance. . . . Washington wanted native regimes that would act as surrogates for American power. The goal was to achieve the sway over allies and dependencies which every imperial nation needs to work its will in world affairs without the structure of old-fashioned colonialism."[153] While this approach was not particularly successful in Vietnam, it has apparently continued to undergird U.S. foreign policy, with its "benevolent" goals justifying both the self-laudatory and self-exempting aspects of American exceptionalism. As Mary Ellen O'Connell observes:

> Officials in the Reagan Administration . . . applied this [exceptionalist] thinking to international law on the use of force. The belief also appears in the Clinton Administration policies . . . regarding the North Atlantic Treaty Organization (NATO) and its right to use force without [UN] Security Council authorization. American exceptionalism is fully evident on the part of those who proposed invading Iraq in the aftermath of September 11th.[154]

With the end of the Cold War and the apparent extension of U.S. influence across the globe, one can see both unilateral and multilateral approaches to international law as consistent with an approach that places priority on the protection of perceived American interests. During this era the United States promoted and shaped international organizations and norms, generally advocating that all states should comply with the global rule of law, while selectively choosing to exempt itself from those institutions and treaty regimes when it appeared that participation would be detrimental to ensuring American primacy. Viewed through this ideological lens of "America First,"[155] what might otherwise be criticized as hypocrisy or "flip-flopping" was justified by the assertion that U.S. interests are sometimes best served by unilateral action and sometimes by multilateral action, and that, in either case, democracy and freedom were being advanced for humanity as a whole. The following section considers some of the problematic aspects of this claim.

The Contemporary World Order: Reconsidering the Benefits of U.S. Hegemony

The Postwar Vision of Global Peace and Security

What has happened to the vision of worldwide peace and security with which the postwar era began? Has the selective participation of the United States in international institutions and treaty regimes succeeded in furthering its vision not only of American dominance but of global freedom, democracy, and prosperity? As discussed in chapter 7, the dynamics of the Cold War preempted effective constraints on the use of military power by the United Nations, perhaps also averting a third world war through a series of proxy wars and military interventions by the "superpowers." Since the end of the Cold War, wars have been or are being fought in the Persian Gulf, the Balkans, Afghanistan, and Iraq, and armed conflict continues to plague much of the planet. The roots of much of what is termed "intrastate" conflict can be traced to the reality that, in the postwar era, self-determination was limited to the recognition of former colonies as independent states, a recognition contingent upon their acceptance of colonial boundaries. This set the stage for "nationalist" struggles, either for independence or for control of state power within the extant framework of the international legal system.

The extent to which this dynamic has undermined any hope of actual peace or security for the world's peoples in the postwar years was illustrated by cultural geographer Bernard Neitschmann, who found that as of 1993 there were ninety-seven wars between states and the nations over which they were attempting to exercise political control compared to one "state versus state" war and six "nation versus nation" wars.[156] He calculated the average duration of "state versus state" wars waged between 1945 and 1993 as 2.8 years, in contrast to an average of 10.2 years for "state versus nation" wars. Neitschmann also estimated that approximately 36 million refugees were attributable to conflicts between states and nations as of 1993, and that between 1945 and 1993 over 80 percent of all deaths attributable to genocide were the result of state-directed genocides against the peoples of nations.[157]

With President Truman's introduction of the construct in his 1949 Inaugural Address, "development" was identified as the presumptive and inevitable path of human progress, and "underdevelopment" as its "naturally occurring" precondition.[158] This entirely ahistorical framing absolved the colonial powers of responsibility for the effects of centuries of exploitation and precluded recognition that the "development" of the North may have been dependent upon the "underdevelopment" of the South.[159] Rich states assumed no responsibility to compensate former colonies or even to refrain from using their disparate political or economic power in an exploitative manner; poor states did not have even the choice of "opting out" of the global economy but instead were expected to "develop" along a predetermined path with the "assistance" of foreign investment, loans, and occasional infusions of humanitarian aid.

Constrained to operating within the political and economic structures established by the major powers, the hopes and energies that accompanied the wave of the national liberation movements in the 1960s were soon replaced by the realization that "independence" would not be accompanied by significant social restructuring or improvement in economic welfare. Beginning in 1972, international financial institutions shifted their focus to the concept of meeting "basic needs"—needs defined entirely from a Western perspective.[160] Even this proved beyond the capacity of the structures of "development," but it did provide yet another rationale for intervention in the domestic affairs of the states receiving Western "aid."[161] These interventions were intensified by the reintroduction of monetarist policies favoring deregulation and by "structural adjustment" programs introduced in the 1980s, with their requirements that debtor countries eliminate subsidies for local agriculture and industries, and sacrifice social welfare programs in favor of debt service, "free markets," and production for export.[162] The delinking of the dollar from the gold standard allowed the economies of the industrialized North to expand far beyond their productive capacity, but only "debtor" states were subjected to the rigors of the adjustment programs,[163] a double standard that did not pass unnoticed in the wake of the American fiscal collapse of 2008.[164]

Finally, it bears noting that the price paid for a "self-determination" limited to nominal political independence was, to quote Swiss development scholar Gilbert Rist, the loss of "self-definition": "From 1949 onwards, often without realizing it, more than two billion inhabitants of the planet found themselves changing their name, being 'officially' regarded as they appeared in the eyes of others, called upon to deepen their Westernization by repudiating their own values."[165] If one presumes that there is no alternative to the Western model of civilization and development, this may be dismissed as an unfortunate by-product of inevitable progress. However, if the current trajectory of world order is, in fact, unsustainable, this loss of values and identity represents a significant limitation not only of individual options but of the alternatives available to the international community as a whole. Rist concludes his study of the history of the construct of development with the admonition that the "greatest danger we face is a refusal to face reality, be it out of conformity or fear."[166] In that spirit, our assessments of the success and potential of international legal structures must take into account some harsh realities.

Contemporary Global Realities

In June 2008 the *British Medical Journal* reported that approximately 5.4 million people died violently in armed conflict between 1955 and 2002, a figure that did not include related deaths from starvation, disease or injury.[167] According to GlobalSecurity.org, a defense think tank based in Alexandria, Virginia,

> The United Nations defines "major wars" as military conflicts inflicting 1,000 battlefield deaths per year. In 1965 there were 10 major wars under way. The new millennium began with much of the world consumed in armed conflict or cultivating an uncertain peace. As of mid-2005, there were eight major wars under way [down from 15 at the end of 2003], with as many as two dozen "lesser" conflicts ongoing with varying degrees of intensity.[168]

It identifies 206 past wars, all occurring since World War II, and 42 current conflicts as of mid-2008, many of which have lasted for decades, noting that most are intrastate wars in which at least 75 percent of those killed or wounded are civilians.[169] The annual *Conflict Barometer* published by the Heidelberg Institute for International Conflict Resolution documented 328 "political conflicts" in 2007, 6 of which it classified as wars, 25 as severe crises involving massive violence, and 99 as conflicts involving sporadic violence.[170]

The "development" statistics are equally grim. Of the approximately 6 billion people in the world, some 1.1 billion lack access to safe drinking water and 2.6 billion lack basic sanitation, even though household water requirements generally represent less than 5 percent of a country's total water use.[171] The percentage of the population with access to improved sanitation, water, and basic nutrition generally increased between 1990 and 2004, but nonetheless in twenty-two countries classified as "least developed" by the United Nations Development Programme (UNDP), almost two-thirds of the population lacked improved sanitation and were deemed "undernourished."[172] Although the last three decades of the twentieth century saw some improvement in life expectancy, in these countries it had risen only from about forty-five to fifty-three years, and infant mortality in 2005 was almost twenty times higher than it was in high-income countries.[173] According to UN reports, one of every twelve or thirteen children worldwide will die before age five, almost all from preventable causes.[174]

In 2008 the World Bank adjusted its measure of extreme poverty from an income of less than U.S. $1 to less than $1.25 per day, and determined that under this standard there were 1.4 billion people living in extreme poverty.[175] Forty percent of the world's population lives on less than U.S. $2 per day; their income accounts for 5 percent of global income, and the richest 20 percent receive 75 percent of the income.[176] There is a widespread belief—in the United States, at least—that although many people around the world are poor, their living conditions are improving. However, according to the 2003 UNDP human development report, fifty-four countries were poorer than they had been a decade earlier and overall human development, as measured by an amalgam of income, life expectancy, and literacy, fell in twenty-one countries during the 1990s.[177] Its 2007/2008 report notes that "more than 80 percent of the world's population lives in countries where income differentials are widening." Reflecting the presumption that growth rather than redistribution of wealth was to be the solution, it continues, "One consequence is that more growth is needed to achieve an equivalent poverty reduction outcome."[178]

The UNDP also reports that climate change—global warming, in particular—is now "a scientifically established fact" likely to lead to "substantial damage to human well-being and prosperity by the end of this century," even if one were to presume that "the world were a single country, with its citizens all enjoying similar income levels and all exposed more or less to the same effects of climate change."[179] In fact, of course, the projected increase in droughts, devastating storms, and rising sea levels will affect the poorest areas first, and most harshly.[180] Between 2000 and 2004 approximately 262 million people were impacted by "climate disasters," with "over 98 percent of them in the developing world."[181] The immediate effect of such disasters include malnutrition, lack of access to drinking water and basic sanitation, the spread of communicable disease, and all the other problems attending mass displacement of populations. The long-term effects of climate change are likely, of course, to be dramatically more severe.[182]

In the meantime, vast swaths of land have been rendered uninhabitable by the relentless quest for "progress."[183] According to the World Bank, during the twentieth century the planet lost about 20 percent of its forested lands, a loss "concentrated in developing countries, driven by the growing demand for timber and agricultural land."[184] Desertification now affects one-third of the earth's land mass and more than a billion people living in 110 countries.[185] It is estimated that between thirty thousand and fifty thousand species are lost each year, in contrast to "the 'natural' rate of extinction before the advent of the human era, considered to be roughly one species every four years."[186] The World Bank, no less, warns that about 12 percent of the world's bird species, 24 percent of mammal species, and 30 percent of fish species are either in immediate danger of, or vulnerable to, extinction.[187] Human cultures are being eradicated at an even faster pace. As of 2004 there were 204 human languages with "speaker communities" of fewer than ten people, and another 344 languages with fewer than a hundred speakers. At the beginning of the twenty-first century there were approximately 7,000 distinct languages spoken; by the end of the century, it is projected that half these languages will have been lost, along with the cultures, knowledge, and worldviews they hold.[188]

In considering possible responses to the state of the world briefly described in this section, we turn to the United States' assertion that it represents the ideal to be emulated by all other states.

The United States: A Single Sustainable Model?

A premise of the version of American exceptionalism considered throughout this book is that the United States represents Western civilization at its apex, and that the rest of the world is best served by emulating its progress. Two aspects of American "achievements" are generally referenced—the United States' unparalleled economic, political, and military strength, on the one hand, and American "values" and constitutional rights, on the other. In the 1940s Henry Luce extended the notion of America's "manifest destiny" into the postwar era with his description of "America as the dynamic center of ever-widening spheres of enterprise, America as the training center of the skilled servants of mankind, America as the Good Samaritan . . . and America as the powerhouse of the ideals of Freedom and Justice."[189] To paraphrase

Ronald Reagan, how stands this city on the hill? In assessing the appropriateness of the global projection of an American model, it is helpful to consider whether universalization of the American visions and realities is viable or desirable.

Consideration of contemporary realities can begin with acknowledging that the United States has established and maintained its position as the world's military, economic, and political superpower by virtue of controlling a hugely disproportionate share of global wealth and resources. Worldwide, about five hundred billionaires control assets equivalent to those of the bottom half the world's population, and at least half of those billionaires are Americans.[190] American military power is maintained at the cost of about $400 billion per year, an amount exceeding the resources devoted to military strength by all other countries combined.[191] The U.S., with only 5 percent of the world's population, consumes 25 to 30 percent of its natural resources, and creates 25 percent of its pollution.[192] Regardless of how optimistically one projects future economic growth, these numbers on their face undermine the premise that it would be possible for all other countries to replicate the United States' "success," as well as the notion that the world as a whole would be better off if that were possible.

There is an additional problem with this prong of the exceptionalist thesis. Despite the grossly disproportionate control the United States exercises over the world's resources and material wealth, it has not been particularly successful in developing economic, social, or political structures that are sustainable in the long run or that provide adequately for the general welfare. Within the United States, the top 1 percent of the population controls between 33 and 40 percent of the country's wealth and receives more after-tax income than the bottom 40 percent of the population combined.[193] These disparities in both wealth and income have, moreover, grown significantly over the past several decades.[194] The Census Bureau reported that the proportion of Americans living in poverty rose significantly in 2001, and that the income of middle-class households had also fallen. The richest 20 percent of the population received 50 percent of all household income, up from 45 percent in 1985, and the poorest 20 percent received 3.5 percent of the total, down from 4 percent in 1985.[195] Meanwhile the average real annual compensation for the top one hundred U.S. corporate executives rose from forty times the average worker's salary in 1970 to more than one thousand times in 1998.[196]

The result is that those at the bottom of the socioeconomic structure face malnutrition, infant mortality, and unemployment rates equal to those of many "Third World" countries. Thus, for example, according to congressional testimony by Oglala Sioux Tribal President John Yellow Bird Steele in March 2007, on the Pine Ridge reservation in South Dakota life expectancy for men was forty-eight years and for women fifty-two, the unemployment rate was 80 percent, the average annual family income about $3,700, and almost half the population over forty years of age had diabetes.[197] More generally, 30 million people in the U.S. go hungry, 12 million of them children,[198] and an estimated 750,000 Americans are homeless on any given night.[199] The public education system is abysmal, having produced 44 million functionally illiterate adults,[200] and the United States has the poorest public health care system in the industrialized world, leaving about 45 million Americans without health insurance.[201] It would appear that the U.S. has not been able to solve the problems of "underdevelopment" even within its own borders.

While there is much to be said for the "American values" of freedom, democracy, equality, and other constitutional rights in the abstract, the United States falls far short of providing a global model. It is difficult to reconcile the oft-touted virtue of freedom with the fact that as of mid-2007 there were approximately 2.3 million people in American prisons and jails, giving the United States 25 percent of all the world's prisoners and the highest per capita incarceration rate on the planet.[202] With respect to racial equality, people of color in the United States are disproportionately affected by all these issues. One-third to one-half of all young black men in America can expect to be imprisoned before they turn thirty, and although African Americans make up only 13 percent of the population they account for half the prison population.[203] African American and Latino/a poverty rates are about twice the nationwide average,[204] and on many American Indian reservation unemployment rates have ranged from 60 to 90 percent for decades.[205] Although there has been some expansion of constitutional rights over the past several decades, as a result of the so-called wars on crime, drugs, and terrorism, as well as the backlash against many of the gains of the civil rights movement, we have seen significant restrictions of individual rights and liberties during the past generation.[206]

Considering these factors—and the many similar statistics that could be added to this litany—it seems reasonable to conclude that the status quo is neither sustainable from an ecological perspective nor beneficial to the vast majority of the world's peoples, even most Americans. While the post–World War II international order may have developed institutional mechanisms for reducing the potential for mass uprisings or dramatic political change, its stated objectives of achieving a lasting international peace undergirded by improved social and economic conditions have not been met.[207] Viewed from this perspective, is "terrorism" the primary threat to global well-being or a fairly predictable response to increasingly untenable conditions of life? Is the extension of Western civilization through aggressive military action, backed by ever tougher international economic policies, the solution, or an intensification of the problem?

The current American position seems to be one that relies heavily on the statist, or Westphalian, construct to assert the primacy of the United States, yet simultaneously projects both its visions and the institutions it has been instrumental in creating upon the rest of the world.[208] In so doing, U.S. representatives invoke the familiar themes of American exceptionalism that have been the subject of previous chapters: human progress as a unilinear trajectory in which "man" dominates nature through science and technology, Western civilization as the highest stage of human social evolution, and the United States as both the best representative of that civilization and the model for its future development. As noted in previous chapters, national leaders today continue to invoke the exceptionalist imagery of the United States as representing the "shining city upon a hill," that "perfect ideal" of freedom, democracy, and human rights.[209] If this is the story that defines the United States' relationship to international law, its extraordinary influence over international legal institutions, as well as the specific instances in which American officials either insist upon compliance with the rule of law or exempt themselves from its provisions, can be understood not as "bullying" or hypocrisy but as intrinsic to a larger and relatively coherent strategy for preserving the gains of Western civilization and ensuring the progressive advance of humanity.

To the extent one accepts the narrative in these terms, one may disagree with particular U.S. policies or practices, but the underlying premises of American exceptionalism need not be contested. As Andrew Bracevitch puts it,

As long as Americans remain in denial . . . they will continue to fancy that some version of global war offers an antidote to Islamic radicalism. The United States will modernize and enhance its nuclear strike capabilities while professing outrage that others should seek similar capabilities. Americans will treat climate change as a problem to be nickel-and-dimed. They will guzzle imported oil, binge on imported goods, and indulge in imperial dreams. All the while, Washington will issue high-minded proclamations testifying to the approaching triumph of democracy everywhere and forever.[210]

If, however, one sees extant problems of global instability—ongoing wars, ecological disintegration, and the growing disparities in income or social well-being—as incapable of being resolved by the current international regime, perhaps even as caused by the policies and practices of "civilized" states, a different story will have to be told, and lived by, that challenges both the contemporary framework of international law and the precepts of American exceptionalism.

9

Confronting American
Exceptionalism

> In a fractured age, when cynicism is god, here is a possible her-
> esy: we live by stories, we also live in them. One way or another
> we are living the stories planted in us early or along the way,
> or we are also living the stories we planted—knowingly or
> unknowingly—in ourselves. We live stories that either give our
> lives meaning or negate it with meaninglessness. If we change
> the stories we live by, quite possibly we change our lives.
> —Ben Okri, *A Way of Being Free*

This book is about the tremendous power of the narrative of American exceptionalism. This narrative presumes that human history is best
understood as a linear progression toward higher stages of civilization, that
Western civilization represents the apex of this history, and that the United
States embodies the best and most advanced stage of Western civilization
and, therefore, human history to date. As discussed in earlier chapters, the
construct of American exceptionalism was invoked to justify the settlement and expansion of English colonies in North America, the creation of
the United States as an independent country, its territorial expansion across
the continent, and the extension of American military and political power
around the globe. In the wake of World War II, as the U.S. has become "an
emergent global empire, the first in the history of the world,"[1] its increasingly
hegemonic power is proffered as evidence of its inherent superiority, its evolutionary "fitness" to remake the world in its image.

The American "creation story," with its framing of origins and purpose,
has remained remarkably consistent over time, rationalizing the superim-
position of the U.S. model onto international economic, political, and legal
systems as well as individual states across the planet. The previous chapters have outlined some of the presumptions, historical origins, and conse-

quences of this ideology, focusing on ways in which the United States has both relied upon and shaped international law while selectively exempting itself from its application with the exceptionalist argument that it represented a higher, more evolved, form of civilization. As the United States' extraordinary influence is exercised over increasingly unified, or "globalized," systems of power in the twenty-first century, a critical analysis of the emerging structures of international governance and the U.S. influence over them is imperative.

The "new paradigm" of international law currently promoted by the United States and acknowledged by many of its allies in the so-called war on terror is not, in fact, a distinct paradigm, for it does not embody fundamental revisions of the premises of the "old" paradigm of law developed by European colonial powers and adapted to accommodate the "decolonization" imperative of the twentieth century. States, as currently recognized, are to remain the primary "actors" in the arenas of international law and politics, while economic power will continue to be channeled through the institutions controlled by the states of the North, particularly the United States. What *is* new may best be characterized as the explicit incorporation of American exceptionalism into international law and structures of governance. Invoking the exigencies of recent changes in unconventional warfare waged by nonstate entities—namely, "global terrorism"—and, more broadly, the discontent manifest by peoples governed by arbitrarily created states incapable of meeting their expectations for improved living conditions, the U.S. has attempted to obtain widespread acquiescence to its "exceptional" power and a less constrained ability to unilaterally change what is accepted as international law.

We can, of course, continue along the current path of intensifying the extension of "Western civilization" and "American values" to the planet, an approach which, while enriching and empowering some, has created, from the perspective of much of the world, more problems than it has solved. As an alternative, this chapter suggests that the current state of the world requires us to reconsider our understandings of "the enemy" posing the greatest danger to human wellbeing, and argues that the decolonization of international law is a necessary prerequisite to a truly sustainable world order. In light of the tremendous influence currently wielded by the United States in the international arena, meaningful change will require challenging the story of American exceptionalism and acknowledging a much broader range of stories reflecting the "pluriverse" of human experience.

Meeting the Enemy
Contextual Considerations

The parameters of the "new paradigm" of international law that many agree is emerging are contested but, given the extraordinary power of the United States, it will be strongly shaped by the "new American internationalism" that was the hallmark of the George W. Bush administration's foreign policy. Accepting the presidential nomination in November 2008, Barack Obama indicated that international relations under his administration may have a kinder, gentler face, but the underlying message was remarkably consistent: you are with us or against us, and America will remain in charge because it represents the highest ideals of Western civilization.[2] In light of the serious problems briefly sketched in the preceding chapter and faced by all peoples today, it is incumbent on us to consider the premises upon which the vision of "American internationalism" relies.

Perhaps the most significant characteristic of the world order that emerged over the past several centuries, and has been consolidated in recent decades, is the extent to which all peoples and lands have been pulled into the orbit of what is commonly called Western civilization. As outlined in chapter 1, the most salient features of this paradigm include its collapsing of all human societies and histories into a universal and linear "story" in which human purpose is equated with "man's" distinction from and domination of nature. In this story there is a linear path of evolutionary development toward more advanced stages of human progress; that progress is measured by "rationality," primarily in terms of scientific and technological advances; and, using these standards, Western civilization represents the capstone of human history. That which embodies Western civilization is most often defined in contrast to what it is *not*—namely, the uncivilized, savage, or barbaric Other.

The premises of the "war on terror" waged by the United States are deeply embedded in this worldview, including as they do the assertions that this is a struggle against "evil"; that evil, or Otherness, is embodied in terrorists and those who support them; that the battle must be waged militarily as well as ideologically; and that, because the enemy is uncivilized, the old rules of engagement have been rendered moot. The bottom line, therefore, is that civilization itself, along with the freedom and democracy it produced, is in danger, and the United States, as the world's foremost representative of Western civilization, is best positioned to lead this war to save civilization and pave the way for collective advance to the next stage of human progress.

Although the ultimate goal is framed in terms of the benefits to humankind as a whole, because of the United States' unique positioning it becomes rational to argue that saving the "American way of life" is critical to the collective project. In turn, this allows the ideology of "America First" to seem reasonable not simply from a selfish perspective but from one that purportedly has the larger interests of humanity at heart. The United States "remain[s] the most prosperous, powerful nation on Earth," President Obama reiterated in his January 2009 Inaugural Address, going on to emphasize that "we will restore science to its rightful place, and wield technology's wonders" to ensure its continued dominance. While outlining a different path from that taken by his predecessor, Obama attempted to reassure the American public that the end he sought was entirely consistent with the familiar and triumphalist narrative of American exceptionalism: "We will not apologize for our way of life, nor will we waver in its defense."[3]

The question is whether—even within the strict confines of a "rational" Western perspective—this approach is supported by contemporary realities. Western science and technology, and the development they have fueled, have brought the planet to the brink of ecological disaster, potentially the sort of disaster from which no one, regardless of wealth, power, or "civilized" status, will be immune. The institutions of world government have failed to prevent military conflicts or deter the creation of weapons capable of increasingly effective human and ecological devastation. The recognition of formerly "backward" or colonized peoples as "independent states" has, in many respects, perpetuated the dynamic of colonialism both by internalizing it within states and by transferring power away from state-based global institutions to military and economic alliances dedicated to maintaining the status quo. The benefits of Western civilization promised to Others in return for their assimilation into its structures—economic development and advances in health care, education, and general social welfare—have not materialized, leaving huge sectors of humanity not only in poverty but without the social systems and community-based institutions that previously ensured their physical and cultural survival.

Is Terrorism the Enemy?

As noted in chapter 1, global terrorism has been defined by U.S. leaders as the primary threat to human civilization, and fighting terrorism is at the heart of their "new paradigm" of international law. As legal scholar Richard Falk reminds us, "The inflammatory use of the word 'terrorism' to associate certain forms of political violence with moral depravity and extreme criminality has had the double effect of repudiating one set of political projects while sanitizing those of adversaries, regardless of the scope and effects of their reliance on violence."[4] An analysis of what should properly be termed terrorism is beyond the parameters of this book, but brief consideration of one example, the evolution of "improvised explosive devices"—often considered the prototypical "terrorist" weapon—illustrates why we need to consider alternative paradigms for the emerging international order.

In *Buda's Wagon: A Brief History of the Car Bomb*, historian and political theorist Mike Davis tells the disturbing story of the rise of the "poor man's air force."[5] After tracing its modern origins to a bomb placed by an Italian anarchist in a horse-drawn wagon on Wall Street in 1920, Davis notes that "the car bomb was not fully conceptualized as a weapon of urban warfare until January 12, 1947, when rightwing Zionist guerrillas, the Stern Gang, drove a truckload of explosives into a British police station in Haifa, Palestine, killing 4 and injuring 140."[6] Used sporadically in the 1960s, notably in Saigon and Algiers, improvised explosive devices reached a new level of destructive capacity in 1970 and 1972, when car bombs utilizing ammonium nitrate were detonated, respectively, by students in Wisconsin protesting U.S. involvement in the war in Vietnam and by the Provisional Irish Republican Army in Belfast. According to Davis,

> Hezbollah's ruthless and brilliant use of car bombs in Lebanon in the 1980s to counter the advanced military technology of the United States and Israel soon emboldened a dozen other groups. . . . Many of the new-generation car bombers were graduates of the sabotage and explosives courses set up by the CIA and Pakistani Inter-Services Intelligence (ISI), with Saudi financing, in the mid-1980s to train *mujahedin* to terrorize the Russians then occupying Kabul. Others learned their skills at training camps sponsored by other governments (India and Iran, especially), or simply cribbed the requisite formulas from explosives manuals in widespread circulation in the United States.[7]

The result, he observes, is "the irreversible globalization of car-bombing know-how"; its most recent resurgence is in Iraq, where the U.S. occupation was met with more than five hundred fatal bombings between 2003 and 2006.[8]

This is but one vignette in the history of the terrorism currently characterized as the primary enemy of "civilization," yet it reminds us of the many factors that must be taken into account in assessing our collective security. Whatever normative judgment one wishes to make about those who employ "irregular" methods to inflict violence on their enemies, they cannot simply be dismissed as "irrational" or "barbaric." It is both rational and predictable that individuals and peoples who see themselves as oppressed will use whatever means are available to them to seek redress of their grievances. The car bomb was a weapon developed by those without access to large-scale military resources, and it was used to counter what were portrayed almost uniformly as political injustices, most often territorial occupation by a hostile power. In response, the more traditional powers provided financing, supplies, and training to counterinsurgency movements—such as the *mujahedin* in Afghanistan—thereby increasing the availability of the technology and often putting it in the hands of those later classified as enemies rather than allies.[9] The result is widely accessible destructive capacity for which there is no "technological fix"; adding armor plating to vehicles or concrete barricades around buildings simply shifts the focus of attacks to "soft" targets, resulting in more civilian casualties.[10] Increasingly frequent and intrusive surveillance and security checkpoints curtail the liberties of the general population and inspire ever more creative responses by those who would circumvent such measures. This creates an entirely predictable downward spiral of attack and counterattack, fear and repression.

Framing terrorism as the primary enemy of all humanity has allowed international visions of a more equitable and sustainable world to be refocused on the creation of an increasingly militarized planet. As Falk puts it, the challenge to the status quo embodied in the "rise of megaterrorism" has "strengthen[ed] the hand of those that insist on an integrated structure of global security, the practical effect of which is to provide a rationale for the reorganization of world order in the form of a post-Westphalian global empire administered by the United States, itself converted into a new hybrid political creature, at once the leading and most sovereignty-oriented territorial state and the nonterritorial overlord of the world."[11] However, just as the focus on terrorism as *the* enemy makes a militarized response seem reasonable, each expansion of unilateral power by the United States fuels "waves of spontaneous opposition,"[12] leaving us with the prospect of "systemic chaos" in Immanuel Wallerstein's words, or "global fascism," to use Richard Falk's phrase.[13]

Looking for Larger Solutions

Considering the current state of the world, it is reasonable to posit that intensification of the approaches which have brought us to this point will not solve the global problems—including but by no means limited to terrorism—documented by various international organizations. If all the "development" programs initiated by UN agencies and international financial institutions such as the IMF and World Bank have resulted in greater gaps between rich and poor, with growing numbers of those in desperate poverty, why initiate yet another "Development Decade" or require more "structural adjustments"? If science and technology have had devastating ecological consequences, why would we rely on those means to resolve the problems they have caused? Why should peoples who have long been deemed Other by the West, and who, prior to their colonization or enslavement, were perfectly clear about their own human worth and dignity, strive to assimilate into Western cultures, relying upon the "rights" to freedom or equality now being proclaimed by those cultures as "universal" values? Why would increasingly repressive governmental measures and the occupation of more peoples' lands reduce the appeal of "self-help" to those with limited access to military resources?[14]

The current framing of "world order" and the potential for change offered within the narrow confines of its Euroderivative paradigm have too many of the hallmarks of the stereotypical image of alchemy: neither the desired end nor the chosen path are interrogated in any meaningful manner; instead, variants of failed strategies are repeated as we are instructed to remain in denial about the consequences, to believe that the resultant toxic by-products or wasted resources, human as well as natural, are simply part of the price of "progress."[15] If one assumes that the existing order is both desirable and sustainable—or that there are no viable alternatives—it may make sense to believe that particular threats to the status quo can be isolated, identified as "the enemy" (i.e., the manifestation of evil that threatens civilization), and destroyed. However, if one sees the status quo as unsustainable, and the ongoing destruction of the natural world, innumerable human societies, and a multiplicity of worldviews as having been caused in significant measure by the advance of Western civilization, "the enemy" takes on a very different shape. Insisting that we, collectively, are on the *only* path to progress, or that there can be only one path, or that "progress" is the ultimate goal, limits our vision and leaves us entrenched in cycles of fear and destruction. Given current global realities and the enormous amounts of human energy and resources going into their maintenance, surely it is worth questioning the presumptions of, and considering alternatives to, the status quo, thereby changing the stories we live by.

Decolonizing International Law

The tremendous influence of European colonization and the expansion of the United States' material wealth and political influence on the current global order—legal, political, and economic—cannot be denied. The point of highlighting these related histories is not to speculate about what might have been had events taken a different course nor to engage in a calculus of redress for historic wrongs. It is, rather, to foster an awareness of the extent to which these histories, and the understandings of the world they embodied, have shaped our current realities and the presumptions we bring to discussions of alternatives to contemporary international legal and political structures.

Legal scholar David Kennedy observes, "International law has seen itself as the voice of civilization, of the center, of the modern, of the future, and of universal humanism and progress against, or in dialog with, the voices of the non-Christian world, the primitive, underdeveloped, non-Western, outlaw world of those who do not yet see things from a high place."[16] Previous chapters have described how the decolonization process of the twentieth century was closely supervised by the colonial powers themselves, and implemented entirely within the framework of international relations they had developed. In other words, both the analysis of the wrongs of colonialism and the means by which they were to be redressed were determined by the perpetrators. In the international legal system, the state-based structures of law and governance initially intended to facilitate relations between "civilized" powers were expanded to incorporate some formerly colonized nations as independent countries, leaving most internally colonized Indigenous peoples as "minorities" within established states. By maintaining control over the mechanisms for the collective imposition of sanctions and the use of force, precluding substantive transformation of international law without their consent, and consolidating significant power within economic institutions, the dominant powers ensured not only that the legacy of colonialism would remain unredressed but that colonial relations would be reproduced in various new forms.[17] The contemporary world order has not been effectively decolonized and, perhaps as a result, faces structural crises of enormous magnitudes.

Recentering Peoples; Decentering States

Substantive decolonization will not be accomplished solely in the realm of law. However, as illustrated by the legal history discussed in chapters 2 and 3, law has always been central to the colonial enterprise, and therefore meaningful decolonization will require a fundamental restructuring of international law and its attendant institutions.[18] In approaching this task, it is helpful to begin with some observations by law professor B. S. Chimni on the work of international lawyers and scholars in India during their first "postcolonial" decades. According to Chimni, Indian scholars "indicted colonial international law for legitimizing the subjugation and oppression of Asian peoples," "emphasized that Asian states were not strangers to the idea of international law" nor culturally incapable of full participation in the international legal system, and developed a strategy of global coalition building to bring about change within, and expansion of, that system.[19]

The benefits of the work undertaken by these scholars, Chimni observes, included the recording of contributions made by Asian peoples to the evolution of law, a more realistic approach to structural changes, and an emphasis on the inclusion of the world's vast majority of Third World peoples. He notes, however, that three basic weaknesses undermined their approach. One was that "the end of colonialism was equated with the end of international relations based on exploitation and violence," with a resulting failure "to see that the structures that had spawned colonialism remained in place."[20] A second was that the adoption of positivist methodology prevented international legal scholars from addressing "the world beyond rules," precluding analyses of how institutions function within historical and political contexts. Finally, Chimni observes that "the first generation of international law scholarship represented the post colonial State as standing above conflicts and classes and the role of the intellectuals was viewed as supporting this State in its nation building tasks."[21] This, he concludes, resulted in a blindness to the violence of the state, an initial neglect of human rights law, an acceptance of lawmaking as the prerogative of government bureaucrats, and exclusion of "consideration of the impact of international legal structures on the lives of ordinary men and women," and therefore the impact of their resistance to the policies and practices imposed by these structures.[22]

Extrapolating from this case study in the decolonization of law, we can posit some new premises from which to begin the reconstruction of our world order. These include, though are not limited to, the recognition that all peoples, not simply the states purporting to represent them, are the rightful subjects of international law; that societies of all different types have rich histories of developing systems to govern their relations with others; that historical context and political effects cannot be detached from legal norms or institutions; and that blindly adopting either the methodologies or structures of the currently hegemonic model will predictably reproduce the relationships upon which it was founded and which it continues to maintain. With this very basic conceptual shift, the claim to universality so central not only to the ideology of Western civilization but also to the contemporary international legal system begins to crumble.

If we take the *all peoples* premise seriously, we see that it refers not simply to the aggregate of individual atomized "units" within the global world order but to *peoples,* with their own multilayered identities, cultures, histories, and worldviews. Gustavo Esteva and Madhu Suri Prakash remind us that "our grassroots experiences continue to teach us that we do not live in a universe, but in a pluriverse; that the universality in the human condition claimed by human rights propagators exists only in their minority worldview."[23] Given the multiplicity of perspectives readily evident to anyone willing to see them, the assertion of any universal Truth requires a concomitant deprecation of the alternatives. Thus, in order for Western civilization to represent the apex of human history, rather than simply one of many possible forms of social organization, it had to define itself in opposition to the Other, for without that Other it could not validate its claims to supremacy.[24] The first step in decolonizing law, therefore, requires suspension of the notion of universality and its concomitant division of humanity into the "civilized" and the Other.

If we understand our surroundings as a pluriverse rather than *the* universe, we can begin to deconstruct the institutions whose purpose is the "globalization" of all humanity, thereby opening up the "space," both literal and conceptual, for a multiplicity of adaptive systems of social organization. This possibility is recognized, at least potentially, in the contemporary notion of self-determination, which, as legal scholar Hurst Hannum reminds us, is in "constant evolution."[25] Hannum chronicles this evolution from the Wilsonian position, which gave "lip service" to national aspirations but included no meaningful right to be free from external domination, to the decolonization phase in which the right of non–self-governing territories to independence was recognized, to a third and contemporary stage in which international law purports to guarantee more extensive human rights but "generally exclud[es] a right to independent statehood."[26] He concludes that "the norm of self-determination in the post-colonial era is both a shield that protects a state (in most cases) from secession and a spear that pierces the governmental veil of sovereignty behind which undemocratic or discriminatory regimes attempt to hide."[27] As this summary illustrates, states are still viewed as the primary "actors" of international law and the goal of national liberation movements is presumed to be statehood. If the liberatory potential of self-determination is to be realized, the sanctity of extant state formations as well as the construct of statehood itself will need to be interrogated.

European states themselves were the product of colonization and conquest, and they used their self-reflective descriptions of what it meant to be a "civilized state" to justify the imposition of colonial regimes upon other parts of the world.[28] The distinctions they drew between those deemed savage or barbarian and those recognized as civilized were critical underpinnings of the international legal order they constructed—one that conditioned rights on state recognition, rationalized conquest with the doctrine of "discovery," and used the "higher purpose" of spreading civilization to justify what were otherwise unconscionable policies.[29]

Thus, for example, as Makau Mutua summarizes, the "'Scramble for Africa,' driven by the need for raw materials and markets for European capitalism and purportedly given 'legal' cover by the 1885 Berlin Conference, was responsible for the imposition of the modern state on Africa."[30] Because in "creating the new states, European powers treated Africa as terra nullius or no-man's land,"[31] the boundaries they drew on their maps had no relationship to the cultural, political, or economic realities of the peoples whom they knew inhabited the lands at issue. The result, of course, was a system in which preexisting nations and communities were both divided between separate colonies and forcibly merged with other peoples. After "independence" the new states were maintained by their internal elites and their "international patrons," their juridical statehood and international legitimacy compensating, in Mutua's terms, for their lack of internal legitimacy.[32] As legal scholar Tayyab Mahmud explains, the transformation of colonial possessions into modern states often

> involved territorial cartographies without regard to cultural, linguistic, historical, or topographical coherence. . . . The resulting postcolonial "contrived state" is often a mockery of the right of self-determination because territory rather than a distinct people become the primary frame of reference of the right. . . . Colonial lineage and the process of territorial demarcation of postcolonial states ensured that internal colonialism became the rule rather than the exception.[33]

Conditioning the right of decolonization on the adoption of colonially imposed state structures and boundaries was therefore not the granting, or recognition, of a right to self-determination but, as Mutua puts it, a process of "legitimiz[ing] the denial of sovereignty to pre-colonial, independent African states and communities."[34]

A predictable result of the imposition of state structures upon colonized territories was the creation of entities that "have more often than not failed to develop into cohesive political units having legitimacy, and have been plagued by separatist movements, civil wars, and seccessions."[35] Having imposed a definition of "success" upon the newly independent states without taking responsibility for ensuring that they had the resources to meet its requirements, much less allowing them to have input into the definition, the powerful states of the North have now declared many of these "failed states," using that label to justify the reimposition of some form of colonial "supervision."[36] Since the early 1990s, proposals have been made for international interventions into states with "governance problems;" proposals that extend and formalize the "good governance" requirements imposed by international development agencies by suggesting that international law be adjusted structurally to accommodate new forms of guardianship or trusteeship over these failed states.[37]

This approach has many problems. It is generally acknowledged that widespread poverty, with its attendant lack of access to basic nutrition, sanitation, housing, health care, and education, underlies the inability of governments to ensure basic security, creating a downward spiral of disintegrating social networks, dysfunctional distribution systems for food and other basic necessities, the rise of predatory crime and private security forces, heightened levels of "ethnic" violence, and a resulting rise in displaced persons and refugees.[38] As law professor Ruth Gordon explains, many Western analysts believe that this is the result of a rush to decolonization (a view that does not necessarily entail acknowledgment that these problems are rooted in the process of colonization itself) and propose some version of international trusteeship as a solution.[39] This would require a redefinition of sovereignty and a repudiation of the principles of self-determination, sovereign equality, and nonintervention so fundamental to contemporary international law.[40] International legal scholar Henry Richardson points out that incorporating the construct of "failed states" into international law in this manner, without addressing the relationship between failures of governance and economic injustice, would effectively "re-legalize" colonialism by reinforcing the authority of Northern states and leading toward "a 'directorate' international order."[41]

The potential for the "failed states" notion to undermine international law, which professors Gordon and Richardson warned of in the mid-1990s, has been manifest not only in the more general ways they predicted but also in the United States' current war on terror. Thus, for example, in attempting to justify the United States' intent not to comply with the Geneva Conventions in the course of its invasion and occupation of Afghanistan, in early 2002 Assistant Attorney General (now federal appellate judge) Jay Bybee wrote a lengthy memorandum to White House and Defense Department attorneys in which he argued that "there are ample grounds for the President to determine that Afghanistan was a failed State, and on that basis to suspend performance of our Geneva III obligations towards it," extending this rationale even to the humanitarian protections generally considered non-derogable.[42] Bybee's argument utilizes the construct of failed states to rationalize U.S. disregard for the rule of law by circling back to the old argument that the law governing "civilized" states need not be applied to those deemed less than fully civilized.

Global institutions could, however, use the need for changes in international law illustrated by the problems of those states described as "failed" or "failing" as an opportunity to acknowledge that the problems of colonialism have not been adequately addressed by contemporary legal institutions. In turn, this acknowledgment could serve as the basis for structural changes that help decolonize the law, rather than reinforcing the disparities of wealth and power that it currently serves to protect.[43] Richardson points out that instead of accepting "the implicit notion among some elites that self-determination is an illicit claim whose proponents are best suppressed in the name of international public order,"[44] we could find in the construct "a duty, specified to those countries of the world community having the sufficient resources, of establishing international transparent process in a declared 'failed' state designed to eliminate, in the short term, all pockets of abject poverty. . . . [And] to support irreversible, locally empowering development process to ensure such poverty would never return."[45]

Or, as Gordon has advocated, we could turn the usual stereotype of the colonial Other "on its head and assume that people are quite capable of governing themselves."[46] She observes that international law, as currently constructed, "focuses on institutions and the privileges and powers of states; the silence of the peoples of these communities, in transforming international law, is deafening."[47] If international legal norms and institutions are to be reconstructed in a truly liberatory fashion there must be room for all voices and a multiplicity of perspectives, and the creation of this space requires stepping back from the fundamental premise that the purpose of international law is to articulate and enforce one universal worldview.[48] In light of this history, as well as the willingness of many contemporary legal scholars to acknowledge that the Westphalian system has outlived its political utility, it seems reasonable to consider solutions that would empower and liberate the peoples and nations upon which state structures have been imposed, rather than limiting our "post-statist" options to the framework created by the most powerful states.

Acknowledging a Pluriverse of Human Values

As discussed in earlier chapters, the legitimacy of the paradigm of Western civilization rests on its claim to be bringing the twin virtues of "development" and "universal rights" to all humanity. From this perspective, challenges to the purportedly Western values of freedom, democracy, and equality are portrayed as attempts to revert to a pre-Enlightenment "stage" of civilization in which societies were ruled by dictators of one sort or another, unconstrained by the need to respect individual rights. On the other hand, the human rights paradigm, like that of development, has been challenged as a "Trojan horse" through which Western powers are attempting to remake all other cultures in their own image.[49]

Even as the rights of peoples to maintain their culture and identity have been recognized,[50] the movement to expand the catalogue of universally agreed-upon rights has gained momentum, leading to debates about the legality and acceptability of particular social practices or legal sanctions such as the death penalty or female genital circumcision (or mutilation, depending on one's perspective).[51] One expects that there are truly universal values common to all peoples, but finding them by exploring the multiverse of actual worldviews and their attendant values is a very different thing from imposing them by fiat.

If international law is to be decolonized the process must be grounded in the perspectives of those who have been colonized and our conceptions of human rights law broadened to recognize the diversity of human perspectives. To begin with, the debates over the "universality" of human rights would be substantially recast—and the resistance generated by the imposition of Western "values" via human rights law significantly alleviated—if states did not exercise almost unlimited power over the peoples and nations within their claimed territorial boundaries. Human rights law has been generated in large measure to counter repressive state action and limit state power, and, as a result, it presumes and, in many ways, reinforces the perceived legitimacy of state structures. The notion of "rights" must also be open to interrogation, if we are to be inclusive of various understandings of human freedom and purpose, and measures of optimal systems of governance. In many cultures, people see themselves as having responsibilities rather than rights—responsibilities to one another, to coming generations, and to the earth itself. From such perspectives, justice may be perceived as the antithesis of what we in the West associate with law. According to social philosopher Robert Vachon, among many traditional Indigenous cultures "it is difficult to understand that rights or entitlements could be homocentrically defined by a human being. That they, furthermore, could be defined by a sovereign state . . . is almost ridiculous."[52]

It is, by definition, impossible to summarize the many understandings of what truly constitutes justice and how "rights" are viewed by different peoples. It is useful, however, to consider a few examples. Some address broad constructs of justice. Esteva and Prakash report that within the "pluriverse" of the sixteen Indian peoples of the Mexican province of Oaxaca, Indigenous traditions of justice have prevailed, even as they have adapted to five centuries of invasions. They quote one Indigenous Oaxacan's observation that Westerners "represent justice with a blindfolded woman. We want her with her eyes well open, to fully appreciate what is happening. Instead of neutrality or impartiality, we want compassion. The person committing a crime needs to be understood, rather than submitted to a trial."[53] Similarly a municipal president in Oaxaca lamented, "I can no longer do what is fair. Every time I try to bring justice to our community, applying our traditional practices to amend wrongdoings, a human rights activist comes to stop me."[54]

Particular "values" such as freedom, or equality, are also contested. Thus, for example, a year after the United States invaded Afghanistan, Sonali Kolhatkar, vice president of the Afghan Women's Mission, contrasted George W. Bush's self-congratulatory statements about having freed Afghan mothers and daughters from the veil with the harsh realities of their daily lives: "What good is an uncovered face if it is starving to death?" she asked.[55] Noting that their most significant problems were starvation, lack of shelter and health care, civil disorder, and ethnic cleansing, Kolhatkar emphasized the priority for women in Afghanistan was not to be freed from the burqa, but "for the U.S. to stop imposing freedom through bombs, stop backing human rights violators and warlords, and stop hindering the security forces from expanding."[56]

Decolonizing human rights discourse means, among other things, asking what "freedom" means and who gets to decide. The United States' 2003 invasion and subsequent occupation of Iraq were named "Operation Iraqi Freedom" and, according to a 2006 White House "fact sheet," Iraq was to be considered "free" upon implementation of a Western-style political democracy in which all sectors of the Iraqi population are represented and the government is secured by police and military forces accountable to the rule of law.[57] For many Iraqis, however, "freedom" is not the term they would use to characterize this invasion and occupation. A study by Iraqi physicians working with epidemiologists at Johns Hopkins University, published in October 2006, estimated that 655,000 more people had died in Iraq since the invasion than would have died had the invasion not occurred,[58] and many sources reported that the civilian death toll had likely exceeded one million by early 2008.[59] According to Human Rights Watch and other organizations, U.S. forces in Iraq failed to curb massive looting of governmental facilities in the aftermath of the invasion, did not guard military arsenals, and disbanded security forces, creating a climate in which theft, car-jackings, kidnappings, and sexual assaults could be committed with impunity.[60] A common complaint was that neither Iraqi civilians nor U.S. soldiers were clearly informed of the rules of engagement, with the result that civilians have been disappeared, detained, and killed, and homes demolished by tank and artillery fire.[61] Some Iraqis like Fatima al-Naddaf, a spokesperson for a women's advocacy organization in Baghdad, consider themselves anything but liberated: "Before, Iraq was under sanctions, but at least it was a free country, not occupied."[62] According to al-Naddaf, the mass detentions of Iraqi men have jeopardized not only their safety but that of women and children, and the incarceration of women has been underreported as well. Similarly sixty-three-year-old Asmaa Ali observes, "now I feel Iraq has become like a big prison."[63]

Such stories illustrate that true self-determination cannot be achieved simply by the imposition, welcomed or not, of independent statehood; instead it must encompass the ability of all peoples to determine the meaning of freedom for themselves. One alternative vision of this construct was presented in author Mari Sandoz's interpretation of Lakota views in her biography of Tesunke Witko, otherwise known as Crazy Horse. Describing treaty talks in which U.S. representatives asked the Lakotas to appoint "one head chief" to negotiate with the federal government, Sandoz says:

> The Indians had held their eagle-wing fans between their faces and the one speaking, not wishing to hear these words. It was not so easy to do this thing that was asked. The Lakotas were not the men to follow like pack mares as it seemed the whites did. Today they might listen to this one, tomorrow to that, or to none at all, for they were free men.[64]

This framing, of course, represents a secondhand understanding of actual Lakota perspectives but nonetheless captures the gulf that can exist between peoples' understandings of both freedom and democratic governance.

Cadwallader Colden, author of the first systematic account in English of Iroquoian social and political life, reported, "The Five [Haudenosaunee] Nations have such absolute Notions of Liberty that they allow of no Kind of Superiority of one over another, and banish all Servitude from their Territories."[65] Similarly, according to the English explorer John Long, "The Iroquois laugh when you talk to them about obedience to kings [because] they cannot reconcile the idea of submission with the dignity of man."[66] As these observations illustrate, for many peoples the version of freedom that the United States has attempted to "bestow" upon them has represented the opposite of freedom, and the attendant civilization promulgated by the U.S. has signified the destruction of all they hold sacred. For similar reasons "progress"—at least when defined as movement up a hierarchy of civilization—is often regarded as inversely correlated with the ability to be truly self-determining.[67]

Articulating alternate visions of human freedom in any comprehensive way, and disentangling them from the many layers of presumptions about history and progress that undergird the master narrative through which contemporary international law defines itself, is a project far beyond the scope of this book. It also would be an inappropriate goal; peoples must be free to tell their own stories on their own terms—a process diametrically opposed to "collecting" worldviews like anthropologically "discovered" artifacts and collapsing them into a master narrative.[68]

Attempts to unleash the liberatory potential of alternative systems of world order need not mean the wholesale destruction of current mechanisms for international consultation and cooperation, but these institutions and procedures must certainly be opened to the wide range of perspectives and histories embodied in the stories of the peoples of the world. Lumbee legal scholar Robert Williams provides one example of the positive effects of opening an international body, the Working Group on Indigenous Peoples, to such stories. Williams explains that the Working Group set aside the usual "screening" mechanisms employed in such venues—determinations of what is considered valid evidence and who has standing to present it—to allow for broader participation. After summarizing just a few of the stories he heard over the course of a decade,[69] Williams concludes that, even within the limits of UN procedures and the statist structures of contemporary international law, this process had a visible impact on the legal institutions through which colonialism continues to function:

> Through such stories told to the Working Group and other international human rights forums . . . indigenous peoples have described the effects of international law's continued adherence to the European doctrine of discovery. Under the exclusive jurisdiction of settler state regimes, indigenous peoples' collective rights as distinct peoples with distinct cultural identities have been denied by settler state governments. The territories they have

traditionally occupied have been invaded and colonized without compensation. Their self-governing autonomy has been systematically destroyed. Their treaties have been declared legal nullities. Such stories told by indigenous peoples for the past decade have raised consciousness in international human rights forums about the continuing genocidal threat of the European doctrine of discovery. . . . And through the power of their stories, indigenous peoples have begun to transform legal thought and doctrine about the rights that matter to them under international law.[70]

Without these stories, it is unlikely that the 2007 Declaration on the Rights of Indigenous Peoples ever would have been passed by the UN General Assembly.

The process was obstructed for more than a quarter-century by resistance from the major settler colonial states, most notably the United States, Canada, Australia, and New Zealand, none of whom voted for the Declaration, but ultimately it did recognize the rights of Indigenous peoples to determine their own identities; to maintain and preserve their own histories, cultures, religions, and systems of health and education; to determine their own political status and, in limited fashion, to exercise political autonomy; to be protected upon their own lands and in controlling their natural resources; to have their treaties recognized and enforced; and to have such redress as is possible for lands and resources taken from them without their free and informed consent.[71] If this much can be accomplished within a system that, quite literally, was created out of, and for the purpose of, exploiting Indigenous peoples, the possibilities for a truly different world order that does not presume the superiority of Western civilization are worth considering.

Breaking out of the unidimensional and highly constricted understanding of rights and freedoms as they have been defined by the purveyors of Western civilization will require nuanced discussions that distinguish between the renunciation of the vision of a grand Eurocentric "march through history" and the notion that one state of affairs cannot be characterized as more desirable than another. As Terry Eagleton warns,

> To argue against History as progressive is not, of course, to claim that there is never any progress at all. . . . [A]nyone who did would be making quite as meta-narrational a claim as someone who thought that history has been steadily on the up since the sack of Rome. But this is different from believing that, say, there is a universal pattern to history characterized by an inexorable growth of productive forces.[72]

Similarly, with respect to the protection of human rights, it is necessary to distinguish arguments against the imposition of one universal set of "rights" from the advocacy of simplistic cultural or moral relativism. As Esteva and Prakash emphasize, "those who have the courage to depart from the Grand March of Human Rights have countless other cultural paths open to them. These cultural alternatives do not entail alliances with the Pinochets, the Pol Pots, the oppressors of Tibet, the Burmese military dictatorship, the propagators of Hindu dowry deaths or Islamic fundamentalism."[73] Pluralism, which acknowledges the significance of deeply held values within particular perspectives or cultures, is in many respects diametrically opposed to relativism, which eviscerates collective values, replacing them with a universe of decontextualized, "free floating" beliefs.[74]

Rather than defining freedom, equality, democracy, and other "values" in terms of rights guaranteed by a system of law "emanat[ing] from the legislative organ of the state, which has the monopoly of legitimate violence to enforce it,"[75] we can consider how they are, and have been, understood by peoples in the many traditions that have been appropriated by and often assimilated into the structures imposed through colonial domination. We can acknowledge the importance of the rule of law—including the rights it purports to guarantee—to the extent we acknowledge the realities of contemporary state power, but we need not concede that the extant balance of political or economic power, or the hegemonic history it would impose upon us, comprises *all* our reality.[76]

Challenging American Exceptionalism

The previous section offered some reflections on the decolonization of international law, a process that will inevitably involve reconsideration of many premises those in the West have come to regard as foundational truths. This book makes no pretense of offering global "solutions" for the crises we face, collectively, in the twenty-first century. Indeed, if the history outlined herein tells us anything, it may be that the search for "universal" answers is misbegotten. Speaking with respect to the deconstruction of development theory, Gilbert Rist says,

> To dwell so much on the Western specificity of the "development" belief would have been rather futile if one were then to claim that one's own conclusions were universal. Respect for cultural diversity, then, prohibits generalizations. There are numerous ways of living a "good life," and it is up

to each society to invent its own. But this in no way justifies the injustices of the present day, when some continue to "develop" while others have to make do with a "happy poverty"—on the false grounds that this corresponds to their particular culture.[77]

Similarly, with respect to international law more generally, it seems clear that we must be receptive to the vast pluriverse of alternative worldviews without falling into a simplistic relativism that precludes addressing concrete injustices.

In an analysis that can be usefully adapted to the problems discussed in this book, Rist proposes three "paths" to address problems resulting from the presumption that human history is inevitably the story of development and growth. The first is to take a rational approach to growth that recognizes the importance of all peoples' living conditions but, rather than relying on the abstract principle of free trade, consciously addresses international inequalities as well as environmental devastation. He summarizes this as "manag[ing] without illusions a system that is known to be perverse."[78] A similar approach to the extant system of international law—one that acknowledges its inherent, historically rooted inequities and "manages" them with an eye to realizing its stated goals of international peace and security, including a genuine right to self-determination—would at least create some space in which the purposes and effects of international law and policies could be more honestly addressed and decisions about the allocation of the system's resources imbued with a higher degree of transparency and accountability.

The second path, which Rist describes as "a wager on the positive aspects of exclusion,"[79] reinforces alternatives developed by "social movements in the South which have stopped expecting everything to come from the good will of those in power, and no longer believe either in aid or in international cooperation."[80] In economic terms, this involves removing the constraints that prevent subordinated communities from becoming self-reliant or reviving their own value systems. From a legal perspective, it could mean rolling back the efforts of states and international institutions to uniformly regulate all aspects of human behavior and social interaction, again providing the space to rediscover and reestablish legal processes whose effectiveness would be measured by the degree to which they result in "justice" as understood by the community at issue. Again, this does not require a retreat into relativism or localized majority rule; each community would still function in relationship to state and international structures, and a balance would have to be worked out as to the role of these larger institutions. However, that could be done, as it were, from the bottom up, with the well-being of all affected peoples as the measure, thus reversing the current trend of ever increasing micro-management of social relations determined by an abstracted and centralized power and enforced by its monopoly on armed force.

Rist's third path involves theory, the development of "strategies of transgression" designed to "extricate thought from the circle of belief."[81] As part of this process he emphasizes the need to step back from our beliefs, to challenge ideas considered self-evident in ordinary discourse, to construct non-hegemonic explanatory models, and to build general understandings of the field (economics in his case, law in ours) that include factors normally considered outside the discipline and that recognize a wide range of historic and cultural realities.[82] As he concludes, "the point is to prepare the ground for post-development—which should not be confused with 'anti-development.' To want to do something different from what has been done so far does not mean doing the opposite." In "preparing the ground" for a reenvisioned and reconstructed system of international law capable of protecting the well-being of all peoples, our "strategies of transgression" must, of course, take into account the ideological and material realities of our time. Given the extraordinary military, economic, and political power currently wielded by the United States, it is unlikely that substantive change can occur without addressing its approach to international law and institutions. This, in turn, means confronting American exceptionalism.

In waging its current war on terror, the U.S. government has taken the position that the new and ever changing threat of global terrorism justifies policies and practices that fail to comply with accepted norms of international law, particularly those governing the use of force and ensuring basic human rights. U.S. representatives have asserted that a new paradigm now governs international law and claim to be implementing a "distinctly American internationalism." While emphasizing the importance of the global rule of law, the U.S. has chosen to exempt itself from many of its particular applications and constraints. In this process, American officials have characterized the opposition as "evil"—embodied in terrorists and rogue states—and argued that established rules of warfare do not apply because this enemy does not behave rationally. More generally, the U.S. claims to be the preeminent representative of Western civilization, waging a war to preserve its most sacred values of freedom and democracy. These values are posited as universally "right and true" and thus, while the United States may appear to be shunning norms and institutions established by the international community, it claims to be doing so for the higher purpose of extending the benefits of civilization to all.[83]

Is the "new internationalism" simply a guise for rejecting the past half-century of international institution building in favor of the exercise of raw power? If so, redress for the injustices wrought by this war on terror could be obtained quite simply by adherence to the rule of law—a straightforward solution, albeit one quite difficult to implement given contemporary political and military realities. While compliance with extant international law would certainly go a long way toward protecting basic human rights and countering allegations of American hypocrisy, I believe that the history discussed thus far illustrates that this proposal, standing alone, is inadequate for two fundamental reasons.

The first goes to the nature of the United States' relationship to international law. U.S. officials are not simply rejecting international law wholesale any more than the "founding fathers" were when declaring their independence from Britain in 1776. Like their predecessors, contemporary American leaders rely upon the international law and legal institutions that justify their control over the lands, peoples, natural resources, and markets which allow them to maintain their hegemonic status. The exceptionalism now being asserted is not fundamentally different from that claimed by the founders when they utilized the colonial law of their era to justify their occupation of North America, but asserted a prerogative to deviate from its strictures for the greater good of bringing Western civilization to a more advanced stage. The claimed need to deviate from otherwise applicable legal standards for the higher purpose of preserving and advancing civilization by combating evil, or savagery, is the same argument proffered by the earliest Crusaders and *conquistadors*, the Puritans in the early American colonies, the settlers and soldiers who slaughtered American Indian peoples, the military forces occupying northern Mexico, and the American general who decided that it might be necessary to exterminate half the Filipino people to bring the benefits of civilization to the other half. The primary distinction is that, in the twenty-first century, American officials are the direct beneficiaries of a century of tremendous U.S. influence over the organizations that articulate and implement this law.

The fundamental premise of American exceptionalism—that it is acceptable and sometimes necessary to violate international law for a "greater good" which can be determined only by American leaders—cannot be successfully countered by the argument that the United States is violating international law. That fact has already been accounted for, explicitly or implicitly. Challenges to the exceptionalist stance will succeed only if they engage the underlying worldview that posits Western civilization as the highest stage of a process of unilinear and inevitable human development, and the American state as its most advanced iteration. Otherwise, one is reduced to accepting the underlying premise and arguing simply that the "greater good" at issue is not sufficiently "good" to justify this or that particular deviation from the rule of law.

The second reason why simply insisting on adherence to international law is inadequate to resolve some of the most fundamental questions of global peace and security, as well as human wellbeing more generally, goes to the nature of the international legal system. As discussed throughout this book, it is an order that was self-consciously designed to accommodate relations between the "civilized" states of Europe and later extended to encompass states recognized by the original members of this "community" as sufficiently assimilated into this system. Although contemporary geopolitical realities must be acknowledged, of course, it is also becoming evident that the political, economic, and military structures created by these states have brought us to a place that is neither just nor sustainable. Simply insisting that the United States "play by the rules" of this international order will not resolve the most fundamental problems that have been generated by that order. This, of course, is the broader project of "decolonizing" international law.

As we are forced to confront the reality that "civilization" may be rapidly rendering the planet uninhabitable,[84] we must rethink the fundamental premises of the deeply embedded notions of manifest destiny, human progress, and American exceptionalism. Few Americans today are willing to justify aggressive wars or genocidal policies on the basis of racial superiority or because "God told us to do it." Such blatant excuses would, one hopes, be quickly dismissed as criminal or pathological. However, when confronted with the history of destruction undertaken in the name of manifest destiny or some variant thereof, many retreat to the "ultimate good" theory in which good is defined in terms of Euroderivative notions of progress, civilization, freedom, and democracy. It is this denial of historical reality that must be confronted in the exceptionalist narrative. The process of decolonizing international law will require addressing many uncomfortable truths, not least of which is that "the enemy" cannot be blithely defined as terrorism or opposition to Western civilization. If we are willing to critically examine and concretely deconstruct the presumptions underlying the contemporary world order, we may find a pluriverse of surviving histories and worldviews that encompass understandings of—perhaps even routes to—freedom and justice long lost to those of us who have been "civilized."

Notes

INTRODUCTION: "A DISTINCTLY AMERICAN INTERNATIONALISM"

1. Obama, Inaugural Address, January 2009.
2. "Obama Acceptance Speech," *The Guardian*; Obama, Inaugural Address.
3. *National Security Strategy*, "Overview of America's International Strategy."
4. See Charter of the United Nations, 1945; Universal Declaration of Human Rights, 1948; Statute of the International Court of Justice, 1945.
5. *National Security Strategy*, Section 1. See also Bush, "A Distinctly American Internationalism"; see also "Bush Outlines Foreign Policy," BBC News. The phrase is said to have been coined by National Security Advisor Condoleeza Rice. See Waller, "Bush Doctrine."
6. See Obama, "The America We Love"; Obama, "The American Moment."
7. Bush, Introduction to *National Security Strategy*.
8. *National Security Strategy*, Section 5.
9. See Henkin, "U.S. Ratification."
10. See generally Bradley, "Unratified Treaties"; Garman, "Children's Human Rights"; Robinson, "Human Rights Challenge"; Cohn, "Resisting Equality"; Henkin, "U.S. Ratification"; Alston, "U.S. Ratification."
11. See Friedman, "Uneasy U.S. Relationship," 213–224.
12. On the ICJ, see van der Vyver, "American Exceptionalism," 784; see generally Chayes, "Nicaragua." On the ICC, see generally van der Vyver, "International Justice"; Franck and Yuhan, "Unilateralism Rampant."
13. See Bisharat, "Sanctions as Genocide," 381.
14. See Saito, *Chinese Exclusion*, 153–200; see generally Paust, *Beyond the Law*; Gassama, "Grotian Moment."
15. See Anghie, *Imperialism, Sovereignty*, 273–309; see generally Barela, "Preemptive or Preventive War."
16 See Stewart, "Military Commissions Act's Inconsistency"; Mayerfeld, "By Our Own Rules"; Gathii, "Torture, Extraterritoriality, Terrorism." See also "U.S. Government Memos," Human Rights First.
17. See generally Sunstein, "Tale of Two Protocols."
18. These subjects are addressed in chapters 3 and 4.
19. The term "American exceptionalism" is defined in this manner because it best captures the particular issues I am addressing. The term has been used in many different ways, and many legal scholars have developed more nuanced and multifaceted

definitions. While these serve other useful purposes, I do not consider it neces-
sary to employ a more complex definition for the purposes of the thesis addressed
in this book. For other approaches, see generally Cleveland, "Foreign Authority,
American Exceptionalism"; Calabresi, "Shining City on a Hill"; Ignatieff, *American
Exceptionalism*; Koh, "On American Exceptionalism"; van der Vyver, "American
Exceptionalism."

20. Taylor, *Nuremberg Trials*, 66 (quoting Jackson). Taylor, of course, was specifically
referring to Germany, but the sentiment applies to any other country.

CHAPTER 1. SAVING CIVILIZATION

1. See Hirschkorn, "9/11 Death Toll."

2. See Cassese, "Terrorism in International Law."

3. Marks, "Branding," 89 (quoting Bush). Marks also quotes Attorney General John
Ashcroft, saying that, "in order to fight and to defeat terrorism the Department of Justice
has added a new paradigm to that of prosecution, and that new priority is the priority of
prevention."

4. Addis, "Autoimmunity Crisis," 325. On the impact of "domestic terrorism" laws, see
generally Scahill, "Domestic Security Enhancement Act"; Saito, "Whose Liberty?" On
the implications for U.S. immigration law and policy, see generally Engle, "Constructing
Good Aliens."

5. "Eurocentric" as used herein refers to that which is reflective of a "conscious or
unconscious process by which Europe and European [or, more recently, Euroamerican]
cultural assumptions are constructed as, or assumed to be, the normal, the natural or
the universal" (Ashcroft, Griffiths, and Tiffin, *Key Concepts*, 90–91; see also Gordon and
Sylvester, "Deconstructing Development," 74).

6. Statement of George W. Bush at the National Cathedral, Washington, D.C., September 14, 2001; quoted in the *National Security Strategy*.

7. Bush, Introduction to the *National Security Strategy*.

8. On the shifting definitions of the enemy, see Hertzbert, "War and Words." On detentions, see generally Cole, *Enemy Aliens*; Fitzpatrick, "Rendition and Transfer."

9. Antony Anghie, for example, focuses on the doctrine of preemptive self-defense, the
concept of rogue states, and the idea of promoting democracy to transform such entities
(*Imperialism, Sovereignty*, 275). In this formulation of precepts, I am indebted to the late
Judge A. Leon Higginbotham Jr.'s "Ten Precepts."

10. "The clever term 'axis of evil' fuses the World War II memory of the Axis powers
to Ronald Reagan's Cold War description of the Soviet Union as the 'Evil Empire'" (May,
"Aftermath," 45).

11. "Excerpted Remarks by the President from Speech at the Graduation Exercises of
the United States Military Academy," West Point, June 1, 2002, in Bush, *We Will Prevail*,
158–163. Of course, this argument can go both ways: "Terrorists may view themselves as
above the prevailing morality, or as possessing a superior morality. The struggle itself is a
moral struggle, in which good and evil are in conflict. . . . The exigencies of their struggle
require them to reject 'normal' standards of behavior" (Cohan, "Political Violence and
Terrorism," 981; citations omitted).

12. "Excerpted Remarks by the President from Speech to Employees at the Federal Bureau of Investigation," September 25, 2001, in Bush, *We Will Prevail*, 22–24.

13. "Excerpted Remarks by the President from Speech at the Department of Defense Service of Remembrance," October 11, 2001, in Bush, *We Will Prevail*, 39–42.

14. Weisberg, *George W. Bushisms*, 48 (quoting speech of January 21, 2000).

15. See Churchill, *Fantasies*, 177–178 (analyzing John Ford's *Stagecoach* and Robert Mulligan's *The Stalking Moon* and observing that the tactic is used to "[build] a tremendous sense of dread long before any Indian is allowed to appear"); see generally Clarens, *Illustrated History*.

16. *National Security Strategy*, Section 3. Cassese defines international terrorism as "a discrete international crime perpetrated in time of peace" which

> (i) is an action normally criminalized in national legal systems; (ii) is transnational in character, i.e. not limited in its action or implications to one country alone; (iii) is carried out for the purpose of coercing a state, or international organization to do or refrain from doing something; (iv) uses for this purpose two possible modalities; either spreading terror among civilians or attacking public or eminent private institutions or their representatives; and (v) is not motivated by personal gain but by ideological or political aspirations. (Cassese, "Terrorism in International Law," 957)

17. *National Security Strategy*, Section 3. For praise of the material support laws, see generally Comerford, "Preventing Terrorism." On the criminalization of financing terrorism, see generally Margulies, "Laws of Unintended Consequences"; Ferrari, "Deep Freeze."

18. Bush, Introduction to *National Security Strategy*.

19. Cole, "Priority of Morality," 1753–1754 (citations omitted).

20. See generally Cryer, "Fine Art of Friendship"; Committee on International Security Affairs, "Legality and Constitutionality."

21. Arend, "Rogue States," 735 ("While almost all states may at times violate international legal rules, a rogue state would be a perennial violator").

22. *National Security Strategy*, Section 5.

23. Ibid.

24. Bush, "Remarks by the President in Photo Opportunity."

25. Quoted in Lobel, "Terrorism and Civil Liberties," 777 (citation omitted).

26. Obama, Inaugural Address.

27. See, e.g., Johnson, *Blowback*, 216–229; Sardar and Davis, *Why Do People*, 193–211; Chomsky, *Hegemony*, 187–216; Churchill, *Roosting Chickens*, 5–37; Scheuer, *Imperial Hubris*, 209–235.

28. On the necessity defense in terrorism cases, see generally Cohan, "Political Violence and Terrorism." On the use of terror tactics by states, including the United States, France, the Soviet Union, and China, see ibid., 926–928; see generally Blum, *Rogue State*.

29. *National Security Strategy*, Section 7.

30. Bush, Introduction to the *National Security Strategy*.

31. *National Security Strategy*, Section 3.

32. Concerning applicable U.S. law, see "Responding to Terrorism," *Harvard Law Review* 1224, no. 60 (describing provisions of 18 U.S.C. §2332b(a)–(b) (2000)). On applicable international law, see Paust, "War and Enemy Status," 327.

33. "More Secure World," *Report to the UN General Assembly*, para. 159.

34. Ibid., esp. paras. 188–192. See also Paust, "Responding Lawfully to Al Qaeda," 762–765.

35. See Cohn, "Human Rights," 318 (describing "the 'shock and awe' military campaign against the Iraqi people, the U.S.'s targeting of the infrastructure, the use by the U.S. of weapons of mass destruction—cluster bombs and depleted uranium—as well as targeted assassinations"). See generally Klein, *Shock Doctrine*.

36. See Virkink and Scheick, "Erosion," 4 ("In many respects, the government's invocation of a military paradigm is a leading cause of the [human rights] abuses documented [by a panel convened by the International Court of Justice]; the language of war serving, above all, as a justification for the use of so-called 'emergency' measures"); Paust, "Addendum" (observing that the U.S. cannot be "at 'war' with an entity that has a status less than that of an insurgent," but that the self-defense provisions of the UN Charter allow for military missions to capture those responsible for armed attacks). See generally Paust, "Use of Armed Force."

37. See Woods and Donovan, "Anticipatory Self-Defense," esp. 494–495. The "madman theory" was invoked by President Richard Nixon in suggesting that the North Vietnamese be pressured into peace negotiations by being led to believe that he might "do anything," even use nuclear weapons, to end the war in Vietnam. See Karnow, *Vietnam*, 582.

38. "Excerpted Remarks by the President from Speech at the Graduation Exercises of the United States Military Academy," West Point, June 1, 2002, in Bush, *We Will Prevail*, 158-163. See also Falk, *Declining World Order*, 189–199, 245–247.

39. In cases of conflicting obligations under other treaties, member states agree that "their obligations under the present Charter shall prevail." Charter of the United Nations, 1945, Art. 103. See also Alvarez, "Hegemonic," 878.

40. See O'Connell, "Myth."

41. Ibid., at 15–18.

42. *National Security Strategy*, Section 3. The rationale is further developed in Section 5.

43. *National Security Strategy*, Section 3.

44. Ibid., Section 5.

45. Ibid.

46. Bush, Introduction to *National Security Strategy*.

47. "Diplomatic historians will long revisit the missed steps that led to the messy start of the Second Gulf War. My view is that a transnational legal process solution—the exercise of multilateral coercive power, led by the United States through the UN mechanism—was available but was tragically bungled" (Koh, "On American Exceptionalism," 1518). See also Anghie, *Imperialism, Sovereignty*, 275–276.

48. Woods and Donovan, "Anticipatory Self-Defense," 495–496.

49. Ibid., 500.

50. Anghie, *Imperialism, Sovereignty*, 278.

51. See Wallach, "Logical Nexus," 549–550 (citing Bush statement of January 18, 2002, and noting that analytical justifications for this position were presented in a memorandum of January 9, 2002, from Assistant Attorney General John Yoo and Special Counsel Robert Delahunty to the General Counsel of the Department of Defense).

52. Gonzales, Memo. See also Wallach, "Logical Nexus," 552. For the full text of related government documents, see generally Jaffer and Singh, *Administration of Torture*; Greenberg and Dratel, *Torture Papers*.

53. See "'United States' Periodic Report," *American Journal of International Law* (noting the committee's conclusions that the United States' indefinite detentions and extrajudically "rendering" of persons to third countries constituted a violation of the Torture Convention); see also Tittemore, "Guantanamo Bay."

54. See Wallach, "Logical Nexus," 546, 599–603. See generally Paust, *Beyond the Law*; Ratner and Ray, *Guantánamo*; Hersh, *Chain of Command*.

55. Article 1 of the Convention Against Torture and Other Cruel, Inhuman or Degrading Treatment or Punishment defines torture as "any act by which severe pain or suffering, whether physical or mental, is intentionally inflicted on a person for such purposes as obtaining from him or a third person information or a confession, punishing him for an act he or a third person has committed or is suspected of having committed, or intimidating or coercing him or a third person, or for any reason based on discrimination of any kind, when such pain or suffering is inflicted by or with the consent or acquiescence of a public official or other person acting in an official capacity."

An August 2002 memorandum of the Department of Justice Office of Legal Counsel limited its definition of torture to actions causing "physical pain . . . equivalent in intensity to the pain accompanying serious physical injury, such as organ failure, impairment of bodily function, or even death" or psychological harm "lasting for months or even years." Further, the torturer would have to have the intent to inflict severe pain, not simply to obtain information. See Goldman, "Trivializing Torture," 3. In December 2004 this was superseded by a memorandum acknowledging that torture violates international law and omitting the narrow definition cited above. However, it was not clear that the administration considered this binding on CIA interrogations. See Drumbl, "Guantánamo," 914–915.

56. See generally Williams, "Your Honor." See also Koh, "Restoring" (noting "extraordinary toll" on the U.S. reputation for compliance with human rights norms).

57. Woods and Donovan, "Anticipatory Self-Defense," 506.

58. Bush, Introduction to *National Security Strategy*.

59. "Excerpted Remarks from Speech to the German Bundestag," May 23, 2002, in Bush, *We Will Prevail*, 156–157.

60. Drinnon, *Facing West*, xviii.

61. Statement of Bradford Berenson, quoted in Virkink and Scheick, "Erosion," at 2.

62. "Excerpted Remarks from Speech to the German Bundestag," May 23, 2002, in Bush, *We Will Prevail*, 156–157.

63. *National Security Strategy*, Section 2.

64. See "Address to a Joint Session of Congress," September 23, 2001, excerpted in Bush, *We Will Prevail*, 14 (noting that "they hate us" because "[t]hey hate our freedoms— our freedom of religion, our freedom of speech, our freedom to vote and assemble and disagree with each other"). Although President Barak Obama's rhetoric has been more tempered than that of his predecessor, in his January 2009 Inaugural Address "he still used the label 'Muslim world,' as if it were homogeneous, and connected it to 'leaders around the globe who seek to sow conflict'" (de Oliveria, "Calling").

65. Anghie, *Imperialism, Sovereignty*, 277. Contesting the U.S. framing in hearings conducted by the International Court of Justice, "ICJ Jurist Hina Jilani asserted that democracy, or its absence, is not the problem. Instead, disenchantment with the conduct of so-called democratic governments poses the greatest threat to the viability of democratic institutions" (Virkink and Scheick, "Erosion," 6).

66. Parry, "Finding a Right," 212 (citations omitted).

67. George W. Bush, "Introduction," *National Security Strategy* (emphasis added).

68. "Excerpted Remarks from Speech at the Graduation Exercises of the United States Military Academy," West Point, June 1, 2002, in Bush, *We Will Prevail*, 162.

69. *National Security Strategy*, Section 1.

70. Ibid., Section 9. See generally Yoo, *War by Other Means*, and Yoo, *Powers of War and Peace* (both providing constitutional rationales for Bush administration policies); Goldsmith, *Terror Presidency* (providing critique of the former Assistant Attorney General who oversaw Bush's Office of Legal Counsel).

71. "West Point Commencement Address," in Bush, *We Will Prevail*, 158–163, quote at 161.

72. Obama, Inaugural Address.

73. Falk, *Declining World Order*, 241.

74. Waswo, *Founding Legend*, 4. See also Durant, *Our Oriental Heritage*, 1–2 (providing a broader definition relating to economic, political, moral, and educational or artistic development).

75. Compact edition of the *Oxford English Dictionary*, 444 (s.v. "civ'tade," "civitas," and "civis").

76. Ibid., 445–446.

77. I use the terms "societies" and "cultures" to represent more diffuse and evolving human groupings, recognizing that these constructs also have been reified in ways that make them vulnerable to critiques similar to the one made herein of "civilization." See Wolf, *People Without History*, 387.

78. Compact edition of the *Oxford English Dictionary*, 448.

79. Fitzpatrick, *Mythology*, 47 (quoting Eliade, *Myth*, 10–11). Fitzpatrick notes that "the mythological city is one form of the powerful symbolism of the centre," a concept that becomes increasingly significant in the construction of colonial empires (ibid., 46).

80. See Smith, *Decolonizing Methodologies*, 20–23 (providing a synopsis of uses of the term "imperialism"). Like Smith, I understand colonialism to be a "more specific expression" of imperialism, and a continuing reality.

81. Ibid., 19.

82. See Waswo, *Founding Legend*, 4–5; see also Roberts, *History of the World*, 24–29.

83. Genesis 1:27–28 (King James Version).

84. Genesis 2:19 (King James Version).

85. See, e.g., Fitzpatrick, *Mythology*, 15 (quoting a creation story of the Riratjingu which identifies the ancestors from whom the people came and attributes to them both "the names of all the creatures" and "our Law"); Torgovnick, *Primitive Passions*, 111–112, quoting Eliade, *Myth* ("Indeed, in certain mystical traditions, 'the fact of giving names or changing them . . . bring about a moral conversion of humanity . . . which characterizes the world fresh from the hand of God.'"); see generally LaDuke, *Recovering the Sacred*.

86. Freire, *Pedagogy of the Oppressed*, chap. 3; see also Smith, *Decolonizing Methodologies*, 157.

87. Deloria, *God is Red*, 82 (citing Cox, *Secular City*, 20).

88. Ibid., 80.

89. Ibid., 81.

90. Waswo, *Founding Legend*, 6. See also Jennings, *Invasion of America*, 74 (noting that until the late 1500s the term "savage" referred equally to plant, animal, and (uncivilized) human life).

91. Fitzpatrick, *Mythology*, 38 (citing Thompson, *Political Forms*, 17).

92. See, e.g., Roberts, *History of the World*, 29 ("The irrationalities of this [twentieth] century show the narrow limits of Man's capacity for conscious control of his destiny. To this extent, he is still determined, still unfree, still a part of nature.").

93. See, e.g., Durant, *Our Oriental Heritage*, 72–78, 98–104; Roberts, *History of the World*, 24–28.

94. See Roberts, *History of the World*, 565–573; Waswo, *Founding Legend*, 186–187.

95. Maragia, "Indigenous Sustainability Paradox," 217–218.

96. Fitzpatrick, *Mythology*, 50.

97. King, *Green Grass*, 40–41.

98. This perspective is distinct from Marxist and capitalist perspectives, both of which define human history in terms of scientific or technological "advances." See, e.g., Fitzpatrick, *Mythology*, 99–100 (noting that Marx, Durkheim, and Weber all contrasted developed societies to traditional ones which, in turn, were essentially primitive); Black Elk, "Observations," 141 ("it seems Marxists are hung up on exactly the same ideas of 'progress' and 'development' that are the guiding motives of those they seek to overthrow"). For a classically Eurocentric capitalist analysis, see generally Rostow, *Stages of Economic Growth*.

99. LaDuke, *Recovering the Sacred*, 15 (quoting San Carlos Apache spiritual leader Franklin Stanley Sr.). See generally Williams, "Large Binocular Telescopes."

100. LaDuke, *Recovering the Sacred*, 21 (quoting George Coyne). See also http://medusa. as.arizona.edu/graham/graham.html (accessed December 15, 2007) (describing the "benefits" of this observatory).

101. See generally United Nations Environment Programme (UNEP), *Outlook*; World Wildlife Fund, *Living Planet Report* (summarizing recent statistics). See also Waswo, *Founding Legend*, 341–343 (describing problems with the UN's methodology, particularly concerning the exclusion of Indigenous peoples).

102. Woods, "Nature's Trust," 245–246 (citations omitted). On the consequences for human health, see ibid., 245; UNEP, *Outlook*, chap. 7.

103. Fitzpatrick, *Mythology*, 93 (also noting that chaos theory appears to an exception to this rule).

104. See generally Wagner, "Congress, Science" (criticizing the U.S. Congress for relying too heavily on scientific and technological solutions to environmental problems). For a cautiously optimistic view on addressing environmental disasters, see generally Gore, *Earth in the Balance*; for a much harsher critique, see generally Jensen, *Endgame*.

105. Obama, Inaugural Address.

106. Roberts, *History of the World*, 3.

107. Ibid.

108. See Fitzpatrick, *Mythology*, ix, 102, 144.

109. Ibid., 44 (quoting Adorno and Horkheimer, *Dialectic of Enlightenment*).

110. Maori scholar Linda Tuhiwai Smith deconstructs imperial history into several core components: that history is a totalizing discourse; that there is a universal history; that it is one large chronology; that it is about development; that it is about a self-actualizing

human subject; that it can be told in one coherent narrative; that it is objective, or factual, and thus the discipline is "innocent"; that it is constructed around binary categories; and that it is patriarchal (Smith, *Decolonizing Methodologies*, 29–32). On the contrast between Western and Indigenous understandings of history, and especially the latter's lack of emphasis on chronology, see also Deloria, *God Is Red*, 98–113.

111. Fitzpatrick, *Mythology*, 92 (quoting Wittgenstein, *Culture and Value*).

112. See generally Wolf, *People Without History*.

113. Trask, *Native Daughter*, 149.

114. Anghie, "Finding the Peripheries," 68.

115. Carmichael, "Dialectics of Liberation," 77–80.

116. Eagleton, *Illusions of Postmodernism*, 55.

117. Roberts, *History of the World*, 555.

118. Wolf, *People Without History*, 5.

119. See Deloria, *God is Red*, 102; Wilson, *The Earth Shall Weep*, 181; see generally Waters, *Book of the Hopi*.

120. See generally Smith, *Decolonizing Methodologies*.

121. See Jackson, *Introduction to African Civilizations*, 118–121 (noting that the library at Alexandria, which contained more than four hundred thousand volumes, was burned by Julius Ceasar's army in 48 B.C., restored by the Romans, and burned again by Christian monks in 389 A.D.).

122. See Lane-Poole, *Moors in Spain*, vii–ix (noting that the Cordova library held a half-million volumes before its destruction during the Crusades).

123. See Mohawk, *Utopian Legacies*, 130–131.

124. Fitzpatrick, *Mythology*, 69; see also 71–72 ("Despite their continuing hold in the West, the stories of progressive stages have never even remotely approximated to the most tolerant conditions of historical enquiry, except for those recent attributions of fiction to history itself.").

125. Roberts, *History of the World*, 121.

126. See Smith, *Decolonizing Methodologies*, 33–37 (discussing the contestation of history, and the respective roles of oral and written traditions).

127. Tompkins, *Great Pyramid*, xiii.

128. On the influence of African civilizations on Europe, see generally Bernal, *Black Athena*, Vols 1–3; Jackson, *Introduction to African Civilizations*; Williams, *Destruction of Black Civilization*. For examples of the intense reactions generated by such challenges to the master narrative, see generally Lefkowitz, *Not Out of Africa*; Lefkowitz and Rogers, *Black Athena Revisited*; Berlinerblau, *Heresy in the University*; see also Bernal, *Black Athena Writes Back*.

129. Roberts, *History of the World*, 58.

130. See generally Lowes, *Indian Giver*; see also Weatherford, *Indian Givers*, 59–115.

131. See generally Hardoy, *Pre-Columbian Cities*.

132. Mann, *Native Americans*, 51.

133. Ibid., 52; see also 52–104.

134. Smith, *Decolonizing Methodologies*, 63. See also Durant, *Our Oriental Heritage*, viii (explaining the incorporation of "Oriental" societies into his history as backdrop for the Greek and Roman civilizations usually portrayed as "the whole source of the modern mind," that is, as precursors of the West).

135. See Olmsted, "Are Things Falling Apart?" 441.

136. See, e.g., Webster, *Fall of the Ancient Maya*, 236–259, 327–348; Minard, "Civilization-Ending Climate Change"; see also Dasgupta and Chattopadhyay, "Ecological Contradictions," 198 (noting lack of support for climatological thesis).

137. See, e.g., Toynbee, *A Study of History*, 190–192 (identifying militarism as "by far the commonest cause of the breakdowns of civilization" and attributing the disintegration of "Sinic Civilization" to overextension and resultant conflicts between states); Roberts, *History of the World*, 128–129 (on the decline of Egypt), 385 (on the decline of the Mayan and Toltec civilizations).

138. See, e.g., Zakaria, *The Post-American World*, esp. 1–3 (describing the "rise of the rest" in terms of economic growth, illustrated by references to the world's tallest building, richest man, largest publicly traded corporation, biggest airplane, etc.).

139. Fitzpatrick, *Mythology*, 41–42.

140. Wolf, *People Without History*, 5.

141. Waswo, *Founding Legend*, 3 (also noting that "most civilizations—as well as most cultures that our tradition would classify as 'primitive'—do not see themselves as having required transportation to their present location").

142. Ibid.

143. Anghie, *Imperialism, Sovereignty*, 4.

144. Fitzpatrick, *Mythology*, 10.

145. Said, *Orientalism*, 1–2.

146. Ibid., 7.

147. "Ideology" is used herein to refer to an overarching and relatively self-contained structure of ideas reflecting the worldview, values, and presumptions of its adherents. For a detailed discussion of the construct, see Eagleton, *Ideology*, 1–31.

148. See Jennings, *Invasion of America*, 76–78 (describing the transition in the early 1600s from an emphasis on Indigenous peoples as "wild," but still people, to "savages" akin to beasts). For background, see generally Sanders, *Lost Tribes*; Williams, *Discourses of Conquest*; Segal and Stineback, *Manifest Destiny*.

149. See, e.g., Williams, *Discourses of Conquest*, 227–286, esp. 246–248 (discussing the American colonists' perceived right to cultivate Indian "waste lands").

150. See generally Manuel and Posluns, *The Fourth World*; see also Churchill, "I Am Indigenist," 275–299.

151. See Deloria, *God is Red*, 78–97.

152. Mohawk, *Lecture at Alfred University*.

153. Esteva and Prakash, *Grassroots Postmodernism*, 125.

CHAPTER 2. CIVILIZING THE OTHER

1. Waswo, *Founding Legend*, 1–3.

2. Fitzpatrick, *Mythology*, 34 (citing Jacques Derrida, *Margins of Philosophy*, 269).

3. Williams, *Discourses of Conquest*, 6.

4. See Tomlins, "Wilderness of Tigers," 468 ("for colonizers, that which lay beyond familiar civil association was a space of deprivation and savagery, inhabited only by barbarism's profound lack of order"); see generally Pendas, "Magical Scent."

5. Fitzpatrick, *Mythology*, 203 (describing the "stock delusions attending colonial rule").

6. See Elliott, *Imperial Spain*, 117 (noting advice given to Queen Isabella of the importance of imposing Spanish laws and language upon the conquered).

7. See "Expanding the Legal Universe," in Deloria, *Metaphysics*, 132–140.

8. See generally Pagden, *European Encounters* (explicating these interactive and often situationally employed tropes).

9. See Korman, *Right of Conquest*, 45 (noting that since at least 1493, "keeping the peace between the great European powers engaged in the competition for overseas territories" motivated the evolution of colonial law).

10. "Media round-up," *BBC International Reports*.

11. "White House apologizes," *AP Online*. Predictably such terminology has aided those who depict the war on terror is an attempt to impose Western or Christian views. See, e.g., Bennhold and Smith, "Twin Car Bombs" (quoting messages claiming that the attacks were aimed at "'the Crusaders and their agents, the slaves of America and the sons of France'").

12. For commentary, see "'Just War' Theory and the Real World," in Chomsky, *Interventions*, 175–180.

13. Williams, *Discourses of Conquest*, 13.

14. On the Augustinian conception of "just war," see Draper, "Grotius' Place," 180–181 (citing Keen, *Laws of War*, 65–66); Nussbaum, *Concise History*, 35–36.

15. Williams, *Discourses of Conquest*, 31. For background, see Cheetham, *History of the Popes*, 91–93; Lotter, "The Crusading Idea," 287.

16. Williams, *Discourses of Conquest*, 25–26; Cheetham, *History of the Popes*, 93–94. See also Durant, *Age of Faith*, 74 (noting Augustinian origin of the "claim of the Church to supremacy over the mind and the state").

17. Williams, *Discourses of Conquest*, 26.

18. Quoted in Jackson, "Introduction" to Lane-Poole, *Moors in Spain*, unnumbered page. On Lady Lugard (1852–1929), see "Lady Flora Lugard," *National Portrait Gallery*.

19. See Lane-Poole, *Moors in Spain*, vii–ix; Durant, *Age of Faith*, 291–307.

20. Williams, *Discourses of Conquest*, 35 (quoting the report of Robert the Monk, said to have been an eyewitness to the speech). See also Payne, *Dream and the Tomb*, 33–35 (providing a somewhat different version of the speech).

21. See Williams, *Discourses of Conquest*, 36 ("In seizing on the pilgrimage tradition as the legal architecture for the Crusades, Urban articulated the first truly colonial-imperialist form of discourse in the West since antiquity in terms designed to appeal to the common people.").

22. Quoted in Payne, *Dream and the Tomb*, 34–35.

23. Williams, *Discourses of Conquest*, 35.

24. Abu-Lughod, *Before European Hegemony*, 21–22. On the Mongol invasion's devastating impact on Islam, which contributed to the subsequent ascendancy of the West, see Payne, *The History of Islam*, 239–240, 243; Durant, *Age of Faith*, 340; Chambers, *The Devil's Horsemen*, 115–135, 172–174.

25. Ironically Innocent was in all likelihood working from translations of Aristotle obtained from Islamic sources, since "the Church [had for centuries] purposely suppressed classical Greek knowledge" on grounds that it was "heretical" (Mohawk, *Utopian Legacies*, 67; see also 70). See also Rodinson, *Mystique*, 15 (noting that by the end of the eleventh century, "the only works by Aristotle available in the West were his brief treatise, *Categories* and his *De Interpretatione*"). On the influence of Arab scholars on "Western"

philosophy, see Durant, *Age of Faith*, 142, 333–338, 911–913; Rodinson, *Mystique*, 16–18; Amin, *Eurocentrism*, 44.

26. See Williams, *Discourses of Conquest*, 43–49. For contemporary Arab perspectives on the Crusades, see generally Aalouf, *Crusades*.

27. Williams, *Discourses of Conquest*, 49–50.

28. "Excerpted Remarks from Speech to the German Bundestag," May 23, 2002, in Bush, *We Will Prevail*, 157.

29. Williams, *Discourses of Conquest*, 14.

30. Bartlett, *Making of Europe*, 1. On the construction of Europe first as a continent in its own right and ultimately as "*The* Continent," see Djait, *Europe and Islam*, 110. See also Davis, *Don't Know Much*, 129.

31. By most accounts, "Europeanization" formally commenced with the coronation of Charlemagne as Holy Roman emperor in 800 C.E., and over the next several centuries "Europe" expanded outward from his capital in Aachen. See Bartlett, *Making of Europe*, 269–291; Herrin, *Formation*, 390–444.

32. See, e.g., Cunningham, *Apples*, 18–37 (analyzing the "Europeanization" of the Celtic peoples of the British Isles); see generally Hector, *Internal Colonialism*.

33. On England's colonization of Ireland, see generally Canny, *Making Ireland*; Pawlisch, *Sir John Davies*. For a broader survey, see generally Teich and Porter, *The National Question*.

34. Williams, *Discourses of Conquest*, 20. See also Gramsci, "The Southern Question," 28–51; Lyttleton, "National Question," 63–105.

35. Williams, *Discourses of Conquest*, 31. See also Harvey, *Islamic Spain*, 9–16 (providing an overview of the *reconquista*); Lane-Poole, *Moors in Spain*, ix (noting the destruction of Moorish infrastructure and public buildings, including seventy libraries). See generally Lomax, *Reconquest*; O'Callaghan, *Reconquest*.

36. Bartlett, *Making of Europe*, 15–18; see also Lotter, "The Crusading Idea," 267–306. For a detailed history, see generally Christiansen, *The Northern Crusades*.

37. See Bartlett, *Making of Europe*, 17; Lotter, "The Crusading Idea," 281.

38. See Williams, *Discourses of Conquest*, 60–61; Bartlett, *Making of Europe*, 17–18; Lotter, "The Crusading Idea," 294–303.

39. Bartlett, *Making of Europe*, 18–19.

40. "Reason," often traced to Aquinas' *Summa contra Gentiles*, is often posited as a unique characteristic of this emerging "European identity," but Aquinas' tract was heavily based upon Averroës' *Tahafut al-Tahafut*, written more than a half-century earlier. See Durant, *Age of Faith*, 336, 338, 966; Rodinson, *Mystique*, 17; Mohawk, *Utopian Legacies*, 89; Atiya, *Crusade*, 218–219.

41. Bartlett, *Making of Europe*, 22.

42. See generally Hector, *Internal Colonialism*; Canny, *Making Ireland*; Otway-Ruthven, *Medieval Ireland*; Frame, *Colonial Ireland*.

43. Bartlett, *Making of Europe*, 262–268.

44. On the Teutonic Knights, or Teutonic Order (*Ordo Theutonicorum*), as they called themselves, see Haverkampf, *Medieval Germany*, 18–20 (on the Teutonic Knights). See also Burleigh, *Germany Turns Eastwards*, 7 (quoting Hitler, *Mein Kampf*, 128–129, 598 [noting the resonance achieved by Hitler's assertion that the "Germans should once again set out on 'the march of the Teutonic Knights of old' toward Russia[, taking up] where we broke off six hundred years ago"]).

45. See Tomaszewski, "The National Question," 293–316 (illustrating ongoing effects on the Poles).

46. Williams, *Discourses of Conquest*, 61–66.

47. See generally Todorov, *Conquest of America*.

48. Williams, *Discourses of Conquest*, 67.

49. See generally Falls, *Elizabeth's Irish Wars*.

50. Portugal's independence from Castile was recognized by the papacy in 1179. In 1580, as a result of disastrous expeditions in Africa and other factors, it was again subordinated to Spain and did not become permanently independent until 1640. See Williams, *Discourses of Conquest*, 68; Elliott, *Imperial Spain*, 264–271, 342–343, 351–354.

51. See Wallerstein, *Modern World-System*, 48–52.

52. Little is known about the people of the Canary Islands, as physical descriptions are conflicting and they were more or less systematically exterminated. See Mohawk, *Utopian Legacies*, 101–102; Sanders, *Lost Tribes*, 30–36; Sale, *Conquest of Paradise*, 50–51.

53. Williams, *Discourses of Conquest*, 69.

54. Sanders, *Lost Tribes*, 35–36, quote at 36.

55. Williams, *Discourses of Conquest*, 69 (quoting Muldoon, *Expansion of Europe*, 54).

56. Williams, *Discourses of Conquest*, 72.

57. On the Portuguese inauguration of Europe's trade in human flesh, see Davidson, *African Slave Trade*, 53–63; Thomas, *Slave Trade*, 48–86.

58. Sanders, *Lost Tribes*, 65–73.

59. Morison, *Admiral*, 96–108; Morison, *European Discovery*, 26–51.

60. Quoted in Morison, *Admiral*, 105.

61. On Columbus, see Williams, *Discourses of Conquest*, 78; Morison, *Admiral*, 43–53; Sale, *Conquest of Paradise*, 51–56; see generally Wilford, *Mysterious History*. On contestation of the Columbus story, see King, *Truth about Stories*, 72–73.

62. See Elliott, *Imperial Spain*, 67 ("Alexander VI in his bull of 1493 conceded the Indies personally to Ferdinand and Isabella for their lifetime, with the intention that America should become a Castilian possession after their death"); also see Sale, *Conquest of Paradise*, 124–125; Mohawk, *Utopian Legacies*, 105.

63. Williams, *Discourses of Conquest*, 80.

64. See ibid., 80–81; Elliott, *Imperial Spain*, 57–58, 67; Morison, *European Discovery*, 97; see also Hemming, *Red Gold*, 7, 527–528; Cocker, *Rivers of Blood*, 14–15.

65. See Sale, *Conquest of Paradise*, 97; Todorov, *Conquest of America*, 47; Morison, *Admiral*, 486–487; see also *Borders v. Rippey* ("Columbus, the Christian gentleman that he was, by force and fraud sent five shiploads of natives from the West Indies to be sold in the slave markets of Spain").

66. Sale, *Conquest of Paradise*, 159 (quoting Las Casas). See also Las Casas, *Devastation*, esp. 42–53.

67. Sale, *Conquest of Paradise*, 155. See also Koning, *Columbus*, 85–86; Stannard, *American Holocaust*, 71.

68. Williams, *Discourses of Conquest*, 82.

69. For population estimates see Cook and Borah, *Essays*, chap. 6; Thatcher, *Christopher Columbus*, 2:348 *et seq*. On Columbus' arrest and return to Spain see Morison, *Admiral*, 570–572; Koning, *Columbus*, 101; Sale, *Conquest of Paradise*, 182–183.

70. See generally Floyd, *Columbus Dynasty*.

71. See chapters 3 and 4 in this volume.

72. Williams, *Discourses of Conquest*, 83–84 (quoting Hanke, *Spanish Struggle*, 20).

73. Hanke, *Spanish Struggle*, 200; see also Sale, *Conquest of Paradise*, 160–161; Stannard, *American Holocaust*, 72.

74. Williams, *Discourses of Conquest*, 174 (referencing the appendix to the 1583 English edition of Las Casas' *The Devastation of the Indies*, then generally referenced as *The Spanish Cruelties*).

75. For a corollary in the contemporary "war on terror" see generally Yee, *For God and Country* (observing that even as the sole Muslim military chaplain at Guantánamo, he was expected to serve the U.S. troops, not the overwhelmingly Muslim prisoners).

76. Williams, *Discourses of Conquest*, 85–86 (noting that although the Dominicans were closely associated with the Spanish Inquisition, they also were strongly influenced by Thomistic humanism).

77. Ibid. By early 1495, prior to formal legal authorization, Columbus had implemented the *encomienda* on Española and had extended the system throughout the Caribbean by 1500. See Sale, *Conquest of Paradise*, 155–156; see also Hanke, *Spanish Struggle*, 19, 131; Stannard, *American Holocaust*, 73; Keal, *European Conquest*, 89–91.

78. Sale, *Conquest of Paradise*, 155.

79. Hanke, *Spanish Struggle*, 11 (quoting Gonzalo Fernández de Oveido, ca. 1517–1518).

80. Hanke, *Spanish Struggle*, 11 (quoting Jeronymite friars, *circa*, 1517).

81. Williams, *Discourses of Conquest*, 88.

82. See Anaya, *Indigenous Peoples*, 23–26.

83. See Dickason, "Concepts of Sovereignty," 189–191 (providing background on Matías de Paz and López and the context in which the *Requerimiento* was drafted).

84. Hanke, *Spanish Struggle*, 28.

85. The full text of the *Requerimiento* is reproduced in Mohawk, *Utopian Legacies*, 107–110 (language quoted at 110).

86. Williams, *Discourses of Conquest*, 92 (quoting Hanke, *Spanish Struggle*, 34).

87. Williams, *Discourses of Conquest*, 93. According to Hanke, the *Requerimiento* was last applied in 1550, to the Indians of Chile, but was not formally retired until 1573 (*Spanish Struggle*, 111–112).

88. See generally Hanke, *Aristotle* (providing a thorough account of the las Casas–Sepúlvida debate).

89. On the influence of Vitoria's formulation on subsequent U.S. federal law governing American Indian nations, particularly as articulated by Chief Justice John Marshall, see chapter 4 in this volume.

90. Williams, *Discourses of Conquest*, 96–97; see also Anghie, *Imperialism, Sovereignty*, 15.

91. For summaries, see Korman, *Right of Conquest*, 52–56; Anghie, *Imperialism, Sovereignty*, 13–28; Williams, *Discourses of Conquest*, 96–108; Green, "Claims to Territory," 39–47. The lectures in English translation are included in Vitoria, *De Indis*. The name is spelled "Victoria" as well as "Vitoria"; for consistency I have employed the latter except in direct quotes and citations.

92. Fitzpatrick, "Terminal Legality," 9.

93. Anghie, *Imperialism, Sovereignty*, 15 (quoting Vitoria, *De Indis*, 123); see also Williams, *Discourses of Conquest*, 93; Green, "Claims to Territory," 39–40.

94. Anghie, *Imperialism, Sovereignty*, 18–19.

95. See generally Williams, *Loaded Weapon*.

96. On the interpretation of the doctrine of *territorium res nullius* to foster the legal fiction that even the territories most heavily populated by Indigenous peoples are "effectively" uninhabited, see Green, "Claims to Territory," 235; Keal, *European Conquest*, 51–52. For an overview of the effects of the doctrine as applied in much of North America, see generally Richardson, *Betrayal and Rebirth*.

97. Williams, *Discourses of Conquest*, 99 (quoting Vitoria, *De Indis*, 138–139).

98. See Anghie, *Imperialism, Sovereignty*, 20; Green, "Claims to Territory," 44; Dickason, "Concepts of Sovereignty," 192, 231. Many subsequent legal theorists, including Grotius and Pufendorf, largely concurred with this view. See, e.g., Ruddy, *Enlightenment*, 88.

99. Vitoria was effectively asserting the central tenet of what has come to be known as customary international law. See generally, Meron, *Human Rights*.

100. Williams, *Discourses of Conquest*, 101.

101. Anghie, *Imperialism, Sovereignty*, 23 (quoting Vitoria, *De Indis*, 156). For somewhat different formulations, see Korman, *Right of Conquest*, 53; Keal, *European Conquest*, 92.

102. Korman, *Right of Conquest*, 53.

103. Williams, *Discourses of Conquest*, 47. It follows that the conversion of Christians to non-Christian beliefs, to say nothing of the "admission of non-Christian missionaries to Spain was, of course, unthinkable" (Nussbaum, *Concise History*, 81).

104. Anghie, *Imperialism, Sovereignty*, 23 (quoting Vitoria, *De Indis*, 156).

105. Williams, *Discourses of Conquest*, 102. See also Korman, *Right of Conquest*, 53 ("the failure of the Indian rulers to protect the 'safety and peace' of those who came from afar or the refusal of Indians to grant the Spaniards such 'natural rights' as the right to trade with them . . . were violations of the natural law of nations which, in Vitoria's view, constituted a just ground for war against them").

106. Williams, *Discourses of Conquest*, 102 (quoting Vitoria, *De Indis*, 153).

107. Williams, *Discourses of Conquest*, 104.

108. Anghie, *Imperialism, Sovereignty*, 21 (quoting Vitoria, *De Indis*, 151).

109. Anghie, *Imperialism, Sovereignty*, 24 (quoting Vitoria, *De Indis*, 155). See also Williams, *Discourses of Conquest*, 103; Korman, *Right of Conquest*, 54–55 ("proceeding on the same ground, Vitoria contended that the right to acquire new territories by conquest might also flow from the right to assist allies in a just war," citing McMahon, *Conquest*, 35).

110. Fitzpatrick, "Terminal Legality," 13.

111. Anghie, *Imperialism, Sovereignty*, 23. See also Schwartzenberger, *Frontiers*, 53; Donelan, "Spain," 78.

112. Anghie, *Imperialism, Sovereignty*, 26. See also Ballis, *Legal Position*, 81 (noting legal assertion of a "distinction between peoples with respect to war" by European states during this period).

113. Anghie, *Imperialism, Sovereignty*, 26–27. On Chief Justice Marshall's arguments, see chapters 3 and 4 in this volume.

114. Anghie, *Imperialism, Sovereignty*, 27 (quoting Vitoria, *De Indis*, 183).

115. See Williams, *Discourses of Conquest*, 103–108. See generally Lindley, *Acquisition and Government*. On application of the principle to Indigenous peoples in the contemporary U.S., see generally Clark, *Lone Wolf*.

116. Williams, *Discourses of Conquest*, 103.

117. Fitzpatrick, "Terminal Legality," 13; see also Fitzpatrick, *Mythology*, 53.

118. Williams, "Algebra," 250 (citing Grotius, Hugo. *De Jure Belli ac Pacis Libi Tres*, 504–506 (1964)).

119. Fitzpatrick, "Terminal Legality," 14 (quoting De Vattel, "Occupation of Territory," 44–45).

120. Westlake, *Principles of International Law*, 140.

121. Ibid., 142–143.

122. On the colonial underpinnings of each major phase of international law since Vitoria, see generally Anghie, *Imperialism, Sovereignty*. For an excellent critique of contemporary human rights law from an anticolonialist perspective, see generally Esteva and Prakash, *Grassroots Postmodernism*.

CHAPTER 3. "A CITY ON A HILL"

1. See Calabresi, "Shining City on a Hill," 1336 (quoting Winthrop, "A Modell of Christian Charity" (1830) and Reagan, "Farewell Address to the Nation," January 11, 1989).

2. Palin, Vice Presidential Debate.

3. From Theodore Roosevelt's *The Strenuous Life*, quoted in Drinnon, *Facing West*, 232.

4. See Merk, *Manifest Destiny*, 32–33 (noting that the phrase was first published in an editorial by John L. O'Sullivan in the *New York Morning News*, December 27, 1845).

5. Merk, *Manifest Destiny*, 265. Merk's seminal work outlines the emergence of the concept in great detail but explicitly declines to draw any connections between race and manifest destiny, a subject addressed in Horsman, *Manifest Destiny*.

6. See Wolfe, "Corporations as Ships," 82.

7. Tomlins, "Law's Empire," 26.

8. See ibid. (noting that the Spanish were primarily concerned with the appropriation of metallic wealth and Indigenous labor to extract it, the Dutch with trade routes, and the English with acquiring territory); Watson, "John Marshall," 499–540 (distinguishing the views of the Spanish, French, Dutch, and English powers); see also Pagden, *Lords of All*, 63–76. On the English creation of settler societies, see Kirkby and Coleborne, "Introduction," 3.

9. See Segal and Stineback, *Manifest Destiny*, 30 ("the best colonial analogy to the period of Manifest Destiny is, in fact, the Puritan-Indian experience"). See also Stephanson, *Manifest Destiny*, 4 (noting the New England influence on American historiography).

10. Segal and Stineback, *Manifest Destiny*, 31 (noting the arrival of one hundred Pilgrims in 1620, and fifteen hundred Puritans in 1630).

11. See Horsman, *Manifest Destiny*, 9–14; Slotkin, *Regeneration*, 37–42.

12. On patents to explore the New World granted by Henry VIII to John Cabot, see Jennings, *Invasion of America*, 5; Pagden, *Lords of All*, 64; Williams, *Discourses of Conquest*, 121–122.

13. See Duffy, "Foundations", 49–81.

14. See Williams, *Discourses of Conquest*, 122–126.

15. See ibid., 133. See generally Andrews, *Elizabethan Privateering*; Adams, "Outbreak," 45–69.

16. Williams, *Discourses of Conquest*, 134.

17. See Lenman, *England's Colonial Wars*, 83 ("Elizabeth . . . invested heavily in the enterprise of [Sir John] Hawkins, which was based on supplying the Spanish settlers in the Caribbean with the West African slaves they needed to replace the collapsing indigenous populations").

18. Adrian IV, the only English pope, issued a bull in 1155 authorizing Henry II to bring the "truth of the Christian faith" to the Irish, who were considered barbarians despite having converted to Christianity centuries earlier. See Williams, *Discourses of Conquest*, 136–137; see also chapter 2 in this volume.

19. See Jennings, *Invasion of America*, 7 (noting similarities between English and Irish cultures); Schmidhauser, "Power," 875 (noting how "the law of conquest devised . . . for Ireland . . . became the prototype of British colonial legal imperialism throughout its expanding empire").

20. Williams, *Discourses of Conquest*, 137 (describing the 1366 Statutes of Kilkenny).

21. On the policies in Ireland, see ibid., 138; on the American practices, see below.

22. See Williams, *Discourses of Conquest*, 139–140. The term "English" is something of a misnomer, as the bulk of the transplanted population was composed of Lowland Scots (or "Scotch-Irish," as they would later be known). See Cunningham, *Apples*, 67–69.

23. Williams, *Discourses of Conquest*, 141; see generally Pawlisch, *Sir John Davies*.

24. See Williams, *Discourses of Conquest*, 146, 151. See also Canny, *Elizabethan Conquest*, 121–135; Lenman, *England's Colonial Wars*, 68–69, 76–82.

25. See Mohawk, *Utopian Legacies*, 146.

26. See chapter 4 in this volume.

27. See Williams, *Discourses of Conquest*, 151–163, 174–177, 180–185. See generally Tomlins, "Legal Cartography."

28. Tomlins, "Law's Empire," 31 (quoting the elder Haklyut).

29. Ibid., 28 (quoting the younger Haklyut).

30. Ibid., 29.

31. Tomlins, "Legal Cartography," 333; "Between 1606 (the first Virginia charter) and 1681 (Pennsylvania) some 28 major territorial charters and grants were promulgated. . . . All used law to hack territory out of space and to depict the institutional and cultural forms in which authority would be applied to (and within) that territory."

32. Tomlins, "Law's Empire," 32.

33. See Williams, *Discourses of Conquest*, 197 (quoting A. Gentili, *De jure belli libri tres* [trans. J. Rolfe, 1964], 41). These days, of course, terrorists are similarly construed as the common enemy of all. See, e.g., Burgess, "Hostis."

34. Williams, *Discourses of Conquest*, 198.

35. Ibid. Williams notes that Lord Chief Justice Edward Coke similarly interpreted English common law to say that "infidels" are by definition perpetual enemies whose laws are automatically abrogated by conquest, a position later rejected by English courts but nonetheless relied upon by English colonizers in the Americas (ibid., 200).

36. See Browne-Marshall, *Race*, 1; Higginbotham, *Matter of Color*, 20–22.

37. See Segal and Stineback, *Manifest Destiny*, 31.

38. Stephanson, *Manifest Destiny*, 6.

39. See Williams, *Discourses of Conquest*, 164–165. For background, see generally Sanders, *Lost Tribes*.

40. Williams, *Discourses of Conquest*, 172 (quoting George Peckham, an early English promoter of American colonization).

41. See Segal and Stineback, *Manifest Destiny*, 29. On the association of Protestant theology with the rise of capitalism, see generally Weber, *Protestant Ethic*; see also Wallerstein, *Modern World-System*, 152–153.

42. Stephanson, *Manifest Destiny*, 7.

43. Because claims based on *res nullius* required prior "discovery," the English relied on mythic accounts of a Welsh Prince Madoc who was said to have arrived in what is now Alabama in the twelfth century, supplemented by claims based on John Cabot's "discovery" of Florida in 1497. See Pagden, *Lords of All*; Williams, *Discourses of Conquest*, 121–122, 178.

44. Pagden, *Lords of All*, 91.

45. See Salisbury, *Manitou*, 178. See also Hanson and Hanson, "The Blame Frame," 430–431 (describing the settlers' ideological transition from viewing American Indians as objects of salvation to threats to civilization).

46. Pagden, *Lords of All*, 77 (also noting that "no less a person than Francis Bacon had demonstrated that 'a country gained by conquest hath no right to be governed by English law'").

47. See ibid., 94 (noting that the "only major exception to this rule was the much discussed conquest of Virginia," where English claims were based on "the claim supposedly grounded in English common law that all infidels were aliens, *perpetui enemici,* 'perpetual enemies'" with whom there could, by definition, be no peace).

48. Fitzpatrick, *Mythology*, 17 (quoting Leach, *Genesis*, 85).

49. Salisbury, *Manitou*, 98, 109.

50. Ibid., 98 (quoting *Travels and Works of Captain John Smith*).

51. Ibid.

52. Segal and Stineback, *Manifest Destiny*, 52.

53. Ibid., 52–53.

54. Quoted in ibid., 50–51.

55. See Jennings, *Invasion of America*, 16–31, 207–208; Salisbury, *Manitou*, 101–106.

56. See Churchill, "'Nits Make Lice,'" 131–137. See also Dobyns, *Their Number*, 34–45 (estimating a preinvasion population of North America perhaps as high as 18.5 million, with a possible hemispheric population of 112 million); Thornton, *American Indian Holocaust*, xvii, 242 (estimating a minimal North American population of 9 million to 12.5 million); Sale, *Conquest of Paradise*, 316 (reflecting the 15 million average now commonly accepted by scholars). In contrast, the Smithsonian estimate has remained at 2 million. See Churchill, "'Nits Make Lice,'" 131.

57. U.S. Bureau of the Census. *Fifteenth Census,* 3 (Table II, "Indian Population by Divisions and States, 1890–1930").

58. See, e.g., Martin et al., *America and Its Peoples*, 17–19 (noting a 90 percent population decline in Mexico following Cortés' invasion).

59. Quoted in Ashburn, *Ranks of Death*, 19.

60. Quoted in Sally, *Narratives*, 284–285.

61. See, e.g., Katz, *Holocaust*, 20 (describing the depopulation of the New World as "largely an *unintended* tragedy" caused by "nature, not malice" [emphasis in original]).

62. Churchill, "'Nits Make Lice,'" 138.

63. Ibid., 139–151; see also Stannard, *American Holocaust*, 76, 81, 134.

64. Although it was known who killed John Oldham, the officer in question, the governors of Massachusetts and Plymouth Plantation publicly blamed the Pequots, who were militarily weaker than the Narrangasetts and had land more immediately coveted by the colonies, leading to a war in which the Pequots were virtually annihilated. See Churchill, "'Nits Make Lice,'" 152; Jennings, *Invasion of America*, 206–227.

65. Quoted in Stearn and Stearn, *Effects of Smallpox*, 44–45.

66. See Mann, *Washington's War*, 11.

67. Williams, *Discourses of Conquest*, 218 (quoting *The Records of the Virginia Company of London*, Vol. 3, *A Justification for Planting Virginia*, 457).

68. Ibid., 217, (quoting *Records of the Virginia Company*, 556).

69. Quoted in Slotkin, *Regeneration*, 38.

70. See ibid., 42–56 (providing more accurate depiction of the culture Bradford claimed to be describing).

71. Jennings, *Invasion of America*, 217.

72. Ibid., 221 (quoting their commander, Captain John Mason).

73. Ibid., 223 (quoting Report of Saybrook Company commander Captain John Underhill); see also Drinnon, *Facing West*, 41–45.

74. Drinnon, *Facing West*, 55.

75. Ibid., 46.

76. Ibid., 55.

77. Ibid. On the transformative power of "the word," see Smith, *Decolonizing Methodologies*, 157; see generally Freire, *Pedagogy of the Oppressed*; Lawrence, "Word and the River."

78. Tomlins, "Law's Empire," 37.

79. See Segal and Stineback, *Manifest Destiny*, 32–36; Jennings, *Invasion of America*, 46–47.

80. On Noriega, see Ma, "Noriega's Abduction," 940–943; Nanda, "Validity," 498–500. On Hussein, see Spectar, "Beyond the Rubicon," 94–102; see also Cooper, "Defending Liberty," 556–557 (describing George W. Bush's invasion of Iraq as "the punishing of evil and an act of liberation" in furtherance of "the same ideals recognized by the initial Puritan colonies").

81. Segal and Stineback, *Manifest Destiny*, 37.

82. Tomlins, "Law's Empire," 42.

83. See Drinnon, *Facing West*, 9–13.

84. Ibid., 12.

85. Ibid., xv.

86. Watson, "John Marshall," 496.

87. Ibid., 497–498; see also 487–498.

88. Segal and Stineback, *Manifest Destiny*, 38.

89. Coskun, "Religious Skepticism," 595 (quoting Cassirer, *Myth of the State*, 74).

90. Stephanson, *Manifest Destiny*, 8 (emphasis omitted).

91. For critiques of the tendency to equate "democracy" with voting, see generally Guinier, "Supreme Democracy." See also Howland, "U.S. Law," esp. 66–67 (illustrating the use of a federally imposed tribal election to override traditional Hopi decision-making processes).

92. Wolfe, "Corporations as Ships," 82 (quoting Bercovitch, *Puritan Origins*, 108).

93. See Williams, *Discourses of Conquest*, 228; see generally Jennings, *Empire of Fortune*.

94. See generally Stagg, *Anglo-Indian Relations*.

95. Quoted in Williams, *Discourses of Conquest*, 237 (emphasis added).

96. Williams, *Discourses of Conquest*, 216.

97. See ibid., 235–246. See also Grey, "Origins," 884–890 (discussing expansion of this argument to say that the British had no right to impose any laws upon unrepresented colonists).

98. Williams, *Discourses of Conquest*, 243 (quoting a resolution drafted by Samuel Adams and approved by the Massachusetts House of Representatives in 1765).

99. Declaration of Independence, 4.

100. Peterson, *Thomas Jefferson*, 62–63.

101. See Declaration of Independence. While issues of taxation, trade, immigration, and access to American Indian lands were clearly motivating the signers, it is notable that the bulk of their complaints are phrased in terms of the king's refusal to comply with established processes of governance.

102. See generally Declaration of Independence.

103. Peterson, *Thomas Jefferson*, 57.

104. Williams, *Discourses of Conquest*, 267 (summarizing Jefferson's arguments in a 1774 pamphlet titled *A Summary View of the Rights of British America*).

105. Grey, "Origins," 891.

106. Declaration of Independence, 6.

107. See Nirmal, *Right to Self-Determination*, 27–28 (noting that the political ideology of both the American and French Revolutions emphasized a right to self-determination). However, the right of *colonized* peoples to self-determination only began to be recognized in the aftermath of World War I, and then only in extremely limited form and only with respect to the colonies of defeated powers. See ibid., 31–36; Anghie, *Imperialism, Sovereignty*, 115–195; Hannum, *Autonomy*, 27–49. See also chapter 7 in this volume.

108. Declaration of Independence, 6.

109. See Pagden, *Lords of All*, 77–78; see also Williams, *Discourses of Conquest*, 246–248 (emphasizing that Locke's philosophy was regarded as "common sense" among the colonial leaders of this period).

110. Quoted in Pagden, *Lords of All*, 78. Vattel drew heavily on Vitoria's *De Indis et De Jure Belli Reflectiones* in drafting his treatise, *The Laws of Nations*. See generally Parry, *Spanish Theory*; Hanke, *Spanish Struggle*; Nussbaum, *Concise History*.

111. Pagden, *Lords of All*, 79.

112. See Hurt, *Indian Agriculture*, 1–76; see also Weatherford, *Indian Givers*, 79–115.

113. Deloria, Foehner, and Scinta, *Spirit & Reason*, 209.

114. In 1831 Justice John Marshall characterized Indian tribes as "an anomaly . . . which the law of nations would regard as nothing more than wandering hordes, held together only by ties of blood and habit, and having neither laws or government, beyond what is required in a savage state" (*Cherokee Nation v. Georgia*). A remarkably similar characterization was employed by Justice William Rehnquist in 1980, dissenting in *United States v. Sioux Nation of Indians*: "'The effective unit was the band or village of a few hundred souls, which might be seen in the course of its wanderings encamped by a water-course with tipis erected. . . . They lived only for the day, recognized no rights or property, robbed

or killed anyone if they thought they could get away with it, inflicted cruelty without a qualm" (ibid., 437, quoting Morison, *Oxford History*, 539–540).

115. For an excellent and detailed analysis of these interests and the compromises effected between them, see Williams, *Discourses of Conquest*, 229–317.

116. Washington's family helped found the Ohio Company in 1747, and Washington was reputed to be the richest man in the colonies by virtue of their land acquisitions. See Mann, *Washington's War*, 38–39; Eckert, *Bloody River*, 13–14, 440.

117. As detailed in the National Archive's *Revolutionary War Pension and Bounty-and-Warrant Application Files*, Virginia, Connecticut, and other states conveyed claims beyond the line demarcated by the Proclamation of 1763 to the Continental Congress in exchange for federal grants of the same land. See Churchill, *Perversions of Justice*, 209–210; Eckert, *Bloody River*, 440–441; see generally Horsman, *Expansion*.

118. Eckert, *Bloody River*, 440.

119. See Williams, *Discourses of Conquest*, 231, 290–291; see also Giunta, *The Emerging Nation*, 27–34, quote at 31 (reproducing correspondence concerning French claims to the Louisiana territory noting that "since the 13 States were not in agreement on their own respective boundaries, it was not surprising that they clashed at some points with the claims of some other power").

120. See Williams, *Discourses of Conquest*, 271–272, 293–295.

121. See, e.g., "Conde d'Aranda to Conde de Floridablanca: Memorandum on Boundary Discussions," in Giunta, *The Emerging Nation*, 490–492 (report of d'Aranda's discussion with John Jay in Paris in 1782, noting American assertions that they "claimed for themselves the rights of England").

122. Williams, *Discourses of Conquest*, 272–273; see also 296–305 (noting that many influential political leaders' positions were influenced by their standing as land speculators).

123. See Williams, *Discourses of Conquest*, 305–306 (also noting that North Carolina and Georgia did not cede their western claims to the central government for many years, and that this provision did not prevent states like New York or Massachusetts from directly negotiating purchases of land from Indian nations within their state boundaries).

124. Williams, *Discourses of Conquest*, 307.

125. Wunder, "'Merciless Indian Savages,'" 66 (also noting that the founders of the United States "are known as the 'Ecunnaunuxulgee' to the Creeks of Georgia, meaning those 'people greedily grasping after the lands of red people'").

126. See Paust, "The Human Right," 550–561 (discussing the "right to revolution" proffered by the American colonists).

127. *Marbury v. Madison*, 163.

CHAPTER 4. ESTABLISHING THE REPUBLIC

1. Cassirer, *Myth of the State*, 97–105.

2. Crawford, *Creation of States*, 6–28.

3. Cassirer, *Myth of the State*, 265 (quoting *Philosophy of Right*, 258).

4. See Zinn, *People's History*, 94 (quoting Jefferson, "I hold it that a little rebellion now and then is a good thing. . . . The tree of liberty must be refreshed from time to time with the blood of patriots and tyrants").

5. See generally Barreiro, *Indian Roots*; Grinde, *Iroquois*; Grinde and Johansen, *Exemplar of Liberty*; Johansen, *Forgotten Founders*; Mohawk, *Exiled*.

6. The Constitution of the Iroquois Confederacy is reproduced in Grinde, *Iroquois*, at Appendix A, 147–167.

7. Johansen, *Forgotten Founders*, 27–29.

8. Ibid., 61–62 (quoting Cassanatego).

9. See Grinde, *Iroquois*, 169–171 (Appendix B, reproducing the Albany Plan); see also 130–132; Grinde, "Iroquoian Political Concept," 47–60; Grinde and Johansen, *Exemplar of Liberty*, 195–250.

10. Johansen, *Forgotten Founders*, 102.

11. Grinde, "Iroquois Political Theory," 235. See also Grinde, *Iroquois*, 136–137 (noting that "the Iroquois Council must meet once every five years for the purpose of reaffirming its goals, and have an opportunity to dissolve . . . Thus, the freedom to continue in the confederate structure is guaranteed, and the people know they have the right to decide, indeed the *right to self-determination*").

12. Grinde, "Iroquois Political Theory," 263 (quoting Adams, *Defence of Constitutions*, xvxvi); see also Grinde and Johansen, *Exemplar of Liberty*, 241–242.

13. Grinde and Johansen, *Exemplar of Liberty*, 195 (quoting Pinckney).

14. See generally Williams, *Linking Arms Together*.

15. Bowers, *Jefferson and Hamilton*, 31 (quoting Frederick Scott Oliver, *Alexander Hamilton: An Essay on the American Union* [1907]).

16. Beard, *Economic Interpretation*, 73–151.

17. Zinn, *People's History*, 90.

18. See Beard, *Economic Interpretation*, 152–188.

19. See U.S. Constitution, Preamble, Amend. X, and Arts. I, II, and III.

20. See U.S. Constitution, Art. VI § 2 ("This Constitution, and the Laws of the United States which shall be made in Pursuance thereof; and all Treaties made, or which shall be made, under the Authority of the United States, shall be the supreme Law of the Land"); see also Paust, *International Law*, 7–11 (documenting the framers' presumption that the Constitution incorporated customary international law).

21. For various formulations, see Dicey, *Introduction*, 179, 185; Raz, "Rule of Law," 210–213; Fuller, *The Morality of Law*, 157; Hernandez-Truyol, "The Rule of Law," 172–173 (summarizing various definitions); see generally Radin, "Reconsidering."

22. See Paust, *International Law*, 200.

23. Hernandez-Truyol, "The Rule of Law", 172.

24. Dworkin, *Matter of Principle*, 11–13.

25. U.S. Constitution, Amend. IX. See also Paust, *International Law*, 200–201 (noting arguments by James Madison and Alexander Hamilton that this was a good reason to avoid specific enumeration of rights).

26. *Marbury v. Madison*, 163; see also U.S. Constitution, Art. III, § 2, cl. 1 ("The judicial Power shall extend to all Cases, in Law and Equity, arising under this Constitution, the Laws of the United States, and Treaties made, or which shall be made, under their Authority").

27. *Chisolm v. Georgia*, 474.

28. See chapter 1 in this volume.

29. See generally Paust, "In Their Own Words"; Paust, *International Law*.

30. U.S. Constitution, Art. III, § 2, cl. 1.

31. U.S. Constitution, Art. VI, cl. 2.

32. Quoted in Paust, *International Law*, 67, 81 n. 2.

33. Ibid., 67.

34. Ibid., 70–71

35. *United States v. Schooner Peggy*, 109.

36. *Talbot v. Jansen*, 161.

37. *Paquete Habana*, 700 (citing *Hilton v. Guyot*, 163, 164, 214, 215).

38. Paust, "In Their Own Words," 212 (quoting Duponceau, *Dissertation*, 3).

39. Churchill, "Perversions of Justice," 5–6.

40. Act to Provide for the Government of the Territory Northwest of the River Ohio.

41. See the Articles of Confederation, Art. IX (addressing treaty making); U.S. Constitution, Art. I, § 8, cl. 3 (giving Congress the power to regulate Commerce with "the Indian Tribes"), U.S. Constitution, Art. I, §10, cl. 3 (limiting treaty making to the federal government); U.S. Constitution, Art. VI, cl. 2 (declaring treaties to be the supreme law of the land); see also Jensen, *Articles of Confederation*, 154–162, 190–232.

42. See generally Kappler, *Indian Treaties*; Deloria and DeMallie, *Documents* (including documents omitted by Kappler). See generally Churchill, "Geographies of Sacrifice," 239–291 (on the U.S. government's continued use of agreements when convenient, e.g., to permit the extraction of radioactive materials or the storage of hazardous wastes on Indian reservations).

43. See chapter 2 in this volume.

44. Ibid.

45. See Churchill, "Perversions of Justice," 2–3.

46. See chapter 2 in this volume.

47. See Churchill, "Perversions of Justice," 3–4; see generally Churchill, "Law Stood Squarely." For background, see generally Peckham and Gibson, *Attitudes*; Davenport, *European Treaties*.

48. Washburn, *Red Man's Land*, 56.

49. See generally Wiessner, "American Indian Treaties."

50. See generally Vaughn, *Early American Indian Documents*; Quinn, *Discovery of America*; Perry, *Establishment*.

51. See Churchill, "Perversions of Justice," 7 (quoting Op. Atty. Gen., April 26, 1821, 354).

52. Wiessner, "American Indian Treaties," 591.

53. See generally Vecsey and Venables, *Native American Environments*.

54. See Wiessner, "American Indian Treaties," 584; Williams, *Discourses of Conquest*, 287–333; see generally Wilkins, *American Indian Sovereignty*.

55. Quoted in Drinnon, *Facing West*, 65.

56. Ibid; see generally Slotkin, *Regeneration* (compiling portrayals of American Indians as "beasts").

57. A third strategy was advocated by Thomas Jefferson, who wrote to William Henry Harrison, then governor of the Indiana Territory: "To promote this disposition to exchange lands . . . we shall push our trading uses, and be glad to see the good and influential individuals among them run in debt, because we observe that when these debts get beyond what the individuals can pay, they become willing to lop them off by a cession of lands." Quoted in Drinnon, *Facing West*, 87.

58. See generally Drinnon, *Facing West*; Slotkin, *Regeneration*.

59. Quoted in Drinnon, *Facing West*, 153–154.

60. Ibid., 153.

61. Ibid., 158.

62. Anghie, *Imperialism, Sovereignty*, 27 (quoting Vitoria, *De Indis*, 183).

63. See Fitzpatrick, *Mythology*, 44–91.

64. Ibid., 44–91.

65. See Smith, *John Marshall*, 74–75 (noting that Marshall and his father each received scrip for ten thousand acres of land in what is now Kentucky, issued by the U.S. government in lieu of payment to troops during the war for independence, and ultimately they jointly acquired more than two hundred thousand acres of western lands); see generally McGrath, *Yazoo*.

66. *Fletcher v. Peck*.

67. See Williams, *Discourses of Conquest*, 308–309.

68. See *Fletcher v. Peck*, 142.

69. See Churchill, "Law Stood Squarely," 665–680.

70. See generally *Johnson v. McIntosh*. The "rights" inhering in "discovery" were, in turn, asserted to have passed from the English Crown to the United States upon the recognition of its independence (Churchill, "Law Stood Squarely," 584–585).

71. Churchill, "Law Stood Squarely," 589–590.

72. Ibid., 590. See generally Miller, *Native America* (discussing roots of the construct of manifest destiny in the doctrine of discovery).

73. Jennings, *Invasion of America*, 60; see also 60–73 (on the invention of the "wandering savage" portrayal).

74. See Churchill, "Nits Make Lice," 146–149; Stannard, *American Holocaust*, 103–118 (on deliberate crop destruction); Woods and Donovan, "Anticipatory Self-Defense," 502–503 (on portrayal of Indigenous peoples as "savage," citing texts by Cotton Mather and other Puritan leaders); Williams, *Discourses of Conquest*, 201–218.

75. See Schaaf, "Great Law of Peace," 324–331; see generally Johansen, *Forgotten Founders*; Grinde, *Iroquois*. See also Jensen, "The Imaginary Connection" (challenging this interpretation).

76. See Strickland, *Fire and the Spirits*, 40–72.

77. Strickland, "Tribal Struggle," 42.

78. See Patterson and Runge, "Smallpox," 220 (noting British commander-in-chief Jeffrey Amherst's instructions to distribute smallpox-infected blankets to American Indians, "as well as to try every other method that can serve to extirpate this execrable race"); see also *Scott v. Sandford*, 407 (describing persons of African descent as having been considered "so far inferior, that they had no rights which the white man was bound to respect"). On the "scientific" theories used to reinforce such perspectives, see Horsman, *Manifest Destiny*, 116–186; Black, *War Against the Weak*, 3–4; Gould, *Mismeasure*, 30–145. For more recent developments, see generally Lombardo, "The 'American Breed'"; Lombardo, *Three Generations*.

79. *Johnson v. McIntosh*, 587. See also Newton, "Federal Power," 248; Churchill, "Law Stood Squarely," 673–675.

80. Gathii, "The American Origins."

81. See Strickland, "Tribal Struggle," 44.

82. Ibid., 41.

83. *Cherokee Nation v. Georgia*, 20; see also U.S. Constitution, Art. III, § 2 (extending federal court jurisdiction to controversies between citizens of different states, or between a state or its citizens and foreign states or their citizens, and giving the Supreme Court original jurisdiction over cases in which a state is a party).

84. *Cherokee Nation v. Georgia*, 52–54.

85. Churchill, "Law Stood Squarely," 677–678.

86. *Cherokee Nation v. Georgia*, 17.

87 See Williams, "Algebra," 253–256; see generally Frickey, "Marshalling Past and Present."

88. *Worcester v. Georgia*.

89. Ibid., 561.

90. See Strickland, "Tribal Struggle," 39–40, 53 (also noting the statement attributed to Jackson, "Marshall has made his law, let him enforce it").

91. See *Worcester v. Georgia,*, 543.

92. *Cherokee Nation v. Georgia*, 27–28. See generally Watson, "John Marshall."

93. See generally Miller, "Doctrine of Discovery" (discussing the continuing application of the doctrine); see generally O'Melinn, "Imperial Origins" (on roots of this jurisprudence in European colonial thought).

94. Fitzpatrick, *Mythology*, 28.

95. Ibid., 30.

96. See Sanders, *Lost Tribes*, 18–19 (noting the *Reconquista*'s "new racial consciousness [that] soon showed its imperialist undertones").

97. See ibid., 55.

98. Ibid., 155 (quoting las Casas, who wrote, among other things, a highly laudatory biography of Columbus).

99. See Churchill, "Deconstructing the Columbus Myth," 81, 85–88; on the demographic effects of these policies, see generally Stannard, *American Holocaust*; Thornton, *American Indian Holocaust*.

100. See Sanders, *Lost Tribes*, 130; Hanke, *Aristotle*, 44–45.

101. See Hanke, *Aristotle*, 44–61, 86–88; Sanders, *Lost Tribes*, 156–165 nn. 1550–1551 (discussing the prolonged debate between las Casas and Juan Ginés de Sepúlveda on the subject).

102. Sanders, *Lost Tribes*, 158–159 (also noting that, in his later *History of the Indies*, las Casas, apparently repulsed by the horrors of African slavery, changed his position, arguing that Africans and Indians should fall under the same law).

103. Higginbotham, *Matter of Color*, 10 (quoting Thomas Jefferson's *Notes on the State of Virginia*).

104. See Jordan, *White Over Black*, 57.

105. Ibid., 56–66.

106. Higginbotham, *Matter of Color*, 20.

107. Ibid., 21.

108. Ibid.

109. Jordan, *White Over Black*, 94.

110. Higginbotham, *Matter of Color*, 36–37 (emphasis in original); see also Bennett, *Before the Mayflower*, 46.

111. Higginbotham, *Matter of Color*, 163 (this document was never officially approved by the colonists, but it reflected the prevailing legal standard).

112. Ibid., 62

113. Strickland, "Tribal Struggle," 41.

114. Higginbotham, *Matter of Color*, 38.

115. See ibid., 36–40, 169–190; Jordan, *White Over Black*, 52–56.

116. Higginbotham, *Matter of Color*, 160–162.

117. Baldwin, *Evidence*, 29–30.

118. Higginbotham, *Matter of Color*, 42. See also *Loving v. Virginia* (holding that such laws violated the equal protection clause of the Fourteenth Amendment); see generally Malcomson, *One Drop of Blood*.

119. Higginbotham, *Matter of Color*, 43–45 (also noting that in 1705 Virginia amended its laws to provide that "mulatto" children, if not enslaved, would be servants until they were at least thirty-one years of age).

120. See Haney Lopez, *White by Law*, 20, 83. See also *Plessy v. Ferguson*, 538 (finding Homer Plessy appropriately classified as "colored" although he was "seven eighths Caucasian and one eighth African blood"); *Doe v. Louisiana* (affirming the constitutionality of Louisiana's "one thirty-second" rule). See generally Woodward, *Jim Crow*; Roediger, *Wages of Whiteness*; Harris, "Whiteness as Property."

121. See, for example, the development of "blood quantum" rules for the allocation of lands to American Indians. See generally Spruhan, "A Legal History."

122. See generally Haney Lopez, *White by Law*.

123. See Esteva and Prakash, *Grassroots Postmodernism*, 125 (on the concept of "pluriverse"); see also chapter 9 in this volume.

124. Fitzpatrick, "Terminal Legality," 9, 20.

125. See, e.g., *Prigg v. Pennsylvania*, 612 (describing the fugitive slave clause as a "fundamental article" of the Constitution, "without the adoption of which the Union could not have been formed").

126. Finkelman, "Covenant with Death," 21; see also Higginbotham, *Shades of Freedom*, 199.

127. See U.S. Constitution, Art. I, § 9, cl. 1 ("The Migration or Importation of such Persons as any of the States now existing shall think proper to admit, shall not be prohibited by the Congress prior to the Year one thousand eight hundred and eight."); U.S. Constitution, Art. I, § 2, cl. 3 ("Representatives and direct Taxes shall be apportioned among the several States . . . according to their respective Numbers, which shall be determined by adding to the whole number of free Persons . . . three fifths of all other persons"); U.S. Constitution, Art. IV, § 2, cl. 3 ("No Person held to Service or Labour in one State, under the Laws thereof, escaping into another, shall in Consequence of any Law or Regulation therein, be discharged from such Service of Labour, but shall be delivered up on Claim of the Party to whom such Service or Labour may be due"); U.S. Constitution, Art. I, § 8, cl. 3 ("Congress shall have power to provide for calling forth the Militia to . . . suppress Insurrections and repel Invasions"). See generally Phillips, *The Constitution*; Lynd, "Slavery"; Finkelman, "Covenant with Death."

128. See McPherson, *Negro's Civil War*, 11.

129. See generally Litwack, *North of Slavery*.

130. *Scott v. Sandford*, 407.

131. "Address to a Joint Session of Congress," in Bush, *We Will Prevail*, 16.

132. "Speech on the 'Lessons of Liberty Initiative,' October 30, 2001," in ibid., 55. This has also been the theme of the U.S. military operation in Afghanistan initiated in 2001 ("Enduring Freedom"), the May 2003 invasion of Iraq ("Operation Iraqi Freedom"), and the program to intensify domestic security ("Operation Liberty Shield"). See "Presidential Address to the Nation, October 7, 2001," in Bush, *We Will Prevail*, 33 (announcing the commencement of attacks on Afghanistan); "Speech on Operations Liberty Shield and Iraqi Freedom, March 31, 2002," in ibid., 245.

133. Brodie, *Thomas Jefferson*, 92.

134. Ibid., 91–92 (also noting that in 1769 Jefferson had introduced legislation which, if passed, would have allowed Virginia slave owners to emancipate their slaves).

135. *Scott v. Sandford*, 454.

136. Ibid., 403.

137. See U.S. Constitution Amend. XIV ("All persons born or naturalized in the United States, and subject to the jurisdiction thereof, are citizens of the United States and of the State wherein they reside").

138. See *Plessy v. Ferguson* (upholding legalized apartheid); *Elk v. Wilkins*, 102 (holding that American Indians did not acquire birthright citizenship because they were not "subject to the jurisdiction" of the United States).

139. Kim, "An Overview," 2; see also Perea, "Demography and Distrust," 287–292.

140. "Naturalization Act of 1790" (repealed by the Act of January 19, 1795, which reenacted most of its provisions, including its racial restriction).

141. See generally Haney Lopez, *White by Law*.

142. *United States v. Bhagat Singh Thind*, 213.

143. See Fitzpatrick, *Mythology*, 62–63 (quoting Michel Foucault on the shift in intellectual activity from "drawing things together" to discriminating between them, and its influence on both identity and order).

144. Fitzpatrick, "Terminal Legality," 21.

CHAPTER 5. A MANIFEST DESTINY

1. See Horsman, *Manifest Destiny*, 220 (noting that the following week Massachusetts Representative Robert C. Winthrop referred to the phrase in Congress and it was soon widely referenced in popular discourse).

2. "Speech to the Employees of the Department of Labor, October 4, 2002," in Bush, *We Will Prevail*, 30.

3. Lens, *Forging*, 2 (also noting that both Samuel Adams and his cousin John Adams insisted that Canada be incorporated into the Union).

4. See Nugent, *Habits of Empire*, 237–251.

5. See Andrist, *The Long Death*, 350–352; Brown, *Bury My Heart*, 401–402.

6. Merk, *Manifest Destiny*, 9 (quoting letter of November 24, 1801).

7. See Fitzpatrick, *Mythology*, 37 (noting that in the presumed universalization of the West "the subject is joined with the progression of subordination and with that which remains unsubordinated").

8. U.S. Bureau of the Census, *Fifteenth Census*, 3 (Table II, "Indian Population by Divisions and States, 1890–1930"); see also Sale, *Conquest of Paradise*, 316 (providing precontact estimates).

9. See chapter 3 in this volume.

10. Heizer, *Destruction*, 251 (quoting "Exciting News From Tehema-Indian Thefts— Terrible Vengeance of the Whites," *Daily Alta California*, March 6, 1853).

11. See Churchill, "To Judge Them," 303–403.

12. See U.S. Bureau of the Census, *Report on Indians*, 637–638 (noting with respect to the 1890 census that the "frontier" was now closed); Churchill, "Law Stood Squarely," 681.

13. Quoted in Fitzgerald, *Writings*, 189–193.

14. Wallace, *Death and Rebirth*, 141–144.

15. Drinnon, *Facing West*, 332 (quoting an 1838 description by historian William L. Stone).

16. See Hamilton, "The Hamilton Papers"; Drinnon, *Keeper*, 23; Fowke, *Archaeological History*, 478–480; Churchill, "To Judge Them," 304; see generally Eckert, *Bloody River*.

17. See Sugden, *Tecumseh's Last Stand*, 180.

18. Stannard, *American Holocaust*, 121; see also Halbert and Hall, *Creek War*, 276–277.

19. See Axelrod, *Chronicle*, 151.

20. Horsman, *Manifest Destiny*, 279.

21. Anghie, *Imperialism, Sovereignty*, 294 (citing Vitoria, *De Indis*, 170).

22. Ibid., 294.

23. Ibid., 295–296 (citing Immanuel Kant, "Perpetual Peace," in Reiss, *Kant*, 98).

24. Mooney, "Population," 286–287.

25. Stiffarm and Lane, "Demography," 35; see also Churchill, "'Nits Make Lice,'" 178–188.

26. Thornton, *American Indian Holocaust*, 49.

27. Gorn, Roberts, and Bilhartz, *Constructing*, 74 (quoting Editorial, *Aberdeen Saturday Pioneer*, December 20, 1890).

28. 4 Stat. 411 (1830).

29. See Churchill, "Like Sand in the Wind," 335–336; Thornton, "Cherokee Losses," 289–300.

30. Churchill, "Like Sand in the Wind," 337 (noting that Jackson's speech was originally published in 1829 in *Documents and Proceedings relating to the Formation and Progress of a Board in the City of New York, for the Emigration, Preservation, and Improvement of the Aborigines of America*).

31. See "A brief history of the formation of Oklahoma territory" in "From the Report of Ex. Gov. Jenkins," *The Indian Advocate* (describing white settlement of Oklahoma as reading "almost like a fairy tale" of American "achievement"); see also Churchill, "Like Sand in the Wind," 338.

32. See Schultz, *Over the Earth*, 279–283; Brown, *Bury My Heart*, 60, 63–64.

33. On their status as prisoners of war, see *Tsosie v. United States*, 395 (citing *Duran v. United States*). On their conditions of confinement, see generally Bailey, *Bosque Redondo*.

34. Hoig, *Sand Creek Massacre*, 147; see also Churchill, "To Judge Them," 310–313; see generally Ortiz, *From Sand Creek*.

35. U.S. Congress, Senate, *Reports of the Committees: The Chivington Massacre*, 42.

36. Churchill, "To Judge Them," 312. On a subsequent massacre of Black Kettle's non-combatants by George Armstrong Custer, see Axelrod, *Chronicle*, 209; see generally Hoig, *Battle of the Washita*.

37. See Berthrong, *Cheyenne and Arapaho Ordeal*, 27–47; Sandoz, *Cheyenne Autumn*, 27–31; Andrist, *The Long Death*, 321–329.

38. On their status as purported prisoners of war, see *Montoya v. United States*, 270 n (Finding of Fact).

39. See *United States v. Fort Sill Apache Tribe of Oklahoma*, 1361–1362; see generally *Fort Sill Apache Tribe of Oklahoma v. United States*, 1361–1362.

40. See Lieder and Page, *Wild Justice*, 28–29, 37; see generally Turcheneske, *Chiricahua Apache Prisoners*.

41. *United States* ex rel. *Standing Bear v. Crook*, 698.

42. Ibid., 697 (noting that the dictionary definition of a "person" was sufficiently comprehensive "to include even an Indian" and also noting the apparent lack of precedent).

43. Ibid., 700.

44. Ibid. See also Harring, *Crow Dog's Case*, 198–203; see generally Tibbles, *The Ponca Chiefs*.

45. *Bad Elk v. United States*.

46. Ex parte *Bi-a-lil-le*, 151.

47. Ibid., 153 (also rejecting the government's argument that the characterization of Indians as "wards of the government" allowed executive officers summary authority in the absence of enabling legislation).

48. Ibid., 153. See also Parman, "The Big Stick."

49. *United States* ex rel. *Standing Bear v. Crook*, 698–699.

50. Ibid., 698.

51. See Andrist, *The Long Death*, 350–352; Brown, *Bury My Heart*, 401–402; see generally McGregor, *Wounded Knee Massacre*. On the conditions of the Lakota confinement, see generally Hyde, *Red Cloud's Folk*; Hyde, *Spotted Tail's Folk*.

52. Quoted in *Ward v. Race Horse*, 70 F. at 600.

53. Ibid., 604.

54. Ibid,. 613; see also 600.

55. Ibid., 605 (quoting *Worcester v. Georgia*), 607.

56. Ibid., 607 (quoting *Worcester v. Georgia*).

57. See *Ward v. Race Horse*, 163 U.S. 504.

58. Ibid., 517–518 (Brown, J., dissenting).

59. Ibid., 508–509.

60. The Supreme Court did not limit the holding of *Ward v. Race Horse* or hold that statehood did not automatically abrogate treaty rights until 1999, even then reaffirming its continued reliance on that part of *Race Horse* holding that Congress could have abrogated the treaty rights at issue. See *Minnesota v. Mille Lacs Band of Chippewa Indians*, 203–208.

61. *Montoya v. United States*, 265. On the fallacy of this statement, see discussions of the Marshall opinions in chapters 3 and 4 of this volume.

62. *Montoya v. United States*, 265.

63. Ibid.

64. See chapter 3 in this volume.

65. Cohen, "How Long," 222–223. On Cohen as the "unrivaled authority," see Felix Frankfurter's foreword to Cohen, *Legal Conscience*, xiii.

66. *Montoya v. United States*, 265.

67. Ibid.

68. See Williams, *Discourses of Conquest*, 233–280.

69. See *Fletcher v. Peck*; see generally McGrath, *Yazoo*. Justice Marshall and his father had each received some of the scrip at issue for land in what is now Kentucky. See Smith, *John Marshall*, 74–75.

70. See Kades, "The Dark Side," 1172–1174.

71. *Johnson v. McIntosh*, 587; see also Newton, "Federal Power," 209, 248; Churchill, "Law Stood Squarely," 673–675.

72. *Cherokee Nation v. Georgia*, 17. See also Churchill, "Law Stood Squarely," 677–678 ("in practical effect, Marshall cast indigenous nations as entities inherently imbued with a sufficient measure of sovereignty to alienate their territory by treaty when and wherever the U.S. desired they do so, but never with enough to refuse").

73. See *Worcester v. Georgia*.

74. Deloria and Wilkins, *Tribes, Treaties*, 29.

75. 16 Stat. 544, 566 (1871).

76. Deloria, "'Congress in Its Wisdom,'" 107.

77. Ibid. (also listing a series of illustrative statutes).

78. See Ex parte *Kan-gi-shun-ca (otherwise known as Crow Dog)*, 570.

79. Ibid., 571.

80. See generally Harring, *Crow Dog's Case*.

81. See Deloria, "'Congress in Its Wisdom,'" 109 (noting that the Major Crimes Act was passed as part of the Indian Appropriation Act of 1885, ch. 341, 23 Stat. 362, 385 [1885], and was followed by the 1898 Assimilative Crimes Act, which allowed less serious criminal offenses to be prosecuted under state law).

82. *United States v. Kagama*, 381–382.

83. Ibid., 380 (quoting *American Insurance Co. v. Canter*, 542). This did not, of course, address the underlying question of the United States' right to acquire the territory in the first place.

84. Deloria, "'Congress in Its Wisdom,'" 109.

85. 24 Stat. 388 (1887), upheld as constitutional in *Lone Wolf v. Hitchcock*. See generally Clark, *Lone Wolf*.

86. Prucha, *Great Father*, 671 n. 26 (noting that the language was first used by "reformer" Merrill Gates in 1900 and was repeated by Roosevelt in his 1901 message to Congress).

87 Clark, *Lone Wolf*, 2. Those who accepted land simultaneously became U.S. citizens, whether they wanted to or not. See also Prucha, *Great Father*, 668 (noting that those who accepted land were required to accept U.S. citizenship); 673–676 (describing simultaneous efforts to rename American Indians in ways easier for the settlers to comprehend and pronounce).

88. See Strickland, "Genocidal Premise," 329–330; see generally Otis, *Dawes Act*.

89. See Porter, "Pursuing the Path," 13 (noting that American Indian nations historically had flexible membership criteria and describing the use of blood quantum standards as "one of the lasting vestiges of colonialism").

90. *Lone Wolf v. Hitchcock*, 565. See generally Frickey, "Doctrine, Context."

91. See Saito, *Chinese Exclusion*, 13–49; see generally Newton, "Federal Power"; Aleinikoff, *Semblances of Sovereignty*.

92. Churchill, "'Nits Make Lice,'" 246.

93. See Churchill, *"Kill the Indian,"* 13–14. For general background, see ibid.; Curcio, "Civil Claims," esp. 48–71; Adams, *Education for Extinction.*

94. Thompson, *Schooling of Native America.*

95. On the deaths and devastation inflicted by malnutrition, disease, and forced labor at these schools, see Churchill, *"Kill the Indian,"* 29–51; on physical abuse and sexual predation, see ibid., 51–68.

96. See Churchill, *"Kill the Indian,"* 34–37, 68–76. On Canadian residential schools instituted on the U.S. model, see ibid., 37–43; Austen, "Canada Offers" (noting governmental apology acknowledging physical and sexual abuse, and recognizing that the system "was dedicated to eradicating the languages, traditions and cultural practices of Native Canadians and has been linked to the widespread incidence of alcoholism, suicide and family violence in many native communities").

97. Porter, "Demise," 109.

98. Ibid., 108–109. See also Porter-Odawi, "Two Kinds" (further explaining this view of assimilationism).

99. See *Problem of Indian Administration;* see also Prucha, *Great Father,* 808 (noting that the Institute publishing this report later became part of the Brookings Institution).

100. See *Cherokee Nation v. Georgia,* 17; Coulter and Tullberg, "Indian Land Rights," 200.

101. Coulter and Tullberg, "Indian Land Rights," 201 (citing Cohen's, "Indian Wardship: Twilight of a Myth").

102. See also chapter 6 in this volume on the problems associated with the subsequent federal recognition of American Indian "tribes" pursuant to the Indian Reorganization Act of 1934.

103. See Churchill, "Like Sand in the Wind," 357 n. 26 (noting that this was not actually a purchase but an agreement by France quitclaiming such rights as it had acquired from Spain in 1800, rights limited, in turn, by lawful acquisition from Indigenous owners).

104. Drinnon, *Facing West,* 103.

105. See Smith, *Plot to Steal;* see also Currie, "Rumors of War," 7.

106. Merk, *Manifest Destiny,* 7.

107. See Mulroy, *Freedom,* 8 (noting that in 1693 the Spanish king had freed fugitive slaves, and in 1704 the governor of Florida announced that "any *negro* of Carolina, Christian or not, free or slave, who wishes to come fugitive, will be [given] complete liberty").

108. See *Davis v. United States,* 954 (describing the formation of the Seminole Nation). See generally Giddings, *Exiles of Florida;* Saito, "From Slavery."

109. See Giddings, *Exiles of Florida,* 37–43.

110. Ibid., 43.

111. Ibid., 37–38.

112. See generally ibid.; Porter, *The Black Seminoles.*

113. Drinnon, *Facing West,* 103–111 (quotes at 104, 111); see also 106–107 (quoting a proclamation by Andrew Jackson accusing the Seminoles of engaging in "all the horrors of savage massacre" and invoking "the immutable laws of self defence" as justification for taking "possession of such part of the Floridas in which the Spanish authority could not be maintained").

114. Giddings, *Exiles of Florida,* 59; see also *United States. v. Percheman.*

115. See Merk, *Manifest Destiny*, 6, 68, 228–229, 231 (discussing American aspirations to much of North and South America).

116. Acuña, *Occupied America*, 43; see also Perea, "Brief History," 287.

117. See Merk, *Manifest Destiny*, 17, 204, 206, 220; Acuña, *Occupied America*, 49.

118. Acuña, *Occupied America*, 43.

119. Ibid., 44 (noting that settlers circumvented this by declaring their slaves "free" and then signing them to lifelong contracts as indentured servants); see also Campbell, *Empire for Slavery*, 23–24.

120. Acuña, *Occupied America*, 43 (noting that in response to the 1819 treaty Long had declared that "Congress had no right or power to sell, exchange, or relinquish an 'American possession'"); see also Van Alstyne, *Rising American Empire*, 101.

121. Acuña, *Occupied America*, 44; Van Alstyne, *Rising American Empire*, 101.

122. Merk, *Manifest Destiny*, 20–21 (citing *House Exec. Docs.*, 25 Cong. 2d Sess. [Serial 332], No. 351, pages 313–314).

123. Merk, *Manifest Destiny*, 21.

124. Acuña, *Occupied America*, 44; see also Weber, *Foreigners*, 89.

125. Barker, *Mexico and Texas*, 162.

126. Acuña, *Occupied America*, 46–48.

127. Quoted in Horsman, *Manifest Destiny*, 219.

128. Ibid., 220.

129. Ibid.

130. Ibid., 224.

131. Perea, "Brief History," 287–288; see also Acuña, *Occupied America*, 48–49; Zinn, *People's History*, 147–152.

132. Horsman, *Manifest Destiny*, 233.

133. See Acuña, *Occupied America*, 51–52; Zinn, *People's History*, 163–165 (noting that in two days thirteen hundred shells were fired into Vera Cruz, hitting, among other things, a hospital, and that whole blocks of Mexico City were destroyed).

134. Quoted in Zinn, *People's History*, 165.

135. Exceptions included the handful of abolitionists in Congress who voted against all war measures, including Joshua Giddings who said, "In the murder of Mexicans upon their own soil, or in robbing them of their country, I can take no part either now or hereafter" (quoted in ibid., 152).

136. Ibid., 163.

137. Quoted in Acuña, *Occupied America*, 41.

138. Zinn, *People's History*, 151.

139. Horseman, *Manifest Destiny*, 236 (quoting *The Casket* [Cincinatti], June 10, 1846).

140. Ibid., 276 (citing Cong. Record, July 25, 1848). See also Weber, *Foreigners*, 59–60 (noting the widespread Angloamerican belief that the Mexicans "had inherited the worst qualities of Spaniards and Indians to produce a 'race' still more despicable than that of either parent"); Perea, "Brief History," 292.

141. Horsman, *Manifest Destiny*, 239.

142. Ibid., 238.

143. Ibid., 243. See also Perea, "Brief History," 293–295; Merk, *Manifest Destiny*, 191–192. Fuller, *Movement*.

144. Perea, "Brief History," 294 (also noting that, when combined with Texas, this resulted in a loss for Mexico of about half its territory). See generally Griswold del Castillo, "Manifest Destiny."

145. Zinn, *People's History*, 166.

146. See e.g., the 1849 California Constitution, which limited the right to vote to "every white male citizen of the United States, and every white male citizen of Mexico, who shall have elected to become a citizen of the United states, under the treaty of [Guadalupe Hidalgo]." Perea et al., *Race and Races*, 302 (quoting Cal. Const. Art. II, sec. 1 [1849]).

147. Perea, "Brief History," 295; see also Weber, *Foreigners*, 163–164 (reproducing Article VIII of the Treaty of Peace, Friendship, Limits, and Settlement with the Republic of Mexico, February 2, 1848, U.S.–Mex., 9 Stat. 922 [Treaty of Guadalupe-Hidalgo]).

148. Perea, "Brief History," 295–296 (discussing Article IX of the Treaty of Guadalupe Hidalgo); see also Perea et al., *Race and Races*, 299 (noting that Congress used this discretion to deny statehood to New Mexico for sixty-two years, until it had a majority Anglo population).

149. Griswold del Castillo, "Manifest Destiny," 37; see also Acuña, *Occupied America*, 69–71, 117, 144–148.

150. See Perea et al., *Race and Races*, 297–298 (quoting draft Articles IX and X of the Treaty of Guadalupe Hidalgo).

151. See Perea et al., *Race and Races*, 296–298.

152. See ibid., 303–323; see generally Ebright, *Land Grants*.

153. See *United States v. Sandoval*.

154. See Perea et al., *Race and Races*, 311–312.

155. Merk, *Manifest Destiny*, 25 (quoting *New York Morning News*, October 13, 1845, and citing similar expressions in the press and in the Senate).

156. Horsman, *Manifest Destiny*, 271.

157. Quoted in Merk, *Manifest Destiny*, 25.

CHAPTER 6. AMERICAN IMPERIAL EXPANSION

1. Horsman, *Manifest Destiny*, 232.

2. U.S. Constitution, Amend. XIII (abolishing slavery and involuntary servitude, except upon criminal conviction), Amend. XIV (prohibiting states from denying equal protection to persons on the basis of race, and recognizing as U.S. citizens all persons born in the territory of and subject to the jurisdiction of the United States). On the exclusion of American Indians until the 1924 Indian Citizenship Act unilaterally imposed U.S. citizenship upon them, see *Elk v. Wilkins* (holding that the birthright citizenship provision of the Fourteenth Amendment did not apply to American Indians).

3. Merk, *Manifest Destiny*, 227.

4. Horsman, *Manifest Destiny*, 24 (noting that nineteenth-century Americans would discover "that the secret of Saxon success lay not in the institutions but in the blood").

5. Ibid., 10–13.

6. Ibid., 33.

7. Ibid., 25–26.

8. See Stanton, *Leopard's Spots*, 6–14. On the earlier debates, see chapter 2 in this volume.

9. See Horsman, "Scientific Racism," 154.

10. See Gould, *Mismeasure*, 30–39; Stanton, *Leopard's Spots*, 3–6.

11. Horsman, *Manifest Destiny*, 98–100.

12. See ibid., 46–48 (summarizing the racial categories created by Swedish naturalist Carolus Linnaeus and German professor Johan Friedrich Blumenbach).

13. See Horsman, "Scientific Racism," 155–156.

14. Gould, *Mismeasure*, 54; see ibid., 42–69 (summarizing the work of Agassiz and Morton). On polygenesis, see generally Stanton, *Leopard's Spots*.

15. Horsman, *Manifest Destiny*, 48–53.

16. Ibid., 58.

17. Ibid., 59 (quoting the *Phrenological Journal* 19 [July 1846]: 214).

18. Gould, *Mismeasure*, 72. It is significant that the full title of Darwin's book was *On the Origin of the Species: The Preservation of Favoured Races in the Struggle for Life*. See Drinnon, *Facing West*, 236.

19. Gould, *Mismeasure*, 75–77.

20. Black, *War Against the Weak*, 16–17. Combined with Mendelian genetics, this provided a purportedly scientific basis for the "blood quantum" rules used in racial classification to this day. See generally Spruhan, "A Legal History."

21. Black, *War Against the Weak*, 17.

22. Horsman, *Manifest Destiny*, 5.

23. Kühl, *Nazi Connection*, 4 (quoting Galton). See generally Lombardo, *Three Generations*.

24. Black, *War Against the Weak*, 31. See also Horsman, "Scientific Racism," 168 ("by the middle of the nineteenth century science itself had endorsed the earlier popular feeling that the Indians were not worth saving and envisaged a world bettered as the all-conquering Anglo-Saxon branch of the Caucasian race superseded inferior peoples").

25. Skaggs, *Guano Rush*, 68–69.

26. Zinn, *People's History*, 291; see also 399 (discussing use of the "Open Door" policy to ensure access to China's trade and resources and keep troops in Beijing for thirty years).

27. See Burnett, "Edges of Empire," 786, 791 (noting that the term's vagueness allowed the U.S. to claim territories without clarifying the attendant implications or responsibilities).

28. Merk, *Manifest Destiny*, 229 ("It was offered because it had become an encumbrance to the Russian Tsar. . . . Chiefly it was taken because it seemed quite cheap at the price of $7,200,000").

29. Ibid., 230.

30. Skaggs, *Guano Rush*, 11–15.

31. 48 U.S.C. §§ 1411–1419, reproduced in Skaggs, *Guano Rush*, 227–228; see also 57–63. See also *Jones v. United States* (upholding constitutionality of the Guano Islands Act).

32. Skaggs, *Guano Rush*, 200–202 (noting U.S. disregard for Haitian claims to Navassa Island, near the Panama Canal, into the mid-1990s).

33. *Jones v. United States*.

34. See Burnett, "Edges of Empire," 788–790; *Jones v. United States*, 137 U.S. at 211–212.

35. U.S. Constitution, Art. IV § 3, cl. 2; see also Burnett, "Edges of Empire," 791.

36. *Jones v. United States*, 137 U.S. at 212.

37. Ibid.

38. Ibid., 219–220.

39. Ibid., 221.

40. *Johnson v. McIntosh.*

41. See Skaggs, *Guano Rush*, 67–114 (noting international disputes resulting from U.S. claims); see also 230–236 (listing claims and acquisitions under the Act).

42. Ibid., 66.

43. See ibid., 199–225 (noting, among other things, use of the Johnson atoll, approximately seven hundred miles from Honolulu, as a nuclear testing and toxic waste site).

44. *Boumediene v. Bush*, 128 S.Ct. at 2252.

45. See Takaki, *Strangers*, 84–87 (noting that, by 1867, 90 percent of the workers laboring on the Central Pacific Railroad were Chinese).

46. Burlingame Treaty; see also Daniels, *Guarding*, 12; Takaki, *Strangers*, 113–115.

47. See generally Chan, *Entry Denied.*

48. Churchill, "Stolen Kingdom," 77. See also O'Connor, *Pacific Destiny*, 43 (noting that in 1810 sandalwood cost one cent per pound in Hawaii and sold for thirty-four cents per pound in China).

49. See U.S. Congress, House, "Report upon the Relations of the United States with the Hawaiian Islands," 8; Kuykendall, *The Hawaiian Kingdom*, 90; Budnick, *Stolen Kingdom*, 61, 139. For background, see generally Tinker, *Missionary Conquest.*

50. Churchill, *Perversions of Justice*, 408 (reproducing Congressional Apology to Native Hawaiians, S.J. Res. 19, 103d Cong., 1st Sess., 107 Stat. 1510 [1993]).

51. On the annexation of Texas, see chapter 5 of this volume. On the process in Hawai'i, see Trask, *Native Daughter*, 4–20; see generally Churchill and Venne, *Islands in Captivity.*

52. See Stannard, *Before the Horror*, 51 (noting an 87 percent decline in the native Hawaiian population between 1778 and 1893); see also Anaya, "Native Hawaiian People," 311–320.

53. Churchill, "Stolen Kingdom," 78 (noting that Hawai'i's first constitution ensured that Christianity would be the state religion and protected the political power of white settlers); see generally Kelly, *Early Mission Impact.*

54. Quoted in Barnard, "Law, Narrative," 9.

55. Morgan, *Economic Change*, 178. See also Barnard, "Law, Narrative," 5; Kame'eleihiwa, *Native Land*, 298–306; see generally Chinen, *The Great Mahela.*

56. Churchill, "Stolen Kingdom," 70; Kent, *Hawaii*, 39 (contrasting the importation of two hundred thousand Japanese with the Kanak population, which had been reduced to fifty-five thousand by 1850). On the sugar plantations, see generally Mollett, *Hawaiian Sugar*; Kelly, *Hawaii.*

57. Churchill, "Stolen Kingdom," 79.

58. Ibid., 79–80; see generally Stevens, *American Expansion.*

59. Churchill, "Stolen Kingdom," 80; Kent, *Hawaii*, 45.

60. See U.S. Congress, House, *Executive Document: Report to Secretary of State W.Q. Gresham*, 377–384 (investigative report of former Georgia congressman James Blount, including letter from Stevens to Foster, November 20, 1892).

61. Quoted in Barnard, "Law, Narrative," 28; for contemporary parallels, see chapter 8 in this volume.

62. See generally Allen, *Betrayal.* These events are also portrayed in the excellent documentary film, *Act of War.*

63. See *Act of War* (portraying debate); see also Miller, *"Benevolent Assimilation,"* 15–16.

64. Merk, *Manifest Destiny*, 243 (quoting Schurz, "Manifest Destiny," *Harper's New Monthly Magazine* [1893]).

65. Merk, *Manifest Destiny*, 244.

66. Zinn, *People's History*, 293.

67. Merk, *Manifest Destiny*, 255–256. See also Joint Resolution to Provide for the Annexing of the Hawaiian Islands ("Newlands Resolution"); Churchill, "Stolen Kingdom," 75–76.

68. See *Hawaii v. Mankichi*, 222 n. 3 (quoting 30 Stat. 750 [1898]).

69. Act to Provide Government for the Territory of Hawaii; see also *Hawaii v. Mankichi*; Cooper and Daws, *Land and Power*, 2.

70. Churchill, "Stolen Kingdom," 84–85. See also Trask, *Native Daughter*, 138–139 (discussing the economic devastation wrought by the tourist industry).

71. Cooper and Daws, *Land and Power*, 3; see also Kent, *Hawaii*, 76.

72. Churchill, "Stolen Kingdom," 86; see also Ferguson, Turnbull, and Ali, "Rethinking the Military," 183–193.

73. See Dudley and Agard, *Call for Hawaiian Sovereignty*, 25–46 (Message of President Grover Cleveland to the Congress [December 18, 1893]); Weaver, *Hawaii, USA*, 103; see also Russ, *Hawaiian Republic*, 37.

74. Churchill, "Stolen Kingdom," 90; see also Anaya, "Native Hawaiian People," 334–335.

75. Congressional Apology to Native Hawaiians, reproduced in Churchill, *Perversions of Justice*, 408–413.

76. Merk, *Manifest Destiny*, 220–221.

77. Drinnon, *Facing West*, 114 (quoting 1823 statement by Jefferson).

78. Merk, *Manifest Destiny*, 221.

79. Horsman, *Manifest Destiny*, 281–282.

80. Ibid., 283.

81. Zinn, *People's History*, 291; see also 291–295.

82. Ibid., 295.

83. See Horsman, *Manifest Destiny*, 282–284. See also Buchanan, Mason, and Soulé, "Ostend Manifesto" (expressing fears of U.S. foreign ministers that to "permit Cuba to be Africanized and become a second St. Domingo, with all its attendant horrors to the white race," would be "base treason against our posterity").

84. Quoted in Zinn, *People's History*, 296.

85. Drinnon, *Facing West*, 269–270.

86. Merk, *Manifest Destiny*, 250.

87. Drinnon, *Facing West*, 269.

88. Zinn, *People's History*, 302 (quoting letter of protest from Cuban leader General Calixto García).

89. Ibid., 303 (giving, as examples, United Fruit's purchase of 1.9 million acres of land for twenty cents an acre and the acquisition of control over 80 percent of Cuban minerals, mostly by Bethlehem Steel).

90. Merk, *Manifest Destiny*, 258; see also Strauss, "Guantanamo Bay," 494–507.

91. Zinn, *People's History*, 304–305.

92. Merk, *Manifest Destiny*, 258. On the continued U.S. occupation of the base, see Schatz and Horst, "Will Justice"; see also *Rasul v. Bush*, 487 (noting that the lease term is "indefinite and at the discretion of the United States" and, therefore, "from a practical perspective . . . has produced a place that belongs to the United States").

93. Organic Act of 1900 (Foraker Act).

94. Burnett and Marshall, "Between the Foreign and the Domestic," 5.

95. See ibid., 32 n. 44 (critiquing this framing).

96. *Downes v. Bidwell.*

97. Ramos, "Legal Construction of American Colonialism," 246–247 (citing *Downes v. Bidwell*). See also *Downes v. Bidwell*, 382 (Justice White, concurring, stating that "while in an international sense Porto Rico was not a foreign country, since it was . . . owned by the United States, it was foreign to the United States in a domestic sense, because the island had not been incorporated into the United States, but was merely appurtenent thereto as a possession").

98. See generally Burnett, "Territorial Deannexation" (noting that the *Insular Cases* allowed the U.S. to both hold and relinquish unincorporated territories at its discretion).

99. Puerto Rican Federalism Relations Act.

100. See *Balzac v. People of Puerto Rico* (holding that the Jones Act, which conferred citizenship but not representation, did not "incorporate" Puerto Rico into the United States).

101. See generally Malavet, *America's Colony*; Mongé, *Puerto Rico*; Ramos, *Legal Construction of Identity*; Burnett and Marshall, *Foreign in a Domestic Sense.*

102. See Torruella, "One Hundred Years," 241–250; Mongé, *Puerto Rico*, 162–163 (listing the factors which still define Puerto Rico as a colony); Román, "Empire Forgotten." See also Leibowitz, *Defining Status*, 314–315 (concerning Guam's continuing status as an unincorporated territory).

103. Mongé, "Injustice," 230–231.

104. Treaty of Peace between the United States and Spain.

105. Merk, *Manifest Destiny*, 254.

106. Drinnon, *Facing West*, 269.

107. 33 Cong. Rec. 56th Cong., 1st Sess., January 9, 1900, 704–705.

108. Drinnon, *Facing West*, 279; Zinn, *People's History*, 306–307.

109. Drinnon, *Facing West*, 279–280.

110. Ibid., 279; Zinn, *People's History*, 306–307.

111. Zinn, *People's History*, 306.

112. Schirmer and Shalom, *Philippines Reader*, 6.

113. Drinnon, *Facing West*, 288. Senator Beveridge describes this incident quite differently: "We did not strike till they attacked us in force, without provocation. This left us no alternative but war or evacuation" (33 Cong. Rec. 56th Cong., 1st Sess., January 9, 1900, at 708).

114. Schirmer and Shalom, *Philippines Reader*, 7.

115. Drinnon, *Facing West*, 288–289.

116. Schirmer and Shalom, *Philippines Reader*, 11. Nonetheless, as UN Ambassador and future Secretary of State Madeleine Albright was to say about the more than half-million Iraqi children killed as a result of U.S.-imposed sanctions, the U.S. "decided it's worth the cost." Churchill, *Roosting Chickens*, 6 (quoting Albright in a May 12, 1996, interview on *60 Minutes*).

117. Linn, *U.S. Army*, 23 (citation omitted).

118. See Churchill, "To Judge Them," 315–318; Miller, *"Benevolent Assimilation,"* 196–218; Drinnon, *Facing West*, 287–288.

119. Drinnon, *Facing West*, 287.

120. Zinn, *People's History*, 309.

121. Schirmer and Shalom, *Philippines Reader*, 15–19.

122. Ibid., 16.

123. See Churchill, "To Judge Them," 316.

124. Schirmer and Shalom, *Philippines Reader*, 17.

125. Ibid., 19. In a 1902 speech Senator George F. Hoar stated, "The conflict in the Philippines has cost you six hundred million dollars, thousands of American soldiers . . . the health and sanity of thousands more, and hundreds of thousands of Filipinos slain" (Cong. Rec., 57 Cong. 1 sess. [1902], 5788–5798, available at http://www.bartleby.com/268/10/25.html [accessed February 28, 2009]). Nonetheless figures as low as twenty thousand continue to be cited. See, e.g., Zasloff, "Law and the Shaping," 291.

126. Miller, *"Benevolent Assimilation,"* 163–164.

127. Zinn, *People's History*, 308.

128. Cong. Rec., 57th Cong., 1st sess. (May 22, 1902), 5788–5798; see also Welch, "American Atrocities."

129. 33 Cong. Rec. 56th Cong., 1st Sess., January 9, 1900, at 707.

130. Ibid., at 705.

131. Ibid., at 712.

132. Ibid., at 708.

133. Drinnon, *Facing West*, 281.

134. Ibid., 293.

135. Ibid., 295.

136. Ibid., 286.

137. Emphasis in original. The full text is available at http://www.mcs.edu.ph/centennial/benevolent.html (accessed August 31, 2008).

138. Zinn, *People's History*, 308. See generally Zasloff, "Law and the Shaping" (describing Root's legal background).

139. Miller, *"Benevolent Assimilation,"* 169–170.

140. See generally Welch, "American Atrocities."

141. Churchill, "To Judge Them," 317–318.

142. Ibid., 318 (citing U.S. Senate, Committee on the Philippine Islands, *Hearings*).

143. *Dorr v. United States*, 139 ("the full discussion had in the opinions delivered in the so-called 'Insular cases,' renders superfluous any attempt to reconsider the constitutional relation of the powers of the government to territory acquired by a treaty cession to the United States"); see also *United States v. Dorr*, 23 S.Ct. 859 (1900, Supreme Court of the Philippine Islands); Merk, *Manifest Destiny*, 258.

144. See Schirmer and Shalom, *Philippines Reader*, 35–66.

145. Ibid., 35.

146. Ibid., 87; excerpted at 88–90. See also 87–88, 94–96 (1955 Laurel-Langley Agreement expanding recognition of Filipino sovereignty while increasing protection of U.S. capital).

147. Ibid., 88; excerpted at 96–100. See also 100–103 (related agreement concerning U.S. military aid and training); Chanbonpin, "Holding the United States Accountable," 332.

148. See generally Chanbonpin, "Holding the United States Accountable."

149. Schirmer and Shalom, *Philippines Reader*, 290–291.

150. Horsman, *Manifest Destiny*, 291 (citing *De Bow's Review* 12 [June 1852]: 614–631).

151. Ibid.

152. Ibid.

153. Horsman, *Manifest Destiny*, 291 (quoting *Merchant's Magazine* article).

154. 33 Cong. Rec. 56th Cong., 1st Sess., January 9, 1900, at 711.

155. Merk, *Manifest Destiny*, 224.

156. Ibid., 224–225.

157. Drinnon, *Facing West*, 232 (quoting Roosevelt, *The Strenuous Life* [1901]).

158. Quoted in ibid., 241. See Merk, *Manifest Destiny*, 259 n. 44 (on Samoa and the Virgin Islands); see generally Rogers, *Destiny's Landfall* (on Guam).

159. Zinn, *People's History*, 399; see also Churchill, *Roosting Chickens*, 58–62 (listing interventions); Drinnon, *Facing West*, 372 (on the Panama Canal).

160. See Churchill, *Roosting Chickens*, 58–60.

161. Merk, *Manifest Destiny*, 259.

CHAPTER 7. MAKING THE WORLD SAFE FOR DEMOCRACY

1. See generally Rubenfeld, "Unilateralism."

2. See Koskenniemi, *Gentle Civilizer*, 121–127; see generally Ocran, "Clash" (discussing the destruction of African legal systems).

3. See Anghie *Imperialism, Sovereignty*, 11 (quoting Doyle, *Empires*, 45 [defining imperialism as "a relationship, formal or informal, in which one state controls the effective political sovereignty of another political society" and which "can be achieved by force, by political collaboration, by economic, social or cultural dependence"]). On other empires with aspirations to globalization, see Bederman, *Globalization*, 4–9.

4. See Crawford, *Creation of States*, 4.

5. See Statute of the International Court of Justice, Art. 38; *Restatement Third*, 102.

6. Nietschmann, "Fourth World," 227. See also Seton-Watson, *Nations and States*, 1.

7. Nietschmann, "Fourth World," 225–242.

8. See Westlake, *Principles of International Law*, 3 (equating international law with "a society of states"); see also Koskenniemi, *Gentle Civilizer*, 49; Anghie, *Imperialism, Sovereignty*, 47–48.

9. Crawford, *Creation of States*, 14–15.

10. Wheaton, *Elements*, 15 (quoted in Anghie, *Imperialism, Sovereignty*, 54). See also Koskenniemi, *Gentle Civilizer*, 49.

11. Crawford, *Creation of States*, 5 (citing Oppenheim, *International Law*, 108).

12. See *Restatement Third*, 201 ("Under international law, a state is an entity that has a defined territory and a permanent population, under the control of its own government, and that engages in, or has the capacity to engage in, formal relations with other such entities").

13. See Anghie, *Imperialism, Sovereignty*, 57–58. On U.S. Supreme Court opinions depicting American Indians, see chapters 4 and 5 in this volume.

14. Anghie, *Imperialism, Sovereignty*, 60–62, quote at 61 (noting that one strategy was to assert that non-European entities were "barbaric" because they lacked law altogether; another was to acknowledge that "while certain societies may have had their own systems of law these were of such an alien character that no proper legal relations" could be developed with them).

15. Anghie, *Imperialism, Sovereignty*, 65–66 (observing that positivist jurists were "framing the project as though the colonial encounter was about to occur, as opposed to having already taken place").

16. Wright, *Mandates*, 14–15.

17. See ibid., 11 n. 19; see also 7–8 (referencing the *Johnson v. McIntosh* opinion to explain the earlier European colonial theory that "peoples outside of European Christian civilization hardly came within" the sphere of international law, and that the "blessings of Christianity and civilization" rendered colonization "meritorious").

18. Anghie, *Imperialism, Sovereignty*, 70.

19. See chapter 4 in this volume for a discussion of the Marshall cases.

20. Lorimer, *Institutes*, 157; see also Wright, *Mandates*, 16–17 (also discussing Alpheus Snow's emphasis on "trusteeship").

21. See Mutua, "Why Redraw," 1127–1129.

22. Ibid., 1130. See also the I.C.J. *Western Sahara* opinion (acknowledging that the existing treaties with African nations preclude claims that the "discovered" lands were *terra nullius*).

23. General Act of the Berlin Conference on West Africa.

24. Wright, *Mandates*, 17 n. 36a ("Resolution, 1888").

25. Wright, *Mandates*, 9–10; see also Anghie, *Imperialism, Sovereignty*, 69.

26. Quoted in Mutua, "Critical Race Theory," 847. See also Anghie, "Finding the Peripheries," 64 (noting that trade became "the mechanism for advancement and progress").

27. Wright, *Mandates*, 13–14 n. 24; see also 12–13.

28. *Neely v. Henkel*, 120; see also Wright, *Mandates*, 13 n. 23. On U.S. policy in Cuba during this period, see chapter 6 in this volume.

29. Wright, *Mandates*, 13–14 n. 24. See also Turns, "Stimson Doctrine" (noting similar arguments by the Taft administration in promoting its "open door" policy with China); Vagts, "International Economic Law," 771 (discussing embodiment of this policy in a 1903 treaty with China).

30. See Brown, "Humanitarian Intervention," 1694 n. 31 (noting Hans Morgenthau's description of this as "localized imperialism"); see also Nkrumah, *Neo-Colonialism*, ix (describing neo-colonialism as existing when a state is, "in theory, independent and has all the outward trappings of international sovereignty" but "its economic system and thus political policy is directed from outside").

31. Gilman, *James Monroe*, 161 (quoting James Monroe, Seventh Annual Message to Congress, December 2, 1823.

32. Ibid., 162.

33. See Boyle, *Foundations*, 87.

34. Pérez and Weissman, "Public Power," 709 (quoting Theodore Roosevelt's Annual Message to Congress, December 6, 1904).

35. See Carrasco and Thomas, "Encouraging Relational Investment," 547–548.

36. See Miller, *"Benevolent Assimilation,"* 81.

37. See Zasloff, "Law and the Shaping," 241. Root, who has been described as "the Father of National Security Law," subsequently became a senator, president of the American Bar Association and the American Society of International Law, and received the Nobel Peace Prize. See Eckhardt, "Nuremberg—Fifty Years," 3; see generally Zasloff, "Law and the Shaping."

38. See Boyle, *Foundations*, 20.

39. Zasloff, "Law and the Shaping," 297–300; on the war in the Philippines, see chapter 6 in this volume.

40. Boyle, *Foundations*, 22.

41. See ibid., 103–122.

42. See ibid., 113–114.

43. Ibid., 27–28.

44. Ibid., 28–29.

45. Ibid., 192 n. 7 (noting that the U.S. made reservations to the 1899 convention and its 1907 revision to ensure that nothing in the conventions would "be construed to imply a relinquishment by the United States of America of its traditional attitude toward purely American questions").

46. Ibid., 32–33.

47. *The Pious Fund Case.*

48. See Boyle, *Foundations*, 35.

49. Ibid., 42–43.

50. The 1907 Hague Convention IV Respecting the Laws and Customs of War on Land was a revision of the 1899 Hague Convention II of the same name, and is reproduced in Roberts and Guelff, *Documents*, 43–59.

51. Boyle, *Foundations*, 57; see also U.S. War Department, *1863 Laws of War.*

52. See Howard, "Constraints," 6. On the evolving incorporation of international law governing warfare into U.S. Army manuals, see generally Wells, *Laws of Land Warfare.*

53. General Orders No. 100, Section II, paragraphs 33–35, in U.S. War Department, *1863 Laws of War,* 40–41.

54. Section I, paragraphs 22–25, in ibid., 38–39.

55. Section II, paragraphs 60, 75, 80, in ibid., 47, 50, 51.

56. Quoted in Howard, "Constraints," 8.

57. For additional examples of U.S. leadership, see Boyle, *Foundations,* 25–64.

58. See ibid., 82–84.

59. Quoted in Boyle, *Foundations,* 125; see also 123–135.

60. See ibid., 130–135; Zinn, *People's History,* 352–354.

61. See Boyle, *Foundations,* 126; Hofstadter, *American Political Tradition,* 343. See also Zinn, *People's History,* 353 (noting that the *Lusitania* was carrying significant amounts of ammunition).

62. See Hofstadter, *American Political Tradition,* 349 (noting that in March 1917 Wilson stated, "perhaps our going to war is the only way in which our preeminent trade position can be maintained and a [world financial] panic averted").

63. On Wilson's characterization, see Wilson, Request for Declaration of War; on the Espionage Act, see Zinn, *People's History,* 354–367; see also Stone, "Learned Hand," 336–345. Convictions under the Espionage Act of June 15, 1917, as amended, 50 U.S.C.A. '31 *et seq.,* include, e.g., *Schenck v. United States; Sugarman v. United States; Frohwerk v. United States; Debs v. United States; Abrams v. United States;* and *Haywood v. United States.*

64. Wilson, Request for Declaration of War.

65. Wilson, Fourteen Points for Peace; see also in Baker, *Woodrow Wilson,* 42.

66. Wilson, Fourteen Points for Peace.

67. Ibid.

68. Smith, *America Enters*, 720–738.

69. Hofstadter, *American Political Tradition*, 354.

70. See Hannum, "Rethinking Self-Determination," 5–8; see also Franck, "The Emerging Right," 52.

71. Covenant of the League of Nations, Arts. 18, 20; see also Anghie, *Imperialism, Sovereignty*, 115.

72. Covenant of the League of Nations, Arts. 12–16.

73. Ibid., Arts. 10, 11; see also Boyle, *Foundations*, 138–139.

74. See, e.g., Covenant of the League of Nations, Art. 5 (providing that the first meetings of its Assembly and Council were to be "summoned by the President of the United States").

75. See ibid., Arts. 1, 15, 21; see also Boyle, *Foundations*, 138.

76. See Schlesinger, *Act of Creation*, 22–25; see also Boyle, *Foundations*, 138, 145; Smith, *American Enters*, 658–660, 720–738.

77. See Falk, *World Order*, 110; see also Boot, *Savage Wars*, 205–330.

78. See Tuchman, *Stilwell*, 253–278.

79. See Lens, *Forging*, 283.

80. See Smith, *America Enters*, 41–54 (discussing interventions in Venezuela and Colombia), 424–427 (on Haiti, the Dominican Republic, and Nicaragua); see also chapter 6 in this volume.

81. Smith, *America Enters*, 702; see also Falk, *World Order*, 109 ("In one sense, the United States under Wilson attempted to extend the notion of hemispheric liberty to the entire world").

82. See Williams, *From Columbus*, 426.

83. See Boot, *Savage Wars*, 129–204, 231–252; Churchill, *Roosting Chickens*, 59–62 (chronological listing of interventions); see generally Calder, *Impact of Intervention*; for background, see generally Galeano, *Open Veins*.

84. See Falk, *World Order*, 108 (citing Huntington, "Transnational Organizations").

85. Anghie, *Imperialism, Sovereignty*, 119.

86. See Wright, *Mandates*, 24–43.

87. On the minority treaty system, see generally Berman, "Perilous Ambivalence"; see also Berman, "Alternative Is Despair," 1821–1859.

88. Covenant of the League of Nations, Art. 22.

89. Ibid.

90. Ibid. See also Anghie, *Imperialism, Sovereignty*, 120–122; Smith, *America Enters*, 705–706.

91. See Wright, *Mandates*, 43–48 (detailing the assignments).

92. See Covenant of the League of Nations, Art. 1 (limiting membership to initial and invited signatories and "any fully self-governing State, Dominion or Colony" whose admission was agreed to by a two-thirds vote of the League Assembly and who provided certain additional assurances).

93. See Anghie, *Imperialism, Sovereignty*, 122–123.

94. Smith, *America Enters*, 706.

95. See Anghie, *Imperialism, Sovereignty*, 157.

96. Ibid.

97. See Oulahan, "Japan"; see also Anghie, *Imperialism, Sovereignty*, 146.

98. See Wright, *Mandates*, 8–11; Anghie, *Imperialism, Sovereignty*, 144–145.

99. See Anghie, *Imperialism, Sovereignty*, 252; see generally Lugard, *Dual Mandate*; Mellor, *British Imperial Trusteeship*.

100. Covenant of the League of Nations, Art. 22; see also Anghie, *Imperialism, Sovereignty*, 157 n. 168 (noting Lugard's highlighting of Joseph Chamberlin's statement, "We develop new territory as Trustees for Civilization, for the Commerce of the World").

101. See Covenant of the League of Nations, Art. 23; Anghie, *Imperialism, Sovereignty*, 166–167.

102. See Wright, *Mandates*, 252 (quoting a PMC member's observation that those races "unable to work" would disappear and the others should be required to work to fulfill the mission of the mandate).

103. Quoted in Anghie, *Imperialism, Sovereignty*, 165.

104. Ibid., 170 (quoting Minutes of the Third Session of the PMC).

105. See Wright, *Mandates*, 229; see also Anghie, *Imperialism, Sovereignty*, 184–190.

106. Wright, *Mandates*, 187–188.

107. See Anghie, *Imperialism, Sovereignty*, 186 (likening this to philosopher Michel Foucault's concept of "disciplinary governance," through which social control is achieved "by defining the normal, the standard and the truth against which deviations are identified and then remedied").

108. See Wright, *Mandates*, 16 (explicating the status of various states).

109. See ibid., 558–568 (noting differences in perceptions concerning freedom and security, and standards for determining social welfare).

110. Anghie, *Imperialism, Sovereignty*, 107.

111. Ibid., 108.

112. See Wright, *Mandates*, 559, 584.

113. *Civil Rights Cases* (holding the Civil Rights Act to be an unconstitutional extension of legislative power into "private" matters); *Plessy v. Ferguson* (upholding legally mandated segregation on the theory that the facilities were "separate but equal"). See McConnell, "Forgotten Constitutional Moment," 133–140 (discussing the end of Reconstruction as a significant "constitutional moment"); see generally Brandwein, *Reconstructing Reconstruction*.

114. See W. E. B. DuBois, "Another Open Letter to Woodrow Wilson," originally published in *The Crisis* in September 1913 and reprinted in DuBois, *Writings*, 1144–1147. On Wilson's association with D. W. Griffith's notoriously racist film, *The Birth of a Nation*, see Stokes, *Birth of a Nation*, 111–112, 175, 198–200.

115. Furedi, *Ideology of Imperialism*, 13 (quoting Lansing, *Peace Negotiations*, 97); see also Smith, *America Enters*, 634.

116. Quoted in Wright, *Mandates*, 49 (emphasis added). For details on U.S. claims, see ibid., 48–56.

117. See Wright, *Mandates*, 48–56; Anghie, *Imperialism, Sovereignty*, 163 n. 186.

118. See chapter 4 in this volume.

119. Quoted in Cohen, "Colonialism: A Realist Approach," 372. See also "History of the Office of the MIT President."

120. *Lone Wolf v. Hitchcock*, 565–567; see generally Clark, *Lone Wolf*. On U.S. assertions of plenary power, see Saito, *Chinese Exclusion*, 15–22.

121. Churchill, "The Indigenous Peoples," 25; see also Adams, *Tortured People* (applying a similar analysis to Indigenous nations in Canada); Hector, *Internal Colonialism* (applying the concept of internal colonialism to the British occupation of Ireland).

122. Churchill, "The Indigenous Peoples," 25. For a more expansive explanation of "settler societies," see Stasiulis and Yuval-Davis, "Introduction: Beyond Dichotomies," 1–38.

123. See Porter, "Proposal," 927–931.

124. *The Citizenship Act of 1924.* See Churchill, "Indian Assimilation," 58.

125. See, e.g., Porter, "Demise," 127–128 (noting protests by the Grand Council of the Haudenosaunee or Six Nations Iroquois Confederacy). See also Washinawatok, "International Emergence," 42–43 (describing the League of Nations' refusal to acknowledge Cayuga leader Deskaheh's efforts to have Haudenosaunee treaties enforced).

126. Clinton, "Redressing," 104.

127. *Indian Reorganization Act of 1934.*

128. Roosevelt, *First Annual Message to Congress* (quoted in Carpenter, "Contextualizing," 624 n. 116).

129. Clinton, Newton, and Price, *American Indian Law*, 357 (quoting Stein, "Tribal Self-Government").

130. Ibid.

131. Quoted in Ickes, "Foreword," v.

132. See Deloria and Lytle, *American Indians*, 99–100 (noting Felix Cohen's observation that the IRA "had little or no effect upon the substantive powers of tribal self-government"). See also Deloria and Lytle, *Nations Within*, 140–170.

133. The use of the term "tribe" is problematic, both because it has been used instead of "nations" to undermine recognition of Indigenous sovereignty and because it is associated with animal groupings and "primitive or nomadic peoples." See *Webster's Deluxe Unabridged Dictionary*, 1949. Nonetheless, it is the terminology used in relevant federal legislation.

134. See Deloria and Lytle, *American Indians*, 14. The tribes could also adopt corporate charters under which they could manage property and engage in business. See "Comment," in Clinton, Newton, and Price, *American Indian Law*, 358–361.

135. Deloria and Lytle, *American Indians*, 14–15 (also noting that "some tribes voted to accept the act and then refused to organize under it, which made their status somewhat nebulous").

136. See Barsh, "Another Look," in Clinton, Newton, and Price, *American Indian Law*, 362–366. See also Deloria and Lytle, *Nations Within*, 171–178.

137. See generally Porter, "Demise." On the complexity of the federal definitions at issue, see Cohen, *Handbook*, 2–5.

138. For examples, see Deloria and Lytle, *American Indians*, 82–89. On adaptations made following Euroamerican colonization, see ibid., 89–99; O'Brien, *American Indian*, 14–33.

139. Churchill, "Indian Assimilation," 59.

140. Ibid.

141. See, e.g., Philp, *John Collier's Crusade*, 166 (concluding that the Hopi "found it difficult to understand white concepts of self-government").

142. See Deloria and Lytle, *American Indians*, 102 (noting that although some tribal constitutions incorporated "variations" based on their own traditions, all had to be approved by the secretary of the interior and "homogeneity rather than usefulness consequently became the virtue").

143. Williams, "Algebra," 276–277; see also Porter, "Decolonizing," 97–98. On U.S. provision of "models" for other states' constitutions, see generally Carrington, "Writing."

144. Excerpts of transcript of March 6, 2004, interview in Trahant, "Bush."

145. Falk, *World Order*, 111.

146. See, e.g., "The United Nations: The Growing Threat."

147. As of the end of 2007 the United States was approximately $633 million in arrears on its payment for peacekeeping operations, in addition to owing $291 million in UN dues. See United Nations Association of the United States of America, "Restoring." See also Schnoor, "International Law," 1141–1144; "United States Proposes Revised UN Assessment Process" (reprinting congressional testimony of John Bolton, U.S. representative to the United Nations).

148. See Bradley, "Unratified Treaties," 309–313; see generally "U.S. Policy Regarding Landmines," *American Journal of International Law*; Goldstone, "Consequences"; van der Vyver, "American Exceptionalism"; Henkin, "U.S. Ratification."

149. See Schlesinger, *Act of Creation*, 25, 28.

150. Ibid., 30–31.

151. See Roosevelt, *Annual Address to Congress*.

152. Ibid.

153. Ibid.

154. Quoted in Heuvel, "The Four Freedoms"; see also Schlesinger, *Act of Creation*, 11.

155. Schlesinger, *Act of Creation*, 37.

156. See "Towards a 'general international organization,'" *UN Chronicle*.

157. Declaration by the United Nations, January 1, 1942.

158. Ibid; see also Boyle, *Foundations*, 151–152 (the four participants were the United States, the United Kingdom, the Soviet Union, and China).

159. See Schlesinger, *Act of Creation*, 40–51.

160. Ibid., 45.

161. Ibid., 53–55, 67–68.

162. Ibid., 62–63, 276.

163. Ibid., 126; see also 111–126. The United States was monitoring the communications of diplomatic delegations, giving it an additional advantage in the negotiations. See ibid., 93–110; see also Bamford, *Body of Secrets*, 21–23.

164. Charter of the United Nations, Arts. 102–103.

165. Ibid., Art. 2, sections (2) and (7).

166. See Schlesinger, *Act of Creation*, 169, 193–107; Bennis, *Calling the Shots*, 4–6. This gave the permanent members effective veto power over *all* substantive Security Council decisions, leading to the well-known stalemate of the Cold War era. See Murphy, "The Security Council," 207 (noting that until 1990 the Security Council on average passed fewer than 11 resolutions per year but adopted 250 resolutions in the next four years). The major powers initially justified the veto on the basis that they would be primarily responsible for UN military actions. See Schlesinger, *Act of Creation*, 222. However, the statistics do not bear out this presumption. See "Monthly Summary of Contributions,"

UN Department of Public Information (noting that as of June 2008 the five permanent Security Council members had each provided between 0.3% and 2.2% of the total UN peacekeeping observers and troops).

167. Charter of the United Nations, Art. 50.

168. See ibid., Arts. 7–32. Many believed that the League of Nations' ineffectiveness could be attributed to the fact that most non-procedural decisions required a consensus of all members, giving each effective veto power. See Covenant of the League of Nations, Art. 5.

169. Charter of the United Nations, Arts. 33–49.

170. Ibid., Art. 1. The fourth stated purpose is "to be a centre for harmonizing the actions of nations in the attainment of these common ends."

171. Ibid., Arts. 9–22.

172. See Falk, "The United Nations," 618; Nirmal, *Right to Self-Determination*, 47 (General Assembly resolutions "have the force of the law when they interpret the provisions of the UN Charter or when they restate a binding rule of international law or when they have been incorporated into state practice or when they have been so often repeated over time and have been accepted by a majority of states of the world as binding that they have become a rule of customary international law"). See generally Falk, "Quasi-Legislative Competence."

173. The Economic and Social Council was established to report on and draft treaties to address issues of poverty and social welfare but many of these functions have since shifted from the political realm of the UN to the international financial institutions. See Charter of the United Nations, Arts. 61–72; see also Chapter 8.

174. See Meyer, *World Court*, 11–86.

175. Ibid., 88.

176. See Charter of the United Nations, Arts. 92–96.

177. See Meyer, *World Court*, 90–91; Statute of the International Court of Justice.

178. Taylor, *Nuremberg Trials*, 25.

179. Ibid., 26–27.

180. See ibid., 30–32, 39–42.

181. See Smith, *Road to Nuremberg*, 190–246; the text of the Charter of the International Military Tribunal is reproduced in Taylor, *Nuremberg Trials*, 645–653.

182. See Taylor, *Nuremberg Trials*, 4. On the Nuremburg Tribunal, see generally ibid.; Smith, *Road to Nuremberg*; Smith, *American Road to Nuremberg*. On the trials of other Axis leaders, see generally Domenico, *Italian Fascists*; Brackman, *The Other Nuremberg*.

183. See Taylor, *Nuremberg Trials*, 41.

184. See Charter of the International Military Tribunal, Art. 6; see also Smith, *American Road to Nuremberg*, 49 (noting that the treaty structure was used because of the unorthodox nature of the system).

185. The primary exception appears to have been the lack of rules governing aerial bombardment of civilian targets. See Taylor, *Nuremberg Trials*, 13, 19.

186. See ibid., 35–36, 41, 629, 637–638.

187. Biddle, *Brief Authority*, 472; see also 468–473.

188. See ibid., 478–480 (discussing the customary law argument and arguing that criminalization of aggressive war was necessary to preserve civilization); Taylor, *Nuremberg Trials*, 37 (discussing the Kellogg-Briand Pact). See also the full text of the treaty, available at http://avalon.law.yale.edu/20th_century/kbpact.asp (accessed August 1, 2008).

189. Taylor, *Nuremberg Trials*, 629.

190. See Smith, *American Road to Nuremberg,* 113–117, esp. 114 n. 3 (discussing the origin of the construct).

191. Taylor, *Nuremberg Trials,* 294 (quoting French prosecutor François de Menthon's description of crimes against humanity as violations "of the laws of all civilized countries" and Nazi practices as intended to "plunge humanity back into barbarism").

192. See Taylor, *Nuremberg Trials,* 625–626.

193. Biddle, *Brief Authority,* 481.

194. UNGA Res. 95(I).

195. Information about the International Criminal Court is available at http://www.icc-cpi.int/home.html (accessed July 31, 2008).

196. Taylor, *Nuremberg Trials,* 66 (quoting Jackson); see also 629.

197. Biddle, *Brief Authority,* 366 (quoting Jackson's invocation of civilization in his opening argument).

198. Taylor, *Nuremberg Trials,* 294–295 (quoting de Menthon). Those on trial also laid claim to European civilization. Defendant Albert Speer said in his closing argument, "The nightmare of many a man that one day nations would be dominated by technical means was all but realized in Hitler's totalitarian system. . . . May God protect Germany and the culture of the West." Biddle, *Brief Authority,* 366 (quoting Speer's statement of August 31, 1946).

199. See Bennis, *Calling the Shots,* 8. The list of the UN members, currently numbering 192, is available at http://www.un.org/members/list.shtml (accessed July 29, 2008).

200. Sixteen territories are still considered non–self-governing. See UN Decolonization Unit Department of Political Affairs, "The United Nations and Decolonization."

201 Berman, "In the Wake," 1521.

202. Schlesinger, *Act of Creation,* 98 (quoting the explanation of the British foreign minister, as recounted by the French ambassador to Britain).

203. See ibid., 232–234 (noting that U.S. proposals for the trusteeship system were modified as a result of pressure from the Soviet Union, China, and the smaller states).

204. See Charter of the United Nations, Art. 73, esp. section B. See generally Sayre, "Legal Problems."

205. The U.S. also held the Northern Mariana Islands, Micronesia, and the Marshall Islands under a 1947 "strategic trust" agreement; they became nominally independent in 1986. In 1994 Palau entered into a "compact of free association" with the United States, after which the Trusteeship Council suspended operations. See UN Decolonization Unit Department of Political Affairs, "Trust and Non–self-governing Territories, 1945–1999." For background, see Leibowitz, *Defining Status,* 487–493; see generally Rios-Martinez, "Congressional Colonialism"; Hinck, "Republic of Palau."

206. See Charter of the United Nations, Arts. 1, 55; see also Sayre, "Legal Problems," 267–268 (noting that the trusteeship system offered a "yardstick" for measuring "political, economic, and social advancement" in the non–self-governing territories outside the trusteeship system).

207. See Nirmal, *Right to Self-Determination,* 36–37.

208. See Anghie, *Imperialism, Sovereignty,* 196.

209. See Pellet, Book Review, 140–141. For background on the movements for decolonization, see generally Bragança and Wallerstein, *African Liberation Reader;* Miller and Aya, *National Liberation.*

210. Gilly, "Introduction," 1–2; for Fanon's explanation, see 31.

211. See listing in UN Decolonization Unit Department of Political Affairs, "Trust and Non–self-governing Territories, 1945–1999."

212. UNGA Res. 1541 (XV). See also Nirmal, *Right to Self-Determination,* 41–42.

213. See Hinck, "Republic of Palau," 949 (quoting James J. Wadsworth, U.S. Representative to the United Nations).

214. See Nirmal, *Right to Self-Determination,* 40–46; International Covenant on Civil and Political Rights, Art. I; International Covenant on Economic, Social, and Cultural Rights, Art. I ("All peoples have the right of self-determination. By virtue of that right they freely determine their political status and freely pursue their economic, social and cultural development").

215. See, e.g., *Western Sahara (Advisory Opinion)* (finding the peoples of the Western Sahara to have the right to decolonize under Resolution 1514, notwithstanding the claims of Morocco or Mauritania); *Legal Consequences for States of the Continued Presence of South Africa in Namibia* (finding South Africa's occupation of Namibia to violate Namibia's right to self-determination) .

216. See generally Mahmud, "Geography"; Mutua, "Why Redraw," 1134 (citing Brownlie, *African Boundaries*).

217. Mutua, "Why Redraw," 1116.

218. See generally Pakaukau, "The Right," 303–321; Churchill, "Stolen Kingdom," 73–123; Declet, "Mandate"; Román, "Empire Forgotten"; Van Dyke, Amore-Siah, and Berkeley-Coats, "Self-Determination"; Anaya, "Native Hawaiian People."

219. UNGA Res. 1541 (XV). On problematic applications of the "salt water" thesis of colonialism, see Román, "Empire Forgotten," 1138; Haile, "Legality of Secessions," 509–511; Iorns, "Indigenous Peoples," 293–295.

220. See Ngugi, "Decolonization-Modernization," 304 (noting that, as a result, "the initial process of 'homogenization' that of incorporation of the emerging Non-Western States in the 'family of nations' ends up being a process of 'differentiation'").

221. Ibid., 304–305.

CHAPTER 8. THE NEW WORLD ORDER AND AMERICAN HEGEMONY

1. Truman, Inaugural Address.

2. See Esteva, "Development," 6.

3. Truman, Inaugural Address.

4. Ibid. ("For the first time in history, humanity possesses the knowledge and skill to relieve the suffering of these people. . . . Greater production is the key to prosperity and peace. And the key to greater production is a wider and more vigorous application of modern scientific and technical knowledge").

5. See Gordon and Sylvester, "Deconstructing," 9, 16 (noting that "development" has been construed as modernization plus national economic growth, with "modernization" anchored in the belief that humans can—and should—control their environment through reason and science).

6. See ibid. 11, 14–15; Esteva, "Development," 7.

7. UNGA Res. 1710 (XVI). See also Gordon and Sylvester, "Deconstructing," 30 n. 118.

8. See Esteva "Development," 13–17; see also International Development Strategy for the Fourth UN Development Decade.

9. Esteva, "Development," 15–16.

10. See generally Rodney, *How Europe Underdeveloped Africa*; Amin, *Imperialism*; Amin, *Unequal Development*.

11. See Anghie, *Imperialism, Sovereignty,* 242; Esteva, "Development," 17.

12. See Anghie, *Imperialism, Sovereignty*, 211–212.

13. Ibid., 212.

14. See ibid., 213–216.

15. UNGA Res. 1514 (XV).

16. "Permanent Sovereignty over Natural Resources."

17. Ibid., see also Anghie, *Imperialism, Sovereignty*, 217 n. 55.

18. See Churchill, *Perversions of Justice*, 5–14.

19. See Anghie, *Imperialism, Sovereignty*, 220 ("the essential manifestation of self-determination, the assertion of sovereignty, becomes primarily a surrender to obligations. [Legal] personality, as in the case of Vitoria, is invented in order to be bound").

20. See Bennis, *Calling the Shots*, 14–16.

21. See UNGA Res. 3201; UNGA Res. 3202; UNGA Res. 3281.

22. See Weston, "Charter," 437–439.

23. See ibid., 439.

24. See Gathii, "Good Governance," 118–119.

25. See Anghie, *Imperialism, Sovereignty*, 226–227.

26. Ibid., 229–234; see also 241–242.

27. Gordon and Sylvester, "Deconstructing," 59; see also 37–38 (on the impact of the oil crisis).

28. See Head, "Law and Policy," 195–201; see generally Anghie, "Time Present."

29. See Gordon and Sylvester, "Deconstructing," 26; see also Bird, "Suitable Case," 285; Articles of Agreement of the International Monetary Fund.

30. See Feinburg, "Changing Relationship," 546–548. See also Wadrzyk, "Is It Appropriate," 555–556 (explaining that the IBRD is now part of the World Bank Group, which includes the IDA, the International Finance Corporation, the Multinational Investment Guarantee Agency, and the International Center for Settlement of Investment Disputes).

31. See Head, "Law and Policy," 196–197; see Weber and Arner, "New Design," 394.

32. See Head, "Law and Policy," 196–197.

33. See Weber and Arner, "New Design," 395; see also World Trade Organization, "The GATT Years."

34. See Wadrzyk, "Is It Appropriate," 561.

35. Woods, "The United States," 92.

36. Current statistics are available at the IMF and World Bank Group Web sites: http://www.imf.org; and http://web.worldbank.org (accessed August 3, 2008).

37. The Agreements are available at http://www.imf.org/external/pubs/ft/aa/index.htm; and http://sitesources.worldbank.org/EXTABOUTUS/Resources/ibrd–articlesofagreement.pdf (accessed August 4, 2008). Every World Bank president and all deputy managing directors of the IMF have been from the United States (Swedberg, "Doctrine," 379).

38. See Gold, "Interpretation," 256–257.

39. See Wadrzyk, "Is It Appropriate," 559–560 (quoting IBRD Articles of Agreement, Arts. III and IV).

40. See Wadrzyk, "Is It Appropriate," 563.

41. See Gordon and Sylvester, "Deconstructing," 24–25 n. 94.

42. See ibid., 24–25; see also Feinberg, "Changing Relationship," 549.

43. See Gordon and Sylvester, "Deconstructing," 26–27.

44. See Feinberg, "Changing Relationship," 549.

45. See Bello, "Global Economic Counterrevolution," 18; see generally Danaher, *50 Years*; Chon, "Intellectual Property."

46. Rajagopal, "From Resistance," 576 (noting that it is apparently inconsequential that "poverty alleviation programs never alleviate poverty or that conditionalities never achieve their stated goals" because the interventions "redound to the authority and expansion of international financial institutions").

47. See Wadrzyk, "Is It Appropriate," 554, 562–569; Head, "Law and Policy," 198–199.

48. Head, "For Richer," 252.

49. Ibid.

50. See Anghie, *Imperialism, Sovereignty*, 247.

51. Ibid., 249 (also noting that the "good governance" concept is applied to Third World countries, not advanced industrial states); see generally Gathii, "Good Governance."

52. See chapter 7 in this volume; see also Anghie, *Imperialism, Sovereignty*, 263–268.

53. See Anghie, *Imperialism, Sovereignty*, 265 (noting that the sovereignty of Third World states is effectively negated by international influence over their economies); see generally Gathii, "Good Governance").

54. See generally Coleman and Maogoto, "Democracy's Global Quest"; Gordon, "Saving Failed States"; see also Chesterman, "Virtual Trusteeship," 219–233 (discussing Security Council interventions in "failed states").

55. See generally Henkin, *Age of Rights*.

56. See chapter 7 in this volume.

57. See Shelton, "International Human Rights," 492; Richardson, III, "'Failed States,'" 45. For background, see Amin, Re-*Reading*, 105–148 (discussing the "bourgeois national project in the Third World").

58. See Ludwikowski, "Fundamental," 87–92; Alston, "U.S. Ratification," 372–377.

59. See Houbert, "Decolonization," 48–55; see generally Byrne, "Decolonization," 231–237; Sornarajah, "Power and Justice."

60. On the origins of the term "Fourth World," see Griggs, "The Meaning"; see also Hall, *American Empire*, 195–196, 286–292.

61. See Gathii, "Good Governance," 135–139.

62. See International Covenant on Civil and Political Rights, Art. I; International Covenant on Economic, Social, and Cultural Rights, Art. I.

63. Convention on the Prevention and Punishment of the Crime of Genocide; International Convention on the Suppression and Punishment of the Crime of "Apartheid"; Convention Against Torture.

64. Universal Declaration of Human Rights; see also the ICCPR, ICESCR, and the International Convention on the Elimination of All Forms of Racial Discrimination. Regional treaties also recognize these basic rights. See European Convention for the Protection of Human Rights and Fundamental Freedoms; American Convention on Human Rights; African Charter on Human and Peoples' Rights.

65. See Convention on the Elimination of All Forms of Discrimination Against Women; Convention on the Rights of the Child; ICERD. Racial discrimination is broadly defined as "any distinction, exclusion, restriction or preference based on race, colour, descent, or national or ethnic origin which has the purpose or effect of nullifying or impairing the recognition, enjoyment or exercise, on an equal footing, of human rights and fundamental freedoms in the political, economic, social, cultural or any other field of public life," and is universally condemned. See ICERD, Art. 1.

66. See, e.g., Convention Relating to the Status of Refugees; Convention Relating to the Status of Stateless Persons; Standard Minimum Rules for the Treatment of Prisoners; UNGA, "Disappeared Persons."

67. UNGA, "Declaration on the Rights of Indigenous Peoples," adopted on September 13, 2007, with 144 states in favor and 4 (including the United States) against.

68. See Anghie, *Imperialism, Sovereignty*, 260–261; Gathii, "Good Governance," 108–109.

69. See Mutua, "Ideology," 651 (citing the World Bank study on Sub-Saharan Africa); see also Gathii, "Good Governance," 159–160; Anghie, *Imperialism, Sovereignty*, 270 (noting similarities between the positions of the U.S. and the World Bank).

70. See Mutua, "Idealogy," 605–606.

71. Esteva and Prakash, *Grassroots Postmodernism*, 117.

72. "A Report to the National Security Council–NSC 68," 25.

73. See Vega, "Human Rights," 4, 36 (also noting that in 2001 U.S. observer status at the Council of Europe was disputed because the U.S. continues to use the death penalty, and that the U.S. was excluded from the Inter-American Commission of the Organization of American States in 2003 because of various human rights concerns).

74. On the ICC, see below; on the doctrine of preemptive war, see chapter 1 in this volume.

75. See Gruber, "Who's Afraid of Geneva Law?" 1022–1023.

76. On detentions, see Saito, *Chinese Exclusion*, 153–169; see generally Cole, *Enemy Aliens*; on torture, see chapter 1 in this volume.

77. See chapter 1 in this volume.

78. See chapter 7 in this volume.

79. See Charter of the United Nations, Art. 93.

80. See Statute of the International Court of Justice, Arts. 34–38.

81. Meyer, *World Court*, 95–98; see also Statute of the International Court of Justice, Art. 36.

82. See Military and Paramilitary Activities in and against Nicaragua (Judgment on Merits) and (Judgment on Jurisdiction). The ICJ made additional interim rulings as well. See also Chayes, "Nicaragua," 1447; see generally Reichler, "Holding America."

83. See Bilder, "The United States," 253–255; Bernstein, "International Court," 147–148. On the reparations ordered by the Court, see Meyer, *World Court*, 183–186.

84. The United States also supported the establishment, and contributed significantly to the funding, of the International Criminal Tribunal for the Former Yugoslavia and, to a somewhat lesser degree, the International Criminal Tribunal for Rwanda. See Hagan, Levi, and Ferrales, "Swaying," 589; Moghalu, "Image," 25–26.

85. See Edlin, "Anxiety," 3.

86. Rome Statute of the International Criminal Court.

87. See Edlin, "Anxiety," 5; Worth, "Globalization," 245–256.

88. Bickley, "U.S. Resistance," 2; Churchill, "The United States and the Genocide Convention," 214–215 (quoting U.S. Ambassador David Scheffer); see also 215– 216 (describing the U.S. as claiming that its "citizens should stand outside the evolving framework of international law so that the United States could pursue its policies with impunity, unhindered by the rule of law"). See Worth, "Globalization."

89. Quoted in van der Vyver, "International Justice," 142. For an analysis of the procedural arguments used by the United States in rejecting the Rome Statute, see generally Cuéllar, "International Criminal Court."

90. See American Servicemembers' Protection Act; see also Worth, "Globalization," 254; Edlin, "Anxiety," 6.

91. Cerone, "Dynamic Equilibrium," 315.

92. Ibid., 314–315.

93. Convention on the Prevention and Punishment of the Crime of Genocide.

94. See LaBlanc, *United States*, 26–27; see generally Lemkin, *Axis Rule*.

95. See Churchill, "The United States and the Genocide Convention," 364–366.

96. Convention on the Prevention and Punishment of the Crime of Genocide, Art. II.

97. Ibid., Art. III.

98. On the drafting process, see Lippman, "The Convention," 449–463.

99. See Reagan, *Remarks*.

100. Churchill, "The United States and the Genocide Convention," 372–383.

101. See U.S. Reservations and Understandings to the Genocide Convention; Paust, "Remarks," 316–321 (noting as particularly problematic the United States' rewriting of the definition to require "the *specific* intent to destroy, in whole or in *substantial* part" one of the protected groups and its limitation of "mental harm" to "permanent impairment of mental faculties through drugs, torture or similar techniques"). See also Lipman, "The Convention," 463–465, 482–487.

102. Reservations to the Convention on the Prevention and Punishment of the Crime of Genocide; see also Lippman, "The 1948 Convention."

103. Kaufman, *Human Rights Treaties*, 45 (quoting from Senate Committee on Foreign Relations, *Executive Sessions II*, 399); see also 43 (quoting ABA testimony before a Subcommittee of the Senate Committee on Foreign Relations arguing that "[p]eoples who do not know the meaning of freedoms are to be metamorphosed into judges of the freedoms of others").

104. See Dudziak, "Little Rock Crisis," 1643–1646; Kaufman, *Human Rights Treaties*, 57–58 (noting exchange concerning the application of the Convention to lynchings of African Americans or mob actions against Chinese immigrants); see also Churchill, "The United States and the Genocide Convention," 373–374.

105. Quoted in Kaufman, *Human Rights Treaties*, 46. The ABA report on the Genocide Convention played on related fears by asserting, "Consent to and ratification of the treaty would transfer all jurisdiction in civil rights to the Federal field to the exclusion of the States" (ibid., 54).

106. See Washinawatok, "International Emergence," 42–43 (describing the League of Nations' refusal to even allow Deskaheh to observe its proceedings); see generally Richardson III, *Origins*.

107. See Layton, *International Politics*, 49–69; Civil Rights Congress, *We Charge Genocide*.

108. Kaufman, *Human Rights Treaties*, 59 (noting the State Department's efforts to explain that lynchings did *not* fall under the Genocide Convention); see also Browne-Marshall, *Race*, 238–239; see generally Harris, "Equality Trouble."

109. See Kaufmann, *Human Rights Treaties*, 66.

110. Universal Declaration of Human Rights.

111. See Kaufmann, *Human Rights Treaties*, 67.

112. Ibid., 69.

113. Quoted in ibid., 70.

114. Ibid., 74–78 (quote at 74).

115. See ibid., 94–116; Henkin, "U.S. Ratification," 348–349; Worth, "Globalization," 253–255; see generally Richards, "The Bricker Amendment."

116. See Kaufmann, *Human Rights Treaties*, 104; Henkin, "U.S. Ratification," 348–349; Worth, "Globalization," 254.

117. Kaufmann, *Human Rights Treaties*, 119.

118. Ibid., 119–147; on the forced labor convention, see http://www.ilo.org/ilolex/cgi-lex/convde.pl?C105 (accessed October 5, 2008).

119. See Post, "The United States and the Genocide Treaty," 687–688, 695.

120. For the status of ratifications and the texts of the conventions, see http://www1.umn.edu/humanrts/research/ratification-USA.html (accessed October 5, 2008); see also United Nations Treaty Collection, available at http://untreaty.un.org/English/guide.asp (last accessed February 27, 2009).

121. Henkin, "U.S. Ratification," 341; see also Kaufmann, *Human Rights Treaties*, 175–176; see generally Lillich, *U.S. Ratification*.

122. Henkin, "U.S. Ratification," 349; For critical but less harsh assessments, see Bell, "From Laggard," 276; Burguenthal, "Modern Constitutions," 212.

123. Van der Vyver, "American Exceptionalism," 776.

124. See Hay, "Post-Kyoto Stress," 494, 502–504; Deller, Makhijani, and Burroughs, *Rule of Power*, 18; Kuchta, "A Closer Look." See also Lefeber, "From the Hague," 25–54, esp. 26 (noting that with respect to the Protocol intended to enhance the effectiveness of the Biological Weapons Convention, "the United States endorsed the Protocol's framework, negotiated and achieved compromises to protect its perceived interests, and then rejected the draft before it was even finalized, killing the chances of its completion").

125. Mower, Book Review, 335; see also Deller, Makhijani, and Burroughs, *Rule of Power*, xii–xiii, xxix–xxx. See generally Convention on the Prohibition of the Development, Production, Stockpiling and Use of Chemical Weapons and on Their Destruction; Convention on the Prohibition of the Use, Stockpiling, Production and Transfer of Anti-Personnel Mines and on Their Destruction.

126. For texts of these treaties, see the "Legal texts: the WTO agreements," available at http://www.wto.org/english/docs_e/legal_e/ursum_e.htm#mAgreement (accessed October 11, 2008).

127. On the Clinton approach, see Foot, MacFarlane, Mastanduno, "Introduction," 3. On NAFTA, see Terbeek, "Love," 488–492.

128. See "North American Free Trade Agreement," available at http://www.wto.org/english/docs_e/legal_e/ursum_e.htm#mAgreement; see also text of NAFTA at http://www.nafta-sec-alena.org/DefaultSite/index_e.aspx?DetailID'78 (both accessed October 11, 2008).

129. See Vega, "Human Rights," 7, 11; see also Sen, "The United States," 125. On challenges to and justifications for the constitutionality of such executive agreements, see Vega, "Human Rights," 7–11.

130. See, e.g., Carter, *International Law*, 418–420 (reservations to ICCPR), 446–447 (reservations to ICERD), 469–470 (reservations to Convention Against Torture).

131. See Bradley, "Military Commissions," 337–341.

132. On U.S. influence over IMF and World Bank decisions, see Woods, "The United States," 92–114; see also chapter 7 in this volume. On the domination of WTO processes by economically powerful states including the U.S., see Gathii, "High Stakes," 1362–1363.

133. Gathii, "Insulating," 4.

134. See Gassama, "Reaffirming," 1488–1491; Churchill, *Roosting Chickens*, 98; see generally Nagan, "Economic Sanctions."

135. See Bennis, *Calling the Shots*, 27 (on Security Council vetoes); Churchill, *Roosting Chickens*, 98; see generally Chomsky, *Fateful Triangle*; Aruri, *Obstruction*.

136. See Bennis, *Calling the Shots*, 10–11 (on Korea), 24–39 (on Kuwait).

137. See Bennis, *Calling the Shots*, 11.

138. See Blum, *The CIA*, 67–76; Prados, *Presidents' Secret Wars*, 92–98, 107; see generally Kinzer, *All the Shah's Men*.

139. Blum, *The CIA*, 77–89; Prados, *Presidents' Secret Wars*, 98–107.

140. See Blum, *The CIA*, 89–91 (Costa Rica), 206–216 (Cuba), 133–161 (Vietnam and Cambodia), 91–107 (Syria and the Middle East); Churchill, *Roosting Chickens*, 66–68.

141. See Blum, *The CIA*, 174–181 (Congo), 191–194 (Peru), 225–231 (Uruguay), 251–260 (Bolivia), 181–191 (Brazil), 195–206 (Dominican Republic), 217–222 (Indonesia), 223–231, (Ghana), 206–213 (Cuba), 162–163 (Haiti). See also Prados, *Presidents' Secret Wars*, 171–217 (Cuba).

142. See Blum, *The CIA*, 272–274 (Costa Rica), 232–243 (Chile), 299–304 (Jamaica), 330–344 (Nicaragua); Klein, *Shock Doctrine*, 75–97 (Chile); see generally LaFeber, *Inevitable Revolutions*; Manley, *Jamaica*.

143. See Blum, *The CIA*, 292–299 (Zaire), 284–291 (Angola), 304–306 (Seychelles).

144. See ibid., 319–344 (El Salvador and Nicaragua); Prados, *Presidents' Secret Wars*, 378–401 (Nicaragua); see generally Crandall, *Gunboat Democracy*; Bonner, *Weakness & Deceit*.

145. See Hoyt, *America's Wars*, 525–528 (Lebanon), 529 (Libya); see Paust, "Responding Lawfully to International Terrorism," 729–732 (discussing U.S. air strikes on Libya).

146. See Maley, *The Afghanistan Wars*, 78–81 (on U.S. support for the *mujahedin*); see generally Shah, "The U.S. Attacks"; Kolhatkar, "Impact."

147. See Zinn, *People's History*, 462 (quoting a 1952 National Security Council memorandum and a 1953 congressional study noting the strategic importance of Southeast Asia's immense natural resources).

148. For striking parallels between U.S. wars of liberation and pacification in other territories and the domestic pacification of American Indians, Filipinos, and Vietnamese, see, e.g., Shafer, *Deadly Paradigms*, 268 (Vietnamese internments); Blaufarb, *The Counterinsurgency Era*, 114–145 ("hamletization" program in Vietnam); Miller, "*Benevolent Assimilation*," 163–64, 208 (mass internments in the Philippines); see generally Bailey, *Bosque Redondo* (American Indian internment).

149. See Taylor, *Nuremberg and Vietnam*, 186–188; see also Falk, *The Vietnam War*, esp. 1–4.

150. See Zinn, *People's History*, 465–67. See also Schwab, *Defending*, 1 (noting Kennedy's characterization of the war as one of freedom versus evil); Franklin, *Vietnam*, 27–41 (comparing the "dominant fantasies" of Americans during the Vietnam War with the documented history). For deconstructions of standard U.S. accountings of the Cold War, see generally Schrecker, *Cold War Triumphalism*.

151. Karnow, *Vietnam*, 260.

152. Franklin, *Vietnam*, 95. On U.S. war crimes, see generally Vietnam Veterans Against the War, *The Winter Soldier*; Russell, *War Crimes*.

153. Sheehan, *Bright Shining Lie*, 131.

154. O'Connell, "American Exceptionalism," 43 (citations omitted).

155. The phrase is used herein because it captures the dynamic of American exceptionalism in the postwar period, but it is most commonly associated with the America First Committee. Organized in 1940 by Henry Ford, Charles Lindbergh, and others to resist U.S. entry into World War II, it was subsequently discredited by its associations with German Nazis and the Third Reich, Italian and Spanish fascists, the American Eugenics Society, and the Ku Klux Klan. See Wallace, *The American Axis*, 241–321.

156. Nietschmann, "Fourth World," 237.

157. Ibid.

158. See Truman, *Inaugural Address*; see also Rist, *History of Development*, 72–74.

159. See Rist, *History of Development*, 74; see generally Rodney, *How Europe Underdeveloped Africa*; Amin, *Accumulation*.

160. The term "basic needs" was introduced by World Bank president Robert McNamara in 1972. See Rist, *History of Development*, 162.

161. Ibid., 164.

162. See Bello, "Global Economic Counterrevolution," 14–19, esp. 16–18. For specific case studies, see the following, all in Danaher, *50 Years Is Enough*: Marcos Arruda, "Brazil: Drowning in Debt" (interview by Multinational Monitor), 44–50; International NGO Forum, "World Bank and IMF Adjustment Lending in Chile," 51–55; Alicia Korten, "Structural Adjustment and Costa Rican Agriculture," 56–61; International NGO Forum, "World Bank and IMF Adjustment Lending in the Philippines," 62–67; Kathy McAfee, "Jamaica: The Showpiece That Didn't Stand Up," 68–77; Ross Hammond and Lisa McGowan, "Ghana: The World Bank's Sham Showcase," 78–82; Mozambique Information Agency, "Mozambique: In the Coils of Structural Adjustment," 83–84; Abdoulaye Ndiaye, "Food for Thought: Senegal's Struggle with Structural Adjustment," 85–87; Patrick Bond, "From Apartheid to Neoliberalism in South Africa," 88–91; Michael O'Heaney, "Zimbabwe: SAP Means 'Suffering for African People,'" 92–94.

163. See Rist, *History of Development*, 172–173.

164. See MacFarquhar, "Upheaval" (noting that many members of the General Assembly were resentful of what they perceived as the imposition of double standards).

165. Rist, *History of Development*, 79.

166. Ibid., 258.

167. See Reinberg, "Worldwide War."

168. "The World at War: Current Conflicts."

169. See ibid.; see also "Past Wars"; see generally Nietschmann, "Fourth World."

170. Heidelberg Institute for International Conflict Resolution, *Conflict Barometer 2007*.

171. UNDP, "Beyond scarcity."

172. UNDP, "Fighting climate change," 254 (Table 7).

173. Ibid., 264 (Table 10).

174. "We the Children: Meeting the Promises of the World Summit for Children," (noting the one in twelve figure). In 2005 the number appeared to be closer to one in thirteen. See UNDP, "Fighting climate change," 264 (Table 10).

175. See "Developing World 'Poorer Than We Thought,' Report Reveals." Using this measure, it also calculated an overall decline from 1.9 billion in 1981.

176. UNDP, "Fighting climate change," 25.

177. Elliott, "The Lost Decade" (also noting that in 2003 the richest 1 percent of the world's population had as much income as the poorest 57 percent).

178. UNDP, "Fighting climate change," 25. See also Price, "UN finds."

179. UNDP, "Fighting climate change," v.

180. Ibid., v.

181. Ibid., 8.

182. See generally Watson, *Climate Change 2001*.

183. See, e.g., Churchill, "Geographies of Sacrifice," 239–291 (describing federal plans to turn American Indian lands contaminated by uranium mining into depopulated "National Sacrifice Areas").

184. World Bank Group, "World Development Indicators" (also attributing this rate of loss to "weak monitoring institutions").

185. Larsen, "Deserts Advancing."

186. Paehlke, *Conservation and Environmentalism*, 77.

187. World Bank Group, "World Development Indicators." See also "Extinction Rate across The Globe Reaches Historical Proportions" (noting estimate that half of all living bird and mammal species will be extinct within the next two or three centuries); Warrick, "Mass Extinction" (noting that at least one in eight plant species is threatened with extinction, and that nearly all biologists polled attributed the losses to human activity).

188. Harrison, *When Languages Die*, 3–4. See also Nettle and Romaine, *Vanishing Voices*, 40 (noting that 12 percent of the world's languages have fewer than 150 speakers); Living Tongues Institute for Endangered Languages, available at http://www.livingtongues.org/ (accessed September 25, 2008).

189. Quoted in Karnow, *Vietnam*, 14.

190. Krieger, "Economic Justice for All."

191. Ibid.,; see Chomsky, *Keeping the Rabble*, 11.

192. Hochschild, "A Generation" (citing a 30% consumption rate and also noting that the U.S. produces 25% of the world's pollution); U.S. Bureau of the Census, *Statistical Abstract*, Table 1300, "Energy Consumption and Production by Country, 1990 and 1992" (citing a 25% consumption rate).

193. See Box, "Public Service Practitioner," 196; see also Wolff, *Top Heavy* (noting control of almost 40% of the wealth). According to the UN, as of 2000, the richest 10 percent of Americans received or spent about 30 percent of the wealth, while the poorest 10 percent received or spent less than 2 percent (UNDP, "Fighting climate change," 281 [Table 15]).

194. Box, "Public Service Practitioner," 196; Hahnel, *Economic Justice*, 15–18.

195. Pear, "Number of People."

196. Younge, "America Is."

197. See Steele, *Congressional Testimony*; see also Schwartz, "Life, conditions" (also noting teen suicide rate 150% and infant mortality rate 300% higher than national average, teacher turnover 800% of the national average and a school drop-out rate over 70%, housing that is 59% substandard, with over 33% lacking basic water, sewage, and electricity and with an average of seventeen persons in each home, many of which have only two or three rooms). For more general statistics, see Strickland, "You Can't," 53; Churchill, "Unravelling the Codes," xiv–xix.

198. Rizvi, "Hungry," quoting Anurandha Mittal of the Institute for Food and Development Policy (noting also that the U.S. spends only $16 billion per year on welfare). The Census Bureau reported 32.9 million Americans in poverty in 2001, 13.4 million with incomes less than half the official poverty level. Pear, "Number of People"; see also http://www.bread.org/learn/hunger-reports/hunger-report-pdfs/hunger-report-2007/Table-7.pdf (accessed September 6, 2008) (noting similar statistics in 2003–2005).

199. See National Alliance to End Homelessness, "Homelessness Counts" (using data from January 2005, and noting that just over half those counted were in shelters of some kind); see also Shepard, "'State of Cities.'"

200. "Statistics on Adult Literacy" (also noting that the U.S. is forty-ninth in world literacy); "Report: State Spending on Prison Grows at 6 Times Rate of Higher Ed." See also Kisch, *Adult Literacy*, xiii–xiv.

201. See Sherman, Greenstein, and Parrott, "Poverty" (noting that, in 2007, 15.3% of Americans had no health insurance, a decline from 15.8% in 2006 but well above the 14.1% recorded in 2001); see also Krieger, "Economic Justice"; "System Overload: Pondering the Ethics of America's Health Care System" (noting that the U.S. is "unique among the industrialized democracies" in retaining a "free market" health system).

202. See U.S. Department of Justice, "Prison Statistics"; The Sentencing Project, "Facts about Prisons and Prisoners"; "Too Many Prisoners," *Washington Post*; "Anger grows as U.S. jail population," *BBC News*; U.S. Department of Justice Special Report, "Defense Counsel in Criminal Cases."

203. Mauer, *The Race*, 121; see also Fletcher, "'Crisis'"; Miller, *Search and Destroy*.

204. Pear, "Number of People" (citing the Census Bureau figures of a poverty rate of 22.7% for blacks and 21.4% for Hispanics compared to an overall U.S. rate of 11.7%). See also "Study Says White Families' Wealth Advantage Has Grown," *New York Times* (noting that white households now have a median net worth eleven times that of Hispanic households and fourteen times that of black households).

205. See Steele, *Congressional Testimony*; Strickland, "You Can't," 53; Churchill, "Unravelling the Codes," xiv–xix.

206. See generally Rubenfeld, "The End" (noting recent constrictions of the Fourth Amendment); Johnson, "From Brown"; Bell, *And We Are Not Saved*.

207. See Hopkins and Wallerstein, "The World-System," 1–10.

208. See generally Davis, "Citizen Observer's View" (summarizing this dynamic in the context of the war on terror).

209. Palin, Vice Presidential Debate; see also chapter 3.

210. Bacevich, *Limits of Power*, 181.

CHAPTER 9. CONFRONTING AMERICAN EXCEPTIONALISM

1. Falk, *Declining World Order*, 241.

2. See, e.g., "Obama acceptance speech," *The Guardian* (noting that "the dream of our founders" and the "power of our democracy" are still alive, and that "a new dawn of American leadership is at hand. To those who would tear this world down—we will defeat you. To those who seek peace and security—we support you. And to all those who have wondered if America's beacon still burns as bright—tonight we proved once more that the true strength of our nation comes . . . from the enduring power of ideals: democracy, liberty, opportunity, and unyielding hope").

3. Ibid.

4. Falk, *Declining World Order*, x.

5. Davis, *Buda's Wagon*, esp. 4–12.

6. Ibid., 4.

7. Ibid., 5–6.

8. Ibid., 7–8, 171.

9. See ibid., 90–96 (describing CIA and ISI training of terrorists and Russian responses).

10. See ibid., 188–195 (noting, for example, that in July 2006 fifty-one thousand police and soldiers at some six thousand checkpoints in Baghdad could not prevent almost daily car bombings).

11. Falk, *Declining World Order*, 22.

12. Ibid., 233.

13. See Wallerstein, "The Global Possibilities," 239; Falk, *Declining World Order*, 248–251.

14. See Davis, *Buda's Wagon*, 195 (advocating the "decommissioning of minds" rather than implements of destruction but noting that, given the unlikelihood of that possibility, "the car bomb probably has a brilliant future").

15. See Churchill, "Dismantling" (providing a parallel critique of contemporary political activism).

16. Kennedy, "When Renewal Repeats," 359; see also Kennedy, "Primitive Legal Scholarship."

17. See generally Gathii, "Imperialism"; see also chapters 7 and 8 in this volume.

18. See generally Zook, "Decolonizing Law"; Pahuja, "Postcoloniality of International Law."

19. Chimni, "Teaching, Research and Promotion," 369–370.

20. Ibid., 370.

21. Ibid., 372.

22. Ibid. See also Mattei and Nader, *Plunder*, 202–211.

23. Esteva and Prakash, *Grassroots Postmodernism*, 125; see also 27 (emphasizing that "the subject is always historical and specific: he or she cannot be abstracted out of the relation, adopting some divine view from 'nowhere'").

24. See chapter 2 in this volume.

25. Hannum, "Rethinking Self-Determination," 66.

26. Ibid., 67.

27. Ibid., 68. See also Sloane, "Policies of State Succession," 1306 (noting as "the prevailing view, that the modern right to self-determination must, with few exceptions, be

exercised within a framework that respects the territorial integrity of sovereign States");
see also In re *Secession of Quebec.*

28. See Mahmud, "Geography," 534; see generally Bartlett, *Making of Europe.*

29. See Mahmud, "Geography," 541–543; see also chapters 2 and 3 in this volume.

30. Mutua, "Humpty Dumpty," 518.

31. Ibid., 519.

32. Ibid., 523–524.

33. See Mahmud, "Geography," 545.

34. Mutua, "Humpty Dumpty," 523 n. 84.

35. See Mahmud, "Geography," 545–546; see also Nietschmann, "Fourth World," 237.

36. See generally Gordon, "Saving Failed States"; Richardson, "'Failed States.'"

37. See Richardson, "'Failed States,'" 1.

38. See Gordon "Some Legal Problems," 306–309; Sylvester, "Sub-Saharan Africa," 1306.

39. Gordon, "Some Legal Problems," 308–311; Gordon, "Saving Failed States," 904–905.

40. Gordon, "Some Legal Problems," 311–323.

41. See Richardson, "'Failed States,'" 5–7.

42. Bybee, "Memorandum for Alberto R. Gonzales," 23–24 (arguing that the rule prohibiting the suspension of basic human rights protections in treaties "makes little sense" because it rewards noncompliance).

43. See Richardson, "'Failed States,'" 7 (characterizing the "failed state" construct as another iteration "of the perennial dilemma of a state-centric international legal system" of protecting rights within states whose resources are inadequate to the task).

44. Ibid.

45. Ibid., 8.

46. Gordon, "Saving Failed States," 971.

47. Ibid.

48. The potential benefits of incorporating non-Western understandings into international law may be seen in the growing appreciation of Indigenous approaches to environmental problems. See, e.g., Barsh, "Challenge," 278–279 (discussing the Rio Earth Summit's recognition of the importance of Indigenous contributions to environmental sustainability).

49. See Esteva and Prakash, *Grassroots Postmodernism,* 117.

50. See, e.g., International Covenant on Economic, Social and Cultural Rights; Declaration on the Rights of Indigenous Peoples.

51. For a particularly thoughtful attempt to reconcile Islamic law and tradition with universal human rights, see generally An-Na'im, *Cross Cultural Perspectives.*

52. Esteva and Prakash, *Grassroots Postmodernism,* 110 (quoting Vachon, "L'etude du pluralism," 165).

53. Ibid., 111.

54. Ibid.

55. Kolhatkar, "Afghan Women."

56. Ibid., see also Quigley, "Afghanistan War," 550–553 (noting the scope of and damage caused by U.S. bombing in Afghanistan); "Statement of Senator Bob Casey" (noting the resurgence of the Taliban, an "alarming rise" in suicide bombings and IED attacks, and "a ballooning opium trade" in Afghanistan).

57. "Fact Sheet: Strategy for Victory: Freedom in Iraq." This document relies on reports from Freedom House, dedicated to combating "totalitarian ideologies," in concluding that

since 2005 "remarkable democratic change" has helped spread liberty across the globe" (ibid.); see also http://www.freedomhouse.org/template.cfm?page'249 (accessed September 8, 2008).

58. See Brown, "Study Claims" (noting that 601,000 of these deaths were attributable to violence).

59. See, e.g., Susman, "Poll"; "Civilian death toll in Iraq may have surpassed 1 million." But see "Iraq Body Count" (putting the total closer to 100,000).

60. Stork and Abrahams, "Sidelined."

61. Ibid. See generally Allawi, *Occupation of Iraq*.

62. Conley and Rashid, "Iraq."

63. Ibid. See also Petersen, "Apocalypse Now," 163–164 (noting the failure of the U.S. to prevent the looting of some fifteen thousand artifacts from the Iraq Museum, including "some of the greatest treasures from Mesopotamia, the birthplace of civilization"); Campagna, "War or Peace," 274–282.

64. Sandoz, *Crazy Horse*, 11. Sandoz was the daughter of European settlers; this quote is used not to represent Lakota understandings but to illustrate how settlers who paid attention to Indigenous perspectives could gain a very different understanding of freedom from that purveyed by mainstream ideology.

65. Quoted in Johansen, *Forgotten Founders*, 40.

66. Grinde, "Iroquois Political Theory," 235.

67. See Trask, *Native Daughter*, 149 (noting that Westerners have been "burdened by a linear, progressive conception of history"). For a classically Eurocentric analysis positing this trajectory in terms of economic development, see generally Rostow, *Stages of Economic Growth*. Marxist analyses have been criticized as similarly constraining. See, e.g., Black Elk, "Observations," 137, 141 ("it seems Marxists are hung up on exactly the same ideas of 'progress' and 'development' that are the guiding motives of those they seek to overthrow").

68. On the potential of "storytelling" in legal settings, see generally Bell, *And We Are Not Saved*; Delgado, "Storytelling"; Matsuda, "Public Response."

60. Williams, "Encounters," 680–681.

70. Ibid., 682.

71. United Nations Declaration on the Rights of Indigenous Peoples; for background and votes, see http://iwgia.inforce.dk/sw248.asp (accessed September 7, 2008).

72. Eagleton, *Illusions*, 55.

73. Esteva and Prakash, *Grassroots Post-Modernism*, 126.

74. See ibid., 130.

75. Ibid., 131.

76. According to Esteva and Prakash, "Gandhi's politics of liberation epitomized this kind of struggle: appealing to the highest moral ideals of the colonizers, while not renouncing his own culture's moral ideals, defining human well-being or 'the good life'" (ibid., 135).

77. Rist, *History of Development*, 241.

78. Ibid., 248; see also 242.

79. Ibid., 248.

80. Ibid., 243.

81. Ibid., 248; see also 245–248.

82. Ibid., 247.

83. See chapter 1 in this volume.

84. Much that has been written about this devastation assumes that it is a problem for "civilization" to solve. See, e.g., Brown, "Thinking Globally," 178–196; see generally Gore, *Earth in the Balance*. For a perspective calling for the elimination of "civilization" as the only solution for impending ecological disaster, see generally Jensen, *Endgame*.

Works Cited

BOOKS

Aalouf, Amin. *The Crusades Through Arab Eyes*. New York: Schocken Books, 1989.

Abu-Lughod, Janet L. *Before European Hegemony: The World System A.D. 1250–1350*. New York: Oxford University Press, 1989.

Acuña, Rudolfo. *Occupied America: A History of Chicanos*. 4th ed. New York: Longman, 2000.

Adams, David Wallace. *Education for Extinction: American Indians and the Boarding School Experience, 1875–1928*. Lawrence: University Press of Kansas, 1995.

Adams, Howard. *A Tortured People: The Politics of Colonization*. Penticton, B.C.: Theytus Books, 1995.

Adorno, Theodor, and Max Horkheimer. *Dialectic of Enlightenment*. London: Verso, 1979.

Aleinikoff, T. Alexander. *Semblances of Sovereignty: The Constitution, the State and American Citizenship*. Cambridge, Mass.: Harvard University Press, 2002.

Allawi, Ali A. *The Occupation of Iraq: Winning the War, Losing the Peace*. New Haven, Conn.: Yale University Press, 2007.

Allen, Helena. *The Betrayal of Queen Lili'uokalani: Last Queen of Hawaii, 1838–1917*. Honolulu: Mutual, 1982.

Amin, Samir. *Accumulation on a World Scale: A Critique of the Theory of Underdevelopment*. New York: Monthly Review Press, 1974.

———. *Eurocentrism*. New York: Monthly Review Press, 1989.

———. *Imperialism and Unequal Development*. Brighton, U.K.: Harvester, 1977.

———. *Re-Reading the Postwar Period: An Intellectual Itinerary*. New York: Monthly Review Press, 1994.

———. *Unequal Development: An Essay on the Social Formations of Peripheral Capitalism*. New York: Monthly Review, 1976.

An-Na'im, Abdullahi Ahmed, ed. *Human Rights in Cross-Cultural Perspectives: Quest for Consensus*. Philadelphia: University of Pennsylvania Press, 1992.

Anaya, S. James. *Indigenous Peoples in International Law*. New York: Oxford University Press, 1996.

Andrews, Kenneth R. *Elizabethan Privateering: English Privateering During the Spanish War, 1585–1603*. Cambridge: Cambridge University Press, 1964.

Andrist, Ralph K. *The Long Death: The Last Days of the Plains Indian*. New York: Macmillan, 1964.

Anghie, Antony. *Imperialism, Sovereignty and the Making of International Law.* Cambridge: Cambridge University Press, 2005.

Aruri, Naseer. *Obstruction to Peace: The United States, Israel, and the Palestinians.* London: Pluto, 2000.

Ashburn, Percy M. *The Ranks of Death: A Medical History of the Conquest of America.* New York: Coward-McCann, 1947.

Ashcroft, Bill, Gareth Griffiths, and Helen Tiffin. *Key Concepts in Post-Colonial Studies.* New York: Routledge, 1998.

Atiya, Aziz. *Crusade, Commerce and Culture.* New York: Wiley, 1962.

Axelrod, Alan. *Chronicle of the Indian Wars from Colonial Times to Wounded Knee.* New York: Prentice Hall, 1993.

Axtmann, Roland, ed. *Globalization and Europe: Theoretical and Empirical Investigations.* London: Pinter, 1998.

Bacevich, Andrew J. *The Limits of Power: The End of American Exceptionalism.* New York: Metropolitan Books, 2008.

Bailey, Lynn R. *Bosque Redondo: The Navajo Internment at Fort Sumner, New Mexico, 1863–68.* Tucson, AZ: Westernlore, 1998.

Baker, Ray Stannard. *Woodrow Wilson and World Settlement: Written from His Unpublished and Personal Material,* Vol. 3, *Original Documents of the Peace Conference.* Garden City, N.Y.: Doubleday, Page, 1922.

Baldwin, James. *The Evidence of Things Not Seen.* New York: Holt, Reinhart, and Winston, 1985.

Ballis, William. *The Legal Position of War: Changes in Practice and Theory from Plato to Vattel.* The Hague: Nijhoff, 1937.

Bamford, James. *Body of Secrets: Anatomy of the Ultra-Secret National Security Agency.* New York: Anchor Books, 2001.

Barker, Eugene C. *Mexico and Texas, 1821–1835.* New York: Russell & Russell, 1965.

Barreiro, Jose, ed. *Indian Roots of American Democracy.* Ithaca, N.Y.: Akwe:kon Press, Cornell University, 1992.

Bartlett, Robert. *The Making of Europe: Conquest, Colonization and Cultural Change, 950-1350.* Princeton, N.J.: Princeton University Press, 1994.

Bartlett, Robert, and Angus MacKay, eds. *Medieval Frontier Societies.* Oxford: Clarendon, 1989.

Beard, Charles. *An Economic Interpretation of the Constitution.* New York: Free Press, 1986.

Bederman, David J. *Globalization and International Law.* New York: Palgrave Macmillan, 2008.

Bell, Derrick. *And We Are Not Saved: The Elusive Quest for Racial Justice.* New York: Basic Books, 1989.

Bennett, Lerone, Jr. *Before the Mayflower: A History of Black America.* 6th ed. New York: Penguin, 1986.

Bennis, Phyllis. *Calling the Shots: How Washington Dominates Today's UN.* New York: Olive Branch, 1996.

Bercovitch, Sacvan. *The Puritan Origins of the American Self.* New Haven, Conn.: Yale University Press, 1975.

Berlinerblau, Jacques. *Heresy in the University: The* Black Athena *Controversy and the Responsibilities of American Intellectuals.* New Brunswick, N.J.: Rutgers University Press, 1999.

Bernal, Martin. *Black Athena: The Afroasiatic Roots of Classical Civilization*, Vol. 1, *The Fabrication of Ancient Greece 1785–1985*; Vol. 2, *The Archaeological and Documentary Evidence*; Vol. 3, *The Linguistic Evidence*. New Brunswick, N.J.: Rutgers University Press, 1987, 1991, 2006.
———. *Black Athena Writes Back: Martin Bernal Responds to His Critics*, ed. David Chioni Moore. Durham, N.C.: Duke University Press, 2001.
Berthrong, Donald J. *The Cheyenne and Arapaho Ordeal: Reservation and Agency Life in the Indian Territory, 1875–1907*. Norman: University of Oklahoma Press, 1976.
Biddle, Francis. *In Brief Authority*. Garden City, N.Y.: Doubleday, 1962.
Black, Edwin. *War Against the Weak: Eugenics and America's Campaign to Create a Master Race*. New York: Four Walls Eight Windows, 2003.
Blaufarb, Douglas S. *The Counterinsurgency Era: U.S. Doctrine and Performance*. New York: Free Press, 1977.
Blum, William. *The CIA: A Forgotten History, U.S. Global Interventions Since World War 2*. London: Zed, 1986.
———. *Rogue State: A Guide to the World's Only Superpower*. 3rd ed. London: Zed, 2006.
Bonner, Raymond. *Weakness & Deceit: U.S. Policy and El Salvador*. New York: Times Books, 1984.
Boot, Max. *The Savage Wars of Peace: Small Wars and the Rise of American Power*. New York: Basic Books, 2002.
Bowers, Claude G. *Jefferson and Hamilton: The Struggle for Democracy in America*. Boston: Houghton Mifflin, 1925.
Box, Richard C. ed. Democracy and Public Administration. Armonk, N.Y.: M. E. Sharpe, 2007.
Boyle, Francis Anthony. *Foundations of World Order: The Legalist Approach to International Relations (1898–1922)*. Durham, N.C.: Duke University Press, 1999.
Brackman, Arnold C. *The Other Nuremberg: The Untold Story of the Tokyo War Crimes Trials*. New York: William Morrow, 1987.
Bragança, Aquino de, and Immanuel Wallerstein, eds. *The African Liberation Reader*. 2 vols. London: Zed, 1982.
Brandwein, Pamela. *Reconstructing Reconstruction: The Supreme Court and the Production of Historical Truth*. Durham, N.C.: Duke University Press, 1999.
Brodie, Fawn M. *Thomas Jefferson: An Intimate History*. New York: W. W. Norton, 1974.
Brown, Dee. *Bury My Heart at Wounded Knee: An Indian History of the American West*. New York: Holt, Rinehart & Winston, 1970.
Browne-Marshall, Gloria J. *Race, Law, and American Society*. New York: Routledge, 2007.
Brownlie, Ian. *African Boundaries: A Legal and Diplomatic Encyclopaedia*. London: C. Hurst, 1979.
Budnick, Rich. *Stolen Kingdom: An American Conspiracy*. Honolulu: Aloha, 1992.
Bull, Hedley, Benedict Kingsbury, and Adam Roberts, eds. *Hugo Grotius and International Relations*. Oxford: Clarendon. 1990.
Bull, Hedley, and Adam Watson, eds. *The Expansion of International Society*. Oxford: Clarendon, 1984.
Burleigh, Michael. *Germany Turns Eastwards: A Study of* Ostorschung *in the Third Reich*. Cambridge: Cambridge University Press, 1988.
Burnett, Christina Duffy, and Burke Marshall, eds. *Foreign in a Domestic Sense: Puerto Rico, American Expansion, and the Constitution*. Durham, N.C.: Duke University Press, 2001.

Bush, George W. *We Will Prevail: President George W. Bush on War, Terrorism, and Freedom*. New York: Continuum, 2003.

Cadwalader, Sandra L., and Vine Deloria Jr., eds. *The Aggressions of Civilization: Federal Indian Policy since the 1880s*. Philadelphia: Temple University Press, 1984.

Calder, Bruce J. *The Impact of Intervention: The Dominican Republic during the U.S. Occupation of 1916–1924*. Austin: University of Texas Press, 1984.

Campbell, Randolph B. *An Empire for Slavery: The Peculiar Institution in Texas, 1821–1865*. Baton Rouge: Louisiana State University Press, 1989.

Canny, Nicholas P. *The Elizabethan Conquest of Ireland: A Pattern Established, 1565–76*. Hassocks: Harvester, 1976.

———. *Making Ireland British, 1580–1650*. Oxford: Oxford University Press, 2001.

Carmichael, Stokely. *Stokely Speaks: Black Power Back to Pan-Africanism*. New York: Vintage Books, 1971.

Carter, Barry E. *International Law: Selected Documents*. 2007–2008 ed. New York: Aspen, 2007.

Cassirer, Ernst. *The Myth of the State*. New Haven, Conn.: Yale University Press, 1946.

Chambers, James. *The Devil's Horsemen: The Mongol Invasion of Europe*. London: Cassell, 1988.

Chan, Sucheng, ed. *Entry Denied: Exclusion and the Chinese Community in America, 1882–1943*. Philadelphia: Temple University Press, 1991.

Cheetham, Nicolas. *A History of the Popes*. New York: Dorset, 1982.

Chinen, J. J. *The Great Mahele*. Honolulu: University of Hawai'i Press, 1958.

Chomsky, Noam. *Fateful Triangle: The United States, Israel and the Palestinians*. 2nd ed. Cambridge, Mass.: South End, 1999.

———. *Hegemony or Survival: America's Quest for Global Dominance*. New York: Metropolitan Books, 2003.

———. *Interventions*. San Francisco: City Lights, 2007.

———. *Keeping the Rabble in Line: Interviews with David Barsamian*. Monroe, Me.: Common Courage, 1994.

Christiansen, Eric. *The Northern Crusades: The Baltic and the Catholic Frontier, 1100–1525*. Minneapolis: University of Minnesota Press, 1980.

Churchill, Ward. *Acts of Rebellion: The Ward Churchill Reader*. New York: Routledge, 2003.

———. *Fantasies of the Master Race: Literature, Cinema and the Colonization of American Indians*. San Francisco: City Lights Books, 1998.

———. *"Kill the Indian, Save the Man": The Genocidal Impact of American Indian Residential Schools*. San Francisco: City Lights Books, 2004.

———. *A Little Matter of Genocide: Holocaust and Denial in the Americas, 1492 to the Present*. San Francisco: City Lights Books, 1997.

———, ed. *Marxism and Native Americans*. Boston: South End, 1983.

———. *On the Justice of Roosting Chickens: Reflections on the Consequences of U.S. Imperial Arrogance and Criminality*. San Francisco: AK Press, 2003.

———. *Perversions of Justice: Indigenous Peoples and Angloamerican Law*. San Francisco: City Lights Books, 2003.

———. *Struggle for the Land: Native North American Resistance to Genocide, Ecocide and Colonization*. San Francisco: City Lights Books, 2002.

Churchill, Ward, and Sharon Venne, eds. *Islands in Captivity: The Record of the International Tribunal on the Rights of Indigenous Hawaiians.* Boston: South End, 2004.

Civil Rights Congress. *We Charge Genocide: The Historic Petitions to the United Nations for Relief from a Crime of the United States Government Against the Negro People.* New York: International, 1970. First published by the Civil Rights Congress in 1951.

Clarens, Carlos. *An Illustrated History of Horror and Science Fiction Films: The Classic Era, 1895–1967.* New York: De Capo, 1997.

Clark, Blue. *Lone Wolf v. Hitchcock: Treaty Rights and Indian Law at the End of the Nineteenth Century.* Lincoln: University of Nebraska Press, 1999.

Clinton, Robert N., Nell Jessup Newton, and Monroe E. Price. *American Indian Law: Cases and Materials.* 3rd ed. Charlottesville, Va.: Michie, 1973.

Cocker, Mark. *Rivers of Blood, Rivers of Gold: Europe's Conquest of Indigenous Peoples.* New York: Grove, 1998.

Cohen, Felix S. *Handbook of Federal Indian Law.* Buffalo, NY: William S. Hein, 1988 [1942].

Cohen, Lucy Kramer, ed. *The Legal Conscience: Selected Papers of Felix S. Cohen.* New Haven, Conn.: Yale University Press, 1960.

Cole, David. *Enemy Aliens: Double Standards and Constitutional Freedoms in the War on Terrorism.* New York: New Press, 2003.

———. *No Equal Justice: Race and Class in the American Criminal Justice System.* New York: New Press, 1999.

The Compact Edition of the Oxford English Dictionary. Vol. 1. Oxford: Oxford University Press, 1971.

Cook, Sherburn F., and Woodrow Borah. *Essays in Population History.* Vol. 1. Berkeley: University of California Press, 1971.

Cooper, George, and Gavan Daws. *Land and Power in Hawaii.* Honolulu: University of Hawai'i Press, 1990.

Cox, Harvey. *The Secular City.* New York: Macmillan, 1965.

Crandall, Russell. *Gunboat Democracy: U.S. Interventions in the Dominican Republic, Grenada, and Panama.* Lanham, Md.: Rowman & Littlefield, 2006.

Crawford, James. *The Creation of States in International Law.* 2nd ed. Oxford: Clarendon, 2006.

Cunningham, Rodger. *Apples on the Flood: The Southern Mountain Experience.* Knoxville: University of Tennessee Press, 1987.

Curtin, P.D., ed. *Imperialism.* London: Macmillan, 1971.

Danaher, Kevin, ed. *50 Years Is Enough: The Case Against the World Bank and the International Monetary Fund.* Boston: South End, 1994.

Daniels, Roger. *Guarding the Golden Door: American Immigration Policy and Immigrants Since 1882.* New York: Hill and Wang, 2004.

Davenport, Francis Gardiner, ed. *European Treaties Bearing on the History of the United States and Its Dependencies.* 2 vols. Washington, D.C.: Carnegie Institution, 1917.

Davidson, Basil. *The African Slave Trade.* Rev. ed. Boston: Atlantic, Little, Brown, 1980.

Davis, Kenneth C. *Don't Know Much About Geography: Everything You Need to Know About the World but Never Learned.* New York: William Morrow, 1992.

Davis, Mike. *Buda's Wagon: A Brief History of the Car Bomb.* London: Verso, 2007.

Deller, Nicole, Arjun Makhijani, and John Burroughs, eds. *Rule of Power or Rule of Law? An Assessment of US Policies and Actions Regarding Security-Related Treaties.* New York: Apex, 2003.

Deloria, Barbara, Kristen Foehner, and Sam Scinta, eds. *Spirit & Reason: The Vine Deloria, Jr., Reader.* Golden, Colo.: Fulcrum, 1999.

Deloria, Vine, Jr. *God Is Red: A Native View of Religion.* 2d ed. Golden, Colo.: Fulcrum, 1994.

——. *The Metaphysics of Modern Existence.* New York: Harper & Row, 1979.

Deloria, Vine, Jr., and Clifford M. Lytle. *American Indians, American Justice.* Austin: University of Texas Press, 1983.

——. *The Nations Within: The Past and Future of American Indian Sovereignty.* New York: Pantheon Books, 1984.

Deloria, Vine, Jr., and Raymond J. DeMallie. *Documents of American Indian Diplomacy; Treaties, Agreements, and Conventions, 1775–1979.* 2 vols. Norman: University of Oklahoma Press, 1999.

Deloria, Vine, Jr., and David E. Wilkins. *Tribes, Treaties and Constitutional Tribulations.* Austin: University of Texas Press, 1999.

Demko, George J., and William B. Wood, eds. *Reordering the World: Geopolitical Perspectives on the Twenty-First Century.* 1ˢᵗ ed. Boulder, Colo: Westview, 1994.

Derrida, Jacques. *Margins of Philosophy.* Chicago: University of Chicago Press, 1982.

Dicey, A. V. *Introduction to the Study of the Law of the Constitution,* ed. Roger E. Michener. Indianapolis: Liberty Fund, Inc., 1982 [1885].

Djait, Hichem. *Europe and Islam: Cultures and Modernity.* Berkeley: University of California Press, 1985.

Dobyns, Henry F. *Their Number Become Thinned: Native American Population Dynamics in Eastern North America.* Knoxville: University of Tennessee Press, 1983.

Dodge, Frederick W., ed. *Handbook of the Indians North of Mexico,* Vol. 2. Washington, D.C.: Bureau of American Ethnology, Bulletin No. 30, Smithsonian Institution, 1910.

Domenico, Roy Palmer. *Italian Fascists on Trial, 1943–1948.* Chapel Hill: University of North Carolina Press, 1991.

Doyle, Michael W. *Empires.* Ithaca, N.Y.: Cornell University Press, 1986.

Drimmer, Melvin, ed. *Black History: A Reappraisal.* New York: Bantam Doubleday Dell, 1968.

Drinnon, Richard. *Facing West: The Metaphysics of Indian-Hating and Empire-Building.* New York: New American Library, 1980.

——. *Keeper of Concentration Camps: Dillon S. Myer and American Racism.* Berkeley: University of California Press, 1987.

DuBois, W. E. B. *Writings.* New York: Literary Classics of the United States, 1986.

Dudley, Michael Kioni, and Keoni Kealoha Agard, eds. *A Call for Hawaiian Sovereignty.* Waipahu, Hi.: No Kano O Ka Malo Press, 1990.

Dudziak, Mary L., ed. *September 11 in History: A Watershed Moment?* Durham, N.C.: Duke University Press, 2003.

Duffy, Michael, ed. *The Military Revolution and the State, 1500-1800.* Exeter, U.K.: University of Exeter Studies in History No. 1, 1980.

Durant, Will. *The Age of Faith: A History of Medieval Civilization—Christian, Islamic, and Judaic—from Constantine to Dante, A.D. 325–1300.* New York: Simon and Schuster, 1950.

———. *Our Oriental Heritage.* New York; Simon and Schuster, 1935.

Dworkin, Ronald. *A Matter of Principle.* Cambridge, Mass.: Harvard University Press, 1985.

Eagleton, Terry. *Ideology: An Introduction.* London: Verso, 1991.

———. *The Illusions of Postmodernism.* Oxford: Blackwell, 1996.

Ebright, Malcolm. *Land Grants and Lawsuits in Northern New Mexico.* Albuquerque: University of New Mexico Press, 1994.

Eckert, Allen W. *That Dark and Bloody River: Chronicles of the Ohio River Valley.* New York: Bantam, 1995.

Eliade, Mircea. *The Myth of the Eternal Return; or, Cosmos and History.* Princeton, N.J.: Princeton University Press, 1965.

———. *Myths, Dreams, and Realities: The Encounter Between Contemporary Faiths and Archaic Realities.* Translated by Philip Mairet. New York: Harper Torchbooks, 1960.

Elliott, J. H. *Imperial Spain, 1469–1716.* New York: St. Martin's, 1964.

Esteva, Gustavo, and Madhu Suri Prakash. *Grassroots Postmodernism: Remaking the Soil of Cultures.* London: Zed, 1998.

Falk, Richard A. *The Declining World Order: America's Imperial Geopolitics.* New York: Routledge, 2004.

———. *The End of World Order: Essays on Normative International Relations.* New York: Holmes & Meier, 1983.

———, ed. *The Vietnam War and International Law.* Princeton, N.J.: Princeton University Press, 1976.

Falls, Cyril. *Elizabeth's Irish Wars.* Syracuse, N.Y.: Syracuse University Press, 1950.

Fanon, Frantz. *Studies in a Dying Colonialism.* New York: Monthly Review Press, 1965.

Fitzgerald, John C., ed. *Writings of George Washington.* Washington, D.C.: U.S. Government Printing Office, 1936.

Fitzpatrick, Peter. *The Mythology of Modern Law.* London: Routledge, 1992.

Floyd, Troy. *The Columbus Dynasty in the Caribbean, 1492–1526.* Albuquerque: University of New Mexico Press, 1973.

Foot, Rosemary, S. Neil MacFarlane, and Michael Mastanduno, eds. *US Hegemony and International Organizations.* Oxford: Oxford University Press 2003.

Fowke, Gerard. *Archaeological History of the Ohio: The Mound Builders and Later Indians.* Columbus: Ohio State Archaeological and Historical Society, 1902.

Frame, Robin. *Colonial Ireland, 1169–1369.* Dublin: Educational Company of Ireland, 1981.

Franklin, H. Bruce. *Vietnam and Other American Fantasies.* Amherst: University of Massachusetts Press, 2000.

Freire, Paolo. *Pedagogy of the Oppressed.* Thirtieth anniversary edition. London: Continuum, 2000.

Fuller, John Douglas Pitts. *The Movement for the Acquisition of All Mexico, 1846–1848.* Baltimore, Md.: Johns Hopkins University Press, 1936.

Fuller, Lon L. *The Morality of Law.* Rev. ed. New Haven, Conn.: Yale University Press, 1969.

Furedi, Frank. *The New Ideology of Imperialism.* London: Pluto, 1994.

Galeano, Eduardo H. *Open Veins of Latin America: Five Centuries of Pillage of a Continent.* New York: Monthly Review Press, 1973.

Giddings, Joshua R. *The Exiles of Florida: Or, The Crimes Committed By Our Government Against the Maroons, Who Fled from South Carolina and Other Slave States, Seeking Protection Under Spanish Law.* Columbus, OH: Follett Foster, 1964 [1858].

Gilman, Daniel C. *James Monroe*. Boston: Houghton Mifflin, 1883.

Giunta, Mary A., ed. *The Emerging Nation: A Documentary History of the Foreign Relations of the United States under the Articles of Confederation, 1780–1789*. Washington, D.C.: National Historical Publications and Records Commission, 1996.

Goldsmith, Jack. *The Terror Presidency: Law and Judgment Inside the Bush Administration*. New York: W. W. Norton, 2007.

Gore, Al. *Earth in the Balance: Ecology and the Human Spirit*. New York: Rodale, 1992.

Gorn, Elliott J., Randy Roberts, and Terry D. Bilhartz. *Constructing the American Past: A Source Book of a People's History*. New York: HarperCollins, 1972.

Gould, Stephen Jay. *The Mismeasure of Man*. New York: W. W. Norton, 1981.

Gramsci, Antonio. *The Modern Prince and Other Writings*. New York: International, 1957.

Green, L. C., and Olive P. Dickason, eds. *The Law of Nations and the New World*. Edmonton: University of Alberta Press, 1989.

Greenberg, Karen J., and Joshua L. Dratel, eds. *The Torture Papers: The Road to Abu Ghraib*. Cambridge: Cambridge University Press, 2005.

Grinde, Donald A., Jr. *The Iroquois and the Founding of the American Nation*. San Francisco: Indian Historian Press, 1977.

Grinde, Donald A., Jr., and Bruce Johansen. *Exemplar of Liberty: Native America and the Evolution of Democracy*. Los Angeles: American Indian Studies Center, University of California, 1991.

The Hague Yearbook of International Law. Vol. 14. The Hague, Netherlands: Martinus Nijhoff, 2001.

Hahnel, Robin. *Economic Justice and Democracy: From Competition to Cooperation*. New York: Routledge, 2005.

Halbert, H. S., and T. H. Hall. *The Creek War of 1813 and 1814*. Tuscaloosa: University of Alabama Press, 1969.

Hall, Anthony J. *The American Empire and the Fourth World*. Montreal: McGill-Queen's University Press, 2003.

Haney Lopez, Ian F. *White by Law: The Legal Construction of Race*. Rev. ed. New York: New York University Press, 2006.

Hanke, Lewis. *Aristotle and the Indians: A Study in Race Prejudice in the Modern World*. Chicago: Henry Regnery, 1959.

———. *The Spanish Struggle for Justice in the Conquest of America*. Philadelphia: University of Pennsylvania Press, 1947.

Hannum, Hurst. *Autonomy, Sovereignty, and Self-Determination: The Accommodation of Conflicting Rights*. University of Pennsylvania Press, 1990.

Hardoy, Jorge E. *Pre-Columbian Cities*. New York: Walker, 1973.

Harring, Sidney L. *Crow Dog's Case: American Indian Sovereignty, Tribal Law, and the United States in the Nineteenth Century*. Cambridge: Cambridge University Press, 1994.

Harrison, K. David. *When Languages Die: The Extinction of the World's Languages and the Erosion of Human Knowledge*. Oxford: Oxford University Press, 2007.

Harvey, L. P. *Islamic Spain, 1250–1500*. Chicago: University of Chicago Press, 1990.

Hasager, Ulla, and Jonathan Friedman, eds. *Hawai'i: Return to Nationhood*. Copenhagen: IWGIA Doc. 75, 1994.

Haverkampf, Alfred. *Medieval Germany, 1056–1273*. Oxford: Oxford University Press, 1992.

Hector, Michael. *Internal Colonialism: The Celtic Fringe in British National Development, 1536–1966.* Berkeley: University of California Press, 1975.

Heizer, Robert F., ed. *The Destruction of the California Indians.* Lincoln: University of Nebraska Press, 1993.

Hemming, John. *Red Gold: The Conquest of the Brazilian Indians, 1500–1760.* Cambridge, Mass.: Harvard University Press, 1978.

Henkin, Louis. *The Age of Rights.* New York: Columbia University Press, 1990.

Herrin, Judith. *The Formation of Christendom.* Princeton, N.J.: Princeton University Press, 1987.

Hersh, Seymour. *Chain of Command: The Road from 9/11 to Abu Ghraib.* New York: HarperCollins, 2004.

Higginbotham, A. Leon, Jr. *In the Matter of Color: Race and the American Legal Process: The Colonial Period.* New York: Oxford University Press, 1978.

———. *Shades of Freedom: Racial Politics and Presumptions of the American Legal Process.* New York: Oxford University Press, 1996.

Hitler, Adolf. *Mein Kampf.* London: Hutchinson, 1974.

Hofstadter, Richard. *The American Political Tradition: And the Men Who Made It.* New York: Knopf, 1989 [1948].

Hoig, Stan. *The Battle of the Washita.* Garden City, N.Y.: Doubleday, 1976.

———. *The Sand Creek Massacre.* Norman: University of Oklahoma Press, 1961.

Hopkins, Terence K. and Immanuel Wallerstein, eds. *The Age of Transition: Trajectory of the World-System, 1945–2025.* London: Zed, 1996.

Horsman, Reginald. *Expansion and American Policy, 1783–1812.* Lansing: Michigan State University Press, 1967.

———. *Race and Manifest Destiny: The Origins of American Racial Anglo-Saxonism.* Cambridge, Mass.: Harvard University Press, 1981.

Howard, Michael, George J. Andreopoulos, and Mark R. Shulman, eds. *The Laws of War: Constraints on Warfare in the Western World.* New Haven, Conn.: Yale University Press, 1994.

Hoyt, Edwin P. *America's Wars and Military Excursions.* New York: McGraw-Hill, 1987.

Hurt, R. Douglas. *Indian Agriculture in America: Prehistory to the Present.* Lawrence: University Press of Kansas, 1987.

Hyde, George. *Red Cloud's Folk: A History of the Oglalla Sioux Indians.* Norman: University of Oklahoma Press, 1937.

———. *Spotted Tail's Folk: A History of the Brule Sioux.* Norman: University of Oklahoma Press, 1961.

Ignatieff, Michael, ed. *American Exceptionalism and Human Rights.* Princeton, N.J.: Princeton University Press, 2005.

Jackson, John G. *Introduction to African Civilizations.* Secaucus, N.J.: Citadel, 1970.

Jaffer, Jameel, and Amrit Singh. *Administration of Torture: A Documentary Record from Washington to Abu Ghraib and Beyond.* New York: Columbia University Press, 2007.

Jaimes, M. Annette, ed. *The State of Native America: Genocide, Colonization and Resistance.* Boston: South End, 1992.

Jennings, Francis. *Empire of Fortune: Crowns, Colonies and Tribes in the Seven Years War in America.* New York: W. W. Norton, 1988.

————. *The Invasion of America: Indians, Colonialism, and the Cant of Conquest.* Chapel Hill: University of North Carolina Press, 1975.

Jensen, Derrick. *Endgame.* 2 vols. New York: Seven Stories, 2006.

Jensen, Merrill. *The Articles of Confederation: An Interpretation of the Socio-Constitutional History of the American Revolution, 1774–1788.* Madison: University of Wisconsin Press, 1940.

Johansen, Bruce E. *Forgotten Founders: Benjamin Franklin, the Iroquois, and the Rationale for the American Revolution.* Ipswich, Mass.: Gambit, 1982.

————. *Forgotten Founders: How the American Indian Helped Shape Democracy.* Boston: Harvard Common Press, 1987.

Johansen, Bruce E., and Barry M. Pritzker, eds. *Encyclopedia of American Indian History.* Vol. 1. Santa Barbara, Calif.: ABC-CLIO, 2008.

Johnson, Chalmers. *Blowback: The Costs and Consequences of American Empire.* New York: Metropolitan Books, 2000.

Jordan, Winthrop D. *White Over Black: American Attitudes Toward the Negro, 1550–1812.* Chapel Hill: University of North Carolina Press, 1968.

Kameʻeleihiwa, Lilikala. *Native Land and Foreign Desires: Pahea La E Pono Ai?* Honolulu: Bishop Museum Press, 1992.

Kappler, Charles J., ed. *Indian Treaties: 1778–1883.* New York: Interland, 1972 [1904].

Karnow, Stanley. *Vietnam: A History.* New York: Viking, 1983.

Katz, Steven T. *The Holocaust in Historical Context,* Vol. 1, *The Holocaust and Mass Death Before the Modern Age.* New York: Oxford University Press, 1992.

Kaufman, Natalie Hevener. *Human Rights Treaties and the Senate: A History of Opposition.* Chapel Hill: University of North Carolina Press, 1990.

Keal, Paul. *European Conquest and the Rights of Indigenous Peoples.* Cambridge: Cambridge University Press, 2003.

Keen, Maurice H. *The Laws of War in the Late Middle Ages.* London: Routledge, 1965.

Kelly, John. *Hawaii: Showcase of Imperialism, Land Alienation, and Foreign Control.* Honolulu, 1874. Self-published.

Kelly, Marion. *Early Mission Impact on Hawaiians and their Culture.* Honolulu: Church of the Crossroads, 1988.

Kelly, Walt. *Pogo: We Have Met the Enemy and He Is Us.* New York: Simon and Schuster, 1972 .

Kent, Noel J. *Hawaii: Islands under the Influence.* 2nd ed. Honolulu: University of Hawaiʻi Press, 1993.

Kim, Hyung-Chan, ed. *Asian Americans and the Supreme Court: A Documentary History.* New York: Greenwood, 1992.

King, Thomas. *Green Grass, Running Water.* New York: Houghton Mifflin, 1993.

————. *The Truth About Stories: A Native Narrative.* Minneapolis: University of Minnesota Press, 2003.

Kinzer, Stephen. *All the Shah's Men: An American Coup and the Roots of Middle East Terror.* Hoboken, N.J.: Wiley, 2008.

Kirkby, Diane, and Catharine Coleborne, eds. *Law, History, Colonialism: The Reach of Empire.* Manchester, U.K.: Manchester University Press, 2001.

Kisch, Irwin S., ed. *Adult Literacy in America: A First Look at the Results of the National Adult Literacy Survey.* Darby, Pa.: Diane, 1994.

Klein, Naomi. *The Shock Doctrine: The Rise of Disaster Capitalism*. New York: Henry Holt, 2007.

Koning, Hans. *Columbus: His Enterprise*. New York: Monthly Review Press, 1976.

Korman, Sharon. *The Right of Conquest: The Acquisition of Territory by Force in International Law and Practice*. Oxford: Clarendon, 1996.

Koskenniemi, Martti. *The Gentle Civilizer of Nations: The Rise and Fall of International Law, 1870–1960*. Cambridge: Cambridge University Press, 2001.

Kühl, Stefan. *The Nazi Connection: Eugenics, American Racism, and German National Socialism*. New York: Oxford University Press, 1994.

Kuykendall, Ralph S. *The Hawaiian Kingdom, 1778–1854*. Honolulu: University of Hawai'i Press, 1938.

LaBlanc, Lawrence J. *The United States and the Genocide Convention*. Durham, N.C.: Duke University Press, 1991.

LaDuke, Winona. *Recovering the Sacred: The Power of Naming and Claiming*. Boston: South End, 2005.

LaFeber, Walter. *Inevitable Revolutions: The United States in Central America*. 2nd rev. ed. New York: W. W. Norton, 1993.

Lane-Poole, Stanley. *The Story of the Moors in Spain*. Baltimore, Md.: Black Classic Press, 1990 [1886].

Lansing, Robert. *The Peace Negotiations: A Personal Narrative*. New York: Macmillan, 1921.

Las Casas, Bartolomé de. *The Devastation of the Indies: A Brief Account*. Baltimore, Md.: Johns Hopkins University Press, 1992.

Layton, Azza Salama. *International Politics and Civil Rights in the United States, 1941–1960*. Cambridge: Cambridge University Press, 2000.

Leach, Edmund. *Genesis as Myth and Other Essays*. London: Jonathan Cape, 1969.

Lefkowitz, Mary. *Not Out of Africa: How Afrocentrism Became an Excuse to Teach Myth as History*. New York: Basic Books, 1996.

Lefkowitz, Mary, and Guy MacLean Rogers, eds. *Black Athena Revisited*. Chapel Hill: University of North Carolina Press, 1996.

Lefort, Claude. *The Political Forms of Modern Society: Bureaucracy, Democracy, Totalitarianism*. Cambridge: Polity, 1986.

Leibowitz, Arnold H. *Defining Status: A Comprehensive Analysis of United States Territorial Relations*. Dordrecht, The Netherlands: Martinus Nijhoff, 1989.

Lemkin, Raphael. *Axis Rule in Occupied Europe: Laws of Occupation, Analysis of Government, Proposals for Redress*. Washington, D.C.: Carnegie Endowment for International Peace, 1944.

Lenman, Bruce. *England's Colonial Wars, 1550–1688: Conflicts, Empire and National Identity*. London: Longman, 2001.

Lens, Sidney. *The Forging of the American Empire*. New York: Thomas Y. Crowell, 1971.

Lieder, Michael, and Jake Page. *Wild Justice: The People of Geronimo vs. the United States*. New York: Random House, 1997.

Lillich, Richard B., ed. *U.S. Ratification of the Human Rights Treaties: With or Without Reservation?* Charlottesville: University Press of Virginia, 1981.

Lindley, Mark F. *The Acquisition and Government of Backward Territories in International Law*. London: Longmans, Green, 1926.

Linn, Brian McAllister. *The U.S. Army and Counterinsurgency in the Philippines War, 1899–1902.* Chapel Hill: University of North Carolina Press, 1989.

Litwack, Leon F. *North of Slavery.* Chicago: University of Chicago Press, 1965.

Lomax, Derek W. *The Reconquest of Spain.* London: Longman, 1978.

Lombardo, Paul A. *Three Generations, No Imbeciles: Eugenics, the Supreme Court and* Buck v. Bell. Baltimore, Md.: Johns Hopkins University Press, 2008.

Lorimer, James. *The Institutes of the Law of Nations: A Treatise of the Jural Relations of Separate Political Communities.* Clark, N.J.: Lawbook Exchange, 2005 [1883].

Lowes, Warren. *Indian Giver: A Legacy of North American Native Peoples.* Penticton, B.C.: Theytus Books, 1986.

Lugard, Lord F. D. *The Dual Mandate in British Tropical Africa.* Edinburgh, U.K.: William Blackwood, 1922.

Malavet, Pedro. *America's Colony: The Political and Cultural Conflict between the United States and Puerto Rico.* New York: New York University Press, 2004.

Malcomson, Scott L. *One Drop of Blood: The American Misadventure of Race.* New York: Farrar Straus and Giroux, 2000.

Maley, William. *The Afghanistan Wars.* New York: Palgrave Macmillan, 2002.

Malone, David M., ed. *The UN Security Council: From the Cold War to the 21st Century.* Boulder, Colo.: Lynne Rienner, 2004.

Manley, Michael. *Jamaica: Struggle in the Periphery.* London: Writers & Readers, 1983.

Mann, Barbara Alice. *George Washington's War on Native America.* Westport, Conn.: Praeger, 2005.

———. *Native Americans, Archaeologists, and the Mounds.* New York: Peter Lang, 2003.

Manuel, George, and Michael Posluns. *The Fourth World: An Indian Reality.* New York: Free Press, 1974.

Martin, James Kirby, Randy Roberts, Steven Mintz, Linda O. McMurray, and James H. Jones. *America and Its Peoples: A Mosaic in the Making to 1877.* 2nd ed. New York: HarperCollins College, 1993.

Mattei, Ugo, and Laura Nader. *Plunder: When the Rule of Law is Illegal.* Malden, Mass.: Blackwell, 2008.

Mauer, Marc. *The Race to Incarcerate.* New York: New Press, 1999.

McGrath, C. Peter. *Yazoo: The Case of* Fletcher v. Peck. New York: W. W. Norton, 1996.

McGregor, James H. *The Wounded Knee Massacre from the Viewpoint of the Survivors.* Baltimore, Md.: Wirth Brothers, 1940.

McMahon, Matthew M. *Conquest in Modern International Law: The Legal Limitations on the Acquisition of Territory by Conquest.* Washington, D.C.: Catholic University of America Press, 1940.

McPherson, James M. *The Negro's Civil War: How American Blacks Felt and Acted during the War for the Union.* New York: Random House, 1991.

Mellor, George R. *British Imperial Trusteeship, 1783–1850.* London: Faber and Faber, 1951.

Merk, Frederick. *Manifest Destiny and Mission in American History: A Reinterpretation.* New York: Knopf, 1963.

Meron, Theodor. *Human Rights and Humanitarian Norms as Customary Law.* Oxford: Clarendon, 1989.

Meyer, Howard N. *The World Court in Action.* Lanham, Md.: Rowman & Littlefield, 2002.

Miller, Jerome G. *Search and Destroy: African American Males in the Criminal Justice System.* Cambridge: Cambridge University Press, 1996.

Miller, Norman, and Roderick Aya, eds. *National Liberation: Revolution in the Third World.* New York: Free Press, 1971.

Miller, Robert J. *Native America, Discovered and Conquered: Thomas Jefferson, Lewis & Clark, and Manifest Destiny.* Westport, Conn.: Prager, 2006.

Miller, Stuart Creighton. *"Benevolent Assimilation": The American Conquest of the Philippines, 1899–1903.* New Haven, Conn.: Yale University Press, 1982.

Mohawk, John C., ed. *Exiled in the Land of the Free: Democracy, Indian Nations and the U.S. Constitution.* Santa Fe, N.M.: Clear Light, 1992.

———. *Utopian Legacies: A History of Conquest and Oppression in the Western World.* Santa Fe, N.M.: Clear Light, 2000.

Mollett, John Anthony. *Capital in Hawaiian Sugar: Its Formation and Relation to Labor and Output.* Honolulu, 1961. Self-published.

Mongé, José Trías. *Puerto Rico: The Trials of the Oldest Colony in the World.* New Haven, Conn.: Yale University Press, 1997.

Moran, Rachel F., and Devon W. Carbado, eds. *Race Law Stories.* New York: Foundation Press, 2008.

Morgan, Theodore. *A Century of Economic Change.* Cambridge, Mass.: Harvard University Press, 1948.

Morison, Samuel Eliot. *Admiral of the Ocean Sea: A Life of Christopher Columbus.* Boston: Little, Brown, 1942.

———. *The European Discovery of America: The Southern Voyages, 1492–1616.* New York: Oxford University Press, 1974.

———. *The Oxford History of the American People.* New York: Oxford University Press, 1965.

Muldoon, James, ed. *The Expansion of Europe: The First Phase.* Philadelphia: University of Pennsylvania Press, 1977.

Mulroy, Kevin. *Freedom on the Border: The Seminole Maroons in Florida, the Indian Territory, Coahuila, and Texas.* Lubbock: Texas Tech University Press, 1993.

National Security Strategy of the United States of America. Falls Village, Conn.: Winterhouse Editions, 2002.

Nettle, Daniel, and Suzanne Romaine. *Vanishing Voices: The Extinction of the World's Languages.* New York: Oxford University Press, 2000.

Nirmal, B.C. *The Right to Self-Determination in International Law.* New Delhi, India: Deep & Deep, 1999.

Nkrumah, Kwame. *Neo-Colonialism: The Last State of Imperialism.* New York: International, 1965.

Nugent, Walter. *Habits of Empire: A History of American Expansion.* New York: Knopf, 2008.

Nussbaum, Arthur. *A Concise History of the Law of Nations.* Rev. ed. New York: Macmillan, 1954.

O'Brien, Sharon. *American Indian Tribal Governments.* Norman: University of Oklahoma Press, 1989.

O'Callaghan, Joseph F. *Reconquest and Crusade in Medieval Spain.* Philadelphia: University of Pennsylvania Press, 2004.

O'Connor, Richard. *Pacific Destiny: An Informal History of the U.S. in the Far East, 1776-1968*. Boston: Little, Brown, 1969.

Okri, Ben. *A Way of Being Free*. London: Phoenix House, 1997.

Oppenheim, Lassa. *International Law: A Treatise*. Vol. 1. 1st ed. New York: Longmans, Green, 1905.

Ortiz, Simon J. *From Sand Creek*. Oak Park, N.Y.: Thunder's Mouth, 1981.

Otis, D. S. *The Dawes Act and the Allotment of Indian Lands*. Norman: University of Oklahoma Press, 1973.

Otway-Ruthven, A. J. *A History of Medieval Ireland*. London: Palgrave Macmillan, 1980.

Paehlke, Robert. *Conservation and Environmentalism: An Encyclopedia*. New York: Routledge, 1995.

Pagden, Anthony. *European Encounters with the New World: From Renaissance to Romanticism*. New Haven, Conn.: Yale University Press, 1993.

———. *Lords of All the World: Ideologies of Empire in Spain, Britain and France, c.-500–c.1800*. New Haven, Conn.: Yale University Press, 1995.

Paine, Albert Bigelow. *Mark Twain: A Biography*. Vol. 3. New York: Harper & Brothers, 1912.

Parry, John Horace. *The Spanish Theory of Empire in the Sixteenth Century*. Cambridge: Cambridge University Press, 1940.

Paust, Jordan J. *Beyond the Law: The Bush Administration's Unlawful Responses in the "War" on Terror*. New York: Cambridge University Press, 2007.

———. *International Law as Law of the United States*. 2nd ed. Durham, N.C.: Carolina Academic Press, 2003.

Pawlisch, Hans S. *Sir John Davies and the Conquest of Ireland: A Study in Legal Imperialism*. Cambridge: Cambridge University Press, 1985.

Payne, Robert. *The Dream and the Tomb: A History of the Crusades*. Chelsea, Mich.: Scarborough House, 1991.

———. *The History of Islam*. New York: Dorset, 1990.

Peckham, Howard, and Charles Gibson, eds. *Attitudes of the Colonial Powers Towards American Indians*. Salt Lake City: University of Utah Press, 1969.

Perea, Juan F., Richard Delgado, Angela P. Harris, and Stephanie M. Wildman, eds. *Race and Races: Cases and Resources for a Diverse America*. St. Paul, Minn.: West Group, 2000.

Perry, John Horace. *The Establishment of European Hegemony, 1415–1713*. Rev. ed. New York: Harper & Row, 1966.

Peterson, Merrill D. *Thomas Jefferson and the New Nation: A Biography*. New York: Oxford University Pres, 1970.

Phillips, Wendell, ed. *The Constitution: A Pro-Slavery Compact: Or, Extracts from the Madison Papers, Etc*. Ithaca, N.Y.: Cornell University Library, 1856.

Philp, Kenneth R. *John Collier's Crusade for Indian Reform: 1920–1954*. Tucson: University of Arizona Press, 1977.

Porter, Kenneth W. *The Black Seminoles: History of a Freedom-Seeking People*. Edited and revised by Alcione M. Amos and Thomas P. Senter. Gainesville: University Press of Florida, 1996.

Prados, John. *Presidents' Secret Wars: CIA and Pentagon Covert Operations Since World War II*. New York: William Morrow, 1986.

Prucha, Francis Paul. *The Great Father: The United States Government and the American Indians, Volumes I and II*. Lincoln: University of Nebraska Press, 1984.

Quinn, David Beers. *England and the Discovery of America, 1481–1620*. New York: Knopf, 1974.

Ratner, Michael, and Ellen Ray. *Guantánamo: What the World Should Know*. White River Junction, Vt.: Chelsea Green, 2004.

Raz, Joseph. *The Authority of Law: Essays on Law and Morality*. New York: Oxford University Press, 1979.

Restatement of the Law Third, Foreign Relations Law of the United States. Vols. 1 and 2. St. Paul, Minn.: American Law Institute Publishers, 1987.

Richardson, Boyce. *People of* Terra Nullius: *Betrayal and Rebirth in Aboriginal Canada*. Vancouver: Douglas & McIntyre, 1993.

Richardson, Henry J., III. *The Origins of African-American Interests in International Law*. Durham, N.C.: Carolina Academic Press, 2008.

Rist, Gilbert. *The History of Development: From Western Origins to Global Faith*. Translated by Patrick Camiller. London: Zed, 1997.

Rivera Ramos, Efrén. *The Legal Construction of Identity: The Judicial and Social Legacy of American Colonialism in Puerto Rico*. New York: American Psychological Association, 2001.

Roberts, Adam, and Richard Guelff, eds. *Documents on the Laws of War*. Oxford: Clarendon, 1982.

Roberts, J. M. *History of the World*. New York: Oxford University Press, 1993.

Rodinson, Maxime. *Europe and the Mystique of Islam*. Seattle: University of Washington Press, 1987.

Rodney, Walter. *How Europe Underdeveloped Africa*. Rev. ed. Washington, D.C.: Howard University Press, 1981.

Rodriguez-Salgado, Mia J., and Simon Adams, eds. *England, Spain and the Gran Armada, 1585–1604*. Edinburgh: John McDonald, 1991.

Roediger, David R. *Wages of Whiteness: Race and the Making of the American Working Class*. New York: Verso, 1992.

Rogers, Robert F. *Destiny's Landfall: A History of Guam*. Honolulu: University of Hawai'i Press, 1995.

Rostow, W. W. *The Stages of Economic Growth: A Non-Communist Manifesto*. New York: Cambridge University Press, 1960.

Ruddy, Francis S. *International Law in the Enlightenment: The Background of Emmerich de Vattel's "Le Droit des Gens."* Dobbs Ferry, N.Y.: Oceana, 1975.

Russ, William Adam, Jr. *The Hawaiian Republic and Its Struggle to Win Annexation (1894–98)*. 2nd ed. London: Associated University Presses, 1992.

Russell, Bertrand. *War Crimes in Vietnam*. New York: Monthly Review Press, 1967.

Sachs, Wolfgang, ed. *The Development Dictionary: A Guide to Knowledge as Power*. London: Zed, 2007.

Said, Edward W. *Orientalism*. New York: Vintage Books, 1979.

Saito, Natsu Taylor. *From Chinese Exclusion to Guantánamo Bay: Plenary Power and the Prerogative State*. Boulder: University Press of Colorado, 2006.

Sale, Kirkpatrick. *The Conquest of Paradise: Christopher Columbus and the Columbian Legacy*. New York: Knopf, 1990.

Salisbury, Neal. *Manitou and Providence: Indians, Europeans, and the Making of New England, 1500–1643*. New York: Oxford University Press, 1982.

Sally, Alexander S., Jr., ed. *Narratives of Early Carolina, 1650–1708.* New York: Original Narratives of American History, 1911.

Sanders, Ronald. *Lost Tribes and Promised Lands: The Origins of American Racism.* Boston: Little, Brown, 1978.

Sandoz, Mari. *Cheyenne Autumn.* New York: Avon, 1964 [1953].

————. *Crazy Horse: The Strange Man of the Oglalas.* Lincoln: University of Nebraska Press, 1942.

Sardar, Ziaddin, and Merryl Wyn Davis. *Why Do People Hate America?* New York: Disinformation, 2002.

Scheuer, Michael. *Imperial Hubris: Why the West Is Losing the War on Terror.* Washington, D.C.: Bassey's, 2004.

Schirmer, Daniel B., and Stephen Rosskamm Shalom, eds. *The Philippines Reader: A History of Colonialism, Neocolonialism, Dictatorship, and Resistance.* Boston: South End, 1987.

Schlesinger, Stephen C. *Act of Creation: The Founding of the United Nations.* Boulder, Colo.: Westview, 2003.

Schrecker, Ellen, ed. *Cold War Triumphalism: The Misuse of History after the Fall of Communism.* New York: New Press, 2004.

Schultz, Duane. *Over the Earth I Come: The Great Sioux Uprising of 1862.* New York: St. Martin's, 1992.

Schwab, Orrin. *Defending the Free World: John F. Kennedy, Lyndon Johnson, and the Vietnam War, 1961–1965.* Westport, Conn.: Praeger, 1998.

Schwartzenberger, Georg. *The Frontiers of International Law.* London: Stevens, 1962.

Segal, Charles M., and David C. Stineback. *Puritans, Indians, and Manifest Destiny.* New York: Putnam's, 1977.

Seton-Watson, Hugh. *Nations and States: An Enquiry into the Origins of Nations and the Politics of Nationalism.* Boulder, Colo.: Westview, 1977.

Shafer, D. Michael. *Deadly Paradigms: The Failure of U.S. Counterinsurgency Policy.* Princeton, N.J.: Princeton University Press, 1988.

Sheehan, Neil. *A Bright Shining Lie: John Paul Vann and America in Vietnam.* New York: Vintage Books, 1988.

Skaggs, Jimmy M. *The Great Guano Rush: Entrepreneurs and American Overseas Expansion.* New York: St. Martin's, 1994.

Slotkin, Richard. *Regeneration Through Violence: The Mythology of the American Frontier: 1600–1860.* Norman: University of Oklahoma Press, 1973.

Smith, Bradley F. *The American Road to Nuremberg: The Documentary Record, 1944–1945.* Stanford, Calif.: Hoover Institution, 1982.

————. *The Road to Nuremberg.* New York: Basic Books, 1981.

Smith, Jean Edward. *John Marshall: Definer of a Nation.* New York: Henry Holt, 1996.

Smith, Joseph Burkholder. *The Plot to Steal Florida: James Madison's Phony War.* New York: Arbor House, 1983.

Smith, Linda Tuhiwai. *Decolonizing Methodologies: Research and Indigenous Peoples.* Dunedin, N.Z.: University of Otago Press, 1999.

Smith, Page. *America Enters the World: A People's History of the Progressive Era and World War I.* Vol. 7. New York: McGraw-Hill, 1985.

Stagg, Jack. *Anglo-Indian Relations in North America to 1763 and an Analysis of the Royal Proclamation of 7 October 1763*. Ottawa: Indian and Northern Affairs Ministry of Canada, 1981.

Stannard, David E. *American Holocaust: Columbus and the Conquest of the New World*. New York: Oxford University Press, 1992.

——. *Before the Horror: The Population of Hawai'i on the Eve of Western Contact*. Honolulu: Social Science Institute, University of Hawai'i, 1989.

Stanton, William. *The Leopard's Spots: Scientific Attitudes toward Race in America, 1815–59*. Chicago: University of Chicago Press, 1960.

Stasiulis, Daiva, and Nira Yuval-Davis, eds. *Articulations of Gender, Race, Ethnicity and Class*. London: Sage, 1995.

Stearn, E. Wagner, and Allen E. Stearn. *The Effects of Smallpox on the Destiny of the Amerindian*. Boston: Bruce Humphries, 1945.

Stephanson, Anders. *Manifest Destiny: American Expansion and the Empire of Right*. New York: Hill and Wang, 1995.

Stevens, Sylvester. *American Expansion in Hawaii, 1842–1898*. New York: Russell and Russell, 1945.

Stokes, Melvyn. *D. W. Griffith's The Birth of a Nation: A History of "The Most Controversial Motion Picture of All Time."* New York: Oxford University Press, 2007.

Strickland, Rennard. *Fire and the Spirits: Cherokee Law from Clan to Court*. Norman: University of Oklahoma Press, 1975.

——. *Tonto's Revenge: Reflections on American Indian Culture and Policy*. Albuquerque: University of New Mexico Press, 1997.

——, ed. *Felix S. Cohen's Handbook of Federal Indian Law*, Charlottesville, Va.: Michie, 1982.

Sugden, John. *Tecumseh's Last Stand*. Norman: University of Oklahoma Press, 1985.

Takaki, Ronald. *Strangers from a Different Shore: A History of Asian Americans*. Boston: Little, Brown, 1989.

Taylor, Telford. *The Anatomy of the Nuremberg Trials: A Personal Memoir*. New York: Knopf, 1992.

——. *Nuremberg and Vietnam: An American Tragedy*. Chicago: Quadrangle Books, 1970.

Teich, Mikuláš, and Roy Porter, eds. *The National Question in Europe in Historical Context*. Cambridge: Cambridge University Press, 1993.

Thatcher, John Boyd. *Christopher Columbus: His Life, His Work, His Remains*. 3 vols. New York: Putnam's, 1903–1904.

Thomas, Hugh. *The Slave Trade*. New York: Simon and Schuster, 1997.

Thompson, Thomas, ed. *The Schooling of Native America*. Washington, D.C.: American Association of Colleges for Teacher Education, 1978.

Thornton, Russell. *American Indian Holocaust and Survival: A Population History Since 1492*. Norman: University of Oklahoma Press, 1987.

Tibbles, Thomas Henry. *The Ponca Chiefs: An Account of the Trial of Standing Bear*. Lincoln: University of Nebraska Press, 1972.

Tinker, George E. *Missionary Conquest: The Gospel and Native American Cultural Genocide*. Minneapolis: Fortress, 1993.

Todorov, Tzvetan. *The Conquest of America: The Question of the Other*. New York: Harper & Row, 1984.

Tompkins, Peter. *Secrets of the Great Pyramid.* New York: Harper & Row, 1971.

Torgovnick, Marianna. *Primitive Passions: Men, Women, and the Quest for Ecstasy.* Chicago: University of Chicago Press, 1998.

Toynbee, Arnold J. *A Study of History.* Vols. 1–6. Abridged by D. C. Somervell. Oxford: Oxford University Press, 1946.

Trask, Haunani-Kay. *From a Native Daughter: Colonialism and Sovereignty in Hawai'i.* Honolulu: University of Hawai'i Press, 1993.

Tuchman, Barbara W. *Stilwell and the American Experience in China, 1911–1945.* New York: Macmillan, 1970.

Turcheneske, John A., Jr. *The Chiricahua Apache Prisoners of War: Fort Sill, 1894–1914.* Boulder: University Press of Colorado, 1997.

Van Alstyne, Richard W. *The Rising American Empire.* New York: W. W. Norton, 1974.

Van Dijk, Ruud, ed. *Encyclopedia of the Cold War.* New York: Routledge, 2008.

Vattel, Emmerich de. *The Laws of Nations.* Philadelphia: T. & J. W. Johnson, 1855.

Vaughn, Alden T. *Early American Indian Documents: Treaties and Laws, 1607–1789.* Washington, D.C.: University Publications of America, 1979.

Vecsey, Christopher, and Robert W. Venables, eds. *Native American Environments: Ecological Issues in American Indian History.* Syracuse, N.Y.: Syracuse University Press, 1980.

Vitoria, Franciscus de. *De Indis et de Ivre Belli Relectiones.* Washington, D.C.: Carnegie Institution of Washington, 1917.

Vietnam Veterans Against the War. *The Winter Soldier Investigation: An Inquiry into American War Crimes.* Boston: Beacon, 1972.

Wallace, Anthony. *The Death and Rebirth of the Seneca.* New York: Knopf, 1970.

Wallace, Max. *The American Axis: Henry Ford, Charles Lindberg, and the Rise of the Third Reich.* New York: St. Martin's, 2003.

Wallerstein, Immanuel. *The Modern World-System I: Capitalist Agriculture and the Origins of the European World-Economy in the Sixteenth Century.* San Diego, Calif.: Academic Press, 1974.

Washburn, Wilcomb E. *Red Man's Land, White Man's Law: The Past and Present Status of the American Indian.* Norman: University of Oklahoma Press, 1995.

Waswo, Richard. *The Founding Legend of Western Civilization: From Virgil to Vietnam.* Hanover, N.H.: Wesleyan University Press, 1997.

Waters, Frank. *Book of the Hopi.* New York: Penguin Books, 1977.

Watson, Robert T., ed. *Climate Change 2001: Third Assessment Report of the Intergovernmental Panel on Climate Change.* Cambridge: Cambridge University Press, 2002.

Weatherford, Jack. *Indian Givers: How the Indians of the Americas Transformed the World.* New York: Crown, 1988.

Weaver, Samuel. *Hawaii, USA.* New York: Pageant, 1959.

Weber, David J., ed. *Foreigners in Their Native Land: Historical Roots of the Mexican Americans.* Albuquerque: University of New Mexico Press, 1973.

Weber, Max. *The Protestant Ethic and the Spirit of Capitalism.* New York: Scribner, 1958 [1904–1905].

Webster, David. *The Fall of the Ancient Maya: Solving the Mystery of the Maya Collapse.* London: Thames and Webster, 2002.

Webster's Deluxe Unabridged Dictionary. 2nd ed. New York: Dorest & Baber, 1983.

Weisberg, Jacob, ed. *George W. Bushisms: The Slate Book of the Accidental Wit and Wisdom of our 43rd President.* New York: Fireside, 2001.

Wells, Donald A. *The Laws of Land Warfare: A Guide to the U.S. Army Manuals.* Westport, Conn.: Greenwood, 1992.

Westlake, John. *Chapters on the Principles of International Law.* Littleton, Colo.: Fred B. Rothman, 1982 [1894].

Wheaton, Henry. *Elements of International Law.* Boston: Little, Brown, 1866.

Wilford, John Noble. *The Mysterious History of Columbus: An Exploration of the Man, the Myth, the Legacy.* New York: Knopf, 1991.

Wilkins, David E. *American Indian Sovereignty and the U.S. Supreme Court: The Masking of Justice.* Austin: University of Texas Press, 1997.

Williams, Chancellor. *The Destruction of Black Civilization: Great Issues of a Race from 4500 B.C. to 2000 A.D.* Chicago: Third World, 1987.

Williams, Eric. *From Columbus to Castro: The History of the Caribbean, 1492–1969.* London: André Deutsch, 1970.

Williams, Robert A., Jr. *The American Indian in Western Legal Thought: The Discourses of Conquest.* New York: Oxford University Press, 1990.

———. *Like a Loaded Weapon: The Rehnquist Court, Indian Rights, and the Legal History of Racism in America.* Minneapolis: University of Minnesota Press, 2005.

———. *Linking Arms Together: American Indian Treaty Visions of Law and Peace, 1600–1800.* New York: Oxford University Press, 1997.

Wilson, James. *The Earth Shall Weep: A History of Native America.* New York: Atlantic Monthly, 1999.

Wittgenstein, Ludwig. *Culture and Value.* Oxford: Basil Blackwell, 1980.

Wolf, Eric R. *Europe and the People Without History.* Berkeley: University of California Press, 1982.

Wolff, Edward N. *Top Heavy: A Study of the Increasing Inequality of Wealth in America.* New York: New Press, 1996.

Woodward, C. Vann. *The Strange Career of Jim Crow.* New York: Oxford University Press, 1974.

Wright, Quincy. *Mandates under the League of Nations.* New York: Greenwood, 1968 [1930].

Yee, James. *For God and Country: Faith and Patriotism under Fire.* New York: Public Affairs, 2005.

Yoo, John. *Powers of War and Peace: The Constitution and Foreign Affairs after 9/11.* Chicago: University of Chicago Press, 2005.

———. *War by Other Means: An Insider's Account of the War on Terror.* New York: Atlantic Monthly, 2006.

Zakaria, Fareed. *The Post-American World.* New York: W. W. Norton, 2008.

Zinn, Howard. *A People's History of the United States.* Rev. ed. New York: Harper Perennial, 1995.

ARTICLES, CHAPTERS, SPEECHES, AND FILMS

Act of War: The Overthrow of the Hawaiian Nation (documentary film). Honolulu: No
Maka o ka Aina, in association with the Center for Hawaiian Studies, University of
Hawai'i at Manoa, 1993.

Adams, Simon. "The Outbreak of Elizabethan Naval War Against the Spanish Empire:
The Embargo of May 1585 and Sir Francis Drake's West Indies Voyage." In Rodriguez-
Salgado and Adams, *England, Spain,* 45–69.

Addis, Adeno. "Informal Suspension of Normal Processes: The 'War on Terror' as an
Autoimmunity Crisis." *Boston University Law Review* 87 (2007): 323–346.

Alston, Philip. "U.S. Ratification of the Covenant on Economic, Social and Cultural
Rights: The Need for an Entirely New Strategy." *American Journal of International Law*
84 (1990): 365–393.

Alvarez, José E. "Hegemonic International Law Revisited." *American Journal of International Law* 97 (2003): 873–888.

Anaya, S. James. "The Native Hawaiian People and International Human Rights Law:
Toward a Remedy for Past and Continuing Wrongs." *Georgia Law Review* 28 (1994):
309–320.

"Anger grows as U.S. jail population." *BBC News,* February 15, 2000.

Anghie, Antony. "Finding the Peripheries: Sovereignty and Colonialism in Nineteenth-
Century International Law." *Harvard International Law Journal* 40 (1999): 1–80.

———. "Time Present and Time Past: Globalization, International Financial Institutions,
and the Third World." *New York University Journal of International Law and Politics* 32
(2000): 243–290.

Arend, Anthony Clark. "International Law and Rogue States: The Failure of the Charter
Framework." *New England Law Review* 36 (2002): 735–753.

Austen, Ian. "Canada Offers an Apology for Native Students' Abuse." *New York Times,*
June 12, 2008.

Barela, Steven J. "Preemptive or Preventive War: A Discussion of Legal and Moral Standards." *Denver Journal of International Law and Policy* 33 (2004): 31–42.

Barnard, David. "Law, Narrative, and the Continuing Colonialist Oppression of Native
Hawaiians." *Temple Political and Civil Rights Law Review* 16 (2006): 1–45.

Barsh, Russel Lawrence. "Another Look at Reorganization: When Will Tribes Have a
Choice?" *Indian Truth* 247 (October 1982): 4–12.

———. "The Challenge of Indigenous Self-Determination." *University of Michigan Journal
of Law Reform* 22 (1993): 277–312.

Bell, Koren L. "From Laggard to Leader: Canadian Lessons on a Role for U.S. States in
Making and Implementing Human Rights Treaties." *Yale Human Rights and Development Law Journal* 5 (2002): 255–291.

Bello, Walden. "Global Economic Counterrevolution: Northern Economic Warfare Dev-
astates the South." In Danaher, *50 Years,* 14–19.

Bennhold, Katrin, and Craig S. Smith. "Twin Car Bombs Strike Algiers, Killing Dozens."
New York Times, December 12, 2007.

Berman, Nathaniel. "'But the Alternative Is Despair': European Nationalism and the Mod-
ernist Renewal of International Law." *Harvard Law Review* 106 (1993): 1792–1903.

———. "In the Wake of Empire." *American University International Law Review* 14 (1999): 1521–1555.

———. "A Perilous Ambivalence: Nationalist Desire, Legal Autonomy and the Limits of the Interwar Framework." *Harvard International Law Journal* 33 (1992): 353–379.

Bernstein, David. "International Court of Justice—*Case Concerning Military and Paramilitary Activities in and Against Nicaragua (Nicaragua v. United States)*." *Harvard International Law Journal* 28 (1987): 146–156.

Bickley, Lynn Sellers. "U.S. Resistance to the International Criminal Court: Is the Sword Mightier than the Law?" *Emory International Law Review* 14 (2000): 213–276.

Bilder, Richard B. "The United States and the World Court in the Post-'Cold War' Era." *Catholic University Law Review* 40 (1991): 251–263.

Bird, Graham. "A Suitable Case for Treatment? Understanding the Ongoing Debate about the IMF." *Third World Quarterly* 22, no. 5 (October 2001): 823–848.

Bisharat, George E. "Sanctions as Genocide." *Transnational Law & Contemporary Problems* 11 (2001): 379–425.

Black Elk, Frank. "Observations on Marxism and Lakota Tradition." In Churchill. *Marxism and Native Americans*, 137–159.

Box, Richard C. "The Public Service Practitioner as Agent of Social Change." In Box, *Democracy*, 194–211.

Bradley, Curtis A. "The Military Commissions Act, Habeas Corpus, and the Geneva Conventions." *American Journal of International Law* 101 (2007): 322–344.

———. "Unratified Treaties, Domestic Politics, and the U.S. Constitution." *Harvard International Law Journal* 48 (2007): 307–336.

Brown, Bartram S. "Humanitarian Intervention at a Crossroads." *William and Mary Law Review* 41 (2000): 1683–1741.

Brown, David. "Study Claims Iraq's 'Excess' Death Toll Has Reached 655,000." *Washington Post*, October 11, 2006, A12.

Brown, Donald A. "Thinking Globally and Acting Locally: The Emergence of Global Environmental Problems and the Critical Need to Develop Sustainable Development Programs at State and Local Levels in the United States." *Dickinson Journal of Environmental Law and Policy* 5 (1996): 175–196.

Buchanan, James, J.Y. Mason, and Pierre Soulé. "Ostend Manifesto." October 15, 1854. Available at http://www.historyofcuba.com/history/havana/Ostend2.htm (accessed June 30, 2008).

Burgess, Douglas R., Jr. "Hostis Humani Generi: Piracy, Terrorism and a New International Law." *University of Miami International and Comparative Law Review* 13 (2006): 293–341.

Burguenthal, Thomas. "Modern Constitutions and Human Rights Treaties." *Columbia Journal of Transnational Law* 36 (1997): 212–223.

Burnett, Christina Duffy. "The Edges of Empire and the Limits of Sovereignty: American Guano Islands." *American Quarterly* 53, no. 3 (2005): 779–803.

———. "Untied States: American Expansion and Territorial Deannexation." *University of Chicago Law Review* 72 (2005): 797–879.

Burnett, Christina Duffy, and Burke Marshall. "Between the Foreign and the Domestic: The Doctrine of Territorial Incorporation, Invented and Reinvented." In Burnett and Marshall, *Foreign in a Domestic Sense*, 1–36.

Bush, George W. "A Distinctly American Internationalism." Speech at Ronald Reagan Presidential Library, Simi Valley, California, November 19, 1999. Available at http://www.mtholyoke.edu/acad/intrel/bush/wspeech.htm (accessed November 15, 2007).
——. Introduction to *The National Security Strategy*.
——. "Remarks by the President in Photo Opportunity with the National Security Team." Office of the Press Secretary, September 12, 2001. Available at http://www.whitehouse.gov/news/releases/2001/09/20010912-4.html (accessed December 9, 2007).
"Bush Outlines Foreign Policy." *BBC News*, November 20, 1999. Available at http://news.bbc.co.uk/2/hi/business/default.stm (accessed November 10, 2007).
Bybee, Jay S. "Memorandum for Alberto R. Gonzales, Counsel to the President, and William J. Haynes II, General Counsel for the Department of Defense, Re: Application of Treaties and Laws to al Qaeda and Taliban Detainees." U.S. Department of Justice, Office of Legal Counsel. January 22, 2002.
Byrne, Daniel. "Decolonization." In van Dijk, *Encyclopedia*, 231–237.
Calabresi, Steven G. "'A Shining City on a Hill: American Exceptionalism and the Supreme Court's Practice of Relying on Foreign Law." *Boston University Law Review* 86 (2006): 1335–1416.
Campagna, Juliana V. "War or Peace: It Is Time for the United States to Ratify the 1954 Hague Convention for the Protection of Cultural Property in the Event of Armed Conflicts." *Florida Journal of International Law* 17 (2005): 271–344.
Carmichael, Stokely. "The Dialectics of Liberation," In Carmichael, *Stokely Speaks*, 77–99.
Carpenter, Kristen A. "Contextualizing the Losses of Allotment through Literature." *North Dakota Law Review* 82 (2006): 605–626.
Carrasco, Enrique R., and Randall Thomas. "Encouraging Relational Investment and Controlling Portfolio Investment in Developing Countries in the Aftermath of the Mexican Financial Crisis." *Columbia Journal of Transactional Law* 34 (1996): 539–620.
Carrington, Paul D. "Writing Other Peoples' Constitutions." *North Carolina Journal of International Law and Commercial Regulation* 33 (winter 2007): 167–217.
Cassese, Antonio. "The Multifaceted Criminal Notion of Terrorism in International Law." *Journal of International Criminal Justice* 4 (2006): 933–958.
Cerone, John P. "Dynamic Equilibrium: The Evolution of US Attitudes Toward International Crimnal Courts and Tribunals." *European Journal of International Law* 18 (2007): 277–315.
Chanbonpin, Kim David. "Holding the United States Accountable for Environmental Damages Caused by the U.S. Military in the Philippines, a Plan for the Future." *Asian-Pacific Law & Policy Journal* 4 (2003): 320–380.
Chayes, Abram. "Nicaragua, the United States, and the World Court." *Columbia Law Review* 85 (1985): 1445–1482.
Chesterman, Simon. "Virtual Trusteeship." In Malone, *UN Security Council*, 219–233.
Chimni, B. S. "Teaching, Research and Promotion of International Law in India: Past, Present and Future." *Singapore Journal of International and Comparative Law* 5 (2001) 368–387.
Chon, Margaret. "Intellectual Property and the Development Divide." *Cardozo Law Review* 27 (2006): 2821–2912.
Churchill, Ward. "Deconstructing the Columbus Myth: Was the 'Great Discoverer' Italian or Spanish, Nazi or Jew?" In Churchill, *Little Matter of Genocide*, 81–96.

————. "Dismantling the Politics of Comfort." Interview in *Satya*, April 2004. Available at http://www.satyamag.com/apr04/churchill.html (accessed October 21, 2008).

————. "Geographies of Sacrifice: The Radioactive Colonization of Native North America." In Churchill. *Struggle for the Land*, 239–291.

————. "I Am Indigenist: Notes on the Ideology of the Fourth World." In Churchill, *Acts of Rebellion*, 275–299.

————. "Indian Assimilation and Reorganization (1900 to 1945)." In Johansen and Pritzker, *Encyclopedia*, 50–64.

————. "The Indigenous Peoples of North America: A Struggle Against Internal Colonialism." In Churchill, *Struggle for the Land*, 15–22..

————. "The Law Stood Squarely on Its Head: U.S. Legal Doctrine, Indigenous Self-Determination and the Question of World Order." *Oregon Law Review* 81 (2002): 663–706.

————. "Like Sand in the Wind: The Making of an American Indian Diaspora in the United States." In Churchill, *Struggle for the Land*, 330–364.

————. "'Nits Make Lice': The Extermination of North American Indians, 1607–1996." In Churchill, *A Little Matter of Genocide*, 129–288.

————. "Perversions of Justice: Examining the Doctrine of U.S. Rights to Occupancy in North America." In Churchill, *Perversions of Justice*, 1–32.

————. "Stolen Kingdom: The Right of Hawai'i to Decolonization." In Churchill, *Perversions of Justice*, 73–124.

————. "'To Judge Them by the Standards of Their Time': America's Indian Fighters, the Laws of War and the Question of International Order." In Churchill, *Perversions of Justice*, 303–403.

————. "The United States and the Genocide Convention: A Half-Century of Obfuscation and Obstruction." In Churchill, *A Little Matter of Genocide*, 363–398.

————. "Unravelling the Codes of Oppression." In Churchill, *Fantasies of the Master Race*, ix–xix.

"Civilian Death Toll in Iraq May Have Surpassed 1 Million." *Agence France Presse*, March 25, 2008. Available at http://fairuse.100webcustomers.com/itsonlyfair/dstar02.html (accessed September 1, 2008).

Cleveland, Sarah H. "Foreign Authority, American Exceptionalism, and the Dred Scott Case." *Chicago-Kent Law Review* 82 (2007): 393–455.

Clinton, Robert N. "Redressing the Legacy of Conquest: A Vision Quest for a Decolonized Federal Indian Law." *Arkansas Law Review* 46 (1993): 77–159.

Cohan, John Alan. "Political Violence and Terrorism." *Stetson Law Review* 35 (2006): 903–981.

Cohen, Felix S. "Colonialism: A Realistic Approach." In Cohen, *Legal Conscience*, 364–383.

————. "How Long Will Indian Constitutions Last?" In Cohen, *Legal Conscience*, 222–229.

Cohn, Marjorie. "Human Rights: Casualty of the War on Terror." *Thomas Jefferson Law Review* 25 (2003): 317–365.

————. "Resisting Equality: Why the U.S. Refuses to Ratify the Women's Convention." *Thomas Jefferson Law Review* 27 (2004): 15–26.

Cole, David. "The Priority of Morality: The Emergency Constitution's Blind Spot." *Yale Law Journal* 113 (2004): 1753–1800.

Coleman, Andrew, and Jackson Maogoto. "Democracy's Global Quest: A Noble Crusade Wrapped in Dirty Reality?" *Suffolk Transnational Law Review* 28 (2005): 175–242.

Comerford, Brian P. "Preventing Terrorism by Prosecuting Material Support." *Notre Dame Law Review* 80 (2005): 723–757.

Committee on International Security Affairs of the Association of the Bar of the City of New York. "The Legality and Constitutionality of the President's Authority to Initiate An Invasion of Iraq." *Columbia Journal of Transnational Law* 41 (2002): 15–32.

Conley, Brian, and Isam Rashid. "Iraq: No Day Is a Woman's Day." *Inter Press Service*, March 13, 2006. Available at http://www.ipsnews.net/news.asp?idnews=32476 (accessed September 5, 2008).

Cooper, Bradley Aron. "Defending Liberty and Defeating Tyrants: The Reemergence of Federal Theology in the Rhetoric of the Bush Doctrine." *University of Detroit Mercy Law Review* 85 (2008): 521–559.

Coskun, Deniz. "Religious Skepticism, Cambridge Platonism, and Disestablishment." *University of Detroit Mercy Law Review* 83 (2006): 579–595.

Coulter, Robert T., and Steven M. Tullberg. "Indian Land Rights." In Cadwalader and Deloria, *Aggressions of Civilization*, 185–213.

Cryer, Robert. "The Fine Art of Friendship: Jus in Bello in Afghanistan." *Journal of Conflict & Security Law* 7 (2002): 37–83.

Cuéllar, Mariano-Florentino. "The International Criminal Court and the Political Economy of Antitreaty Discourse." *Stanford Law Review* 55 (2003): 1597–1632.

Curcio, Andrea A. "Civil Claims for Uncivilized Acts: Filing Suit Against the Government for American Indian Boarding School Abuses." *Hastings Race and Poverty Law Journal* 4 (2006): 45–129.

Currie, David P. "Rumors of War: Presidential and Congressional War Powers, 1809–1829." *University of Chicago Law Review* 67 (2000): 1–40.

Dasgupta, Tapati, and R. N. Chattopadhyay. "Ecological Contradictions Through Ages: Growth and Decay of the Indus and Nile Valley Civilizations." *Journal of Human Ecology* 16:3 (2004): 197–201.

Davis, Benjamin G. "A Citizen Observer's View of the U.S. Approach to the War on Terrorism." *Transnational Law and Contemporary Problems* 17 (2008): 465–502.

Declet, Rafael A., Jr. "The Mandate under International Law for a Self-Executing Plebiscite on Puerto Rico's Political Status, and the Right of U.S. –Resident Puerto Ricans to Participate." *Syracuse Journal of International Law and Commerce* 28 (2001): 19–60.

Delgado, Richard. "Storytelling for Oppositionists and Others: A Plea for Narrative." *Michigan Law Review* 87 (1989): 2411–2441.

Deloria, Vine, Jr. "'Congress in Its Wisdom': The Course of Indian Legislation." In Cadwalader and Deloria, *Aggressions of Civilization*, 105–130.

"Developing World 'Poorer Than We Thought,' Report Reveals." Press Release. Bread for the World. Available at http://www.bread.org/press-room/releases/developing-world-poorer-than-we-thought-report-reveals.html (accessed September 5, 2008).

Dickason, Olive P. "Concepts of Sovereignty at the Time of First Contacts." In Green and Dickason, *Law of Nations*, 143–295.

Donelan, Michael. "Spain and the Indies." In Bull and Watson, *Expansion*, 75–86.

Draper, G. I. A. D. "Grotius' Place in the Development of the Legal Ideas about War." In Bull, Kingsbury, and Roberts, *Hugo Grotius*, 177–207.

Drumbl, Mark A. "Guantánamo, Rasul, and the Twilight of Law." *Drake Law Review* 53 (2005): 897–922.

DuBois, W. E. B. "Another Open Letter to Woodrow Wilson." In DuBois, *Writings*, 1144–1147.

Dudziak, Mary L. "The Little Rock Crisis and Foreign Affairs: Race, Resistance, and the Image of American Democracy." *Southern California Law Review* 70 (1997): 1641–1716.

Duffy, Michael. "The Foundations of British Naval Power." In Duffy, *Military Revolution*, 49-85.

Duponceau, Peter S. *A Dissertation on the Nature and Extent of the Jurisdiction of the Court of the United States.* A valedictory address to the students of the Law Academy of Philadelphia, April 23, 1824.

Eckhardt, William George. "Nuremberg—Fifty Years: Accountability and Responsibility." *University of Missouri–Kansas City Law Review* 65 (1996): 1–14.

Edlin, Douglas E. "The Anxiety of Sovereignty: Britain, the United States and the International Criminal Court." *Boston College International and Comparative Law Review* 29 (2006): 1–22.

Elliott, Larry. "The Lost Decade." *Guardian*, July 9, 2003.

Engle, Karen. "Constructing Good Aliens and Good Citizens: Legitimizing the War on Terror(ism)." *University of Colorado Law Review* 75 (2004): 59–114.

Esteva, Gustavo. "Development." In Sachs, *Development Dictionary*, 6–25.

"Extinction Rate across the Globe Reaches Historical Proportions." *Science Daily*, January 10, 2002. Available at http://www.sciencedaily.com/releases/2002/01/020109074801.htm (accessed September 25, 2008).

"Fact Sheet: Strategy for Victory: Freedom in Iraq." White House. Available at http://www.whitehouse.gov/news/releases/2006/03/20060329-5.html (accessed September 1, 2008).

Falk, Richard A. Editorial Comment. "On the Quasi-Legislative Competence of the General Assembly." *American Journal of International Law* 60 (1966): 782–791.

———. "The United Nations and the Rule of Law." *Transnational Law & Contemporary Problems* 4 (1994): 611–642.

Feinberg, Richard E. "The Changing Relationship between the World Bank and the International Monetary Fund." *International Organization* 42, no. 3 (summer 1988): 545–560.

Ferguson, Kathy, Phyllis Turnbull and Mehmed Ali. "Rethinking the Military in Hawai'i." In Hasager and Friedman, *Hawai'i*, 183–193.

Ferrari, Erich. "Deep Freeze: Islamic Charities and the Financial War on Terror." *Scholar* 7 (2005): 205–227.

Finkelman, Paul. "A Covenant with Death: Slavery and the Constitution." *American Visions* 1 (May–June 1968): 21–27.

Fitzpatrick, Joan. "Rendition and Transfer in the War Against Terrorism: Guantánamo and Beyond." *Loyola of Los Angeles International and Comparative Law Review* 25 (2003): 457–492.

Fitzpatrick, Peter. "Terminal Legality: Imperialism and the (De)Composition of Law." In Kirkby and Coleborne. *Law, History*, 9-25.

Fletcher, Michael A. "'Crisis' of Black Males Gets High-Profile Look: Rights Panel Probes Crime, Joblessness, Other Ills." *Washington Post*, April 17, 1999, A02.

Foot, Rosemary, S. Neil MacFarlane, and Michael Mastanduno. "Introduction" to Foot, MacFarlane, and Mastaduno, *US Hegemony*, 1–22.

Franck, Thomas M. "The Emerging Right to Democratic Governance." *American Journal of International Law* 86 (1992): 46–91.

Franck, Thomas M., and Stephen H. Yuhan. "The United States and the International Criminal Court: Unilateralism Rampant." *New York University Journal of International Law and Politics* 35 (2003): 519–558.

Frickey, Philip P. "Doctrine, Context, Institutional Relationships, and Commentary: The Malaise of Federal Indian Law Through the Lens of Lone Wolf." *Tulsa Law Review* 38 (2002): 5–36.

———. "Marshalling Past and Present: Colonialism, Constitutionalism, and Interpretation in Federal Indian Law." *Harvard Law Review* 107 (1993): 381–440.

Friedman, Michelle S. "The Uneasy U.S. Relationship with Human Rights Treaties: The Constitutional Treaty System and Nonself-Execution Declaration." *Florida Journal of International Law* 17 (2005): 187–257.

"From the Report of Ex. Gov. Jenkins." *The Indian Advocate* 14, no. 1 (January 1902). Available at http://users.icnet.net/~frizzell/advocteokterhist.html (accessed June 17, 2008).

Garman, John J. "International Law and Children's Human Rights: International, Constitutional, and Political Conflicts Blocking Passage of the Convention on the Rights of the Child." *Valparaiso University Law Review* 41 (2006): 659–695.

Gassama, Ibrahim J. "International Law at a Grotian Moment: The Invasion of Iraq in Context." *Emory International Law Review* 18 (2004): 1–52.

———. "Reaffirming Faith in the Dignity of Each Human Being: The United Nations, NGOs, and Apartheid." *Fordham International Law Journal* 19 (1996): 1464–1541.

Gathii, James Thuo. "The American Origins of Liberal and Illiberal Regimes of International Economic Governance in the Marshall Court." *Buffalo Law Review* 54 (2006): 765–801.

———. "Good Governance as a Counter Insurgency Agenda to Oppositional and Transformative Social Projects in International Law." *Buffalo Human Rights Law Review* 5 (1999): 107–174.

———. "The High Stakes of WTO Reform." *Michigan Law Review* 104 (2006): 1361–1386.

———. "Imperialism, Colonialism, and International Law." *Buffalo Law Review* 54 (2007): 1013–1066.

———. "Insulating Domestic Policy Through International Legal Minimalism: A Re-Characterization of the Foreign Affairs Trade Doctrine." *University of Pennsylvania Journal of International Economic Law* 25 (2004): 1–105.

———. "Torture, Extraterritoriality, Terrorism, and International Law." *Albany Law Review* 67 (2003): 335–369.

Gilly, Adolfo. "Introduction," to Fanon. *Studies*, 1-21.

Gold, Joseph. "The Interpretation by the International Monetary Fund of Its Articles of Agreement." *International and Comparative Law Quarterly* 3, no. 2 (April 1954): 256–276.

Goldman, Robert K. "Trivializing Torture: The Office of Legal Counsel's 2002 Opinion Letter and International law Against Torture." *Human Rights Brief* 12, no. 1 (2004): 1–4.

Goldstone, Justice Richard J. "The Consequences of the United States Abdicating Its Moral and Political Leadership of the Free World." *Arizona Journal of International and Comparative Law* 24 (2007): 587–607.

Gonzales, Alberto. Memo from White House Counsel Alberto Gonzales to President George W. Bush. January 25, 2002. Available at http://news.lp.findlaw.com/hdocs/docs/torture/ gnzls12502mem2gwb2.html (accessed December 10, 2007).

Gordon, Ruth E. "Saving Failed States: Sometimes a Neocolonialist Notion." *American University Journal of International Law and Policy* 12 (1997): 903–974.

——. "Some Legal Problems with Trusteeship." *Cornell International Law Journal* 28 (1995): 301–347.

Gordon, Ruth E., and Jon H. Sylvester. "Deconstructing Development." *Wisconsin International Law Journal* 22 (2004): 1–98.

Gramsci, Antonio. "The Southern Question." In Gramsci, *Modern Prince*, 28–51.

Green, L.C. "Claims to Territory in North America." In Green and Dickason, *Law of Nations*, 1–139

Grey, Thomas C. "Origins of the Unwritten Constitution: Fundamental Law in American Revolutionary Thought." *Stanford Law Review* 30 (1978): 843–890.

Griggs, Richard. "The Meaning of 'Nation' and 'State' in the Fourth World." Excerpt from Center for World Indigenous Studies Occasional Paper #18 (1992). Available at http://www.cwis.org/fourthw.htm (accessed February 27, 2009).

Grinde, Donald A., Jr. "Iroquoian Political Concept and the Genesis of American Government." In Barreiro, *Indian Roots*, 47–66.

——. "Iroquois Political Theory and the Roots of American Democracy." In Mohawk et al., *Exiled in the Land of the Free*, 227–280.

Griswold del Castillo, Richard. "Manifest Destiny: The Mexican-American War and the Treaty of Guadalupe Hidalgo." *Southwestern Journal of Law and Trade in the Americas* 5 (1998): 31–43.

Gruber, Aya. "Who's Afraid of Geneva Law?" *Arizona State Law Journal* 39 (2007): 1017–1085.

Guinier, Lani. "Supreme Democracy: Bush v. Gore Redux." *Loyola University Chicago Law Journal* 34 (2002): 23–75.

Hagan, John, Ron Levi, and Gabrielle Ferrales. "Swaying the Hand of Justice: The Internal and External Dynamics of Regime Change at the International Criminal Tribunal for the Former Yugoslavia." *Law and Social Inquiry* 31 (2006): 585–616.

Haile, Minasse. "Legality of Secessions: The Case of Eritrea." *Emory International Law Review* 8 (1994): 479–537.

Hamilton, Henry. "The Hamilton Papers." *Michigan Pioneer and Historical Collections* No. 9 (1886): 501–502.

Hannum, Hurst. "Rethinking Self-Determination." *Virginia Journal of International Law* 34 (1993): 1–69.

Hanson, John, and Kathleen Hanson. "The Blame Frame: Justifying (Racial) Injustice in America." *Harvard Civil Rights–Civil Liberties Law Review* 41 (1991): 413–431.

Harris, Angela P. "Equality Trouble: Sameness and Difference in Twentieth-Century Race Law." *California Law Review* 88 (2003): 1923–1993.

Harris, Cheryl. "Whiteness as Property." *Harvard Law Review* 106 (1993): 1707–1795.

Hay, Derald J. "Post-Kyoto Stress Disorder: How the United States Can Influence International Climate Change Policy." *Missouri Environmental Law and Policy Review* 15 (2008): 493–529.

Head, John W. "For Richer or for Poorer: Assessing the Criticisms Directed at the Multilateral Development Banks." *University of Kansas Law Review* 52 (2004): 241–324.

——. "Law and Policy in International Financial Institutions: The Changing Role of Law in the IMF and the Multilateral Development Banks." *Kansas Journal of Law and Public Policy* 17 (winter 2007–2008): 194–229.

Heidelberg Institute for International Conflict Resolution, *Conflict Barometer 2007*. Heidelberg, Germany. Available at http://www.hiik.de/de/konfliktbarometer/pdf/ ConflictBarometer_2007.pdf (accessed September 25, 2008).

Henkin, Louis. "U.S. Ratification of Human Rights Conventions: The Ghost of Senator Bricker." *American Journal of International Law* 89 (1995): 341– 350.

Hernandez-Truyol, Berta Esperanza. "The Rule of Law and Human Rights." *Florida Journal of International Law* 16 (2004): 167–194.

Hertzbert, Hendrik. "War and Words." *New Yorker*, February 13, 2006. Available at http:// www.newyorker.com/archive/2006/02/13/060213ta_talk_hertzberg (accessed December 9, 2007).

Heuvel, William J. Vanden. "The Four Freedoms." Available at http://www.fourfreedoms. nl/index.php?lang=eng&id=13 (accessed July 27, 2008).

Higginbotham, A. Leon, Jr. "The Ten Precepts of American Slavery Jurisprudence: Chief Justice Roger Taney's Defense and Justice Thurgood Marshall's Condemnation of the Precept of Black Inferiority." *Cardozo Law Review* 17 (1996): 1695–1710.

Hinck, Jon. "The Republic of Palau and the United States: Self-Determination Becomes the Price of Free Association." *California Law Review* 78 (1990): 915–971.

Hirschkorn, Phil. "New York Reduces 9/11 Death Toll by 40." CNN. http://www.cnn. com/2003/US/Northeast/10/29/wtc.deaths/ (accessed December 7, 2007).

"History of the Office of the MIT President." Institute Archives, MIT Libraries. November, 1995. Available at http://libraries.mit.edu/archives/mithistory/biographies/walker.html (accessed July 20, 2008).

Hochschild, Arlie Russell. "A Generation without Public Passion." *Atlantic Monthly*, February 2001.

Hopkins, Terence K., and Immanuel Wallerstein. "The World-System: Is There a Crisis?" In Hopkins and Wallerstein, *Age of Transition*, 1–10.

Horsman, Reginald. "Scientific Racism and the American Indian in the Mid-Nineteenth Century." *American Quarterly* 27, no. 2 (May 1975): 152–168.

Houbert, Jean. "Decolonization in Globalization." In Axtmann, *Globalization*, 43–58.

Howard, Michael. "Constraints on Warfare." In Howard, Andreopoulos, and Shulman, *Laws of War*, 1–11.

Howland, Todd. "U.S. Law as a Tool of Forced Social Change: A Contextual Examination of the Human Rights Violations by the United States Government against Native Americans at Big Mountain." *Boston College Third World Law Journal* 7 (1987): 61–96.

Huntington, Samuel P. "Transnational Organizations in World Politics." *World Politics* 25 (April 1973): 342–347.

Ickes, Harold L. "Foreword" in Cohen, *Handbook of Federal Indian Law*, v–vi..

Iorns, Catherine J. "Indigenous Peoples and Self Determination: Challenging State Sovereignty." *Case Western Reserve Journal of International Law* 24 (1992): 199–348.

"Iraq Body Count." Available at http:www.iraqbodycount.org/ (accessed September 6, 2008).

Jackson, John G. "Introduction" to Lane-Poole, *Story of the Moors*, n.p.

Jensen, Erik M. "The Imaginary Connection Between the Great Law of Peace and the United States Constitution: A Reply to Professor Schaaf." *American Indian Law Review* 15 (1990): 295–298.

Johnson, Kevin R. "From Brown to Bakke to Grutter: Constitutionalizing and Defining Racial Equality." *Constitutional Commentary* 21 (2004): 171–190.

Kades, Eric. "The Dark Side of Efficiency: Johnson v. M'Intosh and the Expropriation of American Indian Lands." *University of Pennsylvania Law Review* 148 (2000): 1065–1189.

Kennedy, David. "Primitive Legal Scholarship." *Harvard International Law Journal* 27 (1986): 1–57.

———. "When Renewal Repeats: Thinking Against the Box." *New York University Journal of International Law and Politics* 32 (2000): 335–500.

Kim, Hyung-Chan. "An Overview." In Kim, *Asian Americans*, 1–76.

Kirkby, Diane, and Catharine Coleborne. "Introduction" to Kirkby and Coleborne, *Law, History*, 1–5.

Koh, Harold Hongju. "On American Exceptionalism." *Stanford Law Review* 55 (2003): 1479–1527.

———. "Restoring America's Human Rights Reputation." *Cornell International Law Journal* 40 (2007): 635–658.

Kolhatkar, Sonali. "Afghan Women: Enduring American 'Freedom.'" *Z Magazine Online* 15, no. 12 (December 2002). Available at http://zmagsite.zmag.org/Dec2002/kolhatkar1202.htm (accessed July 28, 2008).

———. "The Impact of U.S. Intervention on Afghan Women's Rights." *Berkeley Women's Law Journal* 17 (2002): 12–30.

Krieger, David. "Economic Justice for All." *Common Dreams*, May 23, 2003.

Kuchta, Angelique R. "A Closer Look: The U.S. Senate's Failure to Ratify the Comprehensive Test Ban Treaty." *Dickinson Journal of International Law* 19 (2001): 333–361.

"Lady Flora Lugard." *National Portrait Gallery*. Available at http://www.npg.org.uk/live/search/person.asp?LinkID'mp65594. (accessed December 12, 2007).

Larsen, Janet. "Deserts Advancing, Civilization Retreating." *Earth Policy Institute*. March 27, 2003. Available at http://www.earth-policy.org/Updates/Update23.htm (accessed September 5, 2008).

Lawrence, Charles R., III. "The Word and the River: Pedagogy as Scholarship as Struggle." *Southern California Law Review* 65 (1992): 2231–2298.

Lefeber, René. "From The Hague to Bonn to Marrakesh and Beyond: A Negotiating History of the Compliance Regime Under the Kyoto Protocol." In *The Hague Yearbook*, 25–54.

Lippman, Matthew. "The Convention on the Prevention and Punishment of the Crime of Genocide: Fifty Years Later." *Arizona Journal of International and Comparative Law* 15 (1998): 415–514.

———. "The 1948 Convention on the Prevention and Punishment of the Crime of Genocide: Forty-Five Years Later." *Temple International and Comparative Law Journal* 8 (1994): 1–84.

Lobe, Jim. "'New American Century' Project Ends with a Whimper." June 13, 2006. Available at http://www.commondreams.org/headlines06/0613-05.htm (accessed October 21, 2008).

Lobel, Jules. "The War on Terrorism and Civil Liberties." *University of Pittsburgh Law Review* 63 (2002): 767–790.

Lombardo, Paul A. "The 'American Breed': Nazi Eugenics and the Origins of the Pioneer Fund." *Albany Law Review* 65 (2002): 743–830.

Lotter, Friedrich. "The Crusading Idea and the Conquest of the Region East of the Elbe." In Bartlett and MacKay, *Medieval Frontier*, 267–306.

Ludwikowski, Rett R. "Fundamental Constitutional Rights in the New Constitutions of Eastern and Central Europe." *Cardozo Journal of International and Comparative Law* 3 (1995): 73–162.

Lynd, Staughton. "Slavery and the Founding Fathers." In Drimmer, *Black History*, 117–131.

Lyttleton, Adrian. "The National Question in Italy." In Teich and Porter. *National Question*, 63–105.

Ma, Frances Y. F. "Noriega's Abduction from Panama: Is Military Invasion an Appropriate Substitute for International Extradition?" *Loyola of Los Angeles International and Comparative Law Journal* 13 (1991): 925–953

MacFarquhar, Neil. "Upheaval on Wall St. Stirs Anger in the U.N." *New York Times,* September 24, 2008.

Mahmud, Tayyab. "Geography and International Law: Towards a Postcolonial Mapping." *Santa Clara Journal of International Law* 5 (2007): 525–561.

Maragia, Bosire. "The Indigenous Sustainability Paradox and the Quest for Sustainability in Post-Colonial Societies: Is Indigenous Knowledge All That Is Needed?" *Georgetown International Environmental Law Review* 18 (2006): 197–247.

Margulies, Peter. "Laws of Unintended Consequences: Terrorist Financing Restrictions and Transitions to Democracy." *New York International Law Review* 20 (2007): 65–100.

Marks, Stephen P. "Branding the 'War on Terrorism': Is there a 'New Paradigm' of International Law?" *Michigan State Journal of International Law* 12 (2006): 71–119.

Matsuda, Mari. "Public Response to Racist Speech: Considering the Victim's Story." Michigan *Law Review* 87 (1989): 2320–2381.

May, Elaine Tyler. "Echoes of the Cold War: The Aftermath of September 11 at Home." In Dudziak. *September 11,* 35–54.

Mayerfeld, Jamie. "Playing By Our Own Rules: How U.S. Marginalization of International Human Rights Law Led to Torture." *Harvard Human Rights Journal* 20 (2007): 89–140.

McConnell, Michael W. "The Forgotten Constitutional Moment." *Constitutional Commentary* 11 (winter 1994): 115–144.

"Media round-up: Bush's 'crusade' seen as war on Muslims." *BBC International Reports,* September 19, 2001.

Miller, Robert J. "The Doctrine of Discovery in American Indian Law." *Idaho Law Review* 42 (2005): 86–103.

Minard, Anne. "Maya May Have Caused Civilization-Ending Climate Change." *National Geographic News,* August 31, 2008. Available at http://news.natonalgeorgraphic.com/news/2008/02/020229-servir-maya.html.

Moghalu, Kingsley Chiedu. "Image and Reality of War Crimes Justice: External Perceptions of the International Criminal Tribunal for Rwanda." *Fletcher Forum of World Affairs* 26 (summer/fall 2002): 21–43.

Mohawk, John C. Lecture at Alfred University. Alfred, N.Y.: November 19, 1990. (Tape on file with author.)

Mongé, José Trías. "Injustice According to Law: The *Insular Cases* and Other Oddities." In Burnett and Marshall, *Foreign in a Domestic Sense,* 226–240.

Mooney, James M. "Population." In Dodge, *Handbook of the Indians,* 286–287.

Mower, Paul. Book Review of *Rule of Power or Rule of Law,* ed. Nicole Deller, Arjun Makhijani, and John Burroughts. *Journal of Conflict & Security Law* 12 (2007): 334–338.

Murphy, Sean D. "The Security Council, Ligitimacy, and the Concept of Collective Security after the Cold War." *Columbia Journal of Transnational Law* 32 (1994): 201–288.

Mutua, Makau Wa. "Critical Race Theory and International Law: The View of an Insider-Outsider." *Villanova Law Review* 45 (2000): 841–853.

———. "The Ideology of Human Rights." *Virginia Journal of International Law* 36 (1996): 589–657.

———. "Putting Humpty Dumpty Back Together Again: The Dilemmas of the Post-Colonial African State." *Brooklyn Journal of International Law* 21 (1995): 505–536.

———. "Why Redraw the Map of Africa: A Moral and Legal Inquiry." *Michigan Journal of International Law* 16 (1995): 1113–1175.

Nagan, Winston P. "Economic Sanctions, U.S. Foreign Policy, International Law and the Anti-Apartheid Act of 1986." *Florida International Law Journal* 4 (1988): 85–229.

Nanda, Ved P. "The Validity of United States Intervention in Panama Under International Law." *American Journal of International Law* 84 (1990): 494–503.

National Alliance to End Homelessness. "Homelessness Counts." January 10, 2007. Available at http://www.endhomelessness.org/content/general/detail/1440 (accessed September 6, 2008).

Newton, Nell Jessup. "Federal Power over Indians: Its Sources, Scope, and Limitations." *University of Pennsylvania Law Review* 132 (1984): 195–248.

Ngugi, Joel. "The Decolonization-Modernization Interface and the Plight of Indigenous Peoples in Post-Colonial Development Discourse in Africa." *Wisconsin International Law Journal* 20 (2002): 297–351.

Nietschmann, Bernard. "The Fourth World: Nations Versus States." In Demko and Wood, *Reordering the World*, 225–242.

"Obama acceptance speech in full." *The Guardian*, November 5, 2008. Available at http://www.guardian.co.uk/commentisfree/2008/nov/05/uselections2008-barackobama (accessed February 6, 2008).

Obama, Barack. *Inaugural Address.* January 20, 2009. Available at http://www.whitehouse.gov/blog/inaugural-address/ (accessed February 6, 2009).

———. "The America We Love." Speech in Independence, Mo., June 30, 2008. Available at http://www.barackobama.com/2008/06/30/remarks_of_senator_barack_ obam_86.php (accessed November 28, 2008).

———. "The American Moment." Remarks to the Chicago Council on Global Affairs, Chicago, Ill., April 23, 2007. Available at http://www.barackobama.com/2007/04/23/the_american_moment_remarks_to.php (accessed November 28, 2008).

O'Connell, Mary Ellen. "American Exceptionalism and the International Law of Self-Defense." *Denver Journal of International Law and Policy* 31 (2002): 43–58.

———. "The Myth of Preemptive Self-Defense." American Society of International Law Task Force on Terrorism, August 2002. Available at http://www.asil.org/taskforce/oconnell.pdf (accessed December 10, 2007).

Ocran, Modibo. "The Clash of Legal Cultures: The Treatment of Indigenous Law in Colonial and Post-Colonial Africa." *Akron Law Review* 39 (2006): 465–481.

Oliveria, Patrick de. "Calling an end to the 'clash of civilizations.'" *University Daily Kansan*, January 29, 2009. Available at http://www.kansan.com/stories/2009/jan/29/de_oliveira/?opinion (accessed February 9, 2009).

Olmsted, Matthew. "Are Things Falling Apart? Rethinking the Purpose and Function of International Law." *Loyola of Los Angeles International and Comparative Law Review* 27 (2005): 401–477.

O'Melinn, Liam Seamus. "The Imperial Origins of Federal Indian Law: The Ideology of Colonization in Britain, Ireland, and America." *Arizona State Law Journal* 31 (1999): 1207–1275.

Oulahan, Richard V. "Japan Makes Futile Plea." *New York Times*, April 13, 1919.

Pahuja, Sundhya. "The Postcoloniality of International Law." *Harvard International Law Journal* 46 (2005): 459–469.

Pakaukau, Ka. "The Right of Hawai'i to be Restored to the United Nations List of Non–Self-Governing Territories." In Churchill and Venne, *Islands in Captivity*, 303–321..

Palin, Sarah. Vice Presidential Debate. October 2, 2008. Available at http://latimesblogs.latimes.com/washington/2008/10/sarah-palin-b-1.html (accessed October 4, 2008).

Parman, Donald L. "The Big Stick in Indian Affairs: The Bai-a-lil-le Incident in 1909." *Arizona and the West* 20 (winter 1978): 343–360.

Parry, John T. "Finding a Right To Be Tortured." *Law and Literature* 19 (2007): 207–222.

"Past Wars." GlobalSecurity.org. Available at http://www.globalsecurity.org/ military/ world/war/past.htm (accessed September 25, 2008).

Patterson, Kristine B., and Thomas Runge. "Smallpox and the Native American." *American Journal of the Medical Sciences* 323, no. 4 (2002): 216–222.

Paust, Jordan J. "Addendum: War and Responses to Terrorism." *ASIL Insights*, September 2001. Available at http://www.asil.org/insights/insigh77.htm (accessed December 8, 2007).

———. "Executive Plans and Authorizations to Violate International Law Concerning Treatment and Interrogation of Detainees." *Columbia Journal of Transnational Law* 43 (2005): 811–863.

———. "The Human Right to Participate in Armed Revolution and Related Forms of Social Violence: Testing the Limits of Permissibility." *Emory Law Journal* 32 (1983): 545–561.

———. "In Their Own Words: Affirmations of the Founders, Framers, and Early Judiciary concerning the Binding Nature of the Customary Law of Nations." *University of California, Davis, Journal of International Law and Policy* 14 (2008): 205–254.

———. "Remarks" in "Genocide: The Convention, Domestic Law, and State Responsibility." *American Society of International Law Proceedings* 83 (1989): 314–332.

———. "Responding Lawfully to Al Qaeda." *Catholic University Law Review* 56 (2007): 759–803.

———. "Responding Lawfully to International Terrorism: The Use of Force Abroad." *Whittier Law Review* 8 (1986): 711–733.

———. "Use of Armed Force against Terrorists in Afghanistan, Iraq, and Beyond." *Cornell International Law Journal* 35 (2002): 533–557.

———. "War and Enemy Status after 9/11: Attacks on the Laws of War." *Yale Journal of International Law* 28 (2003): 325–335.

Pear, Robert. "Number of People Living in Poverty Increases in US." *New York Times*, September 25, 2002.

Pellet, Alain. Book Review of *The Charter of the United Nations: A Commentary*, ed. Bruno Simma. *Michigan Journal of International Law* 25 (2003): 135–151.

Pendas, Devin O. "'The Magical Scent of the Savage': Colonial Violence, the Crisis of Civilization, and the Origins of the Legalist Paradigm of War." *Boston College International & Comparative Law Review* 30 (2007): 29–53.

Perea, Juan F. "A Brief History of Race and the U.S.–Mexican Border: Tracing the Trajectories of Conquest." *UCLA Law Review* 51 (2003): 283–312.

———. "Demography and Distrust: An Essay on American Languages, Cultural Pluralism, and Official English." *Minnesota Law Review* 77 (1992): 269–373.

Pérez, Louis A., Jr., and Deborah M. Weissman. "Public Power and Private Purpose: Odious Debt and the Political Economy of Hegemony." *North Carolina Journal of International Law and Commercial Regulation* 32 (2007): 699–747.

Petersen, Kirsten E. "Apocalypse Now: The Loss of the Iraq Museum and a New Proposal for the Wartime Protection of Museums." *Minnesota Journal of International Law* 16 (2007): 163–192.

Porter, Robert B. "Decolonizing Indigenous Governance: Observations on Restoring Greater Faith and Legitimacy in the Government of the Seneca Nation." *Kansas Journal of Law and Public Policy* 8 (winter 1999): 97–135.

———. "The Demise of the Ongwehoweh and the Rise of the Native Americans: Redressing the Genocidal Act of Forcing American Citizenship upon Indigenous Peoples." *Harvard BlackLetter Law Journal* 15 (1999): 107–183.

———. "A Proposal to the Hanodaganyas to Decolonize Federal Indian Control Law." *University of Michigan Journal of Law Reform* 31 (1998): 899–931.

———. "Pursuing the Path of Indigenization in the Era of Emergent International Law Governing the Rights of Indigenous Peoples." *Yale Human Rights and Development Law Journal* 5 (2002): 123–175.

Porter-Odawi, Robert B. "Two Kinds of Indians, Two Kinds of Indian Nation Sovereignty: A Surreply to Professor LaVelle." *Kansas Journal of Law and Public Policy* 11 (2002): 629–652.

Post, Jennifer A. "The United States and the Genocide Treaty: Returning Genocide to Sovereign Concerns." *Suffolk Transnational Law Review* 13 (1990): 686–713.

Price, Susannah. "UN finds global inequality rising." *BBC News*, August 25, 2005. Available at http://news.bbc.co.uk/2/hi/americas/4185458.stm (accessed September 9, 2008).

Project for the New American Century. "Rebuilding America's Defenses: Strategy, Forces and Resources for a New Century." September 2000. Available at http://www.newamericancentury.org/RebuildingAmericasDefenses.pdf (accessed October 4, 2008).

Project for the New American Century. "Statement of Principles." June 3, 1997. Available at http://www.newamericancentury.org/statementofprinciples.htm (accessed October 4, 2008).

Quigley, John. "The Afghanistan War and Self-Defense." *Valparaiso University Law Review* 37 (2003): 541–553.

Radin, Margaret J. "Reconsidering the Rule of Law." *Boston University Law Review* 69 (1989): 781–819.

Rajagopal, Balakrishnan. "From Resistance to Renewal: The Third World, Social Movements, and the Expansion of International Institutions." *Harvard International Law Journal* 41 (2000): 529–579.

Raz, Joseph. "The Rule of Law and Its Virtue." In Raz, *Authority of Law*, 210–232.

Reagan, Ronald. "Remarks on the Signing of the Genocide Convention Implementation Act of 1987." U.S. Department of State Bulletin, January 1989. Available at http://findarticles.com/p/articles/mi_m1079/is_n2142_v89/ai_7018358 (accessed August 29, 2008).

Reichler, Paul S. "Holding America to Its Own Best Standards: Abe Chayes and Nicaragua in the World Court." *Harvard International Law Journal* 41 (2001): 15–46.

Reinberg, Steven. "Worldwide War Deaths Underestimated." *HealthDay News*, June 19, 2008. First published in the *British Medical Journal*. Available at http://www.medicinenet.com/ script/main/art.asp?articlekey'90452 (accessed September 25, 2008).

"Report: State Spending on Prison Grows at 6 Times Rate of Higher Ed." *U.S. Newswire*, August 22, 2002.

"Responding to Terrorism: Crime, Punishment, and War." *Harvard Law Review* 115 (2002): 1217–1238.

Richards, Nelson. "The Bricker Amendment and Congress's Failure to Check the Inflation of the Executive's Foreign Affairs Powers, 1951–1954." *California Law Review* 94 (2006): 175–213.

Richardson, Henry J., III. "'Failed States,' Self-Determination, and Preventive Diplomacy: Colonialist Nostalgia and Democratic Expectations." *Temple International and Comparative Law Journal* 10 (1996): 1–78.

Rios-Martinez, Marie. "Congressional Colonialism in the Pacific: The Case of the Northern Mariana Islands and Its Covenant with the United States." *Scholar* 3 (2000): 41–69.

Rivera Ramos, Efrén. "The Legal Construction of American Colonialism: The Insular Cases (1901–1922)." *Revista Juridica Universidad de Puerto Rico* 65 (1996): 225–328.

Rizvi, Haider. "Hungry in a Wealthy Nation." *Inter Press Service*, March 26, 2003.

Robinson, Mary. "A Human Rights Challenge: Advancing Economic, Social and Cultural Rights." *Hastings Law Journal* 56 (2005): 1059–1065.

Román, Ediberto. "Empire Forgotten: The United States's Colonization of Puerto Rico." *Villanova Law Review* 42 (1997): 1119–1211.

Roosevelt, Franklin D. *Annual Address to Congress: The Four Freedoms.* January 6, 1941. Available at http://www.fdrlibrary.marist.edu/od4frees.html (accessed July 27, 2008).

Rubenfeld, Jed. "The End of Privacy." *Stanford Law Review* 61 (2008): 101–161.

———. "Unilateralism and Constitutionalism." *New York University Law Review* 79 (2004): 1971–2028.

Saito, Natsu Taylor. "From Slavery and Seminoles to AIDS in South Africa: An Essay on Race and Property in International Law." *Villanova Law Review* 45 (2000): 1135–1194.

———. "Whose Liberty? Whose Security? The USA PATRIOT Act in the Context of COINTELPRO and the Unlawful Repression of Political Dissent." *Oregon Law Review* 81 (2002): 1051–1131.

Sayre, Francis B. "Legal Problems Arising from the United Nations Trusteeship System." *American Journal of International Law* 42 (1948): 263–298.

Scahill, Timothy. "The Domestic Security Enhancement Act of 2003: A Glimpse into a Post-Patriot Act Approach to Combating Domestic Terrorism." *John Marshall Law Review* 38 (2004): 327–356.

Schaaf, Gregory. "From the Great Law of Peace to the Constitution of the United States: A Revision of America's Democratic Roots." *American Indian Law Review* 14 (1989): 323–331.

Schatz, Christopher J., and Noah A. F. Horst. "Will Justice Delayed Be Justice Denied? Crisis Jurisprudence, the Guantánamo Detainees, and the Imperiled Role of Habeas Corpus in Curbing Abusive Government Detention." *Lewis & Clark Law Review* 11 (2007): 536–562.

Schmidhauser, John R. "Power, Legal Imperialism, and Dependency." *Law and Society Review* 23 (1989): 857–878.

Schnoor, Britta A. "International Law, the Power of the Purse, and Speaking with One Voice: The Legal Cacophony Created by Withholding U.S. Dues from the United Nations." *Iowa Law Review* 92 (2007): 1133–1181.

Schwartz, Stephanie M. "Life, conditions, and hope on the Pine Ridge Oglala Lakota (Sioux) Reservation of SD." *Native American Times*, November 3, 2006.

Sen, Gautam. "The United States and the GATT/WTO System." In Foot, MacFarlane, and Mastanduno, *US Hegemony*, 115–138..

The Sentencing Project. "Facts about Prisons and Prisoners." July 2008. Available at http://www.sentencingproject.org/PublicationsDetails.aspx?PublicationID'425 (accessed September 9, 2008).

Shah, Sikander Ahmed. "The U.S. Attacks on Afghanistan: An Act of Self-Defense Under Article 51?" *Seattle Journal for Social Justice* 6 (2007): 153–182.

Shelton, Dinah. "International Human Rights Law: Principled, Double, or Absent Standards?" *Law and Inequality* 25 (2007): 467–513.

Shepard, Paul. "'State of Cities' Study Released." *Associated Press*, 19 June 1998.

Sherman, Arloc, Robert Greenstein, and Sharon Parrott. "Poverty and Share of Americans without Health Insurance Were Higher in 2007—and Median Income for Working-Age Households was Lower—Than at Bottom of Last Recession." Center on Budget and Policy Priorities. August 26, 2008. Available at http://www.cbpp.org/8-26-08pov.htm (accessed September 8, 2008).

Sloane, Robert D. "The Policies of State Succession: Harmonizing Self-Determination and Global Order in the Twenty-First Century." *Fordham International Law Journal* 30 (2007): 1288–1317.

Sornarajah, M. "Power and Justice: Third World Resistance in International Law." *Singapore Year Book of International Law* 10 (2006): 19–59.

Spectar, J. M. "Beyond the Rubicon: Presidential Leadership, International Law and the Use of Force in the Long Hard Slog." *Connecticut Journal of International Law* 22 (2006): 47–129.

Spruhan, Paul. "A Legal History of Blood Quantum in Federal Indian Law to 1935." *South Dakota Law Review* 51 (2006): 1–50.

Stasiulis, Daiva, and Nira Yuval-Davis. "Introduction: Beyond Dichotomies—Gender, Race, Ethnicity and Class in Settler Societies." In Stasiulis and Yuval-Davis, *Unsettling Settler Societies*, 1–38.

"Statement of Senator Bob Casey." *U.S. Federal News*, March 8, 2007.

"Statistics on Adult Literacy." *Orange County Register*, September 22, 2002.

Steele, John Yellow Bird. *Congressional Testimony before the Senate Committee on Indian Affairs*, March 23, 2007. Available at 2007 WLNR (Westlaw) 5516390.

Stein, Gary. "Tribal Self-Government and the Indian Reorganization Act of 1934." *Michigan Law Review* 70 (1972): 955–986.

Stewart, James G. "The Military Commissions Act's Inconsistency with the Geneva Conventions: An Overview." *Journal of International Criminal Justice* 5 (2007): 26–38.

Stiffarm, Lenore A., and Phil Lane Jr. "The Demography of Native North America: A Question of American Indian Survival." In Jaimes. *State of Native America*, 23-53.

Stone, Geoffrey R. "Judge Learned Hand and the Espionage Act of 1917: A Mystery Unraveled." *University of Chicago Law Review* 70 (2003): 335–358.

Stork, Joe, and Fred Abrahams. "Sidelined: Human Rights in Postwar Iraq." *Human Rights Watch World Report 2004*. Available at http://hrw.org/wr2k4/6.htm#-Toc58744955 (accessed September 6, 2008).

Strauss, Michael J. "Guantanamo Bay and the Evolution of International Leases and Servitudes." *New York City Law Review* 10 (2007): 407–509.

Strickland, Rennard. "The Genocidal Premise in Native American Law and Policy: Exorcising Aboriginal Ghosts." *Journal of Gender, Race and Justice* 1 (1998): 325–333.

———. "The Tribal Struggle for Indian Sovereignty: The Story of the *Cherokee Cases*." In Moran and Carbado, *Race Law Stories*, 37–57.

———. "'You Can't Rollerskate in a Buffalo Herd Even if You Have All the Medicine': American Indian Law and Policy." In Strickland, *Tonto's Revenge*, 47–61.

"Study Says White Families' Wealth Advantage Has Grown." *New York Times*, October 18, 2004, A13.

Sunstein, Cass R. "Of Montreal and Kyoto: A Tale of Two Protocols." *Harvard Environmental Law Review* 31 (2007): 1–65.

Susman, Tina. "Poll: Civilian toll in Iraq may top 1M." *Los Angeles Times*, September 14, 2007.

Swedberg, Richard. "The Doctrine of Economic Neutrality of the IMF and the World Bank." *Journal of Peace Research* 23, no. 4 (December 1986): 377–390.

Sylvester, Jon H. "Sub-Saharan Africa: Economic Stagnation, Political Disintegration, and the Specter of Recolonization." *Loyola Los Angeles Law Review* 27 (1994): 1299–1325.

"System Overload: Pondering the Ethics of America's Health Care System." *Issues in Ethics* 3 (1999): 114–175.

Terbeek, Calvin. "Love in the Time of Free Trade: NAFTA's Economic Effects Ten Years Later." *Tulane Journal of International and Comparative Law* 12 (2004): 487–506.

Thompson, John B. "Introduction" to Lefort, *Political Forms*, 1–28.

Thornton, Russell. "Cherokee Losses during the Trail of Tears: A New Perspective and a New Estimate." *Ethnohistory* No. 31 (1984): 289–300.

Tittemore, Brian D. "Guantanamo Bay and the Precautionary Measures of the Inter-American Commission on Human Rights: A Case for International Oversight in the Struggle against Terrorism." *Human Rights Law Review* 6 (2006): 378–402.

Tomaszewski, Jerzy. "The National Question in Poland in the Twentieth Century." In Teich and Porter, *National Question*, 293–316.

Tomlins, Christopher. "In a Wilderness of Tigers: Violence, the Discourse of English Colonizing, and the Refusals of American History." *Theoretical Inquiries Law* 4 (2003): 451–490. Available at http://www.bepress.com/cgi/viewcontent.cgi?article'1073&context'til (accessed December 11, 2007).

———. "Law's Empire: Chartering English Colonies on the American Mainland in the Seventeenth Century." In Kirkby and Coleborne, *Law, History*, 26–45.

———. "The Legal Cartography of Colonization, the Legal Polyphony of Settlement: English Intrusions on the American Mainland in the Seventeenth Century." *Law and Social Inquiry* 26 (2001): 315–372.

"Too Many Prisoners." *Washington Post*, July 11, 2008.

Torruella, Juan R. "One Hundred Years of Solitude: Puerto Rico's American Century." In Burnett and Marshall, *Foreign in a Domestic Sense*, 241–250.

"Towards a 'general international organization.'" *UN Chronicle*. December 1993. Available at http://findarticles.com/p/articles/mi_m1209/is_n4_v30/ai_14879138 (accessed July 28, 2008).

Trahant, Mark. "Bush on Native American Issues: 'Tribal Sovereignty Means That. It's Sovereign.'" *Democracy Now!* August 10, 2004. Available at http://www.democracynow. org.2004/8/10/bush_on_native_american_issues_tribal (accessed July 20, 2008).

Truman, Harry S. *Inaugural Address*. January 20, 1949. Available at http://www.yale.edu/lawweb/avalon/presiden/inaug/truman.htm (accessed July 28, 2008).

Turns, David. "The Stimson Doctrine of Non-Recognition: Its Historical Genesis and Influence on Contemporary International Law." *Chinese Journal of International Law* 2 (2003): 105–143.

United Nations Association of the United States of America. "Restoring U.S. Credibility through International Cooperation." December 10, 2007. Available at http://www.unausa.org/site/pp.asp?c'fvKRI8MPJpF&b'328637 (accessed July 28, 2008).

"The United Nations: The Growing Threat." *The New American*, October 22, 2001 (special issue).

"U.S. Government Memos on Torture and International Law." *Human Rights First*. http://www.humanrightsfirst.org/us_law/etn/gov_rep/gov_memo_intlaw.htm. (accessed August 12, 2008).

"U.S. Policy Regarding Landmines." *American Journal of International Law* 102 (2008): 190–191.

"'United States' Periodic Report to Committee Against Torture." *American Journal of International Law* 100 (2006): 703–706.

"United States Proposes Revised UN Assessment Process." *American Journal of International Law* 100 (2006): 699–700.

Vachon, Robert. "L'étude du pluralism juridique: Une approache diatopique et dialogale." *Journal of Legal Pluralism and Unofficial Law* 29 (1990): 163–173.

Vagts, Detlev. "International Economic Law and the American Journal of International Law." *American Journal of International Law* 100 (2006): 769–782.

Van der Vyver, Johan D. "American Exceptionalism: Human Rights, International Criminal Justice, and National Self-Righteousness." *Emory Law Journal* 50 (2001): 775–832.

———. "International Justice and the International Criminal Court: Between Sovereignty and the Rule of Law." *Emory International Law Review* 18 (2004): 133–149.

Van Dyke, Jon M., Carmen Di Amore-Siah, and Gerald W. Berkeley-Coats. "Self-Determination for Nonself-Governing Peoples and for Indigenous Peoples: The Cases of Guam and Hawai'i." *University of Hawaii Law Review* 18 (1996): 623–643.

Vattel, Emmerich de. "Emer de Vattel on the Occupation of Territory." In Curtin, *Imperialism*, 42–45.

Vega, Connie de la. "Human Rights and Trade: Inconsistent Application of Treaty Law in the United States." *UCLA Journal of International Law and Foreign Affairs* 9 (2004): 1–42.

Virkink, Mark W., and Erin M. Scheick. "The 'War on Terror' and the Erosion of the Rule of Law: The U.S. Hearings of the ICJ Eminent Jurist Panel." *Human Rights Brief* 14, no. 1 (2006): 2–6.

Wadrzyk, Mark E. "Is It Appropriate for the World Bank to Promote Democratic Standards in a Borrower Country?" *Wisconsin International Law Journal* 17 (1999): 553–577.

Wagner, Wendy E. "Congress, Science, and Environmental Policy." *University of Illinois Law Review* (1999): 181–286.

Wallach, Evan J. "The Logical Nexus Between the Decision to Deny Application of the Third Geneva Convention to the Taliban and Al Qaeda and the Mistreatment of Prisoners in Abu Ghraib." *Case Western Reserve Journal of International Law* 36 (2004): 541–638.

Waller, J. Michael. "Bush Doctrine on free-world safety." *Insight on the News*, October 15, 2002. http://findarticles.com/p/articles/mi_m1571/is_38_18/ai_93457398/pg_1. (accessed November 10, 2007).

Wallerstein, Immanuel. "The Global Possibilities, 1990–2025." In Hopkins and Wallerstein, *Age of Transition*, 226–243.

Warrick, Joby. "Mass Extinction Underway, Majority of Biologists Say." *Washington Post*, April 21, 1998, A4.

Washinawatok, Ingrid. "International Emergence: Twenty-One Years at the United Nations." *New York City Law Review* 3 (1998): 41–57.

Watson, Blake A. "John Marshall and Indian Land Rights: A Historical Rejoinder to the Claim of 'Universal Recognition' of the Doctrine of Discovery." *Seton Hall Law Review* 36 (2006): 496–549.

Weber, Rolf H., and Douglas W. Arner. "Toward a New Design for International Financial Regulation." *University of Pennsylvania Journal of International Law* 29 (2007): 391–453.

Welch, Richard E., Jr. "American Atrocities in the Philippines: The Indictment and the Response." *Pacific Historical Review* 43, no. 2 (May l974): 233–253.

Weston, Burns H. "The Charter of Economic Rights and Duties of States and the Deprivation of Foreign-Owned Wealth." *American Journal of International Law* 75 (1981): 437–475.

"White House apologizes for using 'crusade' to describe war on terrorism." *AP Online*, September 18, 2001.

Wiessner, Siegfried. "American Indian Treaties and Modern International Law." *St. Thomas Law Review* 7 (1995): 567–591.

Williams, Robert A., Jr. "The Algebra of Federal Indian Law: The Hard Trial of Decolonizing and Americanizing the White Man's Indian Jurisprudence." *Wisconsin Law Review* (1986): 219–298.

———. "Encounters on the Frontiers of International Human Rights Law: Redefining the Terms of Indigenous Peoples' Survival in the World." *Duke Law Journal* (1990): 660–704.

———. "Large Binocular Telescopes, Red Squirrel Piñatas, and Apache Sacred Mountains: Decolonizing Environmental Law in a Multicultural World." *West Virginia Law Review* 96 (1994): 1133–1164.

Williams, Stephanie L. "'Your Honor, I Am Here Today Requesting the Court's Permission to Torture Mr. Doe': The Legality of Torture as a Means to an End v. The Illegality of Torture as a Violation of Jus Cogens Norms Under Customary International Law." *University of Miami International and Comparative Law Review* 12 (2004): 301–360.

Wilson, Woodrow. "Address on the Fourteen Points for Peace." Delivered at a Joint Session of Congress. Washington, D.C.: January 8, 1918. Available from the Woodrow Wilson Presidential Library, http://wwl2.dataformat.com/Document.aspx?doc'30716 (accessed July 17, 2008).

———. "Request for Declaration of War." Delivered at a Joint Session of Congress, Washington, D.C., April 2, 1917. Available from the Woodrow Wilson Presidential Library, http://wwl2.dataformat.com/Document.aspx?doc=29623 (accessed July 17, 2008).

Wolfe, Art. "Corporations as Ships: An Inquiry into Personal Accountability and Institutional Legitimacy." *Pepperdine Law Review* 19 (1991): 49–98.

Woods, Jeanne M., and James M. Donovan. "'Anticipatory Self-Defense' and Other Stories." *Kansas Journal of Law and Public Policy* 14 (2005): 487–508.

Woods, Mary Christina. "Nature's Trust: Reclaiming an Environmental Discourse." *Virginia Environmental Law Journal* 25 (2007): 243–276.

Woods, Ngaire. "The United States and the International Financial Institutions: Power and Influence Within the World Bank and the IMF." In Foot, MacFarlane, and Mastaduno. *US Hegemony*, 92–114.

"The World at War: Current Conflicts." GlobalSecurity.org. Available at http://www.globalsecurity.org/military/world/war/ (accessed September 25, 2008).

World Wildlife Fund. *Living Planet Report 2006.* Gland, Switzerland: World Wildlife Fund, 2006. Available at http://assets.panda.org/downloads/living_planet_report.pdf (accessed December 15, 2007).

Worth, John R. "Globalization and the Myth of Absolute National Sovereignty: Reconsidering the 'Un-Signing' of the Rome Statute and the Legacy of Senator Bricker." *Indiana Law Journal* 79 (2004): 245–265.

Wunder, John R. "'Merciless Indian Savages' and the Declaration of Independence: Native Americans Translate the Ecunnaunuxulgee Document." *American Indian Law Review* 25 (2001): 65–92.

Younge, Gary. "America is a Class Act." *Guardian*, January 27, 2003.

Zasloff, Jonathan. "Law and the Shaping of American Foreign Policy: From the Gilded Age to the New Era." *New York University Law Review* 78 (2003): 239–291.

Zook, Darren C. "Decolonizing Law: Identity Politics, Human Rights, and the United Nations." *Harvard Human Rights Journal* 19 (2006): 95–122.

OFFICIAL DOCUMENTS, INCLUDING STATUTES AND TREATIES

Act to Provide Government for the Territory of Hawaii. April 30, 1900. *United States Statutes at Large* 31 (1900): 141.

Act to Provide for the Government of the Territory Northwest of the River Ohio. August 7, 1789. *United States Statutes at Large* 1 (1789): 50.

African Charter on Human and Peoples' Rights. June 27, 1981. *International Legal Materials* 21 (1981): 59. *Entered into force* October 21, 1986.

American Convention on Human Rights. November 22, 1969. *International Legal Materials* 9 (1969): 673. *Entered into force* July 18, 1978.

American Servicemembers' Protection Act of 2002. August 2, 2002. *United States Statutes at Large* 116 (2002): 820.

Articles of Agreement of the International Monetary Fund. July 22, 1944. *Entered into force* December 27, 1945. Available at http://www.imf.org/external/pubs/ft/aa/index.htm (accessed August 3, 2008).

Articles of Confederation. Second Continental Congress. York, Pa.: November 15, 1777. Ratified March 1, 1781.

Burlingame Treaty. July 28, 1868. *United States Statutes at Large* 16 (1868): 739; *Treaty Ser.* no. 48. (United States and China, amending the 1858 Treaty of Tientsin).

California Constitution. (1849). Available at http://www.sos.ca.gov/archives/level3_const-1849txt.html (accessed July 29, 2008).

Charter of the United Nations. June 26, 1945. *United States Statutes at Large* 59 (1945): 1031; *Treaty Ser.* no. 993.

Congressional Apology to Native Hawaiians. November 23, 1993. .Joint Res. 19, 103d Cong., 1st Sess., *United States Statutes at Large* 107 (1993): Stat. 1510

Convention Against Torture and Other Cruel, Inhuman or Degrading Treatment or Punishment. December 10, 1984. *International Legal Materials* 23 (1984): 1027. *Entered into force* June 26, 1987.

Convention on the Elimination of All Forms of Discrimination Against Women (CEDAW). December 18, 1979. *International Legal Materials* 19 (1980): 33. *Entered into force* September 3, 1981.

Convention on the Prevention and Punishment of the Crime of Genocide. December 9, 1948. *United Nations Treaty Series* 78 (1948): 277. *Entered into force* January 12, 1951.

Convention on the Prohibition of the Development, Production, Stockpiling and Use of Chemical Weapons and on Their Destruction. January 13, 1993. *United Nations Treaty Series* 1974 (1993): 45. *Entered into force* April 29, 1997.

Convention on the Prohibition of the Use, Stockpiling, Production and Transfer of Anti-Personnel Mines and on Their Destruction. September 18, 1997. *United Nations Treaty Series* 2056 (1997): 211. *Entered into force* March 1, 1999.

Convention on the Rights of the Child. November 20, 1989. *International Legal Materials* 28 (1989): 1457. *Entered into force* September 2, 1990.

Convention Relating to the Status of Refugees. December 14, 1950. *United Nations Treaty Series* 189 (1951): 137. *Entered into force* April 22, 1954.

Convention Relating to the Status of Stateless Persons. April 26, 1954. *United Nations Treaty Series* 360 (1954): 117. *Entered into force* June 6, 1960.

Covenant of the League of Nations. June 28, 1919. Full text available at http://fletcher.tufts.edu/multi/www/league-covenant.html#annex (accessed July 18, 2008).

Declaration by the United Nations. January 1, 1942. Available at http://www.yale.edu/law-web/avalon/decade/decade03.htm (accessed July 27, 2008).

Declaration of Independence. Second Continental Congress. Philadelphia, Pa.: July 4, 1776.

European Convention for the Protection of Human Rights and Fundamental Freedoms. April 11, 1950. *United Nations Treaty Series.* 312 (1950): 221. *Entered into force* March 9, 1953.

General Act of the Berlin Conference on West Africa. February 6, 1885. Reproduced at *Supplement American Journal of International Law* 3 (1909): 7.

General Allotment Act (Dawes Act) February 8, 1887. *United States Statutes at Large* 24 (1887): 388.

Indian Appropriation Act. March 3, 1871. *United States Statutes at Large* 16 (1871): 544.

Indian Citizenship Act. June 2, 1924. *United States Statutes at Large* 43 (1924): 253.

Indian Removal Act. May 26, 1830. *United States Statutes at Large* 4 (1830): 411.

Indian Reorganization Act of 1934. June 18, 1934. *United States Statutes at Large* 48 (1934): 984; amended by the "Act of June 15, 1935," *United States Statutes at Large* 49 (1935): 378.

International Convention on the Elimination of All Forms of Racial Discrimination (ICERD). December 21, 1965. *International Legal Materials* 5 (1966): 352. *Entered into force* January 4, 1969.

International Convention on the Suppression and Punishment of the Crime of 'Apartheid.' November 30, 1973. *International Legal Materials* 13 (1974): 50. *Entered into force* July 18, 1976.

International Covenant on Civil and Political Rights (ICCPR). December 16, 1966. *United Nations Treaty Series* 999 (1966): 171. *Entered into force* March 23, 1976.

International Covenant on Economic, Social, and Cultural Rights (ICESCR). December 16, 1966. *United Nations Treaty Series* 993 (1966): 3. *Entered into force* January 3, 1976.

Joint Resolution to Provide for the Annexing of the Hawaiian Islands to the United States. July 7, 1898. *United States Statutes at Large* 30 (1898): 750.

Kellogg-Briand Pact (General Treaty for the Renunciation of War). August 27, 1928. *League of Nations Treaty Series* 94 (1928): 57. Available at http://www.yale.edu/lawweb/avalon/kbpact.htm (accessed July 31, 2008).

Major Crimes Act. March 3, 1885. *United States Statutes at Large* 23 (1885): 362.

"A More Secure World: Our Shared Responsibility." A Report of the High-level Panel on Threats, Challenges and Change to the UN General Assembly. December 1, 2004. Available at http://www.un.org/secureworld/report.pdf. (accessed December 9, 2007).

Naturalization Act of 1790. March 26, 1790. *United States Statutes at Large* 1 (1790): 103.

North American Free Trade Agreement (NAFTA). Available at http://www.wto.org/english/docs_e/legal_e/ursum_e.htm#mAgreement; see also text of NAFTA at http://www.nafta-sec-alena.org/DefaultSite/index_e.aspx?DetailID'78 (accessed October 11, 2008).

Organic Act of 1900 (Foraker Act), April 12, 1900. *United States Statutes at Large* 31 (1900): 77.

The Problem of Indian Administration: Summary of Findings and Recommendations. (Meriam Report). Washington, D.C.: Institute for Government Research, 1928.

Puerto Rican Federal Relations Act. March 2, 1917. *United States Statutes at Large* 39 (1917): 951.

"A Report to the National Security Council—NSC 68." President's Secretary's File, Truman Papers. April 14, 1950. Available at http://www.trumanlibrary.org/whistlestop/ study_collections/coldwar/documents/sectioned.php?pagenumber'1&documentdate'1950-04-12&documentid'10-1 (accessed October 5, 2008).

Standard Minimum Rules for the Treatment of Prisoners, First United Nations Congress on the Prevention of Crime and the Treatment of Offenders. UN Doc. E/3048 (1957).

Statute of the International Court of Justice. June 26, 1945. *United States Statutes at Large* 59 (1945): 1055; *Treaty Ser.* no. 993.

Statute of the International Criminal Court (Rome Statute). July 17, 1998. *United Nations Treaty Series* 2187 (1998): 20. Available at http://www.icc-cpi.int/home.html (accessed July 31, 2008).

Treaty of Peace between the United States of America and the Kingdom of Spain. December, 10, 1898. *United States Statutes at Large* 30 (1898): 1754.

Treaty of Peace, Friendship, Limits, and Settlement with the Republic of Mexico (Treaty of Guadalupe Hidalgo). February 2, 1848. *United States Statutes at Large* 9 (1848): 922.

United Nations. "United Nations Member States: List of Member States." Available at http://www.un.org/members/list.shtml (accessed July 29, 2008).

United Nations Development Programme (UNDP). "Beyond scarcity: Power, poverty and the global water crisis." Human Development Report 2006. Available at http://hdr.undp.org/en/media/HDR06-complete.pdf (accessed September 25, 2008).

———. "Fighting climate change: Human solidarity in a divided world," Human Development Report 2007/2008. Available at http://hdr.undp.org/en/media/HDR_20072008_EN_Complete.pdf (accessed September 25, 2008).

———. *Global Environment Outlook*. Republic of Malta: Progress Press, 2007. Available at http://www.unep.org/geo/geo4/media (accessed December 15, 2007).

United Nations General Assembly (UNGA). Declaration on the Rights of Indigenous Peoples. September 13, 2007. Available at http://www.un.org/esa/socidev/unpfii/en/declaration.html (accessed August 29, 2008).

———. Disappeared Persons. UN Doc. A/RES/33/173 (December 20, 1978). Available at http://www.un.org/documents/ga/res/33/ares33r173.pdf (accessed August 29, 2008).

———. International Development Strategy for the Fourth UN Development Decade. 45th Sess., Annex, UN Doc. A/RES/45/199 (December 21, 1990). Available at http://www.un.org/documents/ga/res/45/a45r199.htm (accessed August 29, 2008).

———. Universal Declaration of Human Rights. Res. 217 (December 10, 1948). Available at http://www.unhchr.ch/udhr/lang/eng.htm (accessed August 29, 2008).

———. Res. 95(I), UN GAOR, 1st Sess., UN Doc. A/64/Add.I. (December 11, 1946). Affirmation of the Principles of International Law Recognized by the Charter of the Nurnberg Tribunal.

———. Res. 1514 (XV), UN GAOR, 15th Sess., Supp. 16, UN Doc A/4684 (December 14, 1960). Declaration on the Granting of Independence to Colonial Countries and Peoples.

———. Res. 1541 (XV), UN GAOR, 15th Sess., Supp. 16, UN Doc A/4684 (December 15, 1960). Principles which Should Guide Members in Determining Whether or Not an Obligation Exists to Transmit the Information Called for under Article 73e of the Charter.

———. Res. 1710 (XVI), UN GAOR, 16th Sess., UN Doc A/5100 (December 19, 1961). United Nations Development Decade.

———. Res. 1803 (XVII), 17 GAOR, Supp. 17, UN Doc. A/5217 (December 14, 1962). Permanent Sovereignty over Natural Resources.

———. Res. 3201 (S-VI), UN GAOR, 6th Special Sess., UN Doc A/RES/3201 (May 1, 1974). Declaration on the Establishment of a New International Economic Order.

———. Res. 3202 (S-VI), UN GAOR, 6th Special Sess., UN Doc. A/9559 (May 1, 1974). Programme of Action on the Establishment of a New International Economic Order.

———. Res. 3281, UN GAOR, 29th Sess., UN Doc. A/RES/3281 (December 12, 1974). Charter of Economic Rights and Duties of States.

UN Decolonization Unit Department of Political Affairs. "Trust and Non–self-governing Territories, 1945–1999." Available at http://www.un.org/depts/dpi/decolonization/trust2.htm (accessed July 31, 2008).

———. "The United Nations and Decolonization." Available at http://www.un.org/Depts/dpi/decolonization/main.htm (accessed July 31, 2008).

UN Department of Public Information. "Monthly Summary of Contributions (Military Observers, Police and Troops)." June 30, 2008. Available at http://www.un.org/Depts/dpko/dpko/ contributors/ 2008/jun08_1.pdf (accessed July 28, 2008).

U.S. Bureau of the Census. Fifteenth Census of the United States, 1930: The Indian Population of the United States and Alaska. Washington, D.C.; U.S. Government Printing Office, 1937.

———. Report on Indians Taxed and Not Taxed, 1890. Washington, D.C.; U.S. Government Printing Office, 1894.

———. Statistical Abstract of the United States 1995: The National Data Book. New York: Bernan, 1995.

U.S. Constitution. Available at http://www.consource.org/index.asp?bid=529 (accessed July 11, 2009).

U.S. Department of Justice. "Prison Statistics." June 30, 2007. Available at http://www.ojp.usdoj.gov/bjs/prisons.htm (accessed September 9, 2008).

———. "Defense Counsel in Criminal Cases." November 2000, NCJ 179023. Available at http://www.ojp.usdoj.gov/bjs/pub/pdf/dccc.pdf (accessed September 9, 2008).

U.S. House of Representatives. Executive Document: Report to Secretary of State W.Q. Gresham on *Recent Events Transpiring in the Hawaiian Islands, July 17, 1893*. 53rd Congress, 2nd Sess., 1895.

———. "Report upon the Relations of the United States with the Hawaiian Islands from the First Appointment of a Consular Officer There by This Government." In *Executive Documents of the House of Representatives*. 53rd Cong., 3rd sess., 1894–95.

U.S. Reservations and Understandings to the Genocide Convention. *International Legal Materials* 28 (1989): 782.

U.S. Senate. *Reports of the Committees: The Chivington Massacre*. 39th Cong., 2d sess., 1867.

U.S. Senate, Committee on the Philippine Islands, Hearings Before the Senate Committee on the Philippine Islands (Washington, D.C.: S. Doc. 331, 57th Cong., 1st Sess., 1902).

U.S. War Department. *The 1863 Laws of War*. Mechanicsburg, Pa.: Stackpole Books, 2005.

"We the Children: Meeting the Promises of the World Summit for Children." United Nations Press Release. ICEF/1853, PI/1409, April 18, 2002.

World Bank Group. "World Development Indicators." 2005 Report. Available at http://devdata.worldbank.org/wdi2005/Section3_1.htm#f1 (accessed September 25, 2008).

World Trade Organization. "The GATT years: from Havana to Marrakesh." Available at http://www.wto.org/english/thewto_e/whatis_e/tif_e/fact4_e.htm (accessed August 3, 2008).

List of Cases

Military and Paramilitary Activities in and Against Nicaragua (Nicaragua v. United
    States) (Judgment on Jurisdiction), 1984 I.C.J. 392, 207.
Minnesota v. Mille Lacs Band of Chippewa Indians, 526 U.S. 172 (1999), 280n60.
Montoya v. United States, 180 U.S. 261 (1901), 280n38.
Neely v. Henkel, 180 U.S. 109 (1901), 166.
The Paquete Habana, 175 U.S. 677 (1900), 84.
The Pious Fund Case (United States v. Mexico), October 14, 1902, Reports of International
    Arbitral Awards. Vol. 9, pp. 1–14. Available at http://untreaty.un.org/cod/riaa/cases/
    vol_IX/1-14.pdf (accessed July 15, 2008), 168–169.
Plessy v. Ferguson, 163 U.S. 537 (1896), 178, 277n120, 294n113.
Prigg v. Pennsylvania, 41 U.S. 536 (1842), 277n125.
Rasul v. Bush, 542 U.S. 466 (2004), 287n92.
Reservations to the Convention on the Prevention and Punishment of the Crime of
    Genocide, 1951 I.C.J. 15, 210.
Schenck v. United States, 249 U.S. 47 (1919), 292n63.
Scott v. Sandford, 60 U.S. 393 (1856), 102–104, 275n78.
Sugarman v. United States, 249 U.S. 182 (1919), 292n63.
Talbot v. Jansen, 3 U.S. 133 (1795), 84.
Tsosie v. United States, 825 F.2d 393 (U.S.C.A. 1987), 279n33.
United States v. Bhagat Singh Thind, 261 U.S. 204 (1923), 104–105.
United States v. Dorr, 23 S.Ct. 859 (1900, Supreme Court of the Philippine Islands), 156.
United States v. Fort Sill Apache Tribe of Oklahoma, 533 F.2d 531 (Ct. Cl. 1976), 113.
United States v. Kagama, 118 U.S. 375 (1886), 121.
United States v. Percheman, 32 U.S. 51 (1833), 282n114.
United States v. Sandoval, 167 U.S. 278 (1897), 130.
United States v. Schooner Peggy, 5 U.S. 103 (1801), 84.
United States v. Sioux Nation of Indians, 448 U.S. 371 (1980), 271–272n114.
United States ex rel. Standing Bear v. Crook, 25 F. Cas. 695 (D. Neb. 1879), 114.
Ward v. Race Horse, 70 F. 598 (D. Wyo. 1895), 116.
Ward v. Race Horse, 163 U.S. 504 (1896), 115–118, 280n60.
Western Sahara (Advisory Opinion), 1975 I.C.J. 12, 291n22, 299n215.
Worcester v. Georgia, 31 U.S. 515 (1832), 93, 94, 116, 117, 120, 146, 164.

Index

Abu Ghraib, U.S. prison at, 15, 16
Abu-Lughod, Janet, 39
Abyssinia, U.S. intervention in, 159
Adams, John, 79, 278n3
Adams, John Quincy, 125, 126, 146-148
Adams, Samuel, 69, 271n98, 278n3
Adrian IV, Pope, 268n18
Afghanistan/Afghan, 11; as "failed state," 241;
  Kabul, 233; *mujehadin*, 218, 233, 234; Taliban,
  11, 13, 16, 218, 310n56; U.S. invasion/war in,
  12, 140, 218, 220, 243, 278n132, 310n56; U.S.
  prisoners in, 15; Women's Mission, 243
Africa/African, 52, 96, 137; colonialism in, 40,
  42-44, 163-165, 175-176, 239; independence
  movements, 191, 192; "Scramble" for, 239. *See
  also* Berlin Conference; Slavery
African Americans, 107, 124-125, 136, 226,
  275n78, 303n104
African Charter on Human and Peoples'
  Rights, 301n64
Agassiz, Louis, 136
Aguinaldo, Emilio, 151, 155
Alaska, 159; U.S. "purchase" from Russia, 107,
  139, 285n28
Albany Plan, 79
Albright, Madeleine, 288n116
Alexander II, Pope, 38, 40
Alexander VI, Pope, bulls issued by, 44, 57, 264n62
Algeria, Algiers, 233; decolonization of, 191
Ali, Asmaa, 244
Allotment Act. *See* General Allotment Act of 1887
Al-Naddaf, Fatima, 244
Al Qaida (*also* al Qaeda), 11, 12, 16
America/American: continentalism, 134;
  "frontier," 111, 165, 279n12; identity, 10, 34, 68,
  76-77, 95, 103-105, 107, 133-135, 138; public,
  attitudes of, 3-5, 10, 35, 54, 89, 182, 185, 223,
  227. *See also* United States
"America First": Committee, 306n155; as con-
  struct, 8, 219, 232
American Bar Association (ABA), 211-212,
  291n37, 303n103, 303n105

American Convention on Human Rights, 213,
  301n64
American Eugenics Society, 306n155
American exceptionalism, 4-8, 10-11, 15, 20, 34,
  36-37, 53, 75, 77, 107, 179, 190, 194, 196, 205,
  225, 227, 228, 247; and American Indians,
  94-95, 110, 117; defined, 4, 253-254n19; and
  English settlers, 54-56, 63; and imperialism,
  135; and international law, 209, 212, 219, 230,
  250-251; narrative of, 229-230, 249-251; and
  race, 101, 103, 110, 158; and United Nations,
  182-183. *See also* Manifest destiny
American Indians, 45, 52, 136, 137, 141, 308n197;
  agriculture of, 62, 72, 109, 275n74; "allotment" of lands, 121-123, 180, 281n89; boarding
  schools, 123, 282n95, 282n96; and "blood
  quantum" rules 122, 277n121, 285n20; and
  disease, 62-66, 108-109, 270n64, 275n78; as
  "domestic dependent nations," 93, 102, 120-
  121, 124, 164, 179; and English settlers, 60-68,
  267n9; forced assimilation of, 119-123; identity
  of, 122, 180, 281n87, 281n89; lands of, 56, 67-69,
  72-75, 77, 81, 87-88, 90-94, 95, 106, 108-116,
  131, 141, 261n149, 271n101, 272n123, 272n124,
  274n57, 307n183; laws of, 78-80, 88, 118-121; as
  "lawless," 110-111, 121; massacres of, 65-66, 103,
  108-111, 113, 115, 250, 279n36; political organization of, 78-80, 91; population decline, 108-109,
  111, 269n56, 269n61; as prisoners of war,
  112-114; "removal" of, 111-112; "reorganization,"
  178, 180-181; reservations, 112-117, 121, 180, 226,
  274n42; resistance to colonization, 64-65, 109,
  133, 180; as "savage"/"uncivilized," 65, 88-90,
  91, 94, 95, 107, 118-119, 121, 125, 128, 131, 163, 179,
  259n90, 269n43, 271-272n114, 275n74; scalp
  bounties on, 111, 112; socioeconomic factors,
  226; traditions of, 22, 118-122, 181; "tribes,"
  295n133; and U.S. law, 90-95, 115-122, 179-182,
  191, 280n42, 281n72; as "wards" of U.S. government, 123, 164, 280n47. *See also* Assimilation;
  Citizenship; Indigenous peoples; Marshall,
  John; Sovereignty; Treaties; Trusteeship

American Institute of International Law, 168
"American internationalism," 1, 2, 5, 37, 231,
249, 250; origin of phrase, 253n5
American Society of International Law, 291n37
Amherst, Jeffrey, 64, 275n78
Anghie, Antony, 9, 16, 17, 27, 33, 51, 110, 164,
176, 199, 254n9
Anglo-Saxon: invasion of Ireland, 41; "race,"
55, 56, 100-101, 134, 135-137, 154, 157, 160,
284n4, 285n24; U.S. claims to heritage, 56,
69-70, 75, 107, 127-129, 135-136, 138, 139, 149-
150; model of governance, 78, 80
Angola, U.S. intervention in, 218
Anti-Ballistic Missile Treaty, 215
Apaches, 113; resistance to observatory, 24
Apartheid, 201, 204, 217; Convention on,
301n63
Aquinas, Thomas, 48, 263n40, 265n76
Arab/Arabs, 263n26; culture appropriated by
West, 30, 262-263n25; leaders, 37; in North
Africa, 96; and oil, 199
Arab Americans, 37
Arbenz, Jacobo, 218
Aristotle, 39, 97, 262n25
Arizona, 112
Arkansas: Territory, 112
Articles of Confederation, 79, 274n41
Aryans, 135, 138, 156
Ashcroft, John, 154n3
Asia/Asians, 52, 142, 151, 156, 157, 219, 237; colo-
nialism in, 163, 165, 176. See also Southeast Asia
Assimilation: of American Indians, 119-123,
180; of Filipinos, 155, 161; into Western civili-
zation, 7, 8, 24, 26, 33, 39, 46, 53, 193-194, 232,
235, 251, 299n220
Assimilative Crimes Act of 1898, 281n81
Atlantic Charter (1941), 184, 198
Atlantis, 30
Augustine, St., 38, 87, 262n16
Austin, Stephen, 127, 131
Australia, and Indigenous peoples, 246
Austria-Hungary, 174
Averroës (Ibn Rushd), 263n40
Axis powers, 192. See also World War II
Aztec civilization, 29, 30; library at Tenochti-
tlán, 29

Bacon, Francis, 269n46
Baldwin, James, 99-100
Balkans, war in, 220
Baltics, Christianization of, 40-41
Bannocks, 115-116
Bartlett, Robert, 40, 41
Baum, Frank L., 111
Beard, Charles, 81

Bell, Franklin J., 153, 156
Bell Trade Act, 156
Bercovitch, Sacvan, 68
Berlin Conference, 164-165, 239
Berman, Nathaniel, 191
Bernard, St., 41
Beveridge, Albert J., 133, 151, 153-154, 158, 288n113
Bickley, Lynn Sellers, 208
Biddle, Francis, 189
Bill of Rights. See U.S. Constitution
Bin Laden, Osama, 11, 12
Biological Weapons Convention, 304n124
Bird, Robert Montgomery, 89, 91
Bismarck, Otto von, 165
Black, Edwin, 138
Black Kettle, 113, 279n36
Blount, James, 286n60
Blumenbach, Johan Friedrich, 285n12
Boccaccio, Giovanni, 43
Bolivia, U.S. intervention in, 218
Bolshevik Revolution. See Russia/Russian
Bolton, John, 208, 296n147
Boone, Daniel, 89
Bosque Redondo, 112
Boyle, Francis, 167
Bracevitch, Andrew, 227
Bradford, William, 65, 270n70
Brazil: colonization of, 44; U.S. intervention
in, 218
Bretton Woods: Conference, 200; institutions,
200-201
Bricker Amendment, 211-214
Bricker, John, 212, 214
Britain/British: colonial law, 56-60, 72, 268n19;
colonialism in Africa and Asia, 176, 191;
colonialism in North America, 4, 58-59,
68-74, 77, 268n31, 271n97; foreign policy, 173;
history, 36, 38, 40, 58; law, 69-70, 80; and
United Nations, 184, 199; and World War
I, 170-171; and World War II, 188. See also
England/English; Ireland/Irish
Brookings Institution, 282n99
Brown, Henry B., 116-118, 149
Bryan, William Jennings, 170, 171
Bureau of Indian Affairs (BIA), 181
Burgos, Council of, 46-47; laws of, 46
Burlingame Treaty (U.S.-China), 142
Burma, 247
Burnett, Peter H., 110
Bush, George W.: and American Indians, 181;
and international law, 1, 2, 208, 209, 231;
and Iraq, 243, 270n80; on U.S. as model for
world, 2, 54; on war on terror, 6, 9-15, 17-19,
37, 39-40, 54, 103, 106
Bybee, Jay, 240-241, 310n42

Cabot, John, 267n12, 269n43
Caldwell, Charles, 136
California, 112, 168; Indians in, 109-111; U.S. acquisition of, 129-130, 139, 284n146
Calvinism, 59
Cambodia, U.S. war in, 218
Canada, 278n3; and Indigenous peoples, 246, 282n96, 295n121; trade with, 215
Canary Islands, 42-43, 44, 264n52
Caribbean, colonization of, 44-45, 146
Carmichael, Stokely. *See* Toure, Kwame
Carnegie, Andrew, 187
Carolina, Colony of, 63
Carter, President Jimmy, 213
Cassese, Anthony, 9
Cassirer, Ernst, 67
Castro, Fidel, 218
Caucasian "race," 137, 138
Cayugas, 79
Celts, 263n32
Central American Court, 168
Central Intelligence Agency (CIA), 13, 218, 233, 257n55
Cerone, John, 209
Chaffee, Adna, 156
Chamberlin, Joseph, 294n100
Chamorros, 148
Charlemagne, Roman emperor, 263n31
Charter of Economic Rights and Duties of States, 199
Chavin culture, of Peru, 29
Chemical Weapons Convention, 215, 304n125
Cheney, Vice President Dick, 17, 37
Cheops, Great Pyramid of, 29
Cherokees, 91-94, 102, 112, 118, 120
Cheyennes, 113
Chickasaws, 112, 118
Chile: Indians in, 265n83; U.S. intervention in, 218
Chimni, B. S., 236-237
China/Chinese, 31, 208; civilization, 30, 261n137; immigrants to U.S., 142-144, 286n45, 303n104; "Open Door" policy regarding, 139, 173, 285n26; and United Nations, 184, 186, 298n203; U.S. trade with, 139, 142, 151, 286n48; U.S. intervention in, 159, 173
Chinese Exclusion Act of 1882, 142
Chiricahua Apaches. *See* Apaches
Chivington, John M., 113
Choctaws, 112, 118
Churchill, Ward, 86, 90, 93, 179
Churchill, Winston, 184, 188
Citizenship, 20; of American Indians, 104, 134, 180, 278n138, 281n87, 284n2; and international law, 194; of Mexicans in U.S., 130,

284n146; of Puerto Ricans, 150, 288n100; U.S., 104, 134, 278n140
"City on a hill," 6, 54-55, 225, 227
Civil Rights Act, 178, 294n113
Civil Rights Congress, 211
Civil War, U.S. *See* Wars
Civilization: African, 29, 260n128; and agriculture, 20, 22-23, 58-59; American claims to, 18-19, 55, 56, 68, 75, 80, 82, 91, 95, 105, 107, 111, 117, 126, 129, 133-134, 139, 145, 148, 151-152, 166-167; and cities, 20, 58, 258n79; as construct, 5-6, 8-10, 15, 16, 17-31, 52, 105, 108, 157, 163, 199, 258n74, 258n77; dangers of, 251, 312n84; decline of, 30-31, 261n137; and "development," 160, 174-178, 197; English claims to, 60, 61; non-Western, 29-30, 261n141; and "race," 101, 145, 146, 154, 157-158; and slavery, 98. *See also* Western/European civilization
"Civilized" states: in international law, 49, 53, 71, 76, 82-85, 88, 162-163, 165-167, 175, 177, 182, 187, 190-191, 199, 228, 238-239, 251
"Civilizing mission" (*mission civilisatrice*): of European colonialism, 6, 9, 11, 96, 164-165; of French, 219; of international law, 193; of U.S., 6, 7, 20, 31, 55, 77, 219
Cleveland, Grover, 145-146, 147
Clinton, President Bill, 13, 208, 215, 219
Cohen, Felix S., 118, 123, 295n132
Coke, Edward, 268n35
Colden, Cadwallader, 244-245
Cold War, 8, 11, 32, 192, 203, 217, 219, 220, 254n10, 296n166
Cole, David, 12
Collier, John, 180, 181
Colombia, U.S. intervention in, 159
Colón, Cristóbal. *See* Columbus, Christopher
Colonialism: in Africa, 164-165; American, 6-7, 33-34, 45, 77, 80, 109, 133-134, 139-146, 154, 158, 166-167, 288n102; and British "dual mandate," 176, 191; "classic," 179; defined, 258n80; and development, 198, 221; and education, 53; European 6, 20, 32, 33-34, 45, 64, 137, 138, 157, 162-163, 166, 190-193; ideology of, 5-6, 7, 8, 33, 35-36, 39-40, 105, 107, 110, 132, 261n4, 261n5, 271n109; internal, 178-179, 211, 236, 295n121; law governing, 36, 40, 42, 45-53, 59, 71-72, 96-97, 110, 236, 262n9, 266n103, 266n105, 290n14, 291n15; and League of Nations, 171-178; settler state, 179-180, 193, 245-246, 267n8, 295n122; territorial borders imposed by, 193, 220, 239; and United Nations, 191-194, 196. *See also* Decolonization; Imperialism; Neocolonialism; Trusteeship
Colorado, Indians in, 113

Columbus, Christopher, 39, 43-45, 49, 96, 264n61, 264n65, 264n69, 265n77, 276n98
Comprehensive Test Ban Treaty, 215
Congo, "Belgian," U.S. intervention in, 218
Congregational, missionaries, 142
Conquest, 157, 160; law of, 36, 37, 41, 43, 109, 111, 140, 146, 171, 239, 266n109, 268n19, 268n35, 269n46, 269n47
Constance, Council of, 43
Constitution. *See* U.S. Constitution
Constitutional Convention, 79-80, 90, 102
Continental Congress, 86; and land issues, 73-74, 272n117
Convention Against Torture, 15, 213, 257n53, 257n55, 301n63
Convention for the Pacific Settlement of International Disputes, 168
Convention on the Abolition of Forced Labour (ILO), 213
Convention on the Elimination of Discrimination Against Women (CEDAW), 182, 213, 302n65
Convention on the Political Rights of Women, 213
Convention on the Rights of the Child, 2, 182, 213, 302n65
Convention Relating to the Status of Refugees, 302n66
Convention Relating to the Status of Stateless Persons, 302n66
Convention Relative to the Institution of a Court of Arbitral Justice, Draft, 169
Corn Tassell, 92
Costa Rica, U.S. intervention in, 218
Cotton, John, 62-63
Council of Europe, 302n73
Covenant on Human Rights, draft of, 211
Cox, Harvey, 22
Craniology, 137
Crawford, James, 163
Creeks, 112, 118, 272n124. *See also* Muscogee, Red Sticks
Crook, George, 114
Crow Dog, 120
Crusades, 6, 37-39, 42, 51, 53, 55, 250, 260n122, 262n21, 263n26; in Eastern Europe, 40-41; law of, 38, 50, 163; and war on terror, 6, 37
Cuba, 125, 208; U.S. occupation of, 139, 146-149, 151, 166, 287n83, 287n89; U.S. intervention in, 159, 174, 218. *See also* Guantánamo Bay, Cuba
Custer, George Armstrong, 279n36
Customary law. *See* International law

Darwin, Charles, 137-138, 157, 285n18
Davis, Mike, 233

Dawes, Henry, 122
Declaration of Independence, 69-71, 73, 76-80, 101, 103, 135, 178, 271n101
Declaration of the Rights and Duties of Nations, 168
Decolonization, 7, 53, 162, 239; and human rights, 203, 240; of international law, 8, 37, 230, 235-247; movements for, 7-8, 191-192, 220, 221, 236; and natural resources, 198-200; post-World War I, 173-178, 238, 271n107; post-World War II, 182, 190-194, 230, 238, 298n205, 299n215; theories of, 236-241. *See also* Colonialism; United Nations
Delahunty, Robert, 256n51
Deloria, Vine, Jr., 22, 72, 120, 121
Democracy, 1, 2, 6, 7, 8, 17-18, 31, 32, 91, 126, 161, 178, 182, 205, 206, 226, 227, 251; American Indian models of, 79-80; and founding of U.S., 68, 70, 75, 76-77, 81-82, 94, 103, 107, 119, 135; as international concern, 171-172, 184, 205; in Iraq, 243-244; superiority of Western, 31, 103, 242; theories of, 78-79, 247, 270n91; and wars, 171, 183, 192, 219, 249
Denmark/Danes, 174; conquest of Slavs, 40-41
Deskaheh, Haudenosaunee (Cayuga) leader, 211, 295n125, 303n106
Development, 5, 6, 8, 22, 27, 31, 234-235, 242; Decades, 197, 202, 235; and decolonization, 160, 174-177, 194, 196, 198-200, 202-203; endogenous, 197; and human rights, 203-205; and Indigenous peoples, 50, 164; statistics, 222-223; theories of, 196-197, 221-222, 247-249, 257n65, 299n5, 311n67
Dewey, George, 151, 152
Diné. *See* Navajos
Discovery, 62; age of, 6, 39, 40, 42-47, 51; doctrine of, 49, 86, 90-91, 94, 106, 119-120, 140-141, 239, 245-246, 269n43, 275n70, 276n93
Dominican Republic, 44, 167; U.S. intervention in, 159, 174, 218
Dominicans, 46, 265n76
Donovan, James, 15, 16
Drinnon, Richard, 17, 66, 67, 89, 148
Duarte, King of Portugal, 43
DuBois, W. E. B., 211
Dumbarton Oaks, 1944 Conference, 184
Duponceau, Peter, 85
Durkheim, Émile, 259n98
Dutch, 56, 267n8
Dworkin, Ronald, 82

Eagleton, Terry, 27, 246
Eastern Europe, as "pagan," 38
Eckert, Allen, 73
Ecology. *See* Environment

Edwards, Hayden, 126
Egypt/Egyptian: civilization, 29-30; library in Alexandria, 29, 260n121; U.S. intervention in, 218
Eisenhower, Dwight D., 212
Elizabeth I, Queen of England: and colonization of Ireland, 57-58; and slave trade, 57, 268n17
El Salvador, U.S. intervention in, 218
Emma, Queen of Hawai'i, 144
Encomienda system, 45, 46, 265n77; origins of, 46
Enemy: of civilization, 235, 251, 268n35, 269n47; as irrational, 14-15, 256n37; unseen, 12, 255n15; in war on terror, 12-16, 65, 230, 232-234, 249, 251
England/English, 34, 66-69, 267n8; in Caribbean, 97; law, 69-70, 135, 269n46; Norman invasion of, 38, 40. *See also* Britain/British
English settlers: and African slavery, 96-99; in North America, 6, 49, 54-75, 95, 106, 179, 229; claims to land, 61-66, 69, 131. *See also* Pilgrims, in New England; Puritans
Enlightenment, 23, 26, 32, 54, 136, 242
Environment: destruction of, 3, 5, 8, 24-25, 31, 223-224, 225, 227, 228, 232, 235, 248, 251, 259n104, 307n183, 307n187, 307n192, 312n84; Indigenous approaches to, 310n48
Española, 44-46, 265n77
Espionage Act of 1917, 171, 292n63
Esteva, Gustavo, 34, 197, 205, 238, 243, 247, 311n76
Estonians, Christianization of, 40
Eugenics, 135-139; defined, 138
Eugenius IV, Pope, 42-43
Eurocentrism, 11, 29; defined, 254n5
Europe/European, 35, 177; colonial law, 48, 52, 56; as construct, 40, 263n30, 263n40; hegemony, 33, 36, 136; history, 32, 33, 66, 263n31; political theory, 78, 136. *See also* Western/European Civilization
European Convention on Human Rights, 301n64
Evil: "axis of," 11, 254n10; conceptions of, 11-12, 22, 37, 254n11
Evolution: as justification for conquest, 18; theory of, 137-138
Exceptionalism. *See* American exceptionalism
Exodus narrative, 60

Falk, Richard, 19, 234
Fanon, Frantz, 192
Ferdinand, King of Spain, 45-47, 136, 264n62
Figueres, Jose, 218
Filipinos. *See* Philippines/Filipinos

Fillmore, Millard, 147
Finns, Christianization of, 40
First World, 203
Fitzpatrick, Peter, 22, 23, 29, 31, 33, 36, 51, 52, 54, 89-90, 95, 101, 105, 258n79
"Five Civilized Tribes," 112
Fleischer, Ari, 37
Fleming, William, 212
Florida, acquisition by U.S., 7, 107, 124-125, 127, 148. *See also* Seminoles
Foner, Philip, 147
Foraker Act of 1900, 149
Ford, Henry, 306n155
Foster, John, 144, 286n60
Foucault, Michel, 278n143, 294n107
"Founding Fathers," 68-75, 76, 80-84, 88, 119, 134; and international law, 4, 71-72, 250
Fourth World, 34, 203
Framework Convention on Climate Change, Kyoto Protocols to, 3, 182, 215, 304n124
France/French, 34, 39, 84; colonialism, 56, 57, 141, 191, 218-219, 267n8; foreign policy, 173; in North America, 64, 272n119, 282n103; Revolution, 271n107; and United Nations, 186; and World War II, 188
Franciscans, 46
Franklin, Benjamin, 79, 91, 125
Franks, 34
Frederick II, Holy Roman Emperor, 41
Fredonia, Republic of, 126
Freedom, 6, 28, 31, 32, 105, 242; and decolonization, 192; English colonial notions of, 67-68; and founding of U.S., 68, 75, 76-79, 82-83, 94, 103, 119, 131; non-Western understandings of, 243-245, 247, 251, 311n64; U.S. invocation of, 1, 2, 4, 6, 7, 8, 9, 17-18, 56, 103, 108, 128, 133, 135, 158, 178, 183, 219, 226, 227, 249, 251, 257n64, 278n132, 303n103
Freire, Paolo, 21

Galton, Francis, 137
Gandhi, Mahatma, 311n76
García, Calixto, 287n88
Garrison, William Lloyd, 102
Gates, Merrill, 281n86
Gathii, James, 92, 216
General Agreement on Tariffs and Trade (GATT), 201, 215
General Agreement on Trade in Services (TRIPS), 215
General Allotment Act of 1887, 121-122, 180, 281n85
Genesis, book of, 21, 23
Geneva Conventions, 3, 14, 15, 16, 240-241; as "obsolete," 16, 206

International Monetary Fund (IMF), 8, 196, 200-202, 235; and U.S., 201, 215, 300n37
International Trade Organization, 200
Internments: of American Indians, 111-115, 119, 152; of Boers, 153; compared, 305n148; of Filipinos, 152
Iowa Territory, 112
Iran, 11, and terrorism, 233; U.S. intervention in, 218
Iraq, 11, 208, 220; sanctions against, 2-3, 288n116; U.S. invasion/war in, 3, 12-13, 15, 233, 243-244, 256n35, 270n80, 278n132, 309n10, 311n63; U.S. prisoners in, 15, 244
Iredell, James, 84
Ireland/Irish, 42; Belfast, 233; British colonization of, 57-58, 268n19, 268n22, 295n121; Christianization of, 41, 268n18
Iroquois, 211, 244-245; Covenant Chain, 79; Great Law of Peace, 79; as model for U.S., 79-81, 91; Six Nations Confederacy, 79, 109, 118, 273n6, 273n11, 295n125
Isabella, Queen of Spain, 43, 262n6, 264n62
Islam/Islamic, 50, 257n64, 265n75; civilization, 38, 42; empire, 38, 262n24; in Europe, 40; fundamentalism/"radicalism," 11, 227, 247; law, 310n51; states, 17. See also Crusades; Reconquista
Israel/Israelis, 208, 217, 218; and terrorism, 233
Italy/Italian, 40; fascism, 306n155; foreign policy of, 173, 189; and World War II, 188

Jackson, Andrew, 93, 109, 112, 124-125, 127, 148, 276n90, 279n30, 282n113
Jackson, Robert, 5, 188, 190
Jamaica, U.S. intervention in, 218
Jamestown, 60, 65
Japan/Japanese, 30; foreign policy, 173; in Hawai'i, 143-144; and League of Nation, 176-177; U.S. "opening" of, 139; and World War II, 156, 183, 188, 191
Jay, John, 83, 84, 104, 272n121
Jefferson, Thomas, 69-70, 77-79, 82, 87, 106, 124-126, 147, 271n104, 272n4, 274n57; on race and slavery, 97, 100, 103, 107, 278n134
Jennings, Francis, 91
Jerusalem, 39
Jilani, Hina, 257n65
Johnson atoll, 286n43
Johnson, President Lyndon, 213
Jones Act of 1916 (Philippines), 156
Jones Act of 1917 (Puerto Rico), 150, 288n100
Jordan, Winthrop, 98
Judeo-Christian tradition, 20, 22
Julius Caesar, 260n121
Jus cogens norms. See International law

Jus gentium, 47, 49
"Just war," laws of, 37, 38, 50-52, 61-62, 65, 87, 94, 109, 110, 266n109

Kalakaua, David, King of Hawai'i, 144
Kamehameha III, King of Hawai'i, 143
Kanaka Maoli, 143, 146, 286n52, 286n56. See also Hawai'i
Kant, Immanuel, 110
Karnow, Stanley, 219
Kellog-Briand Pact (1928), 173, 174, 189
Kennedy, John F., 197, 213
King, Thomas, 23-24
Kiowas, 122
Kitchener, Herbert, 153
Knox, Philander, 170
Kolhatkar, Sonali, 243
Korea: North, 11; U.S. intervention in, 159, 217
Ku Klux Klan, 306n155
Kuwait: U.S. intervention in, 217
Kyoto Protocols. See Framework Convention on Climate Change, Kyoto Protocols to

Lakotas, 115, 120-121, 226, 244, 311n64
Landmines, convention banning, 182, 215, 304n125
Language(s): and colonial rule, 262n6; disappearing, 224, 307n188; as essential to worldview, 21; as uniquely human, 22-23
Lansing, Robert, 178
Laos, U.S. war in, 218
Las Casas, Bartolomé de, 44, 45, 47, 96-97, 265n74, 276n98, 276n101, 276n102
Latin America, 168, 177; U.S. intervention in, 159, 166-167, 173-174, 218. See also Monroe Doctrine; Organization of American States
Latinas/os, in U.S., 226
Latvians, Christianization of, 40
Law. See Colonialism; International law; Rule of law; U.S. Supreme Court
Law of nations. See International law
Law of the Sea Treaty, 182
Leach, Edmund, 62
League of Nations, 162, 170-173, 179, 183, 184, 188, 207, 211, 295n125, 303n106; Council of, 172; Covenant of, 172-174, 293n74, 293n92, 297n168; Mandate System, 8, 53, 165, 173-179, 180-182, 191, 202, 203; Permanent Mandates Commission (PMC), 175-177, 294n102. See also Permanent Court of International Justice
Lebanon: and terrorism, 233; U.S. intervention in, 218
Lemkin, Raphael, 209-210
Libya, 208, 218

Lieber, Francis, 169
Lieber's Code, 169
Liliʻuokalani, Queen of Hawaiʻi, 144, 146
Lincoln, Abraham, 109, 113, 129, 169
Lindbergh, Charles, 306n155
Linnaeus, Carolus, 285n12
Lithuanians, Christianization of, 40-42, 44
Locke, John, 72, 271n109
London Charter. *See* Nuremberg Tribunal
Lone Wolf, 122
Long, James, 126, 283n120
Long, John, 79, 245
López de Palacios Rubios, Juan, 47, 265n83
Lorimer, James, 164
Louisiana Purchase, 106-107, 124, 126, 130, 282n103
Luce, Henry, 224
Lugard, Flora Louisa Shaw, 38
Lugard, Frederick, 176, 294n100
Lumumba, Patrice, 218
Lunalilo, King of Hawaiʻi, 144
Lusitania, 170, 292n61

MacArthur, Arthur, 152, 156
MacArthur, Douglas, 156
Madison, James, 82, 124, 273n25
Magna Carta, 70, 184
Mahmud, Tayyab, 239
Major Crimes Act of 1885, 121, 281n81
Malaysia, 30
Mandate System. *See* League of Nations
Manifest destiny, 7, 53, 80, 108, 224, 251, 267n5, 267n9; origin of term, 106, 127, 267n4, 278n1; postulates of, 55, 68; and U.S. continental expansion, 106-107, 117, 124, 131-132; and U.S. imperialism, 133, 158-160; and World War I, 171
Manley, Michael, 218
Mann, Barbara, 30
Maragia, Bosire, 23
Marcos, Ferdinand, 156
Marrakesh Agreement. *See* World Trade Organization
Marshall Islands, 298n205
Marshall, John: land claims of, 90, 275n65, 281n69, 281n72; Supreme Court opinions on American Indians, 51, 75, 83, 84, 90-94, 95, 102, 116, 117, 119-121, 123, 141, 146, 149, 150, 164-165, 174, 176, 271n114, 276n90
Marshall Plan, 200
Marx, Karl, 259n98; Marxist analyses, 311n67
Mary, Queen of England, 58
Massachusetts, Colony of, 60, 63, 64, 270n64, 271n98; and slavery, 98
Mason, John, 65-66

Mather, Cotton, 63, 275n74
Mauritania, 299n215
Mayan civilization, 29
McCain, John, 54
McKinley, William, 145, 147-148, 151, 152, 154-155, 166, 167
McNamara, Robert, 306n160
Menthon, François de, 190, 298n191
Meriam Report, 123, 180
Merk, Frederick, 55, 134, 147, 150, 158, 159, 267n5
Mexico/Mexicans: Indigenous peoples of, 243, 269n58; land grants, 130; Oaxaca, 243; trade with, 215; as "savage"/inferior, 129, 283n140; U.S. annexation of 7, 107, 112, 125-131, 133-134, 139, 144, 147, 148, 250, 284n144; U.S. intervention in, 159, 174. *See also* Immigrants/Immigration; Wars
Micronesia, 298n205
Middle Ages, 38-39
Midway Islands, U.S. acquisition of, 139
Mier y Terán, Manuel, 126
Military Bases Agreement (Philippines), 156
Miller, Stuart Creighton
Minneconjous. *See* Lakotas
Missouri Territory, 112
Mohawk, John, 34
Mohawks, 79
Mongols, 262n24; "discovery" of, 39
Monogenism, 136-137
Monroe Doctrine, 126, 143, 166, 168, 173-174; Roosevelt Corollary to, 166, 168, 173
Monroe, James, 107, 166
Moors, 29, 42, 43, 96, 263n35
Morgenthau, Hans, 291n30
Morocco, 38, 299n215; U.S. intervention in, 218
Morton, George, 136-137
Morton, Thomas, 67
Moscow Declaration (1942), 184
Mossadegh. *See* Iran
Mound builders, 30
Mt. Graham, observatory at, 24
Multinational Investment Guarantee Agency, 300n30
Muscogee, Red Sticks, 109
Muslim. *See* Islam
Mutua, Makau, 164, 193, 205, 239

Namibia, 299n215
Naming, power of, 21-24, 258n85, 270n77
Narragansetts, 64, 270n64
Nation(s): defined, 162; wars with states, 220
National Association for the Advancement of Colored People, 211
National liberation movements. *See* Decolonization

National Negro Congress, 211
National Security Council (NSC), 205,
305n147; NSC 68, 205-206
National Security Strategy (NSS), 1-2, 12, 14, 15,
17-19
Native Americans. *See* American Indians;
Indigenous peoples
Native Hawaiians. *See* Kanaka Maoli
Natural law/natural rights: and colonialism,
48, 51-53, 58-61, 105, 177; and Indigenous
peoples, 44, 47, 61, 65, 74, 90, 94, 141,
266n105; and Roman Church law, 38-42; and
slavery, 96-97; U.S. claims under, 4, 70, 72,
76, 78, 103
Nature, human relationship to, 20, 22-26, 28,
33, 36, 67, 72, 82, 105. *See also* Environment
Navajos, 112, 114
Navassa, 140-141, 285n32
Nazis. *See* Germany/German
Neocolonialism, 166, 167, 174, 219, 232, 236-237;
defined, 291n30
Neolithic culture, 23
Netherlands. *See* Dutch
Neutrality Act, 183
Nevada, 112
New Canaan, Puritan notion of, 61
New International Economic Order (NIEO),
199
New Israel, Puritan notion of, 61
New Mexico, 112; U.S. acquisition of, 129
New Zealand: and Indigenous peoples, 246
"New World," 36, 39, 40, 42, 49, 60
Newlands Resolution, 287n67
Ngugi, Joel, 194
Nicaragua: and International Court of Justice,
207; U.S. intervention in, 159, 174, 207, 218;
and World Bank, 201
Nicholas II, Czar, 168
Nicholas II, Pope, 40
Nietschmann, Bernard, 162, 220
Nixon, President Richard: and international
law, 210, 213; and Vietnam, 256n37
Nobel Peace Prize, 291n37
Non-Aligned Movement, 199
Noriega, Manuel, 66
Normans, 40, 74; conquest of England, 38, 57,
62, 70, 73, 135; in Ireland, 41
North Africa: civilizations of, 29, 38; coloniza-
tion of, 61; during Crusades, 38
North American Free Trade Agreement
(NAFTA), 215
North Atlantic Treaty Organization (NATO),
219
North, global, 199-200, 221, 230, 240
Northern Mariana Islands, 298n205

Northwest Ordinance, 86
Nuclear Nonproliferation Treaty, 215
Nuremberg Tribunal, 188-190, 203, 208,
297n184, 298n198

Obama, Barack, 1, 2, 231; inaugural address, 1,
13, 19, 25, 232, 257n64, 309n2
O'Connell, Mary Ellen, 219
Oglala Lakotas. *See* Lakotas
Oklahoma, as Indian territory, 112, 114, 279n12
Okri, Ben, 229
Oldham, John, 270n64
Olmec civilization, 29
Omahas, 114
Onondagas, 79
Oregon: Indian massacres in, 111; territory, 107;
U.S. acquisition of, 112, 127
Organic Act of 1900, 145
Organic Act of 1902, 152
Organization of American States, 168; Charter
of, 207; Inter-American Commission of,
302n66
Orient, construct of, 33, 154, 260n134
Osages, 118
Ostend Manifesto, 287n83
O'Sullivan, John L., 106, 127
Other, the: and American exceptional-
ism, 179; appropriation of culture and
history of, 29-30; assimilation of, 232,
235; conquest of, 42, 59-60, 66, 75, 77; as
"enemy"/"uncivilized," 5-6, 9, 15, 16, 22, 31,
32-33, 36, 77, 90, 95, 105, 108, 114, 134, 157, 231,
238, 241; in Europe, 40; legal status of, 51,
103, 163; racialization of, 97, 107, 134, 190; as
"underdeveloped," 197
Otis, Ewell, 151
Ottawas, and smallpox, 64
Ottoman Empire: colonies of, 174-176

Pacific Islands, 191, 193
Pagden, Anthony, 61
Pakistan/Pakistani: Inter-Services Intelligence
(ISI), 133
Palau, 192, 298n205
Palestine/Palestinians, 217, 233
Palin, Sarah, 54-55
Panama: Canal, 159, 285n32; U.S. intervention
in, 159, 174, 218
Papal bulls, 44, 47, 57. *See also* Alexander VI,
Pope
Patterson, William L., 211
Paust, Jordan, 83, 84, 85
Paz, Matías de, 47, 86, 265n83
Pearl Harbor, 142, 143, 183
Peckham, George, 269n40

Pentagon, attack on, 9, 11
Pepper, Claude, 207
Pequots, 65-66, 270n64
Permanent Court of Arbitration, 168-169
Permanent Court of International Justice
(PCIJ), 169, 170, 172-173, 187-188, 206
Permanent Mandates Commission. *See* League
of Nations
Peru, U.S. intervention in, 218
Peterson, Merrill, 69-70
Pettigrew, Richard F., 144-145
Philip II, King of Spain, 96
Philippines/Filipinos: immigrants, 143; Laurel-
Langley Agreement, 289n146; U.S. coloniza-
tion of, 7, 58, 139, 141, 146, 148, 151-156, 161,
166-167; U.S. Commission, 167. *See also* Wars
Phrenology, 136-137
Physiognomy, 137
Pilgrims, in New England, 56, 60, 62, 97, 267n10
Pinckney, Charles, 79
Pine Ridge Reservation, 226
Pinochet, Augusto, 218, 247
Platt Amendment, 149
Plenary power: doctrine of, 122, 149, 150, 164,
179, 180
Plessy, Homer, 277n120
"Pluriverse" of worldviews, 34, 101, 230, 238,
242, 243, 248, 251
Plymouth Colony, 60, 62, 65, 270n64; and
slavery, 98
Poland: Crusades in, 41-42
Polk, James K., 128-130, 166
Pol Pot, 247
Polygenism, 136-137
Poncas, 114, 115
Ponce de León, Juan, 63
Porter, Robert Odawi, 123
Portugal/Portuguese, 42; and apartheid, 201;
colonialism, 40, 42-44, 55, 57, 97; history,
264n50; immigrants, 144
Positivism, 51, 163, 167, 177, 291n15
Poverty: global, 221-223, 240, 301n46, 307n174,
307n175, 307n177; and terrorism, 14; and
"underdevelopment," 197-198, 221, 248; in
U.S., 225-226
Prakash, Madhu Suri, 34, 205, 238, 243, 247,
311n76
Pratt, Richard Henry, 122
"The Problem of Indian Administration." *See*
Meriam Report
Progress: as American quality, 1,2, 5, 6, 8, 10,
18-19, 55, 108, 148, 158; as control of nature,
22-23, 26, 33-34, 105, 227, 231; as goal of
international institutions, 10, 177, 221-222; as
unilinear, 197, 227, 229, 235, 245; and Western

civilization, 18-19, 20, 22, 26-31, 50, 66, 75,
136, 138, 176-177, 195, 198, 204, 251
Project for a New American Century, 195
Provisional Irish Republican Army, 233
Prussians, Christianization of, 40
Puerto Rico: U.S. colonization of, 7, 139, 141,
146, 148, 149-150, 151, 156, 174, 193, 288n97,
288n98, 288n100, 288n102
Pufendorf, Samuel von, 131, 266n98
Puritans, 54, 55, 56, 60-63, 65, 67, 91, 119, 138,
143, 250, 267n9, 267n10, 275n74; ideology of,
60-68, 74-75, 105, 133, 158, 270n80

Qatar, 208

Race/racism: and American identity, 95,
103-105, 107, 110, 133-139, 144, 147, 148; in
Angloamerican colonies, 97-101; in colonial ideology, 40, 96-97, 154, 157-158, 176;
construct of, 97-101, 119, 277n120, 285n12;
discrimination defined, 302n65; disparities
in U.S., 226; and human rights, 203, 209-211;
"scientific," 134-139, 275n78, 285n20, 285n24
Race Horse, 115-116
Raleigh, Walter, 58-59
Rationality, concept of, 22-23, 25-26
Reagan, Ronald: and Cold War, 11, 254n10;
farewell address of, 54-55, 225; and interna-
tional law, 207, 209, 219
Reconquista, 36, 38, 40, 42, 43, 276n96
Reconstruction, 178, 294n113
Reformation, Protestant, 55, 57
Rehnquist, William, 271-272n114
Relativism, 247, 248
Renaissance, 32, 48
Rendition, by U.S., 47
Requerimiento, 46, 47, 265n83, 265n85, 265n87
Res nullius. See *Territorium res nullius*
Reza Pahlavi, Mohammad, 218
Richardson, Henry S., III, 240, 241
Rio Grande Pueblos, 118
Riratjingu, 258n85
Rist, Gilbert, 221-222, 247-249
Rivera Ramos, Efrén, 149
Roberts, J.M., 25-26, 28, 29
Robeson, Paul, 211
"Rogue state," 87, 249, 255n28; defined, 2, 13,
255n21
Rolfe, John, 97
Rome/Roman: ancient, 30, 32, 34, 35, 260n121,
260n134; Church of, 37-38, 40-42, 52, 55, 57,
135, 262n25; Holy Roman Empire, 41, 263n31;
law of, 37-39, 57, 59, 70; sack of, 17, 27, 246
Rome Statute (Treaty) of the ICC. *See* Interna-
tional Criminal Court

Underhill, John, 270n73

United Nations (UN), 162, 195, 220, 245, 259n101; and apartheid/racial discrimination, 201, 211; and armed conflict, 185-187, 222, 256n36; and decolonization, 146, 190-194; and development, 197, 202, 222-223; establishment of, 7, 182-184, 190; Headquarters, 185, 191; High-Level Panel on Threats, Challenges and Change, 14; Monetary and Financial Conference, 200; U.S. influence on, 182-185, 188, 191-194, 205, 206, 217, 296n147, 296n163, 298n203. *See also* International Court of Justice; *specific UN organs and agencies*

UN Charter, 1, 13, 184-187, 206, 207, 217, 256n39, 297n172; Art. 51 of, 14-15; and colonialism, 191-193; and International Court of Justice, 187-188

UN Declaration on the Rights of Indigenous Peoples, 204, 246, 302n67

UN Decolonization Unit, 191

UN Development Programme (UNDP), 223

UN Economic and Social Council, 210, 211, 297n173

UN Educational, Scientific and Cultural Organization (UNESCO), 197

UN General Assembly, 186-187, 190-193, 196-199, 201, 208, 306n164; declarations and resolutions, 204, 211, 212, 217, 297n172

UN Human Rights Commission, 206, 211, 212

UN Resolution 1514 on the Granting of Independence to Colonial Countries and Peoples (1960 Declaration), 192-193, 198, 299n215

UN Secretariat, 185

UN Security Council, 186, 217, 219, 296n166

UN Trusteeship Council/system, 165, 191-194, 298n203, 298n205

UN Working Group on Indigenous Peoples, 245-246

United Kingdom. *See* Britain/British

United States (U.S.): colonialism, 80, 191, 192, 250, 298n205; continental expansion, 106-107, 229, 281n83; contradictory policies of, 3-5, 8, 107; and decolonization, 191-193; foreign policy, 54, 139, 161, 168, 182-183, 205, 212, 219; formation of, 68, 76-85, 271n107; hegemony, 6, 32, 53, 54, 55, 64, 76, 90, 94, 101, 106, 143, 194, 217, 220, 229, 249; and human rights, 204-205, 209-214, 216; isolationism of, 8, 161, 162, 182-183, 205, 214; military, 16, 19, 113, 142, 144, 145, 183, 217-220, 225, 233, 265n75; as model for world, 2, 18-19, 167, 211, 224-228, 229; multilateralism of, 183, 205, 214, 215, 217, 220; prisons, 226; as settler state, 179-180;

socioeconomic indices, 225-226, 307n193, 308n197, 308n198, 308n199, 308n201, 308n204; as "superpower," 3, 32, 35, 194, 195, 220, 225; unilateralism of, 3, 35, 182, 205-206, 214, 217, 220; and United Nations, 182-187, 194, 199, 205, 246, 296n147. *See also* America/American; American exceptionalism; American Indians; International law; Treaties; War on Terror; Wars; *specific governmental subdivisions*

Universal Declaration of Human Rights, 1, 205, 211-212, 301n64

Urban II, Pope, 38-39, 262n21

Uruguay, U.S. intervention in, 218

U.S. Army, 113, 155, 169, 292n52

U.S. Bureau of the Census, 63, 108, 109, 225, 279n12

U.S. Congress, 84, 86, 149-150, 153, 171, 183, 259n104, 278n1, 283n135; and American Indians, 120-123, 179-181; and citizenship, 104; and Hawai'i, 142-143, 145-146; and land acquisitions, 124-125, 127, 129, 140, 148; Reconstruction, 178; and slavery, 102; and treaties, 120, 216, 280n60. *See also* U.S. House of Representatives; U.S. Senate

U.S. Constitution, 4, 5, 107, 122, 129, 135, 140, 149-150, 156, 212, 213, 277n125; and American Indians, 86, 91, 93, 121, 274n41; Article I, 274n41, 277n127; Article III, 83, 273n26, 276n83; Article IV, 277n127; Article VI, 83-84, 116, 212, 273n20, 274n41; Bill of Rights of, 81-83; formation of, 77, 79-84, 118, 134; Fifth Amendment, 122; Fourteenth Amendment, 7, 104, 277n118, 278n137, 284n2; Ninth Amendment, 83, 273n25; and slavery, 7, 101-102, 104; Tenth Amendment, 83; Thirteenth Amendment, 7, 284n2

U.S. Department of Defense, 240, 256n51

U.S. Department of Interior, 180-181

U.S. Department of Justice, 15, 254n3, 257n55; Federal Bureau of Investigation (FBI), 11

U.S. Department of State, 15, 188, 304n108; and United Nations, 184-185

U.S. Department of War, 152, 155, 188

U.S. House of Representatives, 81, 102, 184

U.S. Senate, 84, 130, 155-156, 168, 184, 284n155; Foreign Relations Committee, 184, 210, 303n103; and treaty ratification, 170, 173, 185, 188, 206, 207, 210-216

U.S. Supreme Court, 4, 81, 83, 84, 90, 93, 94, 102-104, 115-122, 130, 140-141, 156, 163, 166, 168, 178, 179, 280n60

U.S. Trade Representative, Office of, 215

U.S.S. Maine, 146, 147-148, 151

"Vacant" lands. See *Territorium res nullius*
Vachon, Robert, 242-243
Valladolíd, debates at, 47
Vatican, observatory of, 24
Vattel, Emmerich de, 52, 72, 86, 93, 131, 271n110
Vega, Connie de la, 215
Venezuela, 167
Victoria, Franciscus de. *See* Vitoria, Franciscus de
Vietnam: Ben Tre, 219; Saigon, 233; U.S. war in, 210, 218-219, 256n37
Virgil's Aeneas, 35-36
Virginia: Colony of, 59, 73-74, 268n31, 269n47; Company, 65, 73; plantations, 60; and slavery, 97-99, 100, 277n119, 278n134
Virgin Islands: U.S. "purchase" of, 174
Vitoria, Franciscus de, 48-51, 59, 61, 63, 86, 89, 94, 110, 176, 265n91, 266n99, 266n105, 266n109, 271n110
Vyver, Johan van der, 214, 215

Wadsworth, James J., 299n213
Wales/Welsh, Prince Madoc, 269n43
Walker, Francis, 179
Wallerstein, Immanuel, 42, 234
War on terror, 1-3, 5, 9-18, 47, 51, 53, 65, 77, 226, 240, 249, 250, 254n9, 262n11, 265n75; as "crusade," 6, 37; premises of, 11-18, 27, 35, 231; as struggle for civilization, 9-10, 15-18, 31-33
Wars: in Afghanistan, 12, 218, 220; French and Indian, 64, 68; Little Crow's, 112; Napoleonic, 125; Persian Gulf, 220, 256n47; Seminole, 124-125; Spanish-American, 139, 145, 167, 168; U.S. Civil, 7, 133-134, 169; for U.S. independence, 71, 77, 119, 275n65; U.S. "Indian wars," 109, 115, 124, 152-154; U.S. in Mexico, 128-129, 133, 283n133, 283n135; U.S. in Philippines, 151-156, 161, 165, 219, 250, 288n113, 289n125; U.S. in Vietnam, 210, 218-219, 233, 256n37, 306n150, 306n152; World War I (Great War, WWI), 7, 164, 168-174, 176, 271n107. *See also* Cold War; Iraq; World War II
Washington Conference of 1921, 173
Washington, George, 84, 106; and American Indians, 88, 109, 157; land claims of, 73, 271-272n116
Waswo, Richard, 20, 22, 32, 35
Weber, Max, 259n98, 269n41
West, construct of, 32, 34, 36
Westcott, James D., 129
Western/European civilization, 7, 8, 17, 20, 32-34, 35-36, 52-53, 56-57, 63, 132, 135, 137, 189, 206, 230, 232; and human rights, 204; and Indigenous peoples, 89-90, 97, 111, 163; Nazi claims to, 298n198; presumptions of, 20-31, 105, 197, 242;

as superior, 50, 55, 75, 85, 94, 101, 103, 136-137, 177, 227, 229, 238, 246, 250-251; as universal, 40, 66-67, 95, 107, 123, 163, 190, 222, 231, 237, 278n7; U.S. as exemplar of, 76-77, 80, 183, 224, 227, 229, 231, 249-251. *See also* Civilization
Western Sahara, 299n215
West Indies, 264n62, 264n65
Westlake, John, 52, 163
Westphalia. *See* State(s)
Wheaton, Henry, 163
White, Edward D., 117, 288n97
White, William Allen, 184
Wiessner, Siegfried, 88
Wilkins, David, 120
Williams, Robert A., Jr., 37, 39, 42, 44, 48, 50, 51, 57, 58, 69, 70, 74, 181, 245, 268n35
Williams, Roger, 67
Wilson, Woodrow, 170-174, 178, 206, 238, 292n62, 293n81, 294n114
Winthrop, John, 54, 63
Winthrop, Robert C., 278n1
Wirt, William, 87, 92
Wittgenstein, Ludwig, 26
Wolf, Eric, 28, 32, 34
Woods, Jeanne, 15, 16
Woolsey, James, 13
Woolsey, Thomas, 155
Worcester, Dean Conant, 154
Worcester, Samuel, 93
World Bank (IBRD), 7, 196-197, 200-202, 223-224, 235, 300n30, 306n160; and "structural adjustment," 202, 221. 235; U.S. influence over, 201, 215, 300n37
World Bank Group, 300n30
World Trade Center, attacks on, 9, 11
World Trade Organization (WTO), 201, 215, 305n132; Marrakesh Agreement Establishing, 215
World War II, 156, 169, 182-183, 306n155; postwar era, 2, 53, 168, 173, 195, 196, 200, 203, 206, 207, 209, 217, 220, 222, 226; war crimes trials, 187-190, 297n182. *See also* Nuremberg Tribunal
Wounded Knee, 1890 massacre, 107, 111, 115, 152
Wright, Quincy, 164-165, 176
Wunder, John, 74
Wyoming, 115-116

Yee, James, 265n75
Yoo, John, 256n51, 258n70
Yugoslavia: criminal tribunal, 208, 302n84

Zaire, U.S. intervention in, 218
Zinn, Howard, 151, 159

About the Author

NATSU TAYLOR SAITO is Professor of Law at Georgia State University. She is the author of *From Chinese Exclusion to Guantánamo Bay: Plenary Power and the Prerogative State* and numerous law review articles.